Principles of Catholic Moral Life

Principles of Catholic Moral Life

Edited by
William E. May

Franciscan Herald Press
1434 West 51st Street
Chicago, Illinois 60609

Principles of Catholic Moral Life edited by William E. May. Papers presented at a workshop held at Catholic University, June 17–21, 1979, sponsored by William Cardinal Baum and the Archdiocese of Washington. Copyright © 1981 by Franciscan Herald Press, 1434 West 51st Street, Chicago, IL 60609. All rights reserved.

Library of Congress Cataloging in Publication Data
Main entry under title:

Principles of Catholic moral life.

Papers presented at a workshop held at Catholic University, June 17–21, 1979, sponsored by William Cardinal Baum and the Archdiocese of Washington.
1. Christian ethics—Catholic authors—Congresses.
I. May, William E., 1928-   II. Baum, William W.
III. Washington, D.C. (Archdiocese)
BX1758.2.P74   241'.042   80-10969
ISBN 0-8199-0793-6

Nihil Obstat:
Reverend Lorenzo Albacete

Imprimatur:
Rev. Msgr. John F. Donoghue

February 14, 1980

The nihil obstat and imprimatur are official declarations that a book or pamphlet is free of doctrinal or moral error. No implication is contained therein that those who have granted the nihil obstat or imprimatur agree with the content, opinions or statements expressed.

MADE IN THE UNITED STATES OF AMERICA

Contents

Introduction

From June 17-21, 1979 William Cardinal Baum and the Archdiocese of Washington sponsored a workshop on Principles of Catholic Moral Life at The Catholic University of America. The present volume contains the papers given at that workshop.

The principal purpose of the workshop and of this volume is to present a substantive and comprehensive introduction to the basic principles upon which the Christian way of life, as understood by the Roman Catholic Church, is based. A secondary but nonetheless significant purpose of both the workshop and of this volume is to offer considered and intelligent criticism of some recent developments in Catholic moral thought, in particular the development of a consequentialist methodology in the determination of the morality of human acts. This secondary purpose is not reflected in some of the papers given and may not even, in fact, represent the views of some of the participants. It was, nonetheless, one purpose explicitly in the mind of Cardinal Baum, who sponsored the workshop, and of those who were principally responsible for arranging it (Rev. Ronald Lawler, O.F.M. Cap., and William E. May), and it is explicitly brought to the fore in several of the papers (e.g., those by Richard Roach, S.J., John Finnis, William E. May, Germain G. Grisez).

A key goal of the workshop and volume is to set forth as clearly and cogently as possible the principles of Catholic moral life that are in fact authoritatively proposed by the magisterium or teaching authority of the Church. The contributors to the volume recognize that there is an area in which dissent from authoritative Church teaching on moral issues is possible (see the essay by Grisez), but they reject the view that there can be legitimate dissent on questions of principles of the moral life. Several of the contributors likewise hold that the principles of Catholic moral life are not limited to generic precepts but include specific moral norms, such as the norm that one may not rightfully choose with direct intent to kill innocent human life or devastate entire cities with their populations.

The papers given at the workshop have been organized here into six groups. The first group of papers is concerned with the divinely given sources of our knowledge of the principles of Catholic moral life. This group includes the essays by William Cardinal Baum, Richard Roach, S.J., Manuel Miguens, O.F.M.,* Rev. Donald McCarthy, and Louis Bouyer, Cong. Orat., and is concerned with questions touching on the ecclesial, biblical, and doctrinal foundations of the moral life. A second group of essays, smaller in number, is concerned with the question of natural law and its place within Catholic morality as developed by Vatican Council II (John Finnis) and as articulated by St. Thomas Aquinas (William E. May). A third group of essays focuses on the freedom of the human person that is the root source of our ability both to love and to sin (Ronald Lawler, O.F.M. Cap., John Connery, S.J., and Joseph Boyle). Another group of essays is explicitly devoted to a consideration of the subject of a moral methodology and with the resolution of "conflict" situations. In this group is included

---

*Father Miguens did not participate in the workshop in Washington. Another biblical scholar was scheduled to give a paper at the workshop, but he became seriously ill and could therefore not complete his paper or deliver it. Father Miguens graciously accepted the invitation to prepare a paper on the New Testament foundations of Catholic moral theology for this publication.

the only essay in the work by a non-Catholic, that of Professor Frederick S. Carney of the Perkins School of Theology at Southern Methodist University. Professor Carney's approach to this subject, while grounded in a somewhat different conceptual framework from that shared by most of the Roman Catholic participants, is rooted in a rich religious and philosophical tradition and is thoroughly nonconsequentialistic. The other two essays in this section of the volume are those of Germain Grisez and Joseph Mangan, S.J. Grisez here is chiefly concerned with the theological implications of a consequentialist approach to morality, while Mangan provides an account of the principle of double effect as this has been traditionally understood in Roman Catholic moral thought, principally to show that this principle is intelligible only on the supposition that there are certain sorts or kinds of acts that human persons ought not freely choose to do because of their evil nature, despite the good that may come by doing them. The essays by Rev. William Smith and Paul Philibert, O.P. form another group within the volume in which attention is centered on the subject of conscience. Smith examines this issue from the perspective of forming an objectively correct conscience, whereas Philibert is interested in showing how the work of contemporary developmental psychologists needs both to be critically assessed and integrated theologically if it is to be of genuine service to the Catholic moral theologian. The volume concludes with an essay by Jordan Aumann, O.P., on Christian perfection and spirituality, the goal of our life in Christ.

It would be possible to offer many comments about each of the papers—to indicate, for instance, some areas of disagreement among the authors—but the more appropriate course is simply to introduce them and let the reader undertake the task of understanding and appraising them. It is my belief that the reader will find them informative, scholarly, intelligent, and intelligible. Together, they are of particular value to students of theology; indeed, any Catholic who is serious about understanding what the moral life is all about should be able to find in the essays presented here material for prayerful consideration.

Many have worked hard to make this volume possible. Not only did he contribute an essay of his own, Cardinal Baum also enthusiastically and generously supported the entire project. The Reverends Lorenzo Albacete and William Lori of the Archdiocese of Washington did everything they could to help the contributors and to accommodate the needs of the many priests, religious, and laity who attended the workshop. Ann Turner of the Archdiocesan Chancery Office helped everyone involved by duplicating texts efficiently, preparing and distributing outlines, and typing many of the papers for publication. To all of the above, to my fellow contributors, and to all who helped make the days of June, 1979 a challenging and stimulating event I am very grateful. My greatest hope is that this volume may be of service to many more in their endeavor to come to know who we are and what we are to do if we are to be the beings we are meant to be, children of God, brothers and sisters of Jesus, who is, as St. Thomas Aquinas says, "our best and wisest Friend" (*Summa Theologiae*, 1-2, q. 108, a. 4).

William E. May
Associate Professor of Moral Theology
The Catholic University of America
Washington, D.C. 20064

Part One
The Ecclesial, Doctrinal, and Biblical Sources

The Distinctiveness of Catholic Moral Teaching

William Cardinal Baum
Archbishop of Washington

It is my intention to offer you some reflections that could: (a) draw the contours of moral life in Christ Jesus; (b) note the role of the magisterium of the Church in this mystery; and (c) show this mystery to be one in which everything truly human reaches its fulfillment.

Unlike the other papers to be read at this symposium, these reflections are not presented as a scientific, theological treatise. The perspective to which I call your attention is that of the magisterium of the Church.

The Magisterium

Authority

The magisterium of the Church does not depend entirely on the result of scholarship in order to know with certainty what Catholics must believe and how they must live. This certainty is a gift of the Lord. It is a communication of his authority, the authority that evoked the admiration of people confused by the debates among the different schools and experts, as we read in the gospel:

> Jesus finished this discourse and left the crowds spellbound at his teaching. The reason was that he

taught with authority and not like their scribes (Mt.
7: 28-29).

Hermeneutics

Of course, the teachings of the magisterium must be phrased
in human language, in the categories of particular theologies
and philosophies. Of course, as human language the declarations of the magisterium share the limitations of all human
speech. There is above all the limitation of expressing in
human words what cannot be contained by them. The mysteries of which we speak are the mysteries of One who "is in
Himself above every name, above every thing and above every
created intellect ... infinitely beyond all that we can conceive
in human measure" (Pope Paul VI, *Credo of the People of God,*
June 30, 1968).

The teaching of the declaration *Mysterium Ecclesiae* published by the Sacred Congregation for the Doctrine of the Faith
(June 24, 1973) concerning dogmatic statements of the magisterium applies also to moral teachings. These too "depend
partly upon the expressive power of the language used at a
certain point in time and in particular circumstances." These
too "may be expressed at first incompletely (but not falsely),
and at a later date, when considered in a broader context of
faith or human knowledge [they] receive a fuller and more
perfect expression." In interpreting these teachings, it is also
necessary to identify the "certain questions" and errors that
the magisterium had in mind in making these pronouncements. Finally, the truth of these teachings is "distinct from
the changeable conceptions of a given epoch and can be expressed without them." Nevertheless, they could "have been
enunciated by the Sacred Magisterium in terms that bear
traces of such conceptions." (All references in this paragraph
are from *Mysterium Ecclesiae,* 5.)

All these considerations are true, and if they have been mentioned explicitly at this time, it is to reject the charge that the

magisterium is not aware of these problems. Nevertheless, in spite of these limitations (which scholarship can and must examine), the fact remains that the magisterium has been given a share in the authority of that Word which is capable of being recognized in the flesh, and not only exegetes, philosophers, and theologians. The Word became flesh, sharing the limitations of the flesh, but still remaining the divine Word, the eternal Son of God. The Word became flesh precisely to divinize the flesh, to enable it to bear the truth of the thrice holy God. This is the mystery of the Incarnation, upon which our knowledge of everything that concerns humanity depends.

The Incarnation of the truth means that "the faithful must shun the opinion ... that dogmatic formulas ... cannot signify truth in a determinate way, but can only offer changeable approximations to it." It means that the truth cannot be considered "like a goal that is constantly being sought by means of such approximations" (*Mysterium Ecclesiae*, 5). This teaching concerning dogmatic statements applies also to moral teachings because, from the perspective of the magisterium, these teachings identify the Incarnation of the truth in the acts of the human person.

Therefore, just as in making dogmatic statements the Church has never been intimidated by confusion or pluralism among philosophers, theologians, and exegetes, so too the moral teachings of the Church do not depend on the establishment of a consensus concerning the anthropological categories that are thought to define humanity best. In fact, it is quite the other way around. The moral truths taught by the Church, derived from revelation, are to be used in the formulation of such an anthropology and in the correction of existing ones.

Revelation and Moral Knowledge

Let us recall the teaching of the first Vatican Council (reaffirmed by Vatican II in *Dei Verbum* 6). Because of revelation *things in the divine order not of themselves inaccessible to human reason* can also, in the present status of humankind, be known by all. Because of revelation they can be known easily, with a firm certainty and without any admixture of error. One often speaks in dogma about the "revelation of natural truths," but forgets that it is equally true of morality.

Revelation, therefore, plays a constitutive part in the formulation of moral teachings and moral theology. The purpose of these teachings is to identify the way of life that is in accordance with the truth of revelation and Redemption. This truth is "not a human and rational truth, but the truth that comes from God." Still it is the "truth that brings with it the principle of the authentic liberation of man ... the truth which is the only one that offers a solid basis for an adequate praxis" (Pope John Paul II, *Address to the CELAM,* Puebla, Mexico, January 28, 1979).

Purpose of the Magisterium

In my address to the Fellowship of Catholic Scholars in Kansas City on April 28, 1978, the competence and authority of the magisterium was discussed in the context of the bishop's *sacramental* or *liturgical* ministry. Permit me to cite from this address:

> To make the sacramental life a reality by preserving the Church's unity of faith and life: this is the purpose of the episcopal magisterium.
>
> [The episcopal magisterium] pertains to the sacramental transmission of the divine realities, the saving mysteries. ... The episcopal magisterium has the duty of discerning the state of the Church's life and making sure that the faithful are not separated from the mystery into which we have been assimilated. The interventions of the episcopal magisterium ... are justified by this responsibility for the permanence within the Church of the evangelical proclamation of the Word and its interpretation ... according to the paschal mysteries.

It is my belief that this sacramental, liturgical context enables us to understand not only the role of the magisterium in doctrinal and moral matters, but also the "distinctiveness" of the Christian moral life itself.

The Eucharistic Context

Magisterium and Liturgy (I)

When we speak of the sacramental, liturgical realities, the first thing that comes to mind is the celebration of the eucharistic liturgy. It would not be wrong to say that the "unique power and authority of the magisterium, its doxological character, its relation to the apostolic proclamation, and its authority to call for conversion, repentance, and obedience to the will of God exist to safeguard the indispensable conditions for an efficacious participation in the celebration of the liturgy" (ibid.).

To put it bluntly: The magisterium teaches that which is necessary (in accordance with God's revelation) to make possible the efficacious celebration of the Eucharist.

But how is this to be related to the moral life of human beings in the world, to their actions on the world, to their growth as persons? (Note that we are speaking of all human beings, and of what constitutes all human beings as persons, whatever their religious beliefs may be.)

To answer this question we turn to the teaching of our Holy Father Pope John Paul II in his encyclical *Redemptor Hominis*.

Humanity in the Mystery of Christ

Every human being, the Pope writes, from the first moment of his or her existence, "has been redeemed by Christ... With man—with each man without any exception whatever—Christ is in a way united, even when man is unaware of it." Christ provides "each man and every man, with the light and strength to measure up to his supreme calling" (*Redemptor Hominis,* 14).

Obviously, an individual's appropriation of this redemption offered and made possible by the risen Christ depends on many circumstances, such as his or her relation to the life of the Church and the use of the individual's freedom. It is possible for people to reject this offer and so to condemn themselves for all eternity. Moreover, this offer and this possibility are offered to humanity in many ways, some of them concrete and explicit (such as the sacraments). The free relationship of individuals to these offers does indeed determine the ultimate outcome of their lives. Nevertheless, the point is that every single human being discovers the truth about himself or herself, only by sharing in the mystery of Christ.

This is the teaching of the Second Vatican Council that the Holy Father has made the cornerstone of his teaching:

> It is *only* in the mystery of the Word made flesh that the mystery of man truly becomes clear.... Adam, the first man, was a type of him who was to come. Christ the new Adam, in the very revelation of the mystery of the Father and of his love, fully reveals man to himself and brings to light his most high calling (*Gaudium et Spes,* 22).

If we take this teaching seriously, then only two positions are possible concerning the relation of human morality to revelation—and to life in Christ. Either the two are synonymous, such that "life in Christ" is just the *theological* name given to a reality coextensive with creation; or else the gift of life in Christ is the *basic* reality from which the meaning of the natural can be derived as the capacity to receive this gift. Only this last possibity is in accordance with the faith of the Church.

Archetype and Type

In the words of the great Nicholas Cabasilas:

> It was for the new man that human nature was created at the beginning, and for him mind and de-

sire were prepared. We have received our reason in order that we may know Christ, our desire in order that we might hasten to Him. We have memory in order that we may carry Him in us, since He Himself is the archetype for those who are created. It was not the old Adam who was the model for the new, but the new Adam for the old....

For those who have known him first, the old Adam is the archetype because of our fallen nature. But for Him who sees all things before they exist, the first Adam is the imitation of the Second....

To sum it up: the Saviour first and alone showed to us the true man, who is perfect on account of both character and life and in all other respects as well.... It is most absurd to regard the most perfect ...as striving towards the imperfect, and to posit the inferior as the model of the superior, as though the blind were to lead those who see!...

So then, for all these reasons man strives for Christ by nature, by his will, by his thoughts, not only because of His Godhead which is the goal of all things, but because of His human nature as well. He is the nesting place of human desires; He is the food of our thoughts. To love anything besides Him or to meditate on it is a manifest aberration from duty and a turning aside from the first principles of our nature. (*Life in Christ,* trans. Carmino J. de Catinzaio. Crestwood, N.Y.: St. Vladimir's Orthodox Seminary, 1974, p. 150.)

It should not be said, therefore, that revelation teaches nothing concerning human life that could not be discovered without knowledge of Christ Jesus. The purpose of revelation is the divinization of humanity. Revelation is not primarily the basis of a "privileged access to the human" (there existing, in principle, other ways of reaching full knowledge of the *humanum*). Rather revelation is the *only* access to the mystery of the interior life of the Triune God, and *therefore* to the fullness of what being human means. Christian morality presupposes that the integrity of the *humanum* that had been lost by sin has been restored by the paschal mystery, and that this is the case for every human being who does not freely reject the gift of this restoration.

New Form of Existence

On July 26, 1962, at a public audience Pope Paul VI asked the questions that concern us here: "Does a Christian morality exist? Is there an original way of living that is called Christian?" His answer was as follows:

> [Christian morality] is a way of living according to the faith, in the light of the truths and example of Christ. We have learned these truths from the Gospel and from its first apostolic irradiation, the New Testament. It is a way of living in view of a second coming of Christ and a new form of our existence, the so-called Parousia. It is always lived by means of a double aid. One is interior and ineffable: the Holy Spirit. The other is exterior, historical and social, but qualified and authorized: the ecclesiastical magisterium.

Notice the Holy Father's insistence on the "new form of our existence" that Christian morality has in view. Now in the words of Pope John Paul II, "the Eucharist is the Sacrament in which our *new being* is most completely expressed" (*Redemptor Hominis,* 20).

Why? To answer this question, it is necessary to examine in what this "new form of existence" or "new being" consists. To put it in other words, what is the "truth about man" which the "truth concerning Christ" reveals?

The New Humanity

Our Holy Father Pope John Paul II answers this question in terms of the traditional teaching *de triplici munere Christi:*

Jesus Christ is prophet, priest, and king, and in him, humanity is revealed as prophet, priest and king. These three identities are constitutive of the human person (cf. the book *Sign of Contradiction*). Chapters 19, 20, and 21 of the encyclical *Redemptor Hominis* follow this same threefold division of Christ's—and humanity's—identity. In his *Letter to all Priests of the Church on the Occasion of Holy Thursday 1979*, the Holy Father returns to this way of elaborating the mystery of man in the light of the mystery of Christ.

Prophet: Human Dignity and the Truth

As *prophet* Christ is the one who proclaims divine truth. He is also the one who shows the dignity of humanity to be bound up with truth. "It is truth that makes man what he is. His relationship with truth is the deciding factor in his human nature and it constitutes his dignity as person.... [This] integral part of the mystery of man finds confirmation in Christ the prophet" (*Sign of Contradiction*, XIV,2). The prophetic ministry of humanity consists in its witness to the truth: about itself, the world, and God. This truth is engraved in the very structure of humanity and creation. Humanity is a prophet with respect to the truth when it respects and testifies to the integrity or dignity of creation.

But in what does this integrity or dignity consist? The second characteristic of the truth about Christ and about humanity gives us the answer: *priesthood*.

Priest: Creation and the Sacrifice of Praise

"Priesthood," writes the Holy Father:

> is an expression of the meaning given to man and the world by their relationship to God.... The profoundest of truths about man and the world is that they both belong to God, Creator and Redeemer. This truth leads to understanding of the 'sacrificium laudis' (Ps. 50 (40), 14) *natural to the created world* and entrusted to man in order that man may become

a living expression of the glory of God. This 'sac-
rificium laudis' expresses the homage paid to its
Lord by the whole of creation ... and enables man to
become the spokesman, so to speak, for the created
world" (*Sign of Contradiction,* XV,2).... Priesthood
is the supreme prayer of all things: of man and of the
world (ibid. 4).

We know that as a result of sin humanity lost the capacity to
offer this "sacrifice of praise" in the name of all creation. Christ
Jesus is the eternal high priest who offers this sacrifice on our
behalf. Redeemed humanity shares in the priesthood of Christ.

In the case of humanity, the integrity and dignity of its being
lie in its capacity to offer the sacrifice of praise that defines the
relation between creation and the Creator. It is the capacity to
be a priest. In the case of all creation (including humanity),
this integrity and dignity lie in the capacity *to be part* of this
sacrifice of praise.

Now we can see why it is possible to speak of the Eucharist
as "the Sacrament in which our new being is most completely
expressed" (*Redemptor Hominis,* 20). The celebration of the
Eucharist is the summit and font of all the ways of sharing "in
that unique and irreversible restoration of man and the world
to the Father that was carried out once for all by him who is
both the eternal Son and also true Man" (ibid).

Magisterium and Liturgy (II)

That is why to say that the moral teachings of the magisterium identify the way of life that makes possible the celebration of the Eucharist is not to restrict these teachings to practicing Catholics, but to include all human beings—indeed, all
of creation. And *that* is why "the teaching authority of the
Church is competent to interpret even the natural law"
(*Humanae Vitae,* 4). That is why the successors of Peter and
the apostles have the authority, communicated to them by
Christ the prophet and priest, to be "guardians and authentic

interpreters of all the moral law, not only, that is, of the law of the Gospel, but also of the natural law, which is also an expression of the will of God, the faithful fulfillment of which is equally necessary for salvation" (ibid).

Sacramental Existence

Christian morality is sacramental; it is "symbolic." Created realities are the sacrament or symbol of invisible divine realities. Humanity is the one reality in which this sacramental identity is most perfectly realized and displayed. Authentic human acts are therefore prophetic (they testify to the truth of this capacity of Creation), and priestly (they mediate the contact between the symbol and the divine reality signified). And humanity is created in the image of Christ the archetype, prophet, and priest.

The defense of this conviction demands the rejection of the dualism between the human person and the body. The body is the language of the self, the sacrament of the person.

This dualism must be opposed because otherwise the human being loses the capacity to be the symbol of the divine. Otherwise humanity could not be considered the spokesperson and priest of all creatures (cf. Preface to Eucharistic Prayer IV). It is not *physicalism* that the Church teaches (especially in sexual morality, as many dissenters from the teaching of the magisterium charge) but rather *sacramentalism*.

King: Hominization and Spiritualization

There is a third aspect or dimension of the truth concerning Christ and the truth concerning humanity revealed in Christ. This is the *royal* or *kingly* character of humanity revealed in Christ the king.

Creation is not given to human beings who are prophets and priests as something static or completed. In the words of the Second Vatican Council, by their "activity inwardly supported by the grace of Christ," the faithful act in the world:

> so that all the good things created in accordance
> with the plan of the Creator and in the light of his
> Word may be developed thanks to human effort,
> technical skill, and civic culture, for the benefit of all
> men without exception (*Lumen Gentium*, 36).

Human praxis is thus a manifestation of the kingly character of humanity, of its dominion over the earth, nature, and the
world. Yet this mastery over matter is given to human beings
precisely because of the spiritual element inherent in them,
which enables them to constitute the objects of their activity as
expressions of themselves. That is, kingship is given to humanity so that it might humanize creation. Thus man, "in keeping
with the openness of his spirit within and also with the many
diverse needs of his body and his existence in time, writes his
personal history through numerous bonds, contacts, situations,
and social structures linking him with others" and with creation (*Redemptor Hominis*, 14). Thus humanity humanizes the
world by a projection, so to speak, of its spirit. Its spiritual
element enables humanity to assimilate the world to itself.

Once again, Christ Jesus is revealed to us as the archetype of
this character of humanity. By means of the sending forth of
the Spirit by the Father and the Son, "the fruit of the earth and
work of human hands" is incorporated, assimilated into his
body. Thus he exercises his lordship, his dominion, his kingship, of which humanity is the image. And where, if not during
the celebration of the Eucharist, does this process reach its
summit? Once again we discover a reason for the authority of
the magisterium to formulate moral precepts governing humanity's dominion over creation. It is once again a matter of
making possible the eucharistic celebration.

Penance

The kingly character of humanity concerns its *responsibility*
for creation. The Holy Father relates this truth to the mystery
of repentance for our sins. When individuals recognize that

they have sinned, when in repentance they turn to God, they manifest his kingly character by acknowledging that they have a responsibility, a dominion, and a grandeur to which they have been unfaithful.

In connection with sin and repentance, it is necessary to remember that the sacramental or symbolic relation among humanity, God, and the world makes it tragically possible for human beings to violate or reject their vocation and dignity by means of single acts, not just by the orientation of a whole life or by the corruption of their fundamental option.

The teaching of *Persona Humana,* (the *Declaration on Certain Questions Concerning Sexual Ethics*) by the Sacred Congregation for the Doctrine of the Faith makes this point clearly:

> According to the Church's teaching, mortal sin, which is opposed to God, does not consist only in formal and direct resistance to the commandment of charity. It is equally to be found in this opposition to authentic love which is included in every deliberate transgression, in serious matter, of each of the moral laws....
>
> A person therefore sins mortally not only when his action comes from direct contempt for love of God and neighbor, but also when he consciously and freely, for whatever reason, chooses something which is seriously disordered. For in this choice, as has been said above, there is already included contempt for the divine commandment: the person turns himself away from God and loses charity (*Persona Humana*, 10).

The Body and Blood of Christ

My dear friends, it has been my intention to offer to you some reflections that would draw the contours of moral life in Christ Jesus, locate the role of the magisterium of the Church in this mystery, and show it to be the mystery in which everything that is truly human reaches its fulfillment. (Perhaps these observations will also assist the Orthodox and Protestant Christians to understand better the presuppositions behind the moral teachings of the Catholic Church.)

In offering these reflections to you, I am aware that my words—the words of one bishop, the words of one man—cannot begin to capture the reality of love that has been manifested and communicated to us. Even as I speak, the Church in our country has been celebrating the solemnity of the Body and Blood of the Lord. How can any human words compare to what the Word of God reveals to us through this mystery, the mystery of the Real Presence of the Lord in the most Blessed Sacrament! The truth of the Real Presence confirms the inexpressible dignity of redeemed humanity's "new being" or "new form of existence." This doctrine affirms that, by the power of the Spirit and as the result of the Lord's creative decision, the realities of this world and of the flesh can be and are lifted up into a new order of life, a new creation. There they are assimilated into the glorious Body of the Lord without losing their integrity. By means of the Eucharist, because of the Real Presence, our own existence in the flesh is being transformed into existence as the Body of Christ—existence in him and life in the Spirit. Some day our own mortal bodies will be raised up by this same power and belong also to the new creation. "Christ will raise our mortal bodies and make them like his own in glory" (Eucharistic Prayer III). In the risen body of humanity all of creation will be delivered from its slavery to corruption (cf. Rom. 8: 19-22). Is this not a sufficient basis for life in the world, for personal growth and fulfillment, for our defense of the dignity of humanity and the world?

The Blessed Sacrament is indeed the sacrament of love: the "center of the life of the People of God," so that through all the manifestations of worship due to it, Christ shall be given back "love for love" (*Redemptor Hominis*, 20).

It is invoking this vocation of humanity—to love in return for love—that the bishops of the United States concluded their pastoral letter *To Live in Christ Jesus*. Calling you to reread and study the teachings of the bishops found in this important document, I conclude these reflections with their words:

> When we come to die, much we have cherished will seem worthless, many things deemed urgent and attractive now will appear useless or worse. What will matter then is how much we love now and how we live in response to our Father's love for us.... Jesus yielded up His life for us in perfect loving union with the Father's will, and this is the meaning of His life which also gives meaning to our lives as His followers. If we can acknowledge selfishness as folly and self-sacrifice as victory, if we can love enemies, be vulnerable to injustice and, in being so, still say that we have triumphed, then we shall have learned to live in Christ Jesus (*To Live in Christ Jesus*, 3, NCCB, 1976).

Moral Theology and the Mission of the Church: Idolatry in Our Day

Rev. Richard R. Roach S. J.
Marquette University
Milwaukee, Wisconsin

The fundamental responsibility of moral theology within the broader mission of the Church consists of teaching its members to observe what God has commanded. The fundamental command remains forever the <u>prohibition against idolatry</u>. God cannot permit any creature to address any other being, actual or illusory, as god. Upon this prohibition stands all the rest that God has commanded. What is special about this teaching today arises from the delusion that the one and only God could have commanded contradictory things. Put that way, the delusion is easy to see, so naturally the evil one prefers a different wording. He prefers the language of controversy. He would like us to imagine a situation in which two reputedly good theologians, say, Marcion and Clement, both worship the one and only God but differ about what he has commanded. Marcion believed God wanted women to be his priests and Clement did not. The fallacy embedded in the delusion that this is but a controversy among believers consists in the erroneous assumption that who God is can be known apart from what he wants or commands, just as in ordinary life you and I may know who Joe is or who Mary is without knowing what either wants. We do not know God in the way we may know Mary and Joe. We know him only when he is rightly described because he is invisible. And what he wants and commands are essential to a right description. An experiment with our imaginations can make this point clear.

Imagine you are standing before a woman about whom you know nothing except that you can see her clearly. You are told that her name is Mary. You can now use the name *Mary* to refer to that woman. Without further knowledge you can use the name *Mary* to distinguish her from Joe whom you know in the same way and to the same degree. You need fear no error in the reference you make with the names. Even if someone lied to you about the name *Mary* uses for herself, your use of the name truly refers to her because she is visible and known by direct observation. When using the name *Mary* to refer to this woman, it is nonsense to ask how many Marys there are. That question makes sense only if the name is used to refer to any and all who chose to call themselves *Mary*.

The term *god* works more like the latter use of *Mary* than the former, but properly the term is not a name at all. It stands for a description. Because it is a descriptive term, it is sensible to ask how many gods there are.[1] Only after we have acquired enough descriptive knowledge about God through faith and/or natural theology do we know the right answer, which is that there is only one God.

Even when we use the name *Jesus* to refer to our Lord, who is God with us and both true God and true man, we can know his divinity only through a right description, because his divinity remains hidden in the Christ as well as revealed by him. So the Enlightenment fiction called the "Jesus of history" tells us nothing about who Jesus really is; nonetheless, because Jesus walked among us as a man, the fiction can refer to him. It cannot refer to God because, among other reasons, it does not describe Jesus rightly as both true God and true man.

Our linguistic situation is still more complicated. It is not within our power to have a merely theoretical description of God. One of the tragedies of the Church within recent times has been the misreading of St. Thomas as if his brilliance underwrote such a foolish endeavor. According to Thomas, to know God even theoretically is at least to know what he commanded with respect to essentials whether one obeys him or not. No description of God without those commands called the natural law would be an adequate description. In other words, there is in Thomas no logical disjunction between *is* and *ought* because even our scant natural knowledge of who God is tells us something about what we ought to be and to do.[2]

In describing God in this way, St. Thomas was only following the hints regarding what our minds naturally can discover about God that were given in revelation, for example, in the writings of St. Paul. St. Paul said, "Ever since God created the world his everlasting power and deity—however invisible— have been there for the mind of man to see in the things he has made" (Rom. 1: 20). Then he went on to say that this knowledge means we are without excuse for not doing what God has commanded. "That is why such people are without excuse: they knew God and yet refused to honor him as God or to thank him; instead, they made nonsense out of logic and their empty minds were darkened" (Rom. 1:21).[3]

The first sin we commit is idolatry from which all the other sins follow. St. Paul added:

> The more they called themselves philosophers, the more stupid they grew, until *they exchanged the glory* of the immortal God for a worthless imitation, *for the image* of mortal man, of birds, of quadrupeds and reptiles. That is why God left them to their filthy enjoyments and the practices with which they dishonor their own bodies, since they have given up divine truth for a lie and have worshipped and

> served creatures instead of the creator, who is bless-
> ed forever. Amen! (Rom. 1:22-25).

It does not sound as if for Paul our knowledge of God was detached and disinterested, that is, theoretical in the contemporary, liberal sense. Rather such knowledge is the instrument of God's judgment.

A contemporary "reluctant unbeliever" has shown something of the Pauline appreciation of what it is to "know" about God. In his book *The Seven Deadly Sins Today* Henry Fairlie wrote, "But in their secularization of everything else, the unbelieving must be careful not to secularize God. He is more than an Idea. He is more than the Word. He is more than Logos." (By way of clarification, I would add that God is more than Idea, Word, and Logos, as those terms are understood in our post-Enlightenment culture, but he is Logos as that term was understood by the authors of Scripture.) Fairlie continued:

> There are too many unbelievers today—many of
> them even in our temples and churches—who take
> His name in vain. Perhaps no one sins more out-
> rageously in our age or is more characteristic of the
> slackness we tolerate, than the priest and theologian
> who reduce God to no more than a concept but insist
> that they believe enough to remain members of their
> church or temple. They are making it awkward to be
> an atheist. Apparently one may now deny the teach-
> ings of Christianity—even a teaching as fundamen-
> tal as the divinity of Christ, as some theologians
> have done at Oxford in the past year—and yet re-
> serve the privilege of calling oneself a Christian.[4]

He then asked:

> Why stand outside the doors of the church as an
> atheist, and think gravely of the falsehoods
> preached within that one feels compelled to combat,
> when all the time one could just step inside and in
> God's own house preach against them in His name?[5]

In my judgment a number of Roman Catholic moral theologians have answered Fairlie's rhetorical question in a practical way by remaining within the Roman Catholic Church while teaching moral doctrine at variance with Church teaching on substantial matters. They invoke the illusion that they are believers in good standing engaged only in controversy with other believers, when the logic of the disagreement really means that only one party consists of believers in that God who the Roman Catholic Church has believed for nearly two thousand years is the one and only God. The other party worships an idol of their own making. Fairlie concluded his judgment on those who perhaps sin the most outrageously in our age with these words:

> To deny that God is a Being and reduce Him to a mere concept, a figment of our making, a shadow of Himself, may leave one still a religious man in a trivial way, but it does not leave one a believing Jew or a believing Christian.[6]

In sum, I believe it is logically absurd, given the way in which our words refer to God, to pretend that both sides are talking about the same Being when we dispute, for example, whether or not he forbids all directly procured abortion. In the dispute we are conceptually positing two different "gods" only one of which can be the one and only God. I believe he is the one who forbids all directly procured abortion. Furthermore, I believe that when the question has come up, knowing that prohibition is essential to adequately describing him so as really to refer to him when using the descriptive term *God*.*

---

*Understanding the logical fact that the term *god* is descriptive rather than a proper name can be difficult for readers unfamiliar with the idea to grasp it at first bounce—not because the idea is difficult but because familiar theology has treated *god* as a proper name for so long we have become used to this error. This point is essential to my article. Since I have developed it more fully elsewhere—a develop-

The difference Fairlie points out between a Being and a concept complements this logical point. That difference consists, I believe, in the fact that a Being is actual apart from my mind, and a concept depends wholly upon my understanding for its shape and content. Given the way God has made us, the only way he can impress upon us the fact that he actually is God and not a concept or a projection of our minds is to persuade us or force us to render him obedience. Since he has freely created us as free creatures, our relation with him ought to be one of returned and warm love, of complete trust, and of obedience rendered freely as an expression of that love. But sin, original and actual, has brought it about that things are not as they ought to be. Therefore, some accept his graciousness in faith and render him loving obedience; others merely reject his truth and for a time disobey. But eventually all obey him, because if we are not alive when he comes again, we shall all die. Dying is actual, and our minds can do nothing about it. Furthermore, death is God's just judgment upon our lives no matter how we

---

ment on which I somewhat presume as a foundation for the ideas presented in this article (see note 7 at the end of this article)—permit me to offer an imperfect example, but one that I hope will prove adequate as a metaphor to fix this logical fact in your thinking.

Imagine you have one hundred white capsules, perfectly identical in appearance. Ninety-five of them contain strychnine, the other five aspirin. The chemical descriptions are respectively $C_{21}H_{22}N_2O_2$ for strychnine and $CH_3COOC_6H_4COOH$ for aspirin. It is possible to draw up a list of one hundred proper names and assign one to each capsule, but I doubt that you will be able to keep them sorted that way. Nevertheless, before you take a pill for a headache, you had better be able to determine which is its chemical description because strychnine in the proper quantity is deadly.

The term *god* is like one hundred white capsules. From the depths of our sinfulness we can project at least that many "gods" into the empyrean. Yet we may know that there is only one. If we are to address that one and do his will, we had better get his description right.

die. But for those who believe, that is, for those who render him loving obedience in faith, death is not his final judgment because Jesus Christ, our Lord, is also the first-born from the dead.

For those who have disobeyed and rejected his will, even in dying there remains only the second death in which God confirms the alienation from him that they have chosen. Even in that alienation his justice wins out in a strange way, although it is a way I hope never to experience. I surmise that in one respect the way in which damnation gives him glory is that it is disobedience stripped of all its subjective illusions. In at least the mental realm while the damned were among us, their illusions substituted an idol for the one and only God. After death the truth about God prevails, even if his love has been definitively spurned.

Deviant moral theology became a public reality within the Roman Catholic Church when a number of moral theologians who came overwhelmingly from affluent and, in my opinion, decadent social classes in the West chose to reject Church teaching regarding the regulation of birth as Pope Paul VI reiterated it.[7] They did so, although the Pope's teaching was no more his private judgment than the doctrine of the Incarnation. In fact, I believe we may see in theological developments since 1968 that to reject one is tantamount to rejecting the other. I believe we should have expected this development. The source is the same; the evidence for them both overlaps; and the authority confirming their truth is one, namely, the Church in communion with the chair of St. Peter.

To reject the prohibition against direct contraception that the Church has taught since its founding is, I believe, tantamount to rejecting the Incarnation for the following reason, perhaps best given in the epistle to the Hebrews:

> *You who wanted no sacrifice or oblation,*
> *prepared a body for me.*

> *You took no pleasure in holocausts or sacrifices for sin;*
> *then I said,*
> *just as I was commanded in the scroll of the book,*
> *"God, here I am! I am coming to obey your will"*
> (Heb. 10:5-7)

The sentiment revealed in these words belongs to the Incarnate One who is our Lord and Savior Jesus Christ. In case we miss their revelatory import, the inspired "author" continues by asking us to:

> Notice that he says first: *You did not want* what the Law lays down as the things to be offered, that is: *the sacrifices, the oblations, the holocausts and the sacrifices for sin, and you took no pleasure* in them; and then he says: *Here I am! I am coming to obey your will.* He is abolishing the first sort to replace it with the second. And this *will* was for us to be made holy by the *offering* of his *body* made once and for all by Jesus Christ (Heb. 10:8-10).

The offering of his body consists in doing the Father's will in all, even in bodily things. That will is not wholly extraneous to the body the Godhead prepared for Christ. If it were, Christ could have been as the Docetists imagined he was, human merely in appearance. Instead, he was and is true man. As such he really did die. God's will that humanity should die is patently not extraneous to the body. Neither is his will on other matters.

Thus the most fundamental will or commands that Jesus obeyed were given him in the body the Godhead prepared. And this is as true for us as for him, for it is an essential part of what it is to be a true human being, namely, God's will is given us in the bodies he creates for us. We know that will from rationally observing the bodies God has prepared for us, just as we know that God exists from rationally observing what he has made.

St. Paul affirmed this truth in the letter to the Romans mentioned above. In that passage we further noted that he went on to condemn idolatry, the mother lode of all sin, and then turned to the consequences of idolatry in further sinning. Paul chose appropriately to focus attention immediately on the sins that consist of disobeying the commands God gives us in the bodies he has prepared for us. We know those commands from the same kind of observation whereby we may know that he exists. Paul put it this way:

> That is why God has abandoned them to degrading passions: why their women have turned from natural intercourse to unnatural practices and why their menfolk have given up natural intercourse to be consumed with passion for each other, men doing shameless things with men and getting an appropriate reward for their perversion (Rom. 1:26-27).

I believe Roman Catholic moral theology may find in this passage scriptural warrant for one of its most essential concepts, the distinction between natural and unnatural as the distinction between what God permits and prohibits. Furthermore, I believe that any sexual act which is a human act, performed, that is, by a person with sufficient knowledge and self-control to do it freely, and which is *not* a conjugal act, is unnatural in the moral sense of the term. (The evil of direct contraception within an otherwise responsible and procreative marriage is that it deprives the accompanying sexual acts of their conjugal form.)

The drive to practice what is unnatural begins in idolatry. As merely a temptation we can overcome it only by turning with all our hearts in obedience to the one and only God. If acted out, the drive results in sins, which in turn embody idolatry because they are acts whereby we worship an illusory god (minuscule "g"), who is not the Father Almighty Creator of heaven and earth and therefore of our bodies. Through the unnatural practices of nonconjugal sex we capitulate to the idol who commands lust and uses it to lead us to all other sins. "In other words," as St. Paul says:

> since they refused to see it was rational to acknowledge God, God has left them to their own irrational ideas and to their monstrous behavior. And so they are steeped in all sorts of depravity, rottenness, greed and malice, and addicted to envy, murder, wrangling, treachery and spite. Libelers, slanderers, enemies of God, rude, arrogant and boastful, enterprising in sin, rebellious to parents, without brains, honor, love or pity. They know what God's verdict is: that those who behave like this deserve to die—and yet they do it: and what is worse, encourage others to do the same (Rom. 1:28-32).

I believe this ancient text sounds like a description of the "signs of the times," and I further believe that the cause is the same now as then, the rejection of the commands God gave us in the way he prepared our bodies.

We may see the link between the Incarnation and God's commands in the way our Lord revealed himself both in word and deed. While with us before his death, he taught us some ethics, principally by way of reform of what we knew already from the Torah. He put ceremonial and positive law in its proper perspective and exercised his divine sovereignty in such a way that his Church guided by his Spirit could dispense us from most of it. He reprimanded with utter severity the use of technicalities or false traditions as rationalizations for disobeying substantive commands. For example, he exposed the hypocrisy of disobeying the commandment "Honor thy father and thy mother" embodied in the ceremonial practice of pronouncing one's wealth as "Corban (that is, dedicated to God)," and then regarding oneself as forbidden "to do anything for . . . mother and father" (Mk. 7:12). I might add that in this bit of salvation history we have the paradigm for what may be called *legalism* when we use the term pejoratively. In another sense Jesus was first and foremost a legalist. He obeyed his Father's law and taught us to do the same.[8]

We find in Jesus' words reforming the Torah regarding marriage the clearest appeal to the distinction between natural and unnatural that the Church later developed and expounds today as the natural law. For in reforming the Torah, our Lord appeals to the law in our bodies expressing God's original intentions for marriage given with Creation:

> He [Jesus] answered, "Have you not read that the creator from the beginning *made them male and female* and that he said: *This is why a man must leave father and mother, and cling to his wife, and the two become one body*? They are no longer two, therefore, but one body. So then, what God has united, man must not divide" (Mt. 19:4-6).

In this passage our Lord speaks with sovereign authority, knowing inerrantly the Creator's intentions because he is God. But he also speaks as a sinless man who is able therefore to read clearly God's intentions in nature.

The Church has taught rightly from the beginning that a corollary of his command regarding marriage is the prohibition of direct contraception. This may seem least among his commands, even unnecessary, when applied to a Christian married couple who otherwise live a procreative marriage and seek help from technology only to limit responsibly the number of their children while continuing to live the unitive dimension of their conjugal life. Thus the prohibition against direct contraception wrongly seemed to some like the wildest extension of a ceremonial prohibition against boiling the kid in the milk of its mother. But surely after eleven years of treating the prohibition in that light, we can now see from the consequences of the contraceptive mentality that it is a serious command of

God. We need to retrace our reasoning and locate the prohibition in the context revealed by the Lord's command regarding marriage: "What God has united, man must not divide."

God gives commands regarding marriage in virtue of his work as Creator. The sexual and spiritual union of man and woman in marriage is his because it brings to culmination the way he designed our bodies when he made us male and female. He raises marriage to the dignity of a sacrament in virtue of his work as Redeemer. We must understand his commands against the background of these his mighty works.

What God has united we must not divide because only in the union of male and female is his image physically complete among us. We read in Genesis:

> God created man in the image of himself, in the image of God he created him, male and female he created them (Gen. 1:27).

That the physical image not be a caricature of God, all sexual union must meet stringent conditions.

In the first place, as is obvious from relatively simple observation, sex was made for procreation. God has handed over to us his power to initiate human life. Although God makes each and every human soul directly, he hands himself over to us, as it were, to initiate his creation. Thus sex as the power to procreate was made in the image of God as Creator. If this power is not warped by sin so that his image becomes disfigured, whenever we freely will orgasmic sex, we will it in conformity with his will only as a married couple prepared to accept lovingly and rear as well as we can the work of his creative power. The married may use sex and avoid procreating as long as both use and avoidance are natural. He has so made our sex that such avoidance is relatively easy. But in avoiding procreation we may not directly attack that power, for that is to repudiate the image of God in sex. When we repudiate the image of the one and only God, we set up an idol in its place. In sexual matters that idol is the self and its dominance is demonic. So dominant has lust made the self that ours is the culture of narcissism.[9]

It is important to recall that what is forbidden is direct contraception, a specific intentional action whose sole or overriding purpose is to prevent a conception that otherwise might take place.[10] If we could use technology merely to help us avoid conception for good reason—something our bodies avoid most of the time anyway—rather than to help us attack our procreative power, the use would not be directly contraceptive. I know of no technology that meets this requirement other than the natural techniques (as opposed to manipulative techniques) that go to make up natural family planning. They are truly human, and obviously God has provided them to meet the need for restraining births in some measure among some persons in our day.

Thus the physical image of God in us lies in our power to procreate. But sin has entered the world, and has touched that power in particular so that we are driven wildly at times to use it contrary to God's will in a way apart from marriage, that is, directly and even violently contrary to procreation. We seek directly sterilized sex to satisfy our lust, particularly with partners to whom we are not married. We kill the unwanted results of our sex when we forget our methods of sterilization, or when they fail us. Some prefer the perfectly sterilized practices of homosexuality, as was the case in St. Paul's day.[11] In all these ways we disobey what we may know of God's will by observing how he made us. Therefore, we are still without excuse.

God has long offered us remedies for this driving lust, which both original and actual sin have released within us. The first remedy is marriage.[12] Therein we may use sex as he designed it, open to procreation and prepared to meet the responsibilities of sharing his creative power. But of at least equal importance in marriage is the opportunity to live an image of his absolutely faithful and unique love for each one of us. The exclusivity of married love is permissible only as the sign of his fidelity to each. Otherwise and without the openness to procreation, it would be no more than *égoisme à deux*. Thus marriage is more than an institution to meet the necessities of the newly conceived, just as humanity's share in the image of God is more than physical. Marriage is a truly spiritual state.

Nonetheless, as Redeemer, God offers more than marriage as a remedy for lust. If we will willingly forgo our share in his physical creative power, and if we thereby forgo all it entails (while retaining our sense of manhood and womanhood) and accept complete continence for the sake of the kingdom of God, he will deign to use us as his instruments in the re-creation whereby humanity is born again to life in Christ. A few have thrust upon them no choice but to accept or reject this vocation. They cannot choose an alternative. For the majority who publicly profess complete continence for the kingdom, he wills that they choose it freely over the alternative of marriage. Those upon whom the vocation to continence is thrust choose it willingly or reject it, but may not choose an alternative. They are those for whom marriage is, or has become, an impossibility for one reason or another.

One class of those for whom marriage is, practically speaking, impossible has been ruthlessly exploited, albeit unwittingly, by deviant theologians during this past decade. These theologians have proposed that, instead of the sacrifice of complete continence lived through God's love and in the joy of knowing that one is doing his will, homosexuals ought to act out what they are inclined to do. Many of these homosexuals, who are so inclined through no fault of their own, thereby enter the living hell of lust that follows from denying God's creative image and worshipping the idol that takes its place. I consider it a triumph of the evil one unparalleled in history that he has finally persuaded some Catholic theologians to offer this solution as "kinder"—God help us!—than continence and the escape that continence offers from the demimonde, now misnamed the gay world. In the darker days of my own participation in deviant theology, I lent my name to one of the worst of such books, John J. McNeill's *The Church and the Homosexual*.[13] An outstanding Catholic, who happens to be a homosexual, sought my help. In doing so, this man gave help instead of receiving it, for he helped me see the error of my theology.

Complete continence for the kingdom, therefore, goes beyond marriage in living an affirmation of the image of God as Redeemer, *if it is lived for the kingdom.* If it is lived as what might be called today an alternate life-style—particularly if it is lived as if the difference between the sexes is an annoying biological aberration that we should overcome as well as we can by using technology to build a unisex or androgynous culture—the continence will eventually cease to be complete and become merely a way of avoiding the maturity demanded in marriage. Such celibacy is for the devil, not the kingdom of God. But the fact that the aberration exists must not drive us to forget the ideal of complete continence for the kingdom nor drive those who have been called to it to cease to live their continence, or to return to it if they have sinned. Complete continence for the kingdom proclaims among other truths that our hope is a personal, resurrected life with him everlastingly, rather than the natural immortality of living on in our children. It thereby also affirms his creativity in the form he gives it as he begins to create our lives and our worlds anew. It can therefore be the nobler calling for those he chooses. One sign that it is, is the profounder than ordinary sense of manhood and womanhood developed while living the vocation.

This authentic sign is blurred in our day because neofeminism, the so-called gay liberation, the *Playboy* philosophy, and other movements whose ideologies attack the family as God instituted it have the further effect of obliterating as well as they can any cultural signs of the spiritual significance found in the difference between the sexes.

Neofeminism takes one form within the Church as a drive to ordain women, and as such, it is not simply an attack upon the moral order as revealed in the design of our bodies; it is a direct attack upon the whole person, body and soul.

We are ensouled bodies, i.e., bodies whose form is a rational soul. That is what makes us living human bodies. By virtue of our rational soul we have faculties of intellect and will. With these we freely ordain ourselves toward our goal in life, although since the Fall we cannot choose our true destiny unless God's grace frees us from sin. From its inception our soul is ours individually because it is the form of our unique body. This meta-physical union with a body that makes the soul mine is a union with a male body. Therefore, using those faculties I possess in virtue of my rational soul, the vocation I must freely choose, if I do not want to lose myself body and soul in hell, is that of fatherhood. Were mine the soul of a female body, my vocation would be motherhood. If we deny the vocation given us through our bodies, we deny the individuality of our souls. This denial results in our spiritual disintegration as persons, meaning explicitly that it prevents us from using our spiritual faculties to choose our destiny in God. The denial rejects both creation and grace. Only when grace overcomes the denial can we be saved. Thus the Scriptures affirm the distinction between man and woman as well as support for familial authority; they condemn those sexual sins whereby we deny our identities.[14]

In what does the sexual difference consist? First, it is strictly speaking bodily, that is, biological. In procreation a man's physical labor consists of a few moments, usually of great pleasure and all too short, whereas the woman's consists of nine months of gestation, at least a few more months, or even years, of nurturing the infant unless someone else takes over this last task. This either is a dispensation of profound spiritual significance, or it is the "damnedest injustice" in creation. Only in the light of the transcendent goal of human life that Christian faith makes known to us is the division of labor in procreation anything but an injustice to woman, whereas in that light it is her glory.

Knowing in faith that God is our Father Almighty, the Creator of heaven and earth, and that we are destined to live happily with him forever, implies that God must directly create any being capable of knowing and loving him, for to do so is to share a life that is properly his. And if nothing other than God can create from nothing, *a fortiori* no thing created from nothing could make itself in the image of God. If God chooses, as he has, to share this creative power with a creature—i.e., to hand over to a creature the ability to initiate a new life eventually capable of knowing and loving him—then he must divide the labor because God cannot lie. Fatherhood, i.e., the begetting of rational life, is properly the work of God. If we human beings are knowingly to procreate new human life, he could not allow us to do so in such a way as to live a lie. One thing God cannot do is lie. The reproduction of human life via parthenogenesis as a kind of self-initiated self-actualization would be living a lie because of ourselves we do *not* initiate human life. So God divided his image among us, giving to approximately half the species the spiritual vocation of begetter, to the other half the spiritual vocation of provenience. In himself God is both, but as creatures we must acknowledge him first and foremost as initiator because our minds cannot exclude from the notion of provenience alone the possibility of being acted upon, of being passive, and of yielding further reality of necessity rather than freely. A knowledge particularly of how the Gnostics conceived of the mother goddess confirms why we must speak of God as Father.[15]

In order to prevent those who share in his work as begetters from giving in to pride, God reduced their role to very little indeed, and gave to the provenience, i.e., the woman, the more intimate and vital link to new life. The new being is hers exclusively when it is most vulnerable. In addition, we all bear traces not only of her body but also of her traits. The latter are usually more fundamental in our personalities than those of our fathers because our mothers got there first, as it were. Every man is born of woman. We may not know our fathers, but few of us can forget our mothers. Furthermore, women have potentially a spiritual advantage over males because of women's natural obedience. But I must leave it to a woman to speak further of woman's glorious role, since I cannot know it from within. But I can know what it is not, for I am called to fatherhood.

I have chosen to answer that call by answering a further call to the exclusively spiritual fatherhood of religious chastity. Therefore, I have not been able to rely on physical fatherhood to launch me into the adult vocation of us all, which is being a parent. I must know the spiritual significance of manhood and of my fatherhood, and fulfill what they point to, or I must die a warped, broken, and perhaps even damned creature.

Spiritual fatherhood is begetting new life in Christ—something C. S. Lewis preferred to call regenerate life.[16] As a priest I am called to beget that life through word and sacrament. But, to be sure that this calling does not go to my head, the role that is exclusively mine is very, very small indeed. As a priest I am restricted to the only role of a male that symbolizes in the spiritual order the role of the father in the family.[17] Just as God could be with us only as a man because he initiates both creation and redemption, just as only the male can beget, just as only the husband ought to provide for his wife and defend her when she is incapacitated in labor, thereby earning his place at the head of the family, so only the male can preside in our Lord's place at the table of his sacrifice. Spiritual fatherhood in the priesthood consists of exercising the rights and responsibilities of presiding in this way.

All fatherhood is extremely difficult in our day. Today's culture calls males to a state of perpetual adolescence, and has so prevailed in this nation that over a hundred million American males rolled over with barely a murmur and permitted nine persons, ostensibly men, to take from them their rights of fatherhood prior to the birth of their children and many rights after birth. Fatherhood has almost ceased to exist in our national law. Men who live according to its present spirit abdicate their manhood.[18]

This was brought home to me most forcibly when a young medical student at the Medical College of Wisconsin asked me over the telephone what the Church taught concerning artificial insemination by a donor. He had been asked to donate his seed. (The request, I believe, is made in a general way of all male students.) I pointed out to him that the child born of that seed would be his, and that settled the matter for him. It would not have settled the matter for anyone more despoiled by this culture's demonic denial of our bodies. For them fatherhood is an option one takes up more or less if a woman who has or wants a child wants also sustained rather than casual sexual companionship and perhaps some financial assistance while raising the child. Thus the law of our land confirms "philosophical liberalism" with its "erroneous affirmation of the autonomy of the individual,"[19] and begins to reduce the family to a name for an alternate style of life in a unisex culture. Unisex or androgyny is the caricature of God's image within us. We can show forth that image only by preserving the division of labor spiritually and physically which he built into it.

I believe therefore that, if we return to God by rendering loving obedience to him in faith through living out the image in which he made us, we shall perceive the special idolatry of our day expressed in social movements of both the Right and the Left that will seek to usurp his direct sovereignty over us. That sovereignty is our one hope for human decency and dignity in this life. The political, economic, and social organizations of both the Right and the Left, of fascists, secular liberals, and communists, have joined forces to attack the two institutions through which God exercises his liberating sovereignty, the Church and the family.

On the Right the attack takes many forms. In South Africa through apartheid human beings not only systematically commit the sins that make up racism but they also destroy families. Thereby they attack the image of God and worship an idol. In Brazil through the economic system some people deny hope of a living *family* wage to many others. Thereby they attack the image of God and worship an idol. Ironically, one of the most insidious and subtle attacks upon the family arises not in the impoverished outskirts, vast as they are, of our liberal economic system. Rather the attack arises among the more affluent who make up what our Holy Father, Pope John Paul II, called "the consumer civilization."[20]

It was inevitable that this attack would arise among us. After all, one man with a family of six who earns a living family wage is not going to buy the same number of high-profit consumer goods as six others, male or female, without families but with equal wages. Swinging singles make better consumers than family members. Wherever there is an attack upon the family, to the extent that Church members defend the family as they should, there is also an attack upon the Church.

All forms of Marxism attack faith in God and offer instead the idolatry of totalitarianism. Despite overwhelming evidence to this effect, some still follow Marxism in the name of human ideals. Therefore, there remains some hope of dialogue over human rights. But Marxism remains an attack upon God no matter how packaged with what ideals, no matter what human misery it exploits. Since it is an attack upon God, it is an attack upon humanity made in his image.

Thus we may see that one of the subtlest idolatries of our times is the use from within the Church of Christian "social love" not to espouse Christian and human solutions to the social evils rampant in our world but instead to manipulate and co-opt Christians in support of social, economic, and political solutions from the Right and from the Left whose inner logic is anti-God and therefore anti-human.[21]

Christian social action, or what we once called Catholic Action, is one of the most needed works today. It is perhaps the greatest single achievement of deviant theology within the Church to have diverted those energies to secularistic movements either of the Right or the Left. I leave it to my readers to think on their own about the many, many examples. Pope Paul VI marked out the true path of social action in *Octogesima Adveniens*, his apostolic letter commemorating the eightieth anniversary of *Rerum Novarum*. On the map of social activity he clearly indicated the Scylla of Marxism and the Charybdis of "the liberal ideology," and rightly told us to sail the straits between the two.[22] If we would hold up an alternative to these twin horrors of our age, we would draw all persons of good will to ourselves. Instead, the deviant use a veneer of Christian sentiment to steer the unsuspecting toward one or the other for destruction.

Moral theology today should turn all its energies toward exposing the sin of idolatry among us in all its forms. Then with renewed faith all moral theologians may once again hear the great commission our Lord gave his Church within which he proleptically assigned to moralists their job:

> "All authority in heaven and on earth has been given to me. Go, therefore, make disciples of all the

nations; baptize them in the name of the Father and
of the Son and of the Holy Spirit, and teach them to
observe all the commands I gave you. And know that
I am with you always; yes, to the end of time" (Mt.
19:18-20).

The Roman Catholic moral theologian should study what
God has commanded, all else it entails, the motive for obeying
him and then teach all who will hear to observe them.

A Personal Conclusion

I hope that all who read this work will turn to Scripture and
read the text of Romans from Chapter 1, verse 18 through
Chapter 2, verse 11. Of necessity I have had to dwell upon the
first section of that unit, but the second section speaks to me
about myself as well as the first. St. Paul there said, "So no
matter who you are, if you pass judgment you have no excuse.
In judging others you condemn yourself, since you behave no
differently from those you judge" (Rom. 2:1-2). He did not have
in mind my sentiments exactly, but his admonition to some
among the Christians in Rome, probably to some of Jewish
descent who had enjoyed better moral training early in life
than former pagans, reminds me that my judgments on deviant
theologians are no more than judgments I must pass on myself
for the work of most of my professional life. If God's grace can
deliver me from the idolatry of that theology, I trust his grace
can deliver anyone. In writing this, I pray that others will join
me in returning to the truths his Church teaches in lieu of the
soul-destroying errors the evil one has masked with the illusion of newness, progress, and reform.

Notes

1. Cf. Peter T. Geach, *God and the Soul* (London and Henley: Rout-
ledge & Kegan Paul, 1969; rpt., 1978), pp. 57-58.
2. My interpretation rests on the fact that for St. Thomas *ens et*

verum et bonum convertuintur. God is the supreme Being and the cause and source of all other beings; therefore, he is the supreme Good. The rest follows. Cf. St. Thomas Aquinas, *Summa Theologiae* Ia, q.l, a.1 ob2; IIa-IIae, q.109, a.2 ad 1:Ia, q.6.

3. The quotation in this paragraph and all following quotations from the Scriptures in this article are taken from *The Jerusalem Bible.*

4. Fairlie is referring to the book *The Myth of God Incarnate*, edited by J. Hick (London: SCM Press, 1977).

5. Henry Fairlie, *The Seven Deadly Sins Today* (Washington, D.C.: New Republic Books, 1978), pp. 5-6.

6. Ibid.

7. Roman Catholic moral theology becomes deviant when the theologian deviates from Church teaching usually by teaching one or both of the two following errors: Whereas the Church has always taught according to divine law that knowingly and freely willed orgasmic sex is a moral good only when a conjugal act, other forms of orgasmic sex may now be considered permissible, even desirable, under certain circumstances; and whereas the Church has always taught that no private person may directly kill human life at any stage of development and no public person may directly kill innocent human life, we now know that we may directly and privately kill some forms of human life at some stages of development given certain circumstances. The whole business of a so-called new morality really comes down to no more than this. I contend that the deviant theologian has ceased to talk about the one and only God we may know in faith within the Roman Catholic Church and has come instead to talk about an idol of his own making.

8. P. T. Geach, *The Virtues* (Cambridge: Cambridge University Press, 1977) p. 88.

9. Cf. Christopher Lasch, *The Culture of Narcissism* (New York: W. W. Norton & Company, 1978).

10. Pope Paul VI, *Humanae Vitae* (Encyclical Letter, July 25, 1968); translation: *On the Regulation of Birth* (Washington, D.C.: United States Catholic Conference, 1968), section number 14, p. 9. In the summer of 1978 Malcolm Muggeridge delivered an address in San Francisco that is one of the finest appreciations of this teaching I know. Entitled *Malcolm Muggeridge on Humanae Vitae,* it is now available in print from The National Committee of Catholic Laymen, Inc., Room 480, 150 East 35th Street, New York, N.Y. 10016.

11. There is a vitally important difference between sterile and sterilized. A husband and wife, both seventy-five years of age, who

freely express their love through a natural conjugal act, in all probability perform a sterile sexual act. For one man freely to will an
orgasm in an aperture of another man's body is a steril*ized* sexual act.
Where he chose to place the orgasm sterilizes the orgasm. Too often
fuzzy thinking leads those who deviate from Church teaching to reason falsely that if sterile sex is good for aged Abraham and Sarah, it
should be at least potentially good for two men. Between two men the
sex is steril*ized*, not merely sterile.

12. Geach, *The Virtues*, pp. 146 ff.

13. John J. McNeill S. J., *The Church and the Homosexual* (Kansas
City: Sheed Andrews and McMeel, 1976) pp. x-xi.

14. E.g., Genesis 1:27; Ephesians 5:21-33; 1 Peter 3:1; Colossians
3:18; 1 Corinthians 6:9-10; 1 Timothy 1:9-10; Romans 1:26-27.

15. Cf. Elaine Pagels, "Christianity's Male Orientation," in *New Oxford Review*, 46, no. 2 (March 1979): 4-11.

16. C. S. Lewis, *Miracles* (Glasgow: Collins, Fontana Books, 1960;
rpt., 1976) pp. 173-177. N.B. The copies of this work printed by Macmillan in the United States do *not* give the text Lewis revised in 1960.

17. It should not be necessary to mention that offices that are
functions, unlike the roles of husband-father, wife-mother, and
priesthood, which give a particular character to the soul itself, may be
filled either by males or females, other things being equal. This is to
say that Mrs. Thatcher may serve Britain better as Prime Minister
than her male counterparts, although that remains to be seen. Nevertheless, she could not serve the Church of England as Archbishop of
Canterbury unless that church decided to sever all links with the
orthodox and catholic Christian faith. Cf. Pope Paul VI, *Octogesima
Adveniens* (Apostolic Letter, May 14, 1971); translation: *A Call to
Action: On the Occasion of the Eightieth Anniversary of the Encyclical
Rerum Novarum* (Washington, D.C.: United States Catholic Confer-
ence, 1971), section number 13, p. 8; also, the document from the
Sacred Congregation for the Doctrine of the Faith dated October 15,
1976 and entitled *Declaration on the Question of the Admission of
Women to the Ministerial Priesthood* (Washington, D.C.: United States
Catholic Conference, 1977).

18. Cf. Charles E. Rice, *Beyond Abortion: The Theory and Practice of
the Secular State* (Chicago: Franciscan Herald Press, 1979), esp. pp.
101 ff. Despite the reference to Rice, I am indebted for the idea to Mrs.
Raymond Kuffel of Brookfield, Wisconsin.

19. Pope Paul VI, *Octogesima Adveniens,* section number 35, p. 18.

20. Pope John Paul II, *Redemptor Hominis* (Encyclical Letter, March

4, 1979); translation: *Redeemer of Man* (Washington, D.C.: United States Catholic Conference, 1979), section number 16, p. 53.
21. *Ibid.*, p. 52.
22. Pope Paul VI, *Octogesima Adveniens,* esp. sections number 31-37, pp. 16-20.

The Teaching of the Church and Moral Theology

Rev. Donald McCarthy
Mt. St. Mary Seminary
Norwood, Ohio

Three years before he was chosen to serve as Vicar of Christ and head of the Church, Karol Cardinal Wojtyla spoke these words:

> The "magisterium" of the Church does not only represent the transmission of the Word of God but also that *transmission marked by a special duty towards the truth it contains.* It is exactly at this point, where the "magisterium" coincides with the prophetic mission of the whole People of God, that we somehow touch on the crucial point of this responsibility towards the truth of the Word of God.[1]

This reflection will consider that responsibility toward the truth of the Word of God from three perspectives: (1) the teaching of the Church as prophecy; (2) the role of theology within the prophetic Church; and (3) moral theology and the magisterium.

The Teaching of the Church as Prophecy

The Church is prophetic; it speaks for God in the original sense of prophecy, "the mediation and interpretation of the divine mind and will."[2] The Church teaches the "deposit of faith," and the term *faith* indicates that Church teaching is God's teaching. All of Church teaching in some way conveys, interprets, or applies the Word of God.

The Prologue of St. John's Gospel epitomizes the dynamics of God's Word in the world. "He was in the world, and through him the world was made, yet the world did not know who he was. To his own he came, yet his own did not accept him. Any who did accept him he empowered to become children of God" (Jn. 1:10-12).

Before "the Word became flesh and made his dwelling among us" (Jn. 1:14), God had raised up many prophets to speak for him to the Chosen People. Hence the deposit of faith had already begun. The prophetic teaching throughout the Old Testament interprets nature, history, and humanity in the light of God's word, a word of faith.[3]

Jesus came as a prophet and John's Gospel and the Acts of the Apostles identify him as "the prophet" foretold in Deuteronomy 18:15.[4] Jesus communicated the prophetic spirit and mission to those in union with him.[5] Jesus, the Word of God, spoke the word of God to the Church. More than that, Jesus commissioned the Church to carry on the role of prophecy, not in predicting the future, but in speaking for God.

St. Paul described the role of Church prophecy to the Thessalonians in these words: "We thank God constantly that in receiving his message from us you took it, not as the word of men, but as it truly is, the word of God at work within you who believe" (1 Thes. 2:13).

Although the word *magisterium* was not used until the nineteenth century for the unique teaching authority of the Church, that teaching mission began in the first century.[6] Karl Rahner describes that long period of teaching as "the history of the self-understanding of the Church itself, which cannot but understand itself essentially except as the bearer of the gospel message."[7] Rahner maintains that at the end of the apostolic age the monarchical episcopate was firmly established as the decisive court of appeal in the Church with the mandate of handing on the doctrine of the apostles. The material element of Church teaching was the doctrinal content, and the formal element was the claim of the bishops to demand faith as they testified in the name of Christ and with the assistance of the Holy Spirit.[8]

Hence the whole Church is able to enjoy a prophetic character as it professes the Word of God to the world at large. The Church as a whole cannot deny or corrupt the deposit of faith, for it is the pillar and ground of truth (1 Tim. 3:15) against which the jaws of death shall not prevail (Mt. 16:18,cf. Gal. 1:8). The prophetic mission of the Church with the bishops as chief prophets demands the infallible doctrinal authority of the episcopate as a whole when teaching the deposit of faith.

The eschatological character of the prophetic Church derives from the Christ-event which the Church must make historically present to all ages. The Church would not be the eschatological community of salvation if it were not in infallible possession of the truth of Christ.

The teaching authority of the Church is not mere legal or juridical authority but the authority of the Word of God. Hence Athanasius did not argue from the authority of the Council of Nicaea as such, but from the fact that Nicaea expressed the faith received from the apostles.[9] Although the Church has progressed in its understanding of its own teaching role and particularly of the unique place of the Pope in that role, it has always believed in and exercised the role of prophecy.

Recent historical studies have explored the forms of teaching authority employed by the Church throughout history.[10] As a living teacher, the Church adopted the intellectual resources at hand, using the great theological faculties of the medieval universities, for example, just as it had used the secular wisdom of Greek and Roman philosophy in the patristic period. While faith can never be reduced to propositions alone, at least the same degree of success in expressing the divine mysteries as enjoyed in the apostolic era has been found in all successive ages. The Church has sought to reflect divine truth faithfully and truly within the creatureliness and historicity of human truth.[11]

The modern period of Church history beginning with the Council of Trent saw significant changes in the milieu in which the Church exercised its prophetic role. The religious divisions consequent upon the Reformation created massive doctrinal confusion. The invention of printing revolutionized education and communication, and multiplied the doctrinal confusion. The Index of Forbidden Books was established in 1564. Within the Church the powerful movements of Jansenism, Gallicanism, and Febronianism were followed by Modernism. Against this background the First Vatican Council formulated the explicit doctrine of the papal magisterium. The Second Vatican Council repeated this teaching, and completed it by including the infallible doctrinal authority of the episcopate as a whole with and under the Pope.

The Second Vatican Council Constitution on the Church (*Lumen Gentium*) described the magisterial role of the college of bishops in these words:

> The bishops, in as much as they are the successors of the apostles, receive from the Lord, to whom all power is given in heaven and on earth, the mission of teaching all peoples, and of preaching the Gospel to every creature, so that all men may attain to salvation through faith, baptism and the observance of the commandments.[12]

Fr. Louis Bouyer offered this description of the magisterium:

> the function that pertains to the Church, and particularly to her apostolic hierarchy, of perpetually

proclaiming the Word of God in His name and with
His authority, and of defining its meaning whenever
necessary.[13]

The Second Vatican Council sought to renew within the
Church the appreciation of faith as a personal response to
magisterial teaching.[14] Archbishop Robert Coffy of Albi at the
European Bishop's Symposium in 1975 suggested that the
nineteenth-century emphasis on the magisterium as doctrinal
authority "happened in a given historical context in which
faith was seen, above all, as intellectual acquiescence to a body
of truths. And thus emerged a limitation of the meaning of the
concept of Magisterium." He added, "In a form closer to the
truth, the faith is today presented as an assent of the whole
being to the Mystery of Salvation."[15] At the same symposium
Karol Cardinal Wojtyla made the observation with which this
reflection began about the duty toward the truth that the
magisterium transmits.

Significantly, the famous discussion of the teaching authority of the Church in paragraph 25 of *Lumen Gentium* of the
Second Vatican Council treats *first* of the assent to be given
the prophetic teaching of the Church before it discusses the
certitude of truth and the charism of infallibility.

Regarding assent, the Council fathers speak of submission
and "ready and respectful allegiance of mind" to be given by
the faithful to their bishops' decisions made in the name of
Christ and in matters of faith and morals. Furthermore, "this
loyal submission of the will and intellect must be given, in a
special way, to the authentic teaching authority of the Roman
Pontiff, even when he does not speak *ex cathedra*." (This was
written less than four years before Pope Paul VI's *Humanae
Vitae*.)

Before restating the teaching of Vatican Council I about the
infallibility of the Pope the Council fathers of Vatican II described the way bishops collectively share that charism
through the universal ordinary magisterium:

> Although the bishops, taken individually, do not enjoy the privilege of infallibility, they do, however, proclaim infallibly the doctrine of Christ on the following conditions: namely, when, even though dispersed throughout the world but preserving for all that amongst themselves and with Peter's successor the bond of communion, in their authoritative teaching concerning matters of faith and morals, they are in agreement that a particular teaching is to be held definitively and absolutely.

This clear teaching of the Second Vatican Council that the bishops can teach infallibly through the universal ordinary magisterium deserves careful consideration in appreciating the worldwide prophetic teaching of the Church. Some theologians seem to ignore this infallibility. Fr. Timothy O'Connell, for example, states that all the existing moral teachings of the Church fall in the realm of the "ordinary magisterium," and then explains that these are teachings which, "although assisted by the Spirit, are nonetheless susceptible to error and therefore fallible."[16]

On the other hand, two scholarly articles in the June 1978 issue of *Theological Studies* discussed the text of *Lumen Gentium* cited above and both accepted in principle the infallibility of the universal ordinary magisterium of the bishops when the conditions are fulfilled.[17] Joseph Komonchak presented what he called a minimalizing approach in his conclusions and argued that the condemnation of artificial contraception had not been taught infallibly by the ordinary magisterium. John Ford S.J. and Germain Grisez, on the other hand, presented a much more thorough analysis of the text and an impressive argument that the contraception condemnation *had* been infallibly taught.

Through their careful study of the genesis of the critical text in *Lumen Gentium* Ford and Grisez showed two very significant points:

1. Vatican II purposely avoided saying that a strictly collegial act is required for the infallibility of the ordinary magisterium of the bishops.

2. The Council also studiously avoided limiting the infallibility of such teaching to cases in which a point divinely revealed is proposed for acceptance with the assent of divine faith.[18]

They also provided a sound and coherent interpretation of the four conditions set down by *Lumen Gentium* for the exercise of infallibility in the universal, ordinary magisterium. They argued for an interpretation of the critical fourth condition, that the bishops teach a judgment "to be held definitively," as a teaching calling for "an assent of certitude, similar to the assent of divine faith, but not necessarily having the same motive as has the latter assent."[19]

It is obviously possible for the bishops to teach a doctrine infallibly without theologians who take the minimalizing approach of Joseph Komonchak recognizing that fact. However, the discussion of infallibility, or probable infallibility, must not obscure the more basic theme of the prophetic role of all Church teaching on matters of faith and morals. In the tradition of the Old Testament prophets and of Jesus the prophet, the Church speaks prophetically in proclaiming the deposit of *faith*. When the Old Testament prophets taught the Chosen People or when Jesus proclaimed the Word, no one discussed infallibility.[20]

The analogy with Jesus and the prophets cannot be pressed too far. Public revelation closed with the death of the last apostle, and the teaching Church does not pretend to initiate new revelation. The Second Vatican Council constitution on Divine Revelation taught clearly:

> Sacred Tradition and sacred Scripture made up a single sacred deposit of the Word of God, which is entrusted to the Church....

> But the task of giving an authentic interpretation
> of the Word of God, whether in its written form or in
> the form of Tradition, has been entrusted to the liv-
> ing teaching office of the Church alone. Its authority
> in this matter is exercised in the name of Jesus
> Christ. Yet this Magisterium is not superior to the
> Word of God, but is its servant. It teaches only what
> has been handed on to it. At the divine command
> and with the help of the Holy Spirit, it listens to this
> devotedly, guards it with dedication and expounds it
> faithfully.[21]

That last phrase echoes the language of *Lumen Gentium*,
which speaks of the *depositum revelationis* that must be *sancte
custodiendum et fideliter exponendum*. This grammatical construction was given an official explanation at Vatican II as
describing the content of magisterial teaching and "including
those things which are required to guard as inviolable and
expound with fidelity this same deposit."[22]

This point will have implications in the discussion of moral
theology and the applications of moral teachings to concrete
human actions below. In expressing this point Karl Rahner
noted that the magisterium can and must decide the extent of
magisterial explanation of doctrine:

> The object of the magisterium is the content of
> Christian revelation and all that is necessary or use-
> ful for the preaching and the defence of this revela-
> tion. In determining the content of revelation and
> demarcating it off from matter on which the magis-
> terium is not competent, the magisterium is itself
> the judge of its own authority.[23]

Just as prophets spoke the language and addressed the problems of their place and time, so the magisterial teaching of the
Church speaks the language and addresses the problems of
each age. Theological reflection must take place so that the

teaching and prophetic Church can accomplish this. Theology explores all questions of faith and morals for the benefit of the whole Church, both the magisterial college of bishops and the Church as the entire People of God. The next section will discuss the role of theology.

The Role of Theology Within the Prophetic Church

"One rightly insists on the need for collaboration between the magisterium and theology," said the future Pope John Paul II in the address mentioned earlier, "for a modern language, for direct contact with the experience of the men of our generation, for dialogue suggested by Vatican II and the encyclical *Ecclesiam Suam*."[24]

Vatican II clearly recognized diverse gifts in the Church, and scientific theological reflection ranked high among them. The lofty description of the magisterium in *Lumen Gentium* only obliquely refered to the resource of scientific theology when it noted:

> The Roman Pontiff and the bishops, by reason of their office and the seriousness of the matter, apply themselves with zeal to the work of enquiring by every suitable means into this revelation and of giving apt expression to its contents.[25]

Theologians describe that process of enquiring into revelation by every suitable means as "venturing hypotheses, reviewing data, reconsidering presuppositions, listening and learning, and, it may be, having simply to wait for further light at a later time."[26]

The ecclesialogical model of the Church that took shape in the Second Vatican Council proposed that both hierarchical leaders and those with other gifts interrelate within the Church rather than isolating the teaching authority above the

Church. Bishop John Quinn pointed out after the Council that we see the Church "no longer as a pyramid but as the family of God in which each member plays a role of service in loving obedience to the Spirit and dedication to the good of all."[27]

The year after the Council Pope Paul VI summarized the role of theology by citing three duties of theologians within the Church: (1) to examine and comprehend the truths of Revelation more thoroughly; (2) to bring the fruits of their labor to the attention of the Christian community, and, in particular, to the attention of the magisterium itself, so that the whole Christian people may be enlightened by the doctrine which the ecclesiastical hierarchy hands down; (3) to lend its efforts to the task of spreading, clarifying, confirming, and defending the truth which the magisterium authoritatively propounds.[28]

Implicit in that first duty of examining and comprehending the truths of revelation more thoroughly is found the phenomenon of doctrinal development. Such development only occurs within the context of vigorous theological activity. This is desirable, but at times it can proliferate confusion within the Church. This possibility places increased responsibility on the magisterium. Bishop Quinn pointed out in the address mentioned above that the magisterium has a developmental as well as custodial role in its teaching mission. In fact, he pictured the preeminent role of the magisterium as to "preside over the unfolding of the heritage of the faith, to plant and water (1 Cor. 3:6) with joyous hope, with judicious discernment, always with firm reliance on the abiding presence of the Spirit and with that 'love which casts out fear' (1 Jn. 4:18)."[29]

Yet beneath this poetic language lurks the thorny issue of theological pluralism. For every magisterial statement has at least traces of a theological substructure. Whatever theological substructure the magisterial statements use leaves others in limbo if not utterly rejected. The broader the scope of theological diversity—and it is broad today particularly because of the widespread attempts to improve on neo-scholastic philosophy and theology—the more disturbing is this phenomenon.[30]

This problem suggests four specific points of consideration:

First, the bishops bear the heavy burden of discerning appropriate ways of incorporating theological development into magisterial teaching in all areas of faith and morals. They are responsible to see that the *depositum* is *fideliter exponendum,* faithfully explained. This includes faithfulness to the needs and challenges of each generation. Fr. Raymond Brown described this in his address to the National Catholic Education Association in April 1978: "Bishops must listen to theologians and acquire information, and pray over it, and think over it, and then teach pastorally what they judge the Church must hear."[31] Fr. Avery Dulles uses the metaphor of the Pope and bishops as the "lens by which the light, issuing from all who are competent by faith and scholarship, is brought to a focus and expressed."[32]

Second, the need to consult theologians and the faithful in matters of faith and morals must not generate a "consensus mentality." Consensus is desirable but by no means indispensable in a prophetic Church. Hints of this mentality can be found in the following two statements. "If the official doctrine fails to achieve acceptance in the general body of the faithful," Fr. Avery Dulles said in his presidential address to the Catholic Theological Society of America in 1976, "it may be crucially important to have thinkers devising alternate positions."[33] The following year Fr. Richard McCormick wrote in the *New Catholic World,* "It is my judgment that the Holy Father and the college of bishops should not formulate their teaching against a broad or even very significant theological consensus."[34]

The problem of this "consensus mentality" is not a new one. Seventy-two years ago the decree *Lamentabili* of the Holy Office rejected the modernist proposition that "In defining truths the learning Church and the teaching Church so collaborate that there is nothing left for the teaching Church but to sanction the common opinions of the learning Church."[35]

The point is not to exclude learning from the magisterial process but to avoid undermining the prophetic mission of the magisterium. The "consensus mentality" relies on an ecclesiology and an epistemology of revelation in which the body politic rather than the divinely appointed teachers interpret doctrinal teaching.

This problem may be more acute in our contemporary world in which theology is often taught in universities by professors of comparative religion without a firm commitment to either the magisterium or the life of faith itself. Furthermore, the present practice of ignoring the *imprimatur* subtly encourages publishers to promote the work of the more controversial and popularly appealing theological writers. The consensus of the most popular or widely published theological writers offers little assurance of doctrinal reliability today. The need for responsible self-criticism within the Catholic theological community has become increasingly urgent.[36]

In summary, it is clear that the teaching and learning Church (*ecclesia discens et docens*) needs close communication and collaboration. But the teaching Church cannot teach only what the learning Church wants to hear.

Third, the tendency to consider theological teachers as a distinct and independent magisterium can only augment confusion and undermine the prophetic mission of the Church. Fr. Richard McCormick defended the term *magisterium of theologians* in an article for lay readership in *New Catholic World,* saying it is appropriate "as indicating a true competence and authority not possessed by the hierarchy as such."[37] But in March 1979 in his "Notes on Moral Theology" he agreed with Dr. William May that the designation of two magisteria "can be a confusing verbal vehicle," and he stated that he was not wedded to it.[38] Yet he insisted on *independent* competence for theology without noting that such competence does not constitute a true magisterial role in the proper sense of that word in the modern Church. Rosemary R. Ruether used the erroneous concept of two magisteria when she wrote that the Catholic Theological Society of America "opted for an independent magisterial statement issued on its own authority" in the study on *Human Sexuality*.[39]

This notion of an independent magisterium of theologians has no basis whatsoever in the teaching of the Second Vatican Council. Long before the term *magisterium* had acquired its specific sense in the last two centuries, St. Thomas Aquinas indicated why there cannot be two sources of doctrinal authority:

> The very doctrine of Catholic doctors derives its authority from the Church. Hence we should abide by the authority of the Church rather than by that of an Augustine or a Jerome or any doctor whatever.[40]

Fourth, magisterial teaching not only invites the assent of theologians and the faithful but it is also taught *for that very reason*. It was mentioned above that the contemporary understanding of the faith response to the prophetic teaching of the Church calls for a response of the whole person—mind and will, emotions and passions. All authentic Church teaching calls for that response, not merely solemnly defined doctrines.[41]

Because assent is a function of at least ecclesiastical if not divine *faith* the withholding of assent cannot be a purely intellectual process. One should never undertake to withhold assent unless one is genuinely convinced that magisterial teaching is in error, not simply because it seems or begins to seem unconvincing or dissatisfying. While assent can never be unthinking or unreflective, it is not given primarily on the basis of philosophical arguments, and so it should not be withheld simply because philosophical reasons seem or begin to seem unconvincing.[42] Obviously one cannot withhold assent from defined infallible Church teaching without violating divine faith itself. Fr. Karl Rahner quotes an interesting analogy in a statement of the German bishops in 1967 referring to noninfallible teaching. They compared assent in this case to that of a person who accepts the decision of an expert even though he knows this is not infallible.[43]

Infallibility cannot be the only category opposed to falsity. Between infallibility and falsity there is the whole domain of sufficient certitude fostered in the Church by its belief in the assistance of the Spirit.[44] Hence the certitude of the magisterium is not a purely rational certitude as if the magisterium's persuasiveness were only as strong as the arguments it presents. This applies to moral teaching and interpretation of the natural moral law as well as to dogmatic teaching.

Perhaps the term being used today for the ordinary magisterium when speaking in matters noninfallibly—the "authentic" teaching of the Church—should also be used in describing assent to that teaching; it, too, should be "authentic." In cases where a person is not fully convinced intellectually of the truth of a magisterial teaching, "authentic" assent could not include total intellectual conviction, but it would still include personal acceptance. Such acceptance does not exclude investigation of new developments and formulations of teaching. But this personal acceptance—"authentic" assent—is the normal response of a believing Christian to the authentic teaching of the prophetic Church.

The cases of genuine dissent from magisterial teaching based on the conviction of the falsity of a given noninfallible teaching raise the problem of private versus public dissent. Some contemporary theologians argue that dissent to noninfallible teaching must be made public for the good of the Church and the authentic development of its magisterial teaching.[45] However, at the very least, public expressions of dissent must be presented *as such* and not merely as expressions of theological pluralism. It would seem that clear notice must be given that such positions are in opposition to the magisterium, and a sincere effort must be made to reflect magisterial teaching fairly and adequately.

The attitudes of "consensus mentality" and an "independent magisterium" for theologians mentioned above make it easy to neglect the appropriate expression of dissent just described. In this way dissenting opinions are actually seen as emanating from a second magisterium vying for allegiance among the members of the Church. This phenomenon seems to be especially pronounced in publications of Catholic moral theology since *Humanae Vitae* of 1968.[46] Hence the final consideration will discuss moral theology in particular.

Moral Theology and the Magisterium

The familiar phrase *faith and morals* indicates an essential nexus between faith and morals. Books like Schnackenburg's *The Moral Teaching of the New Testament* manifested what he called the "moral demands" of Jesus as well as the moral teaching of the apostolic Church.[47] The gospels teach faith and the moral response of conversion. The Scriptures teach moral virtues and condemn vice with specific examples.

Hence the prophetic mission of the Church includes moral teaching on an equal footing with dogmatic teaching. Scripture and tradition both contain dogmatic and moral content and both make up a single deposit of the Word of God entrusted to the Church in its living, teaching office.[48] While moral teaching has not been a predominant concern of the ecumenical councils of the Church, it has certainly not overlooked morality in its prophetic teaching.

Moral theology, the scientific study of human activity in the light of revelation, has been developing within the Church from the patristic period to the present day. Three methods have been used in moral theology with varying emphases: the natural-law method typified by St. Thomas Aquinas, the ascetical method typified by St. Bernard and St. Bonaventure, and the casuistic method typified by the Jesuit, Fr. Herman Busenbaum.

Both Church teaching and moral theology have recognized that human reason itself can uncover the basic moral norms obliging all human persons; hence, much Catholic moral teaching clarifies what may be known independently of revelation. But revelation teaches the origin of the moral order in the wisdom of divine creation, the renewing of creation in the paschal mystery of Jesus, and the way of Christian moral perfection leading to the ultimate end of beatitude through the sanctifying work of the Holy Spirit.[49]

Furthermore, the deposit of faith includes the moral teaching *developed* within the Church as it lives and witnesses to the scriptural Word of God. The Church began this witness long before the Council of Nicaea initiated the practice of solemn definition of doctrine. The apostolic Church was surely aware of the natural moral law and the discussion of it in the first two chapters of St. Paul's letter to the Romans.[50] Historical studies of the Church's teaching on abortion and contraception show the infant Church confronting and definitively rejecting these practices with its resources of faith and reason.[51]

Cardinal Sheehan of Baltimore proposed some years ago that if the current controversy on contraception had occurred before Newman wrote on the development of doctrine, he would have cited this moral teaching as an example of the legitimate development of scriptural doctrine within the prophetic Church.[52]

The development of moral doctrine within the Church is influenced by a variety of factors, including cultural, political, social, and economic conditions. John Noonan has pointed to a developing moral doctrine in the Church's teaching on usury that reflected economic conditions. It should be noted, though, that Ford and Grisez in their study cited earlier argued that "the moral teaching on the taking of interest proposed infallibility by the ordinary magisterium has *not* changed."[53]

As the Church's insights into human dignity and the full meaning of human sexuality have developed and matured, so has the moral teaching on slavery and conjugal love. Up until recent years the direction of Catholic moral teaching was heavily influenced by the scholastic synthesis of the Middle Ages and its subsequent formulations.

When the teaching magisterium of the Church began to address moral questions in the papal encyclicals of the nineteenth and twentieth centuries, it relied heavily on this established, natural moral-law tradition. The encyclicals used natural-law principles in analyzing political issues like communism and fascism, social issues like race relations and human rights, economic issues like the problems of a just wage and unions, familial issues like divorce and contraception, and medicomoral issues like abortion and euthanasia. Yet almost invariably they indicated also the use of Christian wisdom or vision or evangelical teaching in understanding the natural moral law. This showed that divine revelation has clarified, solidified, and ratified the natural-law approach.[54]

No one presented more urgently this role of the magisterium in interpreting natural law than Pope Paul VI in *Humanae Vitae*:

> No believer will wish to deny that the teaching authority of the Church is competent to interpret even the natural moral law. It is, in fact, indisputable, as our predecessors have many times declared, that Jesus Christ, when communicating to Peter and to the Apostles His Divine authority and sending them

> to teach all nations His commandments, constituted
> them as guardians and authentic interpreters of all
> the moral law, not only, that is, of the law of the
> Gospel, but also of the natural law, which is also an
> expression of the will of God, the faithful fulfillment
> of which is equally necessary for salvation.[55]

The interpretation of natural law made by Pope Paul VI in
Humanae Vitae was in full continuity with past Catholic teaching, although it incorporated more fully into sexual morality
the insights of *Gaudium et Spes* on conjugal love and the recip-
rocal *personal* gift of self in marriage. The theologians who
disagreed with the teaching of the encyclical argued that it
reflected only the scholastic and neo-scholastic view of natural
law, which was often termed "physicalist" and "static."

The attempts to make room for new versions of Catholic
moral teaching and new approaches to natural moral law relied on the famous substance/formulation distinction proposed
by Pope John XXIII in his opening speech to the Second Vatican
Council:

> The substance of the ancient doctrine of the deposit
> of faith is one thing, and the way in which it is pre-
> sented is another. And it is the latter that must be
> taken into great consideration with patience if
> necessary, everything being measured in the forms
> and proportions of a magisterium which is predomi-
> nantly pastoral in character.[56]

In this effort to distinguish the substance of Catholic teaching from reformable formulations of it, it seems clear that the
basic principles of the moral order belong to the substance.
Thus the Vatican Council Declaration on Religious Liberty
(*Dignitatis Humanae*) said of the Church:

> It is her duty to proclaim and teach with authority
> the truth which is Christ and, at the same time, to·

declare and confirm by her authority the principles
of the moral order which spring from human nature
itself.[57]

The International Theological Commission in 1972 stated in
one of its propositions: "The unity of Christian morality is
based on unchanging principles, contained in Sacred Scripture,
clarified by Sacred Tradition, and presented in each age by the
Magisterium."[58]

However, the key issue in contemporary moral theology is
the concrete application of these principles of the moral order.
Some theologians suggest that the Church has never taught
infallibly on concrete moral actions.[59] Furthermore they argue
that teachings like that of *Humanae Vitae* are not only noninfallible but reformable because they concern the formulation
rather than the substance of Church teaching. Is the traditional Church teaching on the intrinsic (essential, irreversible, unredeemable) evil of such actions as contraception,
homosexual genital activity, direct abortion, the direct destruction of innocent human life, and premarital intercourse
reformable since it represents the concrete application of moral
principles to human activity?

A reflection on this vital question might begin with a statement of Pope John XXIII in *Mater et Magistra*:

> For it is the Church's right and duty not only to
> safeguard principles relating to the integrity of reli-
> gion and morals, but also to pronounce authorita-
> tively when it is a matter of putting these principles
> into effect.[60]

Notice what Pope John was saying. He did not say that such
authoritative Church teaching putting moral principles into
effect is infallible or irreformable. But he spoke of a duty that
linked putting the principles into effect with safeguarding the
integrity of the principles themselves.

This echoed the earlier discussion on the content and extent of the universal, ordinary magisterium of the bishops. The official interpretation of the text of *Lumen Gentium* included in the scope of possibly infallible teachings those necessary that the deposit of faith might be guarded as inviolable and expounded with fidelity.

Whether all four conditions necessary for infallible teaching of the universal ordinary magisterium have been fulfilled in applications of moral principles to concrete human actions like contraception can be discussed and evaluated. But of interest here is the notion that the application of moral principles to certain concrete actions may be necessary to safeguard and defend the principles themselves. If that is the case in regard to certain concrete human actions, it would seem that they share in the irreformable *substance* of Catholic moral teaching.

As mentioned above, Ford and Grisez have made a strong case for including the moral teaching condemning contraception in the scope of the infallible, universal, ordinary magisterium. It would seem that a comparable case can be made for the concrete Church teaching on the deliberate killing of the innocent, homosexual genital activity, direct abortion, and premarital intercourse. In other words, the Church's moral teaching has taught the general moral principles that "human sexual activity must be undertaken with respect and responsibility" and that "human life is sacred," but it has also found it necessary to teach about certain concrete applications of these principles and to forbid specific forms of human activity because they are *necessary* formulations of the substance of the moral teaching.

If this were gratuitously asserted, it could be gratuitously denied. But it is asserted on the basis of a Catholic anthropology of the human person and the transcendent dignity of innocent human life as well as the physical-spiritual integrity and significance of human sexual activity and the interpersonal covenant of conjugal love.

Even prescinding from the infallible, universal, ordinary magisterium in the Church's teaching on these issues of intrinsic evil, those who would reform these teachings must ask the question "Why were they not reformed sooner?" Was the Church in error over these many years? I would prefer to say that the Church taught these concrete applications with the help of revealed wisdom and the Christian understanding of life and sexuality. These teachings were not specifically the product of medieval natural law, and they will survive in more contemporary and more personalist versions of natural law that are still in the process of development.

One author who has specifically applied the substance/ formulation distinction to premarital intercourse is Fr. Richard McCormick. He has suggested that the substance of the Church's teaching is that premarital intercourse is evil, namely, there is always something missing; hence, it is to be avoided.[61] But he does *not* believe it is of the substance of Church teaching that premarital intercourse is intrinsically evil or seriously evil in each act. Therefore the latter teaching is, in his judgment, subject to modification or qualification.

The modification of Church teaching proposed by a number of scholars today would introduce the concept of premoral or ontic evil for premarital intercourse.[62] This would introduce a calculus in which other circumstances might outweigh the premoral evil so that the act of premarital intercourse, although undertaken knowingly and willfully, would not be judged morally evil.

This methodology cannot be discussed in depth here. However, in the light of our reflection on the substance/formulation and principle/application distinctions, an observation can be made. The formulation that considers premarital intercourse intrinsically evil is based on the meaning of human sexual activity and the interpersonal relationship of conjugal love. Is this not a necessary formulation based on the substance of the Church's moral teaching about sex and marriage? Does the evil of premarital intercourse disappear when attending circumstances are sufficiently extenuating? Put another way, why is premarital intercourse wrong? Is it wrong because of the reality and truth of sex and love? Or is it wrong only conditionally because enough circumstances have not accumulated to make it right?

Some theologians who reject the intrinsic evil of premarital intercourse would still judge that the evil is virtually exceptionless because there is simply no proportionate reason that could justify premarital relations. Presumably they would have discerned that the disvalues simply outweigh the values when all the long-range consequences are taken into account. The reply of the Catholic tradition would be to agree with the estimate of long-range unfavorable consequences. But it would say these arise because the act violates the meaning of human sexual activity and the interpersonal relationship of conjugal love. In other words, the consequences are there because the act is intrinsically evil rather than because the act can be judged evil since no proportionate reason can be found for placing it.

In conclusion, it seems important to place this critically important question of intrinsically evil human actions back in the context of the "Teaching of the Church and Moral Theology." Clearly the Church has taught and continues to teach in magisterial documents the intrinsic evil of certain actions, among them the deliberate killing of the innocent and contraception.[63] On the other hand books are appearing and selling to a popular market with titles like *Sexual Morality, A Catholic Perspective* and *Principles for a Catholic Morality,* which seem to presume the error of this magisterial teaching from the casual way in which they dismiss it.[64]

Undoubtedly the magisterial position needs further careful study in the light of contemporary Christian personalism. But those who co-opt an alternative magisterial position while choosing to ignore the authentic magisterium are rendering questionable service to the Church. The history of the prophetic Church is dotted with false prophets along the way!

Notes

1. Karol Wojtyla, "Bishops as Servants of the Faith," *Irish Theological Quarterly* 43, no. 4 (1976): 260-273, at p. 267.
2. Bruce Vawter C.M., "The Nature of Prophecy" in *The Jerome Biblical Commentary* (Englewood Cliffs, N.J.: Prentice-Hall, 1968) p. 224.
3. Cf. James J. Mulligan, *The Pope and the Theologians* (Emmitsburg, Md: Mt. St. Mary's Seminary Press, 1968), pp. 14-27. Fr. Mulligan outlines the Old Testament role of prophets, announcing good but more frequently passing a sentence of condemnation to be followed by punishments. Hence prophecy is not merely communicative but productive, not merely noetic but dynamic. The Word of God is presented as an independent, irresistible force. This is the prophetic heritage that the Church received.
4. Jn. 4, 19; 6, 14; 7, 40,52; 9, 17; Acts 3, 22-23; 7, 37 Jesus insisted that he had a prophetic mission: "These very works which I perform testify on my behalf that the Father has sent me" (Jn. 5:36). At the end of the Sermon on the Mount, Matthew records that "he taught with authority and not like their scribes" (Mt. 7:29).
5. Cf. Mulligan, pp. 23-27.
6. Cf. Yves Congar, "Pour une histoire sémantique du term 'magisterium,'" *Revue des Sciences philosophiques et Théologiques* 60 (1976): 85-98, and "Bref historique des formes du 'magistère' et de ses rélations avec les docteurs," ibid.: 99-112.
7. Karl Rahner, "Magisterium" in *Sacramentum Mundi* 3 (New York: Herder and Herder, 1969) pp. 351-58 at p. 351.
8. Ibid.
9. Yves Congar, "The Magisterium and Theologians—A Short History," *Theology Digest* 25 (1977): 15-20 at p. 16.
10. In addition to the articles of Congar already cited, cf. *Chicago Studies* 17, no. 2 (Summer 1978): 149-309 (entire issue). See also T. Howland Sanks S.J., *Authority in the Church: A Study in Changing Paradigms* (Montana: The Scholars Press, 1974).
11. Cf. Vatican Council I, Dogmatic Constitution on the Faith, chap. 4, "Faith and Reason" in *The Teaching of the Catholic Church,* edit. by

Neuner and Roos, reedited by Karl Rahner (Staten Island, N.Y.: Alba House) 1967, pp. 35-38.

12. *Vatican Council II: The Conciliar and Post Conciliar Documents,* Austin Flannery O.P., ed. (Collegeville, Minn.: Liturgical Press, 1975), "The Church" *(Lumen Gentium)*, 24, p. 378.

13. Louis Bouyer, *Dictionary of Theology,* trans. Charles U. Quinn, (New York: Declée, 1965), p. 288.

14. For example, cf. Vatican Council II, "Divine Revelation" *(Dei Verbum)*, 5, p. 752, and "The Church" *(Lumen Gentium)*, 25, p. 379.

15. Robert Coffy, "Magisterium and Theology," *Irish Theological Quarterly* 43, no. 4 (1976): 247-59 at p. 255.

16. Timothy E. O'Connell, *Principles for a Catholic Morality* (New York: Seabury Press, 1978), p. 95.

17. Joseph A. Komonchak, "*Humane Vitae* and Its Reception," *Theological Studies* 39, no. 2 (1978): 221-57; John C. Ford S.J. and Germain Grisez, "Contraception and Infallibility," ibid.: 258-312. Joseph Komonchak supports his minimalizing approach by quoting Canon 1323 of the *Code* for using restrictive interpretations of solemn definitions and uses Occam's razor: "*Infallibilia non sunt multiplicanda,*" p. 240. He also insists on reading magisterial statements in historical contexts, citing *Mysterium Ecclesiae* of the Congregation for the Doctrine of the Faith *(AAS* 65, 1973, 402-3) for some useful hermeneutical principles. Nonetheless, his success in rebutting the case made by Ford and Grisez seems limited to this observer.

Note also that the Catholic scholars in the Catholic-Lutheran dialogue on "Teaching Authority and Infallibility in the Church" concentrated on papal infallibility, and touched only obliquely on the issue of the infallibility of the universal ordinary magisterium. Their considerations appear in *Theological Studies* 40, no. 1 (March 1979): 113-66, cf. p. 150.

18. Ford and Grisez, p. 269.

19. Ibid, pp. 275-76.

20. While there is surely a difference between doctrine taught infallibly and noninfallibly from the point of view of assent and of reformability, there is also surely a continuity between the two categories because of the fact that doctrines taught "definitively" and possibly infallibly (like contraception) must be taken much more seriously than doctrines that are clearly noninfallible. Hence a footnote of Fr. Richard McCormick in which he says, "I am supposing a radical difference between the infallible and noninfallible magisterium . . ." may be a bit too strongly worded. Cf. "Notes on Moral Theology," *Theological Studies* 30 (1969): 663, ftn. 72.

21. Vatican Council II, "Divine Revelation" (*Dei Verbum*), 10, pp. 755-6.

22. Ford and Grisez, pp. 267-8 and nn. 25-29.

23. Karl Rahner, "Magisterium," p. 354.

24. Karol Wojtyla, p. 272.

25. Vatican Council II, "The Church" (*Lumen Gentium*), 25, p. 381.

26. Joseph Komonchak, p. 233.

27. John R. Quinn, "The Magisterium and Theology," *Catholic Theological Society of America Proceedings* 24 (1969): 255-61 at p. 257.

28. Pope Paul VI, "Theology: A Bridge between Faith and Authority," Oct. 1, 1966 (Address to an International Congress on the Theology of Vatican II) in *The Pope Speaks* 11 (1966), pp. 348-55 at p. 351.

29. John R. Quinn, pp. 256-57.

30. Cf. T. Howland Sanks S.J. "Co-operation, Co-optation, Condemnation: Theologians and the Magisterium 1870-1978," *Chicago Studies* 17, no. 2 (Summer 1978): 242-63. At the conclusion of his historical overview Sanks observes: "The issue then, is not magisterial authority as such, but the theology enshrined in official statements" (p. 262).

31. Raymond E. Brown S.S., "The Dilemma of the Magisterium vs. the Theologians—Debunking Some Fictions," *Chicago Studies* 17, no. 2 (Summer 1978): 290-307 at 293.

32. Avery Dulles, *The Survival of Dogma* (Garden City, N.Y.: Doubleday & Company, 1971), p. 106-7.

33. Avery Dulles, "The Theologian and the Magisterium," *Catholic Theological Society of America Proceedings* 31(1976): 235-46 at p. 244.

34. Richard McCormick, "Conscience, Theologians, and the Magisterium," *New Catholic World* 220, no. 1320 (November-December 1977): 268-71 at p. 271.

35. *Sources of Catholic Dogma*, trans. from 30th edit. of Denzinger's *Enchiridion Symbolorum* by Roy J. Deferrari (St. Louis: B. Herder Book Company, 1957), no. 2006, p. 508.

36. Cf. Cahal B. Daly, "Theologians and the Magisterium," *Irish Theological Quarterly* 43, no. 4 (1976): 225-46 at pp. 225-26.

37. Richard McCormick, p. 271.

38. *Theological Studies* 40, no. 1 (March 1979): 95.

39. In *Christian Century*, August 3-10, 1977, p. 682.

40. *Summa Theologiae II, II*, Q. 10, a. 12.

41. An example of nearly total disregard of the notion of assent to the authentic noninfallible magisterium is this statement by Engelbert Gutwenger: "Logic and honesty suggest that statements of the *magis-*

terium authenticum are ultimately invitations to a dialogue in which the pros and cons can be sorted out" (in "Role of the Magisterium," *Concilium* vol. 51, *Dogma and Pluralism* edit. by Edw. Schillebeeckx (New York: Herder and Herder, 1970), pp. 43-55 at p. 52.

42. Cf. the helpful discussion of dissent in the American Bishops' Pastoral Letter of November 15, 1968, "Human Life in Our Day" (Washington, D.C.: U.S. Catholic Conference, 1968), pp. 14-16 and 18-19. They cite Cardinal Newman's letter to the Duke of Norfolk which speaks of obeying the noninfallible teaching of the Pope "unless a man is able to say to himself, as in the Presence of God, that he must not, and dare not, act upon the Papal injunction" (p. 15). Note also the statement of Pope Paul VI in *Humanae Vitae* (Huntington, Ind.: Our Sunday Visitor, 1968) that "Obedience obliges not only because of the reasons adduced, but *rather* because of the light of the Holy Spirit, which is given in a particular way to the pastors of the Church in order that they may illustrate the truth," no. 28, p. 19 (emphasis added).

43. Karl Rahner, "Magisterium", p. 357.

44. Cf. a helpful review of the literature on the notion of the "assistance of the Holy Spirit" in Richard McCormick "Notes on Moral Theology," *Theological Studies* 30 (1969(: 663-68.

45. Cf. Richard McCormick, "Notes on Moral Theology," *Theological Studies* 40, no. 1 (March 1979): 95.

46. Three publications of major influence that many people will regard as expressions of the "second magisterium" are: A. Kosnik et al., *Human Sexuality, New Directions in American Catholic Thought* (New York: Paulist Press, 1977); Philip Keane S.S. *Sexual Morality: A Catholic Perspective* (New York: Paulist Press, 1977); Timothy E. O'Connell, *Principles for a Catholic Morality* (New York: Seabury Press, 1978).

47. Rudolf Schnackenburg, *The Moral Teaching of the New Testament*, (New York: Herder and Herder, 1965).

48. Vatican Council II, "Divine Revelation" (*Dei Verbum*), 10, p. 755.

49. On the need of divine help to remedy the effects of sin and ignorance, cf. Vatican Council II "The Church in the Modern World" (*Gaudium et Spes*), 13-15, pp. 914-16.

50. An interesting historical item from the Council of Arles of 314 A.D. is a letter of submission by a priest, Lucius, who acknowledges the law of nature through which some are saved. Cf. *Sources of Catholic Dogma,* 160 b, p. 66.

51. John Noonan's studies are well known: *Contraception* (New York:

New American Library, 1967, Mentor-Omega book), and "An Almost Absolute Value in History" in *The Morality of Abortion*, edit. by John T. Noonan, Jr. (Cambridge, Mass.: Harvard University Press), pp. 1-59.

52. Lawrence Cardinal Sheehan, "*Humanae Vitae*: 1968-73" in *Homiletic and Pastoral Review* (November 1973), pp. 14-32, 51-54 at p. 23.

53. Ford and Grisez, p. 298.

54. For a comment on this by St. Thomas Aquinas see: *Summa Theologiae* I, II, q. 99, a. 2 ad 2 um.

55. Pope Paul VI, *Humanae Vitae*, 4, p. 6. Note 1 in this passage gives previous magisterial statements on this subject.

56. Printed in *the Documents of Vatican II*, edit. by Walter Abbot S.J. (New York: America Press, 1966), pp. 710-19 at p. 715. Similar statements in Council documents: Cf. *Vatican Council II*, "Church in the Modern World" (*Gaudium et Spes*), 62, p. 966; also "Decree on Ecumenism" (*Unitatis Redintegratio*) 4, p. 458.

57. Vatican Council II, "Religious Liberty" (*Dignitatis Humanae*), 14, p. 811.

58. International Theological Commission (October 11, 1972) in *La Documentation Catholique* 70 (May 20, 1973), p. 460; English trans. in (London) *Tablet,* 227 (July 7, 1973), p. 647.

59. Cf. Note 16 above. Cf. also Daniel Maguire, "Morality and the Magisterium," *Cross Currents* 18 (Winter 1968): 41-65. Also Charles E. Curran and Robert E. Hunt, *Dissent in and for the Church* (New York: Sheed and Ward, 1969), p. 63.

60. Pope John XXIII, *Mater et Maistra* (Washington, D.C.: National Catholic Welfare Conference, 1961), 239, p. 67.

61. Richard McCormick, *New Catholic World,* p. 270-71.

62. For example, Philip Keane, p. 107. (He cites other authors.)

63. For an interesting discussion of the two categories of actions for which Catholic moral theology refuses to admit proportionalism and upholds the notion of intrinsic evil see Richard McCormick, "Notes on Moral Theology," *Theological Studies* 38 (1977): 80.

64. Cf. note 46 above.

The Christian Mystery and Christian Ethics

Rev. Louis Bouyer
The Oratory, Paris

It cannot be denied that there is a crisis in Christian ethics, as in so many other fields of Christian teaching today. Here as elsewhere we can see a connection between the crisis within Christendom and the crisis in the world at large. However, here perhaps more than anywhere else, we must acknowledge that, if the crisis is no less serious among those who should bring the witness of salvation to the world than among the people of a world desperately in need of that salvation, we have to attribute this especially to the fact that something has gone wrong with the witness of the former. And this is not a sudden and fortuitous accident; instead, it is the final outcome of a process of erosion that may well have been developing among us for a long time. The present circumstances have simply revealed the worm that has been inside the fruit long before it was thus made manifest.

I shall not here try to follow the first beginnings and the slow growth of the unseen evil that has suddenly become visible. I shall content myself with pointing out its main roots in order to come as quickly as possible to what should be, in my opinion, the normal process of restoration and, later, of fruitful development of a genuinely Christian ethics.

First of all, we have tended to reduce Christian ethics to a matter of casuistry. Next, we have divorced ethics from spirituality. And finally, we have lost the sense of a close connection existing since the beginnings of Christianity between Christian belief and the Christian way of life. The result has been that Christian belief itself has become, as it were, fragmented into a series of apparently disconnected beliefs. This has led to our present inability either to see how the supernatural end of human life can be related to the demands imposed upon humanity by its very nature, or, more simply, to see what the very idea of the natural law can mean for the Christian. When this point was reached, it must be said that we were and are still back to the fundamental error of gnosticism, which was unable to see how the same God who was first the Creator could also be the Redeemer. To make a little clearer every one of these dissociations and their baleful effect on Christian ethics will be the purpose of our study.

I

First of all, it is clear that we cannot dispense with casuistry, simply because it is impossible to speak of the moral life without taking into account all the concrete details of daily life. But to say this is quite different from thinking that ethics can ever be reduced even to the best kind of casuistry. Ethics is worthless—nothing—if it does not provide humanity with a positive ideal. When casuistry absorbs or tends to absorb the whole of ethics into itself, it *eo ipso* makes ethics appear to be negative, as if the only purpose of ethics in human life is to pronounce interdictions from which casuistry must release us if life is to be livable. Thus a paradox arises: The more casuistry tends to make ethics as little troublesome or burdensome as possible, the more it reinforces the impression that ethics is just a nuisance, something that curbs life and indeed might even choke it altogether unless it is limited and restricted in its application as much as possible by casuistic thinking.

When this impression has been created, ethics becomes separated from spirituality, if not opposed to it. Within the perspective of this distorted view of moral realities, spirituality is positive and even limitless since, in Christianity, it is the pursuit of perfection. Ethics, on the other hand, is comprised of negatives, of things not to be done, of temptations to be rejected. At the same time ethics is made to appear to be compulsory for everyone and, for that very reason, unpalatable. Spirituality, on the contrary, is free: No one is under any obligation to embark upon it. Spirituality is a matter of counsels, not commandments. But when spirituality is viewed this way, it itself becomes debased; for while it appears at first as an ideal and a generous goal, it is soon regarded as not only gratuitous but unnecessary, not to say useless or totally unreal. When this point is reached, it seems clear that not only ethics but spirituality as well have little to do with Christian belief. People might well admit that to be spiritual in a Christian way, we must accept all the Christian dogmas. Nonetheless, while this is commonly accepted as a preliminary requirement and indeed as a common basis for both ethics and spirituality, it turns out that it is a basis with no organic links to what it is called to support or to buttress. One of the most famous exponents of this kind of compartmentalized Christianity in a former generation came to think and to say, toward the end of his life, that we must acknowledge both as a principle and a fact that even the highest spiritual experiences of the Christian saints might just as well have been attained through a proper psychological training by persons of no Christian belief—even by persons of no belief at all. Others who are of this same mentality have even maintained that God could grant the same spiritual and mystical experiences to persons habitually living in what Christians would regard as mortal sin.

The state of affairs described above is indeed absurd. When it is reached, it is clear that Christian dogma has been turned into something purely abstract, an outgrowth of a rationalistic scholasticism that has totally desiccated Christian belief under the pretence of making it fully rational. An immediate result of this dubious achievement is to make irresistible the liberal Protestant distinction (if not opposition) between faith and belief, a distinction that seems to have become a commonplace now for many Catholic (or would-be Catholic) theologians. But this is not the worst aspect of the present situation. For once this point is reached, the notion of revelation, if any idea of it remains at all, means simply a series of autonomous, separate propositions, each of which will have to be developed into a system of consequences drawn from it by purely syllogistic deduction. No connection will be admissible between the alleged "revealed affirmation" without the whole scheme's collapsing into the crudest form of rationalism. Here we can realize how some modern writers have been led to consider a mystery as something that we are to believe but not try to understand. Seen in its proper perspective, this concept shows perfectly how far some kinds of neo-Thomism may have evolved from the Thomism of St. Thomas himself, simply by substituting for his understanding of a theological conclusion something utterly different from it even though it bears the same name. According to Aquinas, a theological conclusion is what an article of faith becomes when it has been related to another as to its own principle; as a result, the whole and final effect of theology, which moves entirely within the domain of revelation and is therefore an exercise of reason within and in utter dependence upon the exercise of Christian faith, tends only to make us conscious, in our grasp of the whole of revelation, of an organic whole. Too many neo-Thomists, from the seventeenth century to the present, have come to consider as a proper form of a theological conclusion the logical combination of a revealed proposition with a supposedly "purely" rational one; the result is the extension of the field of theology beyond that of revelation as such. All this is an exercise of rationalism that any intelligent unbeliever should be just as able to achieve as any believer of the same intellectual acumen.

In my opinion (and, I believe, in the opinion of all the Fathers of the Church as well as of all the great schoolmen of the thirteenth century), this is a completely illusory extension or liberation of theology; it implies a complete stultification of revelation itself. This is because it keeps only an appearance of supernaturality for revelation and theology by fragmenting revelation, or rather the very Word of God of which it is the product, into a mere congregate of unconnected and unrelated affirmations. This is the dismemberment of theology and revelation into a mere heap of *membra disjecta*; each component as well as the whole are now utterly dead as a result of atomizing the revealed truth instead of integrating it organically.

When we have gone this far, the process of Redemption seems totally foreign to that of creation. Once the supernatural becomes fundamentally unnatural, it inevitably comes to be regarded as purely meaningless or as more or less radically antinatural. Either it has no connection whatsoever with the nature of humanity, however this may be conceived, or it cannot be contemplated rationally unless it appears to modify and, therefore, to alter that nature. Grace, in this view, may not suppress nature but, if it has anything to do with it, it cannot be anything like it; grace is seemingly a distortion of nature, even if that distortion is still called an elevation. So conceived, grace gives rise to strange, distorted conceptions of Christianity similar to those set forth even in Renaissance times by thinkers who called themselves Christians. I have in mind people like the humanist Lorenzo Valla (c. 1407-57) for whom Christianity had introduced—along with the cross of Christ and concomitant with its effort to elevate human nature—a countertendency opposed to the natural impulse of human beings to flourish and fructify. In short, according to Valla, Christianity had introduced an instinct of death opposed to the very instinct of life. Ideas of this sort gave rise, even if not consciously, to some theologies of the recent past that opposed more or less openly a theology of terrestrial realities to the supposedly traditional theology of supernatural grace. A pretended creational and positive Christianity open to the world was presented to counteract a so-called ascetical and negative Christianity in flight from the world.

All this, it must be said, is mere nonsense. It is quite clear that Christianity, under its redemptive aspect linked to the cross of Christ, has not introduced suffering and death into the world. On the contrary, Christianity has introduced to the world the redemptive gospel that can alone overcome suffering and death, not by evaporating them into a speculative resolution of the problem of evil but by meeting evil in the full concreteness of its terrible reality in order to introduce the only realistic hope of salvation for human nature. Christianity alone makes it possible for human nature not only to develop to its full maturity but to grow beyond all possible limitations. It thus does not ignore but fulfills the deepest, albeit inexplicable, wish of human nature as created by God and for God.

When we have said this, it would be useless to spend more time in criticizing distorted or false conceptions of Christianity. We are now sufficiently prepared to face in its more positive aspect the mystery (and not just the mysteries) of Christianity, and to realize what a light Christianity projects upon human life and its widest possible fulfillment.

II

There is an intrinsic and in no way artificial connection between Christian faith and the Christian way of life. The Christian way of life, consequently, should be recognized as the only possible, full actualization of all truly human possibilities. This is because Christian belief, first of all, is not concerned with a disjointed series of utterly incomprehensible mysteries but with a single mystery, which cannot appear to be blinding except when, through the very fullness of its light, we come suddenly to its discovery. More precisely, it is essential to the verity of the Christian mystery to be a mystery of life. Of course, it is the mystery of the life of *God*—and of this life as revealed insofar as God intends to make us partakers of it. This should not be seen as an afterthought, as if the Creator were now modifying or altering what might be called our innate nature as this proceeded from his own creativity. The truth is just the opposite. It is not only, as St. Augustine put it, that God made us for himself so that our hearts can find no rest until they come to rest in him but also, and more definitely, that God has created us solely with the view of associating us intimately with his own life. This means that the supernatural life is not superadded, as it were, to our natural life and is thus seemingly detrimental, even if sublimely so, to its proper development. Instead, the supernatural life is the only ultimate goal for which our nature was intended from the very beginning and therefore disposed by its own Creator.

The Fathers of the Church, beginning with St. Irenaeus, applied to what has just been said the statement of Genesis that God had created man to his own image and resemblance. For them the *image* meant that innate capacity of human beings for a life of intercourse and an identification with God, while the *resemblance* meant the eventual fulfillment of that design through the dynamic conjunction of humanity with God in the course of its existence. To translate this patristic view into a later terminology, we can say that the *image* was natural to humanity while the *resemblance* was acquired by humanity's free acceptance of grace as the supernatural gift of God.

It can, of course, be disputed whether the biblical narrative itself implied all that lay behind the patristic use of these words. But it is undoubtedly true that the Bible as a whole implies or rather proclaims that humanity is preadopted by

God from its creation for an encounter. This adoption is viewed as one freely accepted and therefore giving rise to a common life that will be finally discovered as the life of humanity loving God and its fellow creatures as they have been loved by God himself from all eternity. This, St. Paul says, is taking place through the fact that God has radiated or poured forth his own *agape* or divine love—the very soul of his divine life—into our hearts through the Holy Spirit, who was given to us through Christ Jesus. We can say that this describes for the apostle the final outcome of the mystery of Christ.

As all the Fathers say, Christ, the eternal Son of God, was made man so that man might partake of his own sonship. Man was not only *called* a child of God but was actually *made to be* a child of God, as St. John says. St. Thomas made it luminously clear, in recapitulating this biblical and patristic teaching, that revelation was given to us, so that we might be brought to salvation. Thus revelation can only make sense when it is considered in the perspective of faith, a perspective that makes it perfectly understandable. This concept no longer appears, as it seems to have appeared to many (including would-be Thomists of a later date) as a merely pious statement. It is rather the very essence of the affirmations of Christian faith, so that their very meaning is lost for all who do not realize that they are always to be taken within the vision of a God who reveals to us his own life in order to lead us to a participation in its reality.

The mystery of Christ—the mystery that, according to St. Paul, was fundamentally the mystery of the Cross, but of the Cross as seen in the perspective of the resurrection and the communication of the Holy Spirit—was the very mystery of God and of his eternal life of love. This mystery has to be understood also as our own mystery: "Christ in us, the hope of our glory," as Paul says to the Colossians.

A more definite understanding of the Pauline mystery,

however, is necessary if we are to understand the full import of this central and all-dominating object of our faith. It is needed if we are to grasp properly the knowledge of God mediated through this mystery as well as the knowledge of ourselves and of the life given to us by reason of the gift of God's grace through Christ to our nature. In particular, we must discover how this gift is related, above all, to the fullness of the divine revelation, of the divine Word; thereby we must come to see how this gift combines in itself a revelation of the divine life with the revelation of how that life has to come to be the life of humanity.

A half-century ago scholars attempting to explain the meaning and nature of the Pauline mystery tended to find its source in the so-called mystery religions that were flourishing and more or less competing with Christianity during the first few centuries of the Christian period. These religions, which began with the famous Greek mysteries of Eleusis, were centered around a god of vegetation or elementary life, who was seen to die and revive. By associating themselves through rituals, the people initiated into the mysteries were supposed, more or less explicitly, to have become associated with the dying god in such a way that they would be associated permanently with his divine life after their own death. Not only non-Catholic scholars like Richard Reitzenstein but even orthodox theologians like Dom Odo Casel, the great monk of Maria Lach who was influential at the start of the contemporary liturgical revival, came to think that the Christian religion had appropriated to itself the pattern of primitive religion so as to make accessible to humanity a grasp of what the divine life might be as well as its communication to ourselves. It is correct that the mystery religions, to say the least, focused the attention of religious individuals on the centrality of the problem of life as leading to death. It even appeared that death should be accepted as a way to a new and better life. At the same time such scholars implied the possibility of a union between God and humanity through ritual celebration. Still these similarities should not be mistaken for a real analogy, much less for a historical source of the Christian mysteries in the pagan mysteries. First of all, in the pagan religions there was no question of a real resurrection nor of a truly supernatural life that became our own. The dying gods were not transcendent beings but just an embodiment of cosmic life that alternated between death and rebirth. There was no real resurrection, even of the god himself, much less of his worshiper, but only of a rebirth to a life that would be just the same as that which had, of itself, led to death and that therefore could only tend again to death through its own development.

In addition, there were few or no moral or spiritual implications in the mystery religions. They were a mere matter of ritual, and the purely mechanical effect of the ritual was to grant to the worshiper a privileged situation in the afterlife, totally independent of any change in this life or afterwards, in an ethical sense or even in a physical one. The best of the ancient pagan writers emphasized a scandalous fact about the mystery religions: Even a scoundrel who underwent initiation was to be saved whatever might be the nature, however ambiguous, of the state of salvation. At the same time, even a Socrates or any other moral hero should be considered as lost if he had not been initiated.

Nonetheless, it was true that the best philosophers, including even Plato himself in the *Phaedo,* interpreted the ritual of Eleusis symbolically, as an image of the process of assimilation to a god which, according to Plato, was to be seen as one and the same as the discovery and acceptance of a truly good way of life. But this was a private philosophical interpretaion—purely allegorical—of the mysteries. It had nothing to do either with their actual performance or with the beliefs that they traditionally involved. The Eleusian mysteries themselves involved only the secrecy of a mere ritual, which was to be made known only to those undergoing the initiation; it had nothing to do with a higher revelation either of the divine life or of the moral and spiritual transformation through which humanity already could, here and now, be associated with and assimilated to the divine.

It is precisely here that we see the impossibility of finding in the pagan mysteries the source of the Christian mystery. For it is essential to the Christian mystery not to be kept secret but to be made manifest, to be proclaimed to the whole world. The content of this mystery, moreover, is not a ritual reserved for an elite but a revelation of God and of what he has done for us all and intends to make of all of us—his adopted children in his only begotten Son—by an adoption depending on this Son and his unique manifestation in human history, a history of sin and death. It is the revelation of God's great, limitless love for us, a gift of Father, Son, and Spirit, and one that causes us not only to be called children of God but to be his children in full reality.

For this reason the literary and historical source of the Christian mystery is not to be sought in the heathen mysteries but in the biblical Word, more specifically in the Wisdom books of the Bible. Finally, it is to be sought in the supreme transformation of the Wisdom literature assumed into the biblical tradition that produced the apocalyptic literature. This is despite the fact that the apocalyptic literature, at first sight, seems in its exalted supernaturalism to be the very opposite of the earlier form of the Wisdom books, which are so practical, positive, and matter-of-fact.

This conclusion was established by Deden, a theologian at the University of Louvain, in a remarkable work published shortly before World War II. Deden very convincingly showed through a parallel study of chapters 1 and 2 of Paul's first letter to the Corinthians and chapter 1 of the book of Daniel that the biblical and Pauline mystery is the secret of God's

eternal design and plan of salvation for humanity and the entire created world, even though this world seems doomed by sin
and death. This mystery is the ultimate statement of the divine
wisdom, which disposes of everything infallibly and in accord
with its omnipotent goodness. This ultimate statement will
become known to all people at the end of time through God's
final intervention in history. We must keep in mind that this
same God is the source of all things. He will then, at the end of
time, bring back to himself the perverted will of humanity; he
will return to humanity its freedom by offering to it an escape
from the seduction of the evil one, the fallen prince of this world.

As has been the case since the very beginning of God's intervention in the life of Israel, the revelation of God's wisdom and
of his design for humanity and the world will be, at the same
time, a revelation of God himself. More exactly, as Paul makes
clear in the first letter to the Corinthians through a theme that
will become central in the epistles of his captivity—the epistles
to the Colossians, Philippians, and Ephesians—this ultimate
revelation of God's will for us is at the same time the most
perfect revelation of his deepest, most interior life. As the epistle to the Romans had already stated, the most perfect revelation of God is the revelation of his *agape,* that is, of his creative, redemptive, and communicating love. And that supreme
revelation takes place in the revelation of the mystery of the
Cross of Christ, that is to say, of the pure, generous, gratuitous,
and self-surrendering love of God extended not only to all creation but even to sinners. In the manifestation of that love in
which and through which God appears to us as the Father from
whom all fatherhood in heaven and on earth takes its name,
Christ appears himself as *the* Son of God, the eternal Son of his
eternal love. But Christ reveals himself also as a new Adam in
the resurrection that will be the fruit of the tree of the Cross
seen as the very tree of life. Or better yet, he reveals himself as
the last and eschatological Man in whom all men and women

are to be gathered together, reconciled among themselves with
the eternal Father in the body of his Son. In Christ they will
receive, indeed, an adoption that is not merely legal or
figurative but fully real. For in him we become through baptism living members of his body, which is dead to sin and
resurrected for the salvation of the whole world. Nourished on
Christ's own flesh through the Eucharist, we are lifted up from
our degradation through sin and filled with the life and glory of
his own Spirit, who is the Spirit of the Father and the Son, and
who is the Spirit of sonship. This makes fully actual our own
filiation in the Beloved One by pouring into our hearts that
same love, which is the very life of God himself.

III

Once the full significance of the Christian mystery—the
principal and finally the ultimate and sole object of our
faith—has been made known to us through faith, and once we
realize that that faith—through the sacramental experience of
baptism leading to what may be called the eucharistic life—is
properly faith in the mystery of "Christ in us, the hope of our
glory" (as Paul himself says in his letter to the Colossians), it
becomes crystal clear that there is an unbreakable continuity
and unity in Christianity between faith and life. Our Christian
belief, of itself, involves a spirituality. This is precisely our own
renewal in the Spirit; that spirituality, in turn, implies an
ethical program that can be described as a restoration of that
very *image* of God after which our own nature has been pat-
terned since our creation. However, it is no less clear that this
image is not to be understood as something static, nor as something that could be, as it were, enclosed within itself. Just as
the Christian revelation that culminates in the Christian mystery is a discovery of the life and very being of God as *agape*, or
self-giving love, the image of God rooted in our very being
implies that we were born to a life of active and congenial

resemblance with God. This means that we were born for union with him, for a free response to his grace, and for an acknowledgment of his eternal love. This love has not only been extended to us, his creatures, but has diffused itself through the Spirit into our hearts so that we—like his eternal Son—are his members who love him and his whole creation, just as God himself has loved us from all eternity. This will be, in its perfection, what St. Paul calls "to know God as we have been known by him," i.e., a living knowledge, a knowledge that is the actual experience in ourselves of what he is in himself.

I think that, on this basis, we can and are right to build not only a spirituality but an ethics. The spirituality has no other ultimate end than our filial assimilation to God. The ethics, while fully Christian in its inspiration and aspiration, is in no way artificially grafted onto the face of our nature; but instead, it is a revelation or elucidation of the inner law of its own *physis*, in the exact meaning of this Greek word for nature, i.e., its dynamic self-realization.

I will not here try to delineate how this should be done in all its details, first, because I lack the time to do this, and second, because it is not my special field of research. I shall only, in an inconclusive conclusion, try to emphasize how the organic connection between what is most deeply natural to humanity and its vocation to the life of grace may be approached.

St. Thomas Aquinas found in Aristotle a kind of foundation stone for the Christian vocation of humanity. He found this in the idea that humanity, through its inseparable unity of intelligence and free will, is fundamentally able to make itself one with all possible reality; there is no limited scope to be assigned to the activity of human beings. I would say, in the light of Christian revelation, that what is to be understood as the natural basis of any kind of really and fully human ethics should be seen as the radical duty human beings have to respect in themselves and in all other human beings that openness of their own being. Here we have, it seems to me, the basis for all sound ethics in a fully developed awareness of our properly human consciousness as being one with what we call the moral conscience. It means that, for human beings the root of virtue is in the wholly accepted truth of their own being, which must necessarily be developed into a personal fidelity to a personal God. This fidelity will reveal to us through all creation and all human history—the history of fall and sin becoming through divine intervention, the history of salvation—a call. This is the call that God, sooner or later, addresses to all of us, singularly but also in and through our relationship to all humanity and the universe, to make a full response to the fullness of God's love.

This, I would say, means that we are to be led, through a total fidelity to the verity of our being and the whole of our existence in the world, to what can be described as a eucharistic life. This is a life of discovery in exultant praise of the fullness of God and the fullness of his design for us; it is the surrender of ourselves to the totality of the divine gift itself.

On Being a Christian and the Moral Life: Pauline Perspectives

Rev. Manuel Miguens O.F.M.

St. Paul occasionally compiles lists of sins or incorrect moral attitudes. In doing so, his concern is negative in the sense that he emphasizes what pagans do and what Christians should not do. But Paul and his disciples do not consider the moral behavior of a *Christian* as a matter of rules, regulations, and laws; there is nothing legalistic about their concern. The moral behavior of a Christian is a natural "fruit" (Gal. 4:22; Rom. 6:22), born of his or her very being as a Christian. By its own dynamics the power involved in being a Christian leads to what is usually called a moral life, not to its opposite. The Pauline literature emphasizes this point in various ways and from different perspectives, but the fundamental reality is always the same, namely, the very nature of being a Christian. The reason for several variations of perspective is that the nature of the Christian mystery is at the same time justification, incorporation into Christ's body, and life in the Spirit, among other aspects.

Justification and the Moral Life

In the Pauline language *justification* is the divine action through which God, by his grace and forgiving love in Christ, established a Father-son communion of friendship and life with the human being who adheres to Christ by faith (and baptism). For Paul justification is not the acquittal of an innocent, nonguilty person; it is the acquittal of a "sinner" as such (Rom. 3:21-26; 4:5; 5:1-10). Beyond that, it is a particular relationship of love in which, among other gifts, God pours his divine Spirit into humanity (Rom. 5:5; Gal. 4:6).

The natural effects of such justification for practical Christian living are described by Paul, first of all, in Romans 6. Even though God's grace is more powerful and copious than sin's power and humanity's many sinful acts, a Christian cannot continue to keep allegiance to sin—the universal tyrant that "reigned" supreme over the world (Rom. 5: 21; cf. verses 12-21) ever since the first sin at the beginning. Baptism, Paul understands, marks a radical turning point in human existence because through baptism the sinful person "dies" to what he or she was before, to a life in the service of sin. In baptism the Christian confesses and professes that in Christ "all men have died" because he died for all of them (2 Cor. 5: 14 f.); he died for "our" sins (1 Cor. 15:3; see 2 Cor. 5:21). The Christian acknowledges that God's condemnation of sin in Christ's flesh (Rom. 8: 3) was due to himself or herself, not to Christ. This is why Paul states that the Christian baptism is an unto-death baptism through which people are involved in the saving mystery of Christ in two ways; they receive a new life principle as they are ingrafted into the body of Christ from whom a divine energy (Spirit) flows into the Christians; at the same time, through their union with Christ they die to what they were before; their old self is "crucified" (Rom. 6:6) and left behind, just as Christ's mortality and moral dimension died on the cross and were left behind. A "man in Christ" is, Paul understands, a "new creature" (2 Cor. 5:17; Gal. 6:15) and, as such, part of the new creation "created in Christ Jesus" (Eph. 2:10).

The death and re-creation of human beings "with" and "in" Christ is no theoretical consideration. Of course, Paul does not lose sight of the final resurrection at the end of time (Rom. 6:5, 8). But before that, Paul says, the death of "the old self" in a Christian and the new life given him or her must show in a Christian way of living that implies that this person "*no longer is a slave of sin*" (Rom. 6:6), or is at the service of sin. Putting the same thought in positive terms, Paul maintains that after their unto-death baptism Christian people are supposed to "walk in newness of life" (Rom. 6:4), namely, to live according to a new life principle. Just as after his death/resurrection, Christ's life was of a higher quality, so also after the death/re-creation of Christians through baptism, their lives have to be of a higher quality. This must show in a way of life where humanity "no longer is a slave to sin" precisely because "he who dies is free of sin" (Rom. 6:7) in the sense that that person is not under the power of sin any longer.

That is why, after this kind of introduction in the indicative, Paul comes to the imperative, namely to practical rules: "Realize that you are dead to sin but living to God in Christ Jesus" (Rom. 6:11). The concept is that in their practical existence Christians must not allow sin to rule over them. Becoming a Christian marked a radical rebellion against the tyranny of sin and a total inaction and powerlessness to continue in the service of sin. What happened in baptism sacramentally must show as a reality at work in the definite circumstances of the lives of Christians. In Paul's view, throughout their lives Christians must become what he himself is: someone dead for sin but living for God. Christians must keep dying to sin and become more and more alive to God.

In Paul's understanding, human justification by God is not a magic event that happens in an instant without humanity's total involvement in the entire process. It remains true that justification is a total gift of God flowing from his gracious love. But the essential requirement on the part of human beings is to commit themselves totally to their justification by God. God justifies humanity without human "works" or merits. But humanity's subsequent conduct or "works" will show whether or not it is committed to this justification; whether or not humanity's conversion to God has been sincere and wholehearted; whether or not its death to sin has been real and definitive—a real death; whether or not its life is really for God.

This is why Paul insists on the imperative, namely, on the principles that incarnate justification is the Christian living reality: "Sin must not rule over your mortal bodies so as to obey its desires" (Rom. 6:12). Then he gives a new turn to his phrase to signify that it is not just a matter of sin's tyranny; it is also a matter of human willingness. "You must not put your members at the service of sin as weapons of unrighteousness." He goes on to say this: " . . . rather put yourselves at God's service as living beings (risen) from the dead, and your members as weapons of righteousness (fighting) for God: yes, sin must not lord it over you" (Rom. 6:13). During the unredeemed life of the past, human beings had put themselves at the service of impurity and unrighteousness as a slave; but " . . . now put your members (yourselves), as slaves, at the service of righteousness to be holy" (Rom. 6:19).

Justification is, Paul understands, a free gift of God that human beings grasp through faith and possess in faith; but this gift must become real and operative in action and decision in our lives. We must make God's gift effective in the moral effort of our own lives toward holiness. The effectiveness of baptism (death to sin) is nothing magically certain; it is rather a new mode of existence graciously given to us, the ethical quality of which must necessarily show in our effort and determination not to fall slave to sin any longer.

In his reasoning Paul points out a very important detail. The life of a Christian must be at God's service, not at the service of sin, "for Sin must not lord it over you; as a matter of fact, you are not under (any) law but under grace." In other words, the

Christian does not live under any legalistic regime but under the regime of grace. For a Christian, moral attitudes and ethical behavior are not a matter of merely legalistic compliance with a set of rules. Christian behavior is no passive and reluctant slavery to an external norm. It is Paul's view that where there is no law there is no sin (Rom. 5:15; 4:15); that the law is the cause of (divine) wrath (Rom. 4:15); that the law makes the transgression all the greater (Rom. 5:20); that the law is the starting point of sin's activity (Rom. 7:8); that the law is given to be a cause of transgressions (Gal. 3:19). Of course, here he speaks, not in philosophical but in factual terms; he does not speak of the merits of the law in itself but of what actually happens when people are confronted with the law—at some time or other they break it. A law, in fact, is powerless to make people righteous because the law does not add any strength ("spirit") to people, and human "flesh" (i.e., our earth-bound and weak condition) is the weakness of the law, of any legalistic system (Rom. 8:3). That is why Paul cannot found any ethical system on legalistic considerations. He finds a more basic and solid foundation of the Christian effort against the power of sin in the very grace of justification. From the moment of our justification we live under the regime of grace, and that is why "sin must not lord it over you."

The moral problem is not a question of rules, commandments, customs, legalism, or legalities. It is a matter of loyalties—loyalty either to God or to sin. Paul elaborates the gospel principle that "no one can be the servant of two masters." True service (or commitment) is not determined by theoretical definitions, and still less by empty statements, but by real action and "works." Experience taught Paul, as it does everybody, that people are servants of their masters—it is practical and factual obedience that loyalty is all about. The alternatives confronting human loyalty in this area are two only—either service to sin, or service to "obedience" (which in the following verse, Rom. 6:17, is understood as the Christian faith in the gospel message). It comes back to our initial question: Can those who have been baptized still keep allegiance to sin? (Rom. 6:1). Were this the case, the process of conversion/ justification would have meant nothing to such Christians, and everything would now be as it was before. But through conversion and baptism Christians have shifted their allegiance. Christians "were" (past tense) slaves to sin in the past, but through their conversion and baptism they have come wholeheartedly to "obey" the gospel teaching, thus being set "free" from sin's power and becoming slaves to righteousness (Rom. 6:17). Service to righteousness and to God is the only alternative open to Christians.

The notion of slavery in Paul's reasoning should be further defined. The apostle refers to the law of the *bond slave*, which was well known in Paul's days. If someone freely sold himself or herself as a bond slave to a master, such an act was irreversible; it could never be nullified. This person was a slave for life under the absolute authority of the master. Paul sees that such was the condition of a person without Christ—he or she was a bond slave of sin. This renders the act of a person's deliverance by God all the more valuable; it is an extraordinary grace. But by shifting from sin to God, people freely and voluntarily sold themselves as bond slaves to God. Their loyalty to God is both absolute and irreversible. It is God's orders and wishes that determine their lives. That is why moral attitudes are a necessary consequence of humanity's shift of allegiance, namely, of its loyalty to God.

It is from this perspective that, far from being a carte blanche to sin, the regime of "grace" requires moral attitudes and ethic behavior. The regime of grace was brought about by God's "gracious" initiative and living care, but it was also a regime that Christian converts longed for and committed themselves to. God wanted them as his children but, in turn,

they wanted to be children of God; this is why they are supposed to live as God's children. Correctly understood, the regime of grace, under which Christians live, is the true foundation of genuine and uncompromising morality—a morality
that is not a legal imposition but an exercise of inner freedom
and personal commitment. Grace does not release us from responsibility; it always drives us to responsible attitudes.

The regime of grace, however, does not work automatically
or magically. Through conversion and baptism people commit
themselves to it, and this lasting commitment works in two
directions at the same time: the struggle not to fall again under
the slavery of sin, and the effort to grow in righteousness (Rom.
6:16), holiness (v. 19), and life (v. 22 f.). It is here that the
notion of Christian "mortification," as Paul understands it, enters the picture. Because of the death undergone in baptism,
humanity's "old self" enslaved to sin "was crucified with the
result that the body [the total person] in the possession of sin is
done with" (Rom. 6:6). But in Romans 8:13 Paul warns that
there is still in humans something that must be put to death;
the same concept is insisted upon in Colossians 3:5 ff.; Galatians 5:17 states clearly that "the flesh" [the entire person who
is bound to earth] still "has desires against the spirit [the entire person who is obedient to God's Spirit]," and that within
human beings a "fight" is going on between the flesh and the
spirit, with the implication that even regenerated persons can
still comply with the desires of the flesh (Gal. 5:16). Clearly
the apostle understands that, even after baptism, innocence
is not human nature; sin can still take place, even though
a final victory over sin is now possible by God's power that
has been given to people through the justifying process. It is
this condition of justified persons that demands effort and
struggle to live up to their commitment of being no longer at
the service of sin. In other words, regenerated persons must
keep dying to sin.

It is this that Paul points out in Romans 8:13 and other passages. The issue is life according to the "flesh" or according to the "Spirit." Since an existence according to the flesh leads to death, Christians who want to live must "*put to death* the deeds of the body by the spirit." This is the notion of Christian "mortification" (putting to death). But mortification does not just consist in denying oneself some pleasure even if it is lawful and not sinful. Christian mortification consists in sustaining the struggle that rages inside each regenerated person between the "flesh" and the "spirit," in such a way that it is the "spirit" that has the upper hand and leads the person's existence. It is the struggle to which Paul refers in Galatians 5:16-18 (and in Rom. 7:21-25). This sort of mortification is no optional alternative for Christians; it is the essential task of Christians. It is in sustaining this struggle that they can see how "Christian" they are, how powerful the new life principle is that they have received in baptism. If the "spirit" is to lead and Christians are to live, the deeds of the "body" (or the "desires of the flesh") must die; Christians must "put them to death." They can do so by the "spirit," which is their total person insofar as they put the power of God's Spirit to work in their personal lives.

It is important to note that the "body" and the "flesh" are not just anthropological concepts. They are theological projections of the entire person, including the soul, will, and intellect. In these passages of Romans and Galatians, the flesh comprises the entire reality of a person who disregards God and his requirements, and lives according to earthly, worldly interests and inclinations. Although the "body" is not necessarily the same thing as the flesh, it comes down to the same thing in this context. The "deeds" that express such spiritual attitudes—the "old self" at the service of sin—must be put to death. Christians are required to do so by heeding God's commandments and opening up to the guidance and power of the Spirit. It is not a suggestion or advice; it is a must. In Colossians 3:5 Paul uses the imperative mood *nekrosate* ("put to death") which (being an aorist tense) comprises each and all cases where such a need arises. Paul refers to this arduous Christian task when he reminds Christians that they are athletes in a contest who "have to deny themselves all sorts of things," and lets them know that he himself is in the competition and "disciplines his own body and tries to master it" (1 Cor. 9:24-27). Again, when Paul stresses the fact that a "share in Christ's sufferings by being formed into the pattern of his death" is a necessity for a Christian, he portrays the effort needed to achieve that as a competition in a race: "I give no thought to what lies behind but push on to what is ahead ... all of us who are mature must have this attitude" (Phil. 3:10, 13, 15).

If we wonder what are the "deeds" of the body or the "desires" of the flesh that Christians must put to death—and it is here that the moral line of the Christian life comes down to specifics—Paul is not ambiguous at all. In Romans 6:12 he points out the "desires" of our mortal body and, in v. 19, "impurity and lawlessness," all of which should be read together with Romans 1:24-32. In Galatians 5:20 the apostle lists "the works of the flesh" as "fornication, impurity, licentiousness, idolatry, hostilities, bickering, jealousy, outbursts of rage, selfish rivalries, dissensions, factions, envy, drunkenness, orgies, and the like." Then (v. 15) he reminds his readers of the basic principle underlying his list of wrong attitudes: "Those who belong to Christ Jesus (i.e., those who are Christians) crucified the flesh with its passions and desires." In Colossians 3:5 ff. the Pauline teaching is no less explicit:

> Put to death what is earthly in you: fornication, uncleanness, passion, evil desires, and that greediness which is idolatry ... anger, quick temper, malice, insults, foul language; stop lying to one another, since you have put aside your old self with its deeds,

and put on the new self, one that grows in knowledge
as he is formed anew in the image of his Creator.

The Body of Christ

The most characteristic, perhaps, of Paul's conceptualizations of the Christian reality is his teaching that the Christian community, together with Christ himself, constitutes the body of Christ, and each Christian individual is a member of this body. In this particular conceptualization the notion *body* is the entire person, with everything he or she is and has, as expressed through the body.

The body of Christ, of Jesus of Nazareth, is the entire reality of Christ who acted through his body on earth and continues to act through it (not independently of it) even after his resurrection. In this sense the fullness of God's saving power, of divine life, and of the Holy Spirit dwells in the risen Christ as he is, with his body too (Col. 1:19; 2:9; cf. Col. 2:3). Whatever saving grace and life Christians receive, they receive from Christ's "body" [total person], so that the body of Christ becomes the source from which life flows into Christians. This life is the life of Christ's risen body (the "spirit" of 1 Corinthians 15:45; 6:17) which, through the sacraments, shares it with his "members." Paul understands that through baptism (1 Cor. 12:13) a person is ingrafted into Christ (through the body); the channels of communication between both Christ and the person are established and opened, so that the life available in the body of Christ flows into the baptized person, and can be increased through the other sacraments. Since this person is now animated by a life principle that by nature belongs to the risen body of Christ, he or she becomes a "member" of the body of Christ. The same is true of all Christians who, together with Christ as their "head," constitute the total body of Christ.

This mystery of the Christian reality, Paul understands, demands of Christians a particular way of living in the world.

The vital expressions or manifestations of living creatures correspond to the life principle that animates them. This applies to the "nature" of Christians. The projections of their personalities, both internal and external, must flow from the life principle that animates them; these projections must manifest the real nature of that principle. The life principle that Christians are given is a share in the very life of the risen Lord. It follows that the activity of such a principle in human life cannot be different from the activity of Christ himself. It must be of the same quality (though not of the same degree or intensity); it must be an activity that Christ can claim as his own, thereby elevating it to a supernatural level. It is for this purpose that he shares his risen life with his "members," thereby truly becoming a "vivifying spirit" (1 Cor. 15:45). The apostle himself resorts to this principle in order to urge moral attitudes in several areas.

According to 1 Corinthians 6:15 ff., the reality of Christ's body requires of Christians a moral conduct in matters of sexual behavior. In v. 13 Paul stresses that the human body (with the human personality) is not for fornication but for the Lord, and that the Lord is for the human body. This is marital language that points to the intimate relationship that exists between the "vivifying" Lord and Christians. A few lines further down (v. 17) Paul emphasizes, as a matter of fact, that the person who joins the Lord becomes "one spirit" with him, which is the counterpart of the "one flesh" effected by a man who joins a prostitute. This intimate relationship by which a Christian belongs to the Lord is, in Paul's view, a fundamental reason why sexual immorality is against the "nature" of being a Christian; it is against the fundamental realities involved in the Christian mystery. Or "do you not know that your bodies are members of Christ? Would I, then, take Christ's members [members of one's body that belong to Christ] and make them members of a prostitute? God forbid! Or do you not know that he who joins the prostitute is one body [with her] ... but he who joins the Lord is one spirit [with him]?" (v. 15-17). Indeed, "your body is a temple of the Holy Spirit who is in you and whom you have from God" (v. 19).

By becoming Christians, people do not lose their physical nature, but they become "one spirit" with the Lord by being ingrafted into the body of the Lord and sharing the life of the "vivifying spirit," which is the Lord himself. In this sense, by receiving the Spirit of God as a gift, these people become at the same time a "temple" where the Holy Spirit dwells and members of Christ's body. When a Christian man joins his legitimate wife, this happens according to the purpose and plans of the Creator, and this is why Christ approves of the relationship. When a man joins a prostitute [whatever the specific meaning of this term in the present text], this does not happen according to the purpose and orderly plan of the Creator; they do "become one flesh" (1 Cor. 6:16), but in the wrong way, in the wrong relationship—and this is why it is a sin. In this case the life of Christ poured into that Christian cannot contribute to that relationship and, still less, elevate it to any supernatural level. Thus Christ cannot claim such an action as his own. It happens not because of his life but in spite of his life, which has been poured into that man, and in spite of Christ himself. The Christian man uses a body—his own—that belongs to Christ and is animated by Christ's life as one of his "members," and puts it at the service of somebody else who is an unlawful lord/partner (see 1 Cor. 7:4), namely, a prostitute. That is why it is a sin. For Paul, a correct sexual conduct in a Christian is not a matter of legalistic compliance with a rule—Paul agrees that, from a legalistic point of view, the Christian person is free, and "everything is lawful" to him or her (6:12). A moral sexual behavior necessarily flows from the very life principle that a person enjoys as a Christian; "he is not for fornication, he is for the Lord," and everything the person does must express this relationship and the living power on which this relationship is grounded. For this and other reasons Paul concludes that Christians "must glorify God with their bodies" (1 Cor. 6:20).

Parenthetically, it may be added, in this passage (1 Cor. 6:12 ff.) Paul argues about the correct use of human sexuality on some basic reasons other than legal. He mentions that a Christian's body will be raised to God's glory, as Christ's was, just because the "members" belong where the "body" is (v. 14). Another reason is that, since the body is a temple where God's Spirit dwells, it must be respected and held in honor (v. 19)—it should not be profaned by using it for what it is not intended. Paul mentions, furthermore, that Christians are not masters of themselves, "for you were bought by a price" (v. 20), which is none other than the price Christ paid; and this is why Christ is "the Lord" of all Christians. Servants are supposed to comply with the orders of their master.

The reality of the body of Christ is, in addition, the basis for moral, let us say, "Christian," attitudes in the vast area of mutual relations among Christians. The principle of Christian love applies, first of all, to "divisions" in the Christian community (1 Cor. 12:12-13). The problem contemplated in 1 Corinthians 12 seems to have been the correct coexistence of influential members with lower, or less prominent, people in the same community. Some "feet" or "ears" in the community apparently decided not to belong to "the body" because they were not "hands" or "eyes" respectively (v. 15 f.). On the other hand, it should be clear, Paul feels, that "the eye cannot say to the hand 'I do not need you,' any more than the head can say to the feet 'I do not need you'" (v. 21). All "members" in the community should realize that "the body is not one member but many" (v. 14, 19 f.); that it was "God who placed the members, each of them, in the body as he pleased" (v. 18); that it was "God who composed the body and gave additional honor to him who lacks it, that there be no division in the body but the members be equally concerned about each other" (v. 25). Joys and sufferings should be equally shared by all "members." The ultimate reason for all this being that "you are Christ's Body and, individually, his members" (v. 27). Loving coexistence and concord is nothing accidental or superfluous to the Christian. No, it springs from the very nature of being a Christian; all Christians belong to the same body, and are animated by the same life principle. Their very life consists in promoting the well-being of the organism of which they are integral parts.

Along the same line, in Romans 12:3, Paul warns Christians in the Roman community "not to think (of oneself) more highly than one ought to think, but rather so to think as to think soberly." Paul draws on his own experience with his communities and stresses a correct relationship among the members of a Christian church or congregation. There can be little doubt that his warning in this passage covers everything he has to say in chapters 12 and 13 and, particularly in chapters 14 and 15, where quarrels and arguments between the "weak" and the "strong" in faith are pointed out. The problem in Paul's mind concerns the insiders themselves.

Interestingly, the warning not to think more highly than one ought to think finds its fundamental justification in the fact that in the Christian community all different offices, functions, and gifts are God's grace. This grace is intended to be put to work in the conviction that we "the congregation are one body in Christ and, as individuals, we are members of one another" (Rom. 12:4, 5). There is a unity ("one body") in the Christian community, but there is also a diversity of "members" with different functions. The necessary harmony and concord that such a diversity requires is provided by the interrelationship that necessarily exists between the members of one single organism that receive their life supply from the same source, and work toward the same goal of the body's growth. The particular point brought into relief by Paul in this passage is that any "superiority complex" does not promote the well-being of the body of Christ. Some of the practical implications of this principle are expounded in chapters 14 and 15 where, in reference to religious practices, Paul rejects critical attitudes, strife, arrogance, and self-assertiveness in relations among Christians, while stressing the point that "we must no longer pass judgment on one another. Instead your judgment must be to put no stumbling block or hindrance in your brother's way.... We who are strong (in faith) ought to be patient with the weak faith of those who are not strong—and not please ourselves. Let each one of us please his neighbor for his advantage in view of his edification. As a matter of fact, Christ himself did not please himself.... Therefore welcome one another just as Christ welcomed us so as to glorify God" (Rom. 14:13; 15:1-3, 7).

The basic idea is the same in Ephesians 4:16 where the body of Christ is supposed "to build itself up in love," in the realization of the fundamental unity among Christians (4:2-6) in spite of different ministries and gifts from Christ in the community (4:7-11). In Colossians 2:16-19 (see v. 20-23) false and irrelevant expressions of religious faith are excluded, because for a Christian true and correct religious faith consists in "holding fast to the head" of the body by striking deeper roots into Christ ("the head") in order to draw from him an ever increasing flow of life, so as to experience the growth that God wants to bring about. Inter-Christian ecumenism also finds its firm basis in the reality of the body of Christ (Eph. 1:1-22). In this passage the point at issue is that Jews and pagans were "created into one new man" in Christ who "in himself" killed "enmity" and made peace between them (v. 15 f.). Christ did this by reconciling both of them with God "in one body" when he "created" Jews and pagans into one new man "in himself." This is what establishes "peace" between all the members of the community.

Life in the Spirit

It is Paul's understanding that one of the most important aspects of human justification by God is the gift of the Holy Spirit. The security of God's love for the justified person is "the Holy Spirit given to us" (Rom. 5:6; cf. 2 Cor. 1:22; Eph. 1:13 f.; 4:30); a direct implication of this is that the body/person of the Christian is "a temple of the Holy Spirit whom you have from God" (1 Cor. 6:19), "a temple of God, and the Holy Spirit dwells in you" (1 Cor. 3:16 f.; cf. 2 Cor. 6:16). Since the Spirit is the expression of God's love for humanity, he is also the tangible evidence of the Father-son relationship that God establishes between himself and the justified human being. "You have not received a spirit of slavery leading to fear once again; no, you have received a Spirit of sonship who makes us call out 'Abba, oh Father!'. The Spirit himself together with our own spirit bears witness that we are children of God" (Rom. 8:15, 16). "Since you are sons, God has sent forth the Spirit of his Son into our hearts, calling out 'Abba, oh Father!' Thus you are no longer slaves but sons" (Gal. 4:6 f.).

From this fundamental truth of the Christian being, Paul derives practical applications that bear upon the moral attitudes of the Christian. He states that "the law of the Spirit of life in Christ Jesus has set you free from the law of sin and death" (Rom. 8:2). The "law" of the Spirit or of sin and death in this context is a rule; it is a way of living and, more particularly, a religious way of life. The law of the Spirit is not a way of life dominated and ruled by sin and, therefore, death; the law of the Spirit of life is a way of life that happens "in Christ Jesus," a way of life guided and powered by the Spirit who possesses life and, therefore, conveys life and power to a person "in Christ" so that this person is able to live according to the guidance of the Spirit. It is imperative, however, that Christians live according to "the law of the Spirit of life"; it is the only alternative left to them after their conversion and justification by God. The only other alternative is the law of sin and death, i.e., the kind of life Christians gave up by their conversion—a life that "saddens the Holy Spirit" (Eph. 4:30). The law or rule of the Spirit consists in letting ourselves be "driven by the Spirit of God" (Rom. 8:14) which, among other things, implies "putting to death the deeds of the body through the Spirit" (v. 13). This is how Christians show that they are "sons of God" (v. 14).

It is a matter of fundamental realities. The law of God must be complied with, even and particularly by Christians (Rom. 8:4; 3:31). But there is a problem here, and the problem is human flesh, not the nature of God's law (v. 4). As we have seen, "flesh" means the total person as he or she is bound to earth; it disregards God and his wishes, and resists the beneficent action of the Spirit (Gal. 5:17). It is because of such a spiritual attitude in human beings that God's law becomes "powerless," ineffective, in the sense that, as a matter of fact, it is not complied with and does not lead men and women to salvation. But Christians are "those who do not walk according to the flesh, but according to the Spirit" (Rom. 8:4). It is a matter of "being," and the alternatives are two only: "those who 'are' according to the flesh have their minds set on things fleshly, but those who 'are' according to the Spirit have their minds set on things spiritual" (v. 5). The mindset of the flesh is death; and this is why "the mind-set of the flesh spells enmity towards God" (v. 7). This is clear evidence that Christians cannot live according to the flesh, namely, in disregard of God, his demands, and his law. In point of fact, the mindset of the flesh "does not submit to God's law, indeed it cannot" (v. 7). But the painful result of all this is that "those who are in the flesh cannot please God" (v. 8). The ultimate implication, Paul understands, is that Christians cannot live according to the flesh and disregard God's law in their lives.

The only other alternative for Christians is to live according to the "rule of the Spirit of life" and let themselves "be driven by the Spirit of God." The reason is obvious: "You (Christians) are not in the flesh; no, you are in the Spirit if (as it is) the Spirit of God dwells in you" (v. 9). The presence of God's Spirit in humans is the evidence of Christ's indwelling in them, and this is why Paul emphasizes very strongly that the indwelling of the Spirit/Christ in Christians necessarily entails the death of our sinful personality. Our unregenerated, unredeemed dimension is dead—just as sin is dead. On the contrary, the Spirit is life, and he imparts life (Rom. 8:10).

Paul has an even more stern warning for Christians. The presence of the Spirit/Christ in Christians will certainly show in the life of the Spirit because of righteousness; it will also show in the death of the Christians' sinful projection because of sin (v. 10). If this is not the case of humans, they must realize that they are not Christians "If someone does not have the Spirit of Christ, he is not his," i.e., he or she does not belong to Christ, and is not a Christian. Paul's conviction is that a life "according to the Spirit" is the true evidence that people are Christians and are in the Spirit. Moral attitudes tell us a lot about ourselves, and about what we really are.

In Galatians 5:20-22 Paul becomes more specific about what a way of life according to the flesh or the Spirit means. A life according to the Spirit yields a harvest of "love, joy, peace, forbearance, kindness, goodness, faithfulness and self-control." A life according to the flesh yields the opposite result of vices and sinful attitudes listed in Galatians 5:19-21, which Paul calls the "works of the flesh." In this context the apostle stresses that if the life principle of Christians is the Spirit, they must follow the Spirit (v. 24), which, Paul understands, cannot be achieved without effort and struggle because "the flesh has desires contrary to the Spirit" and vice versa, with the result that they fight against one another (v. 17). But Christians must know that "those who are of Christ Jesus crucified the flesh with its passions and desires" (v. 24), and have to keep crucifying it through the guidance and power of the Spirit that are given to them.

When Paul brings the "law" of the Spirit into relief in Romans 8:1 ff., he points out an important aspect of Christian life, namely, the relationship between the leadership of the Spirit and God's law. He stresses the fact that "the flesh" does not submit to God's law; it cannot. On the contrary, a truly Christian life under the Spirit's leadership does take God's law into account. What is more, one of the reasons why the power and guidance of the Holy Spirit were given to Christians was so that the requirements of the law might be fulfilled in Christians (Rom. 8:4). A Christian life necessarily implies compliance with God's will manifested in his law. In no way does Paul suggest that his understanding of God's grace in Christ exempts humans from adjusting their conduct to God's requirements. The "freedom" that Christians were granted cannot be an excuse for them to yield to the "flesh" (Gal. 5:13); and the fact that Christians are under the regime of grace does not mean that they can continue to sin (Rom. 6:14 f.). Paul is adamant in his principle that God's grace and justification through faith alone do not mean abrogation of his law: "God forbid! Far from it, we confirm the law (as valid)" (Rom. 3:31). But the law, though good, holy, supernatural, etc. (Rom. 7:12-14), by itself alone is powerless to bring human beings to justification because it cannot overcome their "fleshly" condition of spiritual weakness (Rom. 8:3, 7:14). This is why the supernatural power of the Spirit is needed; it is this power that helps us overpower our fleshly powerlessness to comply with the demands of God's law. This is a clear indication that, in God's plan, his law stands and is in force even and particularly in regard to Christians—this is the reason why he gives them the power of the Spirit so that "the requirements of the law might find fulfilment in us" Christians.

It is well known that Paul is very emphatic in denying any value to "works of the law" in order to obtain justification and salvation (Rom. 3:20, 27 f.; Gal. 2:16) and even goes as far as to say that the law is the cause of sin (Rom. 4:15; 5:13, 20; 7:8, 10, 13; Gal. 3:17, 19). But there is no contradiction in his teaching. When he stresses the fact that compliance with the law does not justify humanity, he is opposing the Pharisaic religious system. Against this background he maintains that *legalism* is the wrong approach to God and salvation because, as a matter of *factuality,* on account of its fleshly condition humanity does not comply with the entire law at all times. The result is that, whenever humanity breaks the law, legalism (strict observance of the law for its own sake) cannot save it any longer, and the only alternative left to human beings is God's forgiving grace and love offered in Christ.

When Paul emphasizes that God's law stands and keeps its force in the regime of grace, and that Christians must fulfill the requirements of the law, Paul does not commend the legalism he rejects in some other places. The Christian religious system is not based on slavery, fear, and legalism. The Spirit given to humanity is a Spirit of *sonship*; it is the security of God's love for humanity. Through Christ God established a Father-child relationship between himself and humanity by which humanity, moved and enlightened by the Spirit, calls out to God "Abba, Oh Father!" In other words, humanity recognizes God as his father and itself as God's child. The relationship between them is one of *love.* In such a relationship, if and when it is real, humanity complies with the law, not because it is a law but because it is the expression of the wishes of its "Father" whom it loves. Humanity complies with God's law, not out of legalism but out of love—a process in which the Spirit is particularly active. Such is the Christian "freedom" to which Paul refers (Gal. 5:1 ff., 13, etc.)—the freedom of accepting and complying with God's will out of free and liberating love, not out of compulsion. This is why Paul says that one of the results of Christ's redeeming work is that "the requirements of the law might be fulfilled in us (by the Spirit) who walk, not according to the flesh but according to the Spirit" (Rom. 8:14). This is why Christians are not supposed to sin even though they are under a regime of grace and not under law (Rom. 6:15). It is in this sense, first of all, that the apostle dares to say that "if you are driven by the Spirit you are under no law" (Gal. 5:18), because the will of God is complied with, not out of legal or legalistic compulsion but out of love. Still God's law stands and is to be complied with.

Paul brings up another dimension of the Christian reality that requires an ethical conduct. As pointed out above, in Romans 8:9, he states that the Spirit of God "dwells" in Christians, and that persons who do not have the Spirit cannot be Christians. Since the Spirit dwells there, "your body is a *temple* of the Holy Spirit who is in you" (1 Cor. 6:19). The apostle mentions this aspect of the Christian mystery as a powerful reason for urging moral attitudes on Christians, particularly in the area of sexual morality, because, even on a natural level, sexual impurity is a "dishonor of one's own body" (Rom. 1:24). But when the human body is turned into a "temple" of God or of the Spirit, dishonoring our body is a matter of religion; it becomes a profanation or desecration of something holy and sacred, namely, of God's temple. Paul spells this out when in 1 Corinthians 3:17 he states that "if someone corrupts God's temple, God will corrupt him; for God's temple is holy—and you are that temple." Since "we are a temple of the living God," the apostle understands that there must be a "separation" between this temple and the "impurity" tied to the pagan way of life (2 Cor. 6:16 f.). In his own terms, this requires an effort to "clean ourselves of every defilement of flesh and spirit by bringing our sanctification to completion in the fear of God" (7:1).

* * *

For Christians a correct moral life and full compliance with God's law is not a matter of legalism or imposition from outside. Rather it is a necessary consequence of being Christians, and a clear evidence that God's power and love are at work in them—that their "faith is effective through love" (Gal. 5:6). Were it otherwise, Christians should be concerned about whether the Spirit really dwells and is effective in them, and realize that "if someone does not have the Spirit of Christ, he does not belong to him," to Christ; they are not Christians.

Part Two
Natural Law and Christian Morality

The Natural Law, Objective Morality, and Vatican II

Dr. John Finnis
University College
Oxford University
Oxford, England

In 1965, the Second Vatican Council declared in *Gaudium et Spes* (The Pastoral Constitution on the Church in the Modern World):

> Today the human race is entered upon a new era of its history.... Profound and rapid changes, triggered by the intelligence and creative energy of man, recoil on man himself, on his judgments, his individual and collective desires, and his manner of thinking and acting both about things and about people. So we can now speak of a true social and cultural transformation... (*Gaudium et Spes*, 4).
>
> History itself is speeding up on so rapid a course that individuals can scarcely keep pace with it.... And so the human race is passing from a relatively static conception of the scheme of things to a more dynamic and evolutionary conception—whence there arises a new set of problems, calling for new analyses and new syntheses (*Gaudium et Spes*, 5).[1]

The remainder of *Gaudium et Spes* is devoted to just such new analyses and new syntheses. And in the last words of the

Introduction, the Council offers a methodological reflection on all that is to follow:

> The Church believes that Christ, through his Spirit, provides man with light and strength so that man can respond to his high calling.... Likewise she believes that in her Lord and Master are to be found the key, the center and the goal of the whole history of mankind. And the Church affirms, too, that underlying all changes there are many things that do not change, and which have their ultimate foundation in Christ who is the same yesterday, today, and forever. So it is in the light of Christ, the image of the unseen God, and the firstborn of every creature, that the Council is setting out to speak to everyone, to clarify the mystery of man and to cooperate in finding a solution to the principal problems of our time (*Gaudium et Spes,* 10).

Gaudium et Spes and *Dignitatis Humanae* were promulgated on the same day, and we may usefully weave the great themes of those documents together to find the pattern of those underlying realities which, in the teaching of the Council, do not change, being founded on Christ, the Word of God and, as crucified and risen, the center of human history.

The Objectivity of the Natural Law

In the final paragraph of *Gaudium et Spes*, the Council recalled that most awesome saying of Christ: "Not everyone who says 'Lord, Lord' will enter into the kingdom of heaven, but those who *do the will of the Father* ..." (*Gaudium et Spes,* 93 quoting Mt. 7:21; for the full sense, see vv. 22-23 also; cf. *Lumen Gentium*, 14, n.13). As *Dignitatis Humanae* puts it:

> The highest norm of human life is the divine law[2]— eternal, objective and universal—whereby God orders, directs and governs the whole world and the

ways of the human community according to the plan
of his wisdom and love. God makes man a sharer
(*particeps*) in this his law so that, by divine providence's sweet[3] disposing, man can recognize
more and more the unchanging truth (*Dignitatis
Humanae*, 3).

At this point, in a footnote mysteriously suppressed in the Abbott edition of the documents of Vatican II, the Council referred
us to three texts of Aquinas, including one obviously upper-
most in the mind of those who drafted the document:

The eternal law is unchanging truth, and everyone
somehow knows the truth, at least the general principles of the natural law (even though in other matters some people share more and some less in the
knowledge of truth).[4]

So it was no accident that the Council said that the human
person is a sharer (*particeps*) in the eternal law. Aquinas's
"definition" of the natural law is: "the participation of the eternal law in the rational creature"[5]; for, as Aquinas says in the
same place, the rational creature is subject to divine providence in a more excellent way than other creatures, inasmuch
as the rational creature *provides* for himself and others and
thus is a sharer (*particeps*) in divine providence.[6]
The Council's text, where we left it, was speaking of the
unchanging truth that human beings can increasingly recognize. This looks back to the previous paragraph of *Dignitatis
Humanae*: "... all men ... are by their own nature impelled,
and are morally bound, to seek the truth" (*Dignitatis
Humanae*, 2). And the truth that they are to seek is no merely
abstract or speculative truth. For "they are bound, too, to
adhere to the truth they know and to order their whole life
according to the requirements of the truth" (*Dignitatis
Humanae*, 2); their duty is "prudently [i.e. reasonably, by prac-

tical wisdom] to form right and true judgments of conscience"
(*Dignitatis Humanae*, 3). For the human being "perceives and
recognises the dictates of the divine law by means of his conscience" (*Dignitatis Humanae*, 3).

More about conscience in due course. For the moment I want
to reinforce the clear implication of *Dignitatis Humanae* that
these "dictates of the divine law," which are the "supreme
norm of human life," include the requirements of the natural
law.[7] This emerges sufficiently from a later paragraph of the
Declaration: "... by the will of Christ the Catholic Church is
the teacher of truth and it is her responsibility to proclaim and
authentically [or authoritatively: *authentice*] to teach the
truth that is Christ himself and, at the same time, by her
authority to declare and confirm the principles of the moral
order *that flow from human nature itself*" (*Dignitatis
Humanae*, 14). As *Gaudium et Spes* put it: "The Church, in
preaching the Gospel on the basis of her divine mission, contributes to placing the brotherly common life [*consortionis*] of
individuals and peoples on a solid basis: namely, a knowledge
of the *divine and natural law*" (*Gaudium et Spes*, 89), i.e., of a
law that, as natural, is also divine. This is made very clear in
the famous paragraph about birth control: the divine law
which, in the light of the gospel, is unfolded (*Gaudium et Spes*,
51) and authentically interpreted by the Church's magisterium
(*Gaudium et Spes*, 50) provides, or consists of, objective standards based on the nature of the [human] person and of his acts
[*objective criteriis, ex personae eiusdemque actuum natura de-
sumptis*] (*Gaudium et Spes*, 51).

The Council's teaching that the natural law is an aspect of
the divine law is not an idle, arbitrary, or formal assertion. For
the "natural goodness" of things (including human life), their
"value", comes from God (*Apostolicam Actuositatem*, 7), who as
Creator has established them according to his plan (*Christus
Dominus*, 12; cf. also *Lumen Gentium*, 36). And in the finest

paragraph of *Gaudium et Spes* we find that the Lord's command [*mandatum*] is to "spread on earth the goods of human dignity, brotherly unity, and liberty, *that is to say* all the *good fruits of our nature* and of our effort"—the goods which "we will find again..., transfigured" in the completed kingdom of "truth and life, holiness and grace, justice, love and peace" (*Gaudium et Spes,* 39). A group of six Council fathers suggested that this reference to the goods, or good fruits, *of our nature,* be deleted, on the ground that in the context of human culture today it is not too felicitous to speak of "our nature"; these things are the fruits not of our nature but of free human work.[8] Their objection was rightly rejected, though the reference to "our effort [*industria*]" was added to make the point (as traditional as it is modern) that human nature is fulfilled (bears its good fruits) only in action (including, of course, such action as contemplation).[9]

All in all, it is easy to see that, in the teaching of the Council, the objectivity that a judgment has by being in accordance with the divine creative understanding (i.e., in accordance with the divine law) and the objectivity that a judgment has by discerning and/or choosing what is really good for a being constituted as we are (i.e., a being with our nature) are two aspects, only notionally distinguishable, of (a) the objectivity of the "objective moral order" (*Dignitatis Humanae,* 7 and *Inter Mirifica,* 6; cf. also *Gaudium et Spes,* 16: "objective norms of morality"), and (b) the rightness and truth of a "right and true conscience" (*Dignitatis Humanae,* 3).

Against this background we can get a clearly focused understanding of the Council's teaching on conscience, the dignity of the conscience, and indeed on human dignity in general. The Council spoke of human dignity more than sixty times, and always as a kind of shorthand for the complex of reason/freedom/responsibility we find referred to in that sentence I quoted partially a few minutes ago: "In accordance with their dignity, all men—since they are persons, i.e., endowed with reason and free will and thus raised to personal responsibility[10]—are by their own nature impelled, and are morally bound, to seek the truth" (*Dignitatis Humanae*, 2; cf. also *Dignitatis Humanae,* 11).

Reason, freedom, responsibility, obligation: perhaps the nearest the Council gets to a formal account of human dignity is in *Gaudium et Spes,* in the central paragraph of the chapter on the dignity of the human person: "Man attains [his] dignity when, liberating himself from all captivity to the passions, he pursues his end, in the free choice of good and procures for himself, effectively and by skillful effort [*industria*], appropriate aids to that end" (*Gaudium et Spes,* 17). And what is that end? It is, as the Council says in the next sentence, an "ordination toward God." So the Council can venture an even shorter "definition" of what it means by dignity: the dignity of man *is*, consists in, obeying the law written in his heart by God (*Gaudium et Spes*, 16). And here, of course, the Council cited the foundation text for Catholic reflection on natural law, *Romans* 2:15-16: "[When the Gentiles who do not have the Law do by nature [*naturaliter*] what the Law requires] they show that what the Law requires is written on their hearts, while their conscience also bears witness. . . ."

For conscience, too, is another in the cluster of concepts that we use in understanding this subtle intersection ("participation") of the human with the divine. As the Council said in the first sentence of its treatment of "the dignity of moral conscience":

> In the depths of conscience man discerns a law which he does not dictate to himself but which he ought to obey; always summoning him to love and do the good and to avoid evil, the voice of this law [*not*, as "Abbott" mistranslates, the voice of conscience!] sounds

when necessary in the ears of his heart as "Do this, shun that. . . ."

"Conscience," continues the Council, quoting Pius XII, "is the most secret core and sanctuary of man, in which he is alone with God, whose voice resounds in his inwardness" (*Gaudium et Spes,* 16). Fidelity to conscience means a "search for *truth*" and for *true* solutions to moral problems; conscience can indeed err "through invincible ignorance without losing its dignity" (provided there is sufficient "care for the search for the true and the good"); but "to the extent that a correct conscience holds sway, persons and groups are turning away from blind choice and seeking to conform to the objective norms of morality" (*Gaudium et Spes*, 16).

In short, it was the Council's unwavering teaching that the dignity of conscience consists in its *capacity* to disclose the objective truth about what is to be done, both in particular assessments and in general norms,[11] and that that truth has its truth as an intention of God whose voice is our law. This law is knowable by us because we "participate in the light of the divine mind" (*Gaudium et Spes,* 15). The teaching corresponds to this, indeed, it is an explicitation of it, the equally unwavering and even more frequently repeated teaching of the Council that human dignity consists of the capacity to *understand,* to some extent, what God expects of us, and to choose *freely* to relate ourselves to God in faith, hope, and love by acting and living in accordance with that understanding. Let us now add a last statement:

> The outstanding rationale [*ratio*] of human dignity consists in the vocation of the human being to communion with God. To converse [*colloquium*] with God, the human being is invited right from his very origin; for he would not exist were he not constantly

> preserved (as he was created) by God's love, and he
> cannot live fully according to truth unless he freely
> acknowledges that love and commits himself to his
> Creator (*Gaudium et Spes,* 19).

In all the Council's many references to human dignity, there
is no trace of that arbitrary, "picture-thinking" conception of
dignity that we find, for example, in the working paper (dated
27 May 1966) of the "majority theologians" of the Pontifical
Commission on Population, Family, and Birth, in which they
sought to *explain* why, if contraceptive intercourse is morally
good, nevertheless various other masturbatory acts between
spouses are not. In relation to the latter acts, they said:

> The new theory is extremely strict... since it does
> not permit them. For in these acts there is preserved
> neither the dignity of love nor the dignity of the
> spouses as human persons created according to the
> image of God.

This is no explanation at all, since an act accords with human
dignity in the morally relevant sense by being reasonable and
right in accordance with God's call to us. As *Gaudium et Spes*
said (citing 1 Corinthians 6:13–20 on the indignity of fornication): "... human dignity itself involves that one glorify God in
one's body" by "not allowing it to serve the depraved inclinations of one's heart" (*Gaudium et Spes*, 14); that is, once again,
by turning aside from blind choice toward the objective norms
of morality, toward God's law, which is discerned in the conscience (*Gaudium et Spes*, 16) *somehow* by all who have intelligence at all and *fully* by one who has that wisdom which
"perfects the intelligent nature of the human person"
(*Gaudium et Spes,* 15).

And so, when the Council comes to speak in *Gaudium et
Spes*, 51 of the need to reverence the conjugal sexual act as
"directed according to genuine human dignity," it explains this

norm (so to speak) of dignity by exactly the same line of thought as we have just observed in *Gaudium et Spes,* 14-16; indeed it makes its explanation even clearer by beginning the next sentence with a "therefore" [*igitur*]:

> Therefore, the moral character of [this] action, when the harmonizing of conjugal love with the responsible transmission of life is in question, does not depend only on a sincere intention and a consideration of motives, but ought to be determined by objective criteria, derived from the nature of the human person and of the human person's acts. . . .

That is what human dignity demands: an objective (i.e., real) relationship to basic human goods, basic aspects of human personality as they are inevitably involved in certain sorts of human acts: These "objective criteria," therefore, "in an ambience of true love, *respect the whole sense of mutual [self-] giving and of human procreation,*" and this objectively adequate respect for those basic human goods (and thus for authentic human dignity) "cannot be had unless the virtue of conjugal chastity is cultivated serious-mindedly [*sincero animo*]" (*Gaudium et Spes,* 51).

Natural Law: The Ultimate Authority for Christian Life?

It is said by various contemporary theologians that the objective or "natural-law" ethics with which moral theology must work is an "experiential" ethics, that is, an ethics based on ordinary knowledge of the facts.[12] These theologians differ among themselves about what sorts of "facts" really count for these purposes.[13] But their appeals to experience and/or ordinary facts have a common purpose, which is twofold. The *first* purpose is to suggest that it is the relevant sort of experiential or factual knowledge, and not revelation, that provides the "ultimate" foundation of ethical knowledge so that the "ulti-mate" authority in any inquiry into natural law (and thus in human, including Christian, life) is *not* revelation but these experienced facts. And the *second* purpose of these theologians is to argue that the alternative to "experiential" moral knowl-edge is a legalism which, whether it be based on "natural law, understood in some juridical sense" or on "commandments of some kind," is "an injustice to both the Creator and his crea-tion."[14] Let me take up these two arguments.

First, the argument that, if we believe in natural law, we cannot believe that revelation has "ultimate authority" in morals. The argument and its implications are spelled out most clearly by Fr. Gerard Hughes: "Belief in revelation is irra-tional unless that revelation somehow fits our antecedent con-victions, and, in particular, with our antecedent moral convic-tions"; our response to revelation "must inevitably include moral reflection which is not in turn dependent on the revela-tion it is trying to interpret"; such moral reflection is "epis-temologically prior to our appeal to revelation, which cannot therefore be ultimately authoritative"; *therefore,* according to Hughes, appeal to revelation *cannot* "enable us to solve moral dilemmas to which there is no other adequate solution"; there *could not* be "a specifically Christian ethic, the conclusions of which cannot be firmly established without appeal to revela-tion"; and if one can find no *conclusive* arguments, say, against the legitimacy of divorce and remarriage *before* one appeals to revelation, it necessarily follows that there *could not* be any basis in revelation for concluding that divorce and remarriage are illegitimate.[15]

You will have noticed the *non sequitur*; it is, I'm afraid, extremely glaring. Revelation (since it cannot settle the ques-tion whether I ought to believe it and adhere to it—I must have some prior grasp of the moral importance of truth) cannot set-tle *all* questions; "therefore" revelation cannot settle *any* questions. Revelation is not the "ultimate" source of Christian life, which must "ultimately" begin with a free response to what is divinely proposed for belief and acceptance; the "ultimate authority" is the truth, respect for which motivates and justifies that response; "therefore" revelation is not an "ultimate" authority in any aspect of Christian life. Either *all* moral truths receive their ultimate justification or verification from revelation, or *none* do. (Three ways of expressing one and the same invalid reasoning to a false conclusion.)

The middle position—the Catholic position clearly expounded by Vatican I and frequently implied by Vatican II—was simply overlooked or brushed aside by these writers, viz, the position that moral truth about *some* matters *can* be securely known without (supernatural) revelation but the moral truth about *other* matters can be *securely* known only because God has revealed what objectively ought to be done.[16] Both parts of the position were developed in *Dignitatis Humanae*. Prior to their acceptance or even awareness of divine revelation, "all men ... are by their own nature impelled, *and morally bound*, to seek the truth, especially religious truth" (*Dignitatis Humanae*, 2). That this is an objective moral demand can be securely known in advance of hearing the Word. So can the further objective moral demand "to adhere to the truth, once it is known, and to order their whole lives in accord with its demands" (*Dignitatis Humanae*, 2). And then, when the Word has been heard, there arises "the duty of believing the word of God" (*Dignitatis Humanae*, 9, 11), that is, the "gospel, ... source of all saving truth and all moral teaching [*morum* disciplina]" (*Dei Verbum,* 7), including that "sacred and certain doctrine" by which the Church "declares and confirms by her authority those principles of the moral order which have their origin in human nature itself" (*Dignitatis Humanae,* 14).

Thus Vatican II supplied the materials for a more profound

exposition of the relations between natural law, gospel, and conscience than the Council itself formally expressed. Classic expositions of natural law as the participation of God's eternal intention in the human understanding have used, and rightly used, the metaphor of light, "irradiating" our minds, enabling us to "see," e.g., moral truth. Without questioning that metaphor, the Council (while making use of metaphors of see-ing) in effect invited us to consider another. It is not precisely or merely the metaphor of hearing; rather it is the richer metaphor (drawn not from the order of bare "nature" but from the order of social interaction) of coming to understand (and love) a person better through conversation or colloquy. For our dignity, to be found in our obedience to God's law (the voice of which sounds in the depths of our conscience) (*Gaudium et Spes*, 16), is rooted in our vocation, our calling, "*ad colloquium cum Deo*" (*Gaudium et Spes*, 19).[17] That *colloquium* begins in this life with our questions, "our" suppositions and "our" judg-ments (ours, because we are responsible for them; "ours," be-cause we do not simply "make them up"), e.g., about what really is good, and about what response the really good re-quires of us: about the natural law. But that is a conversation in a space crowded with our relatives and acquaintances and communities and enemies, and noisy not only with their voices but also with the voice of our own self-interest. Into that Babel the Word of God has been spoken publicly, so that it may be heard and taken to heart by each of us. That voice can be recognized for what it is, since its tones and its message are not foreign to our anticipations; but it can reply to questions whose answers otherwise seemed muffled and indistinct to us; and it summons us to closer converse—*colloquium, participatio*—with the loving and therefore demanding and judging One whose voice, whether recognized or unrecognized, it always has been, in truth, whenever we judge rightly.

One could pursue and amplify this analogy extensively. But

I want to sharpen the point by turning to the *second* argument of those who oppose "experience" to "revelation"—the argument that the alternative to experiential moral knowledge is *legalism*. Now I have just finished a long book defending the classic theses *not only* that one can understand, without revelation, the basic forms of human good and the basic requirements of practical reasonableness and thus a number of quite precise moral obligations, *but also* that one can understand, without referring to the will or commandments of God, the idea of real moral obligation. So I should like now to show how those classic theses do not imply that a respect for the commandments of God must be inappropriate, childish "legalism." These reflections of mine on legalism will continue through most of the rest of this paper, even when I am discussing other themes.

Why speak about the commandments at all? Well, as you know,[18] a rich young man came up to Jesus one day, and asked him, "Teacher, what must I do to have eternal life?" And (as all the Synoptics report, with interesting but immaterial variations) Jesus began his answer by saying to him, "If you would enter into life, keep the commandments." "Which?" "*You must not kill. You must not commit adultery. You must not bring false witness. Honour your father and mother,* and: *you must love your neighbour as yourself*" (Mt. 19:16-20; Mk. 10:17-19; Lk. 18:18-21).[19]

Now if the rich young man had recently been reading *Principles for a Catholic Morality,* these words of the Lord would have come as quite a surprise. For in that book there is no suggestion that Jesus made the specific moral commandments in the Decalog his own; the most Fr. Timothy O'Connell will allow is that it is a "great exaggeration" to contrast "Jesus' teaching of the two New Commandments" with "the Ten Commandments of the Old Law" which, however, were "not particularly concerned about *individual* morality in any form" and did not have a "precisely ethical" importance.[20] Well, the rich young man might reflect that, whatever may have been the case when the Decalog was originally revealed or incorporated in the inspired Scriptures, and whatever may have been its original relationship with similar moral conceptions in Egypt and Babylon, these commands, *repromulgated to him* by the good teacher who spoke with the authority of the Creator who offers eternal life, are the very paradigm of what in late western society would come to be called "precisely ethical" and "individual morality."

If the rich young man might well have lost confidence in the adequacy of Fr. O'Connell's discussion of the Decalog, so he would be unlikely to listen any longer (if ever he had) to Fr. Hughes's suggestion that Christ's Revelation is not concerned with "the details of morality" but only with "the general importance of being morally good"—the suggestion that, in direct contradiction to the words that the rich young man had just heard, "particular teachings on particular moral issues" are not "taught as salvation-truths" but are "offered simply because it is in general a salvation-truth that to take such issues seriously is required of us. . . ."[21]

But he might have been reading Frs. Schüller, McCormick, and O'Connell on parenetic discourse, inviting him to conclude that Christ's commands here do "not convey information about the specific content of... moral demands" but are merely "hortatory to what is presumed to be known and agreed on,"[22] so that they were "not meant to be taken literally and not intended to be really exceptionless".[23] Rather every command, such as "Do not kill," "Do not commit adultery," can be read subject to a tacit rider of the form: "except when there is a proportionate reason,"[24] i.e., except when killing or committing adultery would "maximize good and minimize evil."[25] An "absolute" or "exceptionless" command would be sheer legalism, i.e., would be a betrayal of the natural law itself.

Can we help the rich young man sort out these claims of the

new "moral theology"? The claims are of two sorts. One is about the need to interpret the promulgated commands (and implicitly, to interpret them in the light of our *prior* grasp of natural law). The other claim is specific: what the natural law requires, or makes appropriate, is a consequentialist interpretation of those "commands." Let us take these two sorts of claims separately.

Natural Law, Revelation, and Interpretation

No one doubts, or has doubted, that the commands of God that Christ entrusted to his apostles to be taught to the ends of the earth and the end of the world (Mt. 28:20; cf. 1 Cor. 7:10, 25) are in need of interpretation. As *Dei Verbum* put it:

> ... through contemplation and study by believers who treasure those [words] in their hearts..., through the intimate understanding of the spiritual things they experience, and through the proclamation of those who with the episcopal succession receive the sure charism of truth, the understanding of the words handed down grows (*Dei Verbum,* 7).

Moreover, this interpretative understanding will be achieved by Christians, i.e., by persons who bring to their contemplation and study of the divine words that (at least) elementary grasp of basic values and fundamental requirements of practical reasonableness which enabled them, under God's grace, to recognize the moral obligation to accept the revelation of Christ by reason of its truth. And if we, prior to that acceptance, can understand that truth is an objective good which, as objective, makes authoritative claims on us, equally we can grasp other basic aspects of human good such as life, and friendship and practical reasonableness, and such basic requirements of practical reasonableness as impartiality. Indeed, it is the grasp of these goods and requirements that ena-

bles us to perceive the publicly offered word as divinely ut-
tered. As Fr. Hughes says, "Revelation commends itself to us in
part because it does harmonize with our moral aspirations,"
which must therefore have been "present antecedently (at
least in a logical sense)."[26] So far so good; but then Fr. Hughes
(openly; and many another theologian tacitly) falls for the
hermeneutical circle:

> The attempt to use the biblical tradition as ulti-
> mately authoritative [i.e., as providing final and cer-
> tain solutions applicable to *us*] is viciously circular,
> since it must invoke precisely those processes of in-
> dependent moral reason which it is the purpose of
> the attempt to circumvent.[27]

Alas, Fr. Hughes's argument would prove that learning, in any
field, is logically impossible! For learning, in any field, very
commonly involves a *self-correcting* process, whereby the
understanding with which one began a particular inquiry (and
which enabled one to undertake the inquiry) is not only
amplified but also partially qualified and partially corrected by
the new understanding yielded by the inquiry.[28]

So, if we accept the Pauline thesis that "Gentiles who do not
have the Law do by nature what the Law requires... [and]
show that what the Law requires is written on their hearts"
(Rom. 2:14, 15), or the equivalent thesis of Irenaeus and the
whole Catholic tradition that the moral precepts of the Decalog
are matters of natural law,[29] we are not thereby challenging
the "ultimate authority" of God's publicly revealed word, i.e.,
(in *this* use of "ultimate") the capacity of that divine word to
reform and correct as well as supplement and make precise our
prior (and continuing!) understanding (whether articulated or
not) of natural law, i.e., of the *same* "eternal, objective, and
universal" plan of God's wisdom and love as is disclosed to us
through our natural capacity to understand the goods to which
we created beings find ourselves inclined.

A command such as "Do not kill" has this capacity and "ultimate" authority to correct and refine (notwithstanding its own need for interpretation) precisely because it is not a single set of words on a page but one part of a larger revelation made by word and deed. It is not my intention to make a foray into either biblical exegesis or biblical hermeneutics. But recent appeals to the notion of parenesis are calculated to suggest that the moral teachings of revelation are all in need of an interpretation which, in respect of all specific and material norms of conduct, must be effectively controlled by some "natural law" (or autonomous, philosophical reasonings; or by "experience" yielding, I suppose, some sort of intuitions). (This argument from the parenetic character of scriptural moral teaching is thus an alternative argument toward the thesis about the "ultimacy" of natural law, which we saw fallaciously defended by Fr. Hughes.) So I wish to give an indication of the *sorts* of reasons there are for supposing that revelation contains within its own resources *sufficient material to control its own interpretation* and thereby sufficient to correct the philosophical or "natural law" reasonings that might have seemed persuasive without it. To say that revelation has these resources and thus this corrective capacity is not to say that the resources of revelation could override a strict demonstration that an alleged moral norm cannot be morally acceptable. Nor is it to say that, where revelation does not confirm what would otherwise have seemed to be required or permitted by natural reasonableness, revelation must be *adding* something over and above the natural law. Rather it is to warn against the all too common slide *from* "the law of God/Christ is fundamentally natural law," or "nothing in revelation can in principle be contrary to reason," *to* "whatever I find morally opaque (or: whatever I cannot demonstrate to be part of natural law) cannot be part of the gospel's saving *disciplina morum*."

So to go back to particular but not fully specific commandments; each of them is one of a number of commandments, one

or more of which are *explained* by Christ and his apostles in
terms that make clear the proper *strategy* for interpreting the
parenetic (nonexplanatory) "Do not kill." For example, as
against the Jewish interpretation, Christ by explanatory discourse makes plain certain aspects of the stringency and "material" content of the command "Do not commit adultery" (Mt.
5:27-28, 31-32; and par.), and this strategy, identified as
Christ's, is applied (as against Gentile incomprehension of the
moral significance of sex) by St. Paul to the whole range of
nonmarital sexual activity.[30] So too, the context of revelation
supplies the materials for an explanatory specification of what
counts as the "killing" forbidden in the commandment which,
when thus made fully specific, applies as an exceptionless rule
of life; the process of specification begins in Exodus itself (the
"Do not kill" of Ex. 20:13 becomes the "Do not kill the innocent
and righteous" of Ex. 23:7); the distinction between direct and
indirect killing can be approached by asking whether Jesus
committed suicide; and so on. The interpretative process always envisions distinctions in terms of real human goods and
real modes of involvement with those goods, but never proposes
a calculus of consequences, and never degenerates into the
merely formal "Do not kill unjustly."

And do not forget that, just as the call of Christ to the rich
young man extended beyond the Decalog itself and indeed beyond the other commandments that I quoted (see Mt. 19:21), so
the resources of revelation that control its own interpretation
extend far beyond the expressed commands, the vice lists, the
house tables, and other overtly moral argumentation. These resources include such fundamental perspectives as Vatican II
recalls for us in the passage I have already partly quoted:

> We do not know the time of the consummation of the
> earth and of humanity, nor do we know how the
> universe will be transformed. The figure of this
> world deformed by sin is passing away.... [But] all

the good fruits of our nature and our effort (after we
have spread them on earth in the Spirit of the Lord
and according to his command) we will find again ...
transfigured, when Christ hands over to the Father
the kingdom ... of truth and life ... now on this
earth present in mystery, and to be consummated
when the Lord comes (*Gaudium et Spes,* 39).

Christians, then, are not to count only the good consequences
that can be humanly seen and foreseen in a world that is passing away; the morality of Christ counts the good that cannot be
seen, that hidden treasure of good works, which is hidden to us
in the calamities of ruin and oppression but known by faith to
be real and really constitutive of the kingdom of God being
now, in mystery, built up by obedience to the Lord (*Gaudium et
Spes,* 39, 93).

Revelation, Natural Law, and Consequentialism

The consequentialist theologians argue that Christ's commands are all subject to riders such as "unless there is proportionate reason for doing (the otherwise forbidden act)," or, less
obscurely though in fact absurdly,[31] "unless doing (the otherwise forbidden act) would maximize good and minimize evil."
They argue that the parenetic form of the commands leaves
them open to such "explanatory" qualifications. But the writings of these moral theologians themselves provide a refutation of this thesis. For do they really have any use for the
commands as formulated in revelation? An audience or congregation that has learned that the commands of the Decalog
"do not give us any information," are "not oriented toward the
material of a particular situation," "are really tautologies" and
"somehow involve circular logic," are "contentless"[32] and just
amount to saying that wrong actions are wrong, is not going to
be impressed or "challenged" or "motivated" by a homiletics
that appeals to such "commands."

By contrast, the architecture of Catholic moral teaching is, I venture to say, profoundly biblical in its methodology; even when presented as if simply an unfolding of the natural law, it has in reality been also an intelligible exposition and development of the words and deeds of revelation. Much of this architecture is visible in the moral teachings of Vatican II. The Council taught that there is a "natural and Gospel law" (*lex naturalis et evangelica*, not well translated in the Abbott edition as "natural law and the Gospel") which establishes "limits" that must be observed even by one who is defending his rights against unjust oppression (*Gaudium et Spes*, 74). It proclaims, not that there is only one universal principle of the natural law with unchanging binding force (as the consistent consequentialist argues) but that there are many (*Gaudium et Spes*, 79). It offers several examples of types of action that "are deliberately opposed" to those universal and unchanging principles: "above all, those actions which by intention and design exterminate a whole people, nation or ethnic minority" (*Gaudium et Spes*, 79); and again, "*every* warlike act which tends indiscriminately to the destruction of entire cities or of extensive areas along with their populations is a crime against God and man ..." (*Gaudium et Spes*, 80). It proclaims that the magisterial unfolding of the divine law can involve the condemnation of particular "ways of regulating births," not surely because the magisterium is in a position to assess "*authoritatively*" the "facts" about good and bad consequences of, say, contraception, but because some "ways of regulating births" fail to preserve the "integral meaning of mutual self-giving and of human procreation ..." (*Gaudium et Spes*, 51). The Council itself condemned abortion and infanticide as dreadful crimes (ibid.). Then, in a context dealing not with revealed divine law but with "the high dignity of the human person ... and his universal and inviolable rights and duties" (*Gaudium et Spes*, 26), the Council spoke in terms that cannot be reconciled with consistent consequentialism: "Whatever is opposed to life itself, such as any sort of homicide, genocide, abortion, euthanasia and willful suicide itself . . . ; all these and others of their like [some of which the Council identifies in the same passage, e.g., slavery, prostitution, and torture] are indeed shameful; while they poison human civilization, *they degrade [or harm] those who so act more than those who suffer the injury . . ."* (*Gaudium et Spes,* 27).

This last observation by the Council is, of course, as well known in the tradition of natural law philosophizing (see Plato, *Gorgias* 469B, 508B) as in the biblical revelation, which would clearly be understood as teaching that "evil may not be done for the sake of good" even if Paul had not expressly said so (Rom. 3:8; cf. 6:1).[33] So too the biblical and conciliar proclamation of prohibitions of types of act meshes in with the tradition of purely human ("natural") reason and custom that Aristotle summed up in the remark that there are actions about which we should never be asking ourselves "When? How? With whom? etc."; the mere commission of such acts (e.g., adultery) is wrong, and circumstances do not affect the matter (*Nicomachean Ethics* II, 6: 1107a 9-18; similarly, *Eudemian Ethics* II, 3: 1221b 18-26). Again, the scholastic maxim "Affirmative precepts are always valid but do not have to be carried out on every occasion; negative precepts have to be respected on every occasion"[34] is an induction from the scriptural data faithfully interpreted—indeed, the distinction between affirmative and negative precepts can be discerned even in the reordering of the commandments by Christ, addressing the rich young man—but it is also a principle of reasonableness, which insists that, though an omission to act can be as murderous, say, as a positive act, the distinction between act and omission is frequently of decisive relevance in assessing one's responsibilities (or guilt).

Thus, between the scripturally controlled theological tradition and the products of philosophical reflections intended to be "without revelation," there is an interpenetration so profound that when we are confronted by, say, Kant's "categorical imperative"—"Act so that you treat humanity, whether in your own person or in another's, always as an end and never as a means only"[35]—we cannot say (even as historians of philosophy) how much this owes to "natural reason" and how much to the revealed commands treasured in the hearts if not the deeds of Europeans for 1750 years. So too it is virtually impossible to determine (and unprofitable to try) whether the consequentialist theologians have been led astray *primarily* by bad philosophy (for consequentialism, which rejects all the principles, maxims, and distinctions I've just mentioned, *is* incoherent and philosophically indefensible)[36] or primarily by a loss of faith in the scriptural/traditional *disciplina morum*.

But there is another side to all this. The controlling clarity of the main lines of revealed moral teaching have encouraged a certain philosophical slackness amongst moral theologians; we are now seeing the bad consequences of that neglect. And we will be unable, I think, to respond adequately to the philosophical/theological crisis unless we identify and correct certain defects in, for example, Aquinas's treatise on natural law, defects left uncorrected, indeed exacerbated, in the neoscholastic revival of moral theology.

For instance, Aquinas distinguished three levels of principles or precepts of natural law: (i) most general principles, "not so much precepts as, so to speak, the ends or point of precepts," recognized by anyone who reaches the age of reason and has enough experience to know what they refer to; (ii) precepts that state the most elementary and easily recognizable moral implications of those first principles; precepts that can nevertheless be obscured or distorted for particular people and indeed for whole cultures; (iii) precepts that state solutions to moral questions that can be answered rightly only by someone who is *wise* and who considers the question searchingly. Now this set of distinctions, though vague, is quite reasonable.[37] But secure in his faithful grasp of revelation, Aquinas was casual in giving examples of the first-level principles, and some of the examples he gave encouraged the neo-scholastic thesis that certain precise, negative moral precepts (corresponding to items expressed or implied in the second table of the Decalog) are intuitively known by an act of intuition that is truly self-validating (i.e., which is not really a conclusion from suppressed premises that could be brought to light by analysis). That neo-scholastic thesis is not true; theologians who have recently discovered that it is not true tend to become (more or less consistent!) consequentialist theologians of the sort I have already mentioned. That is to say, they leap to the conclusion that therefore the strict negative precepts of the Decalog cannot be precepts of natural law; they fail to make the patient survey of the various truly self-authenticating requirements of practical reasonableness (or modes of responsibility) which, when brought to bear on particular basic values (i.e., on the premoral first principles of practical reason which Aquinas spoke of), do yield fully "material" moral precepts such as those of the Decalog as interpreted in the Catholic tradition. For Aquinas, too, failed to identify these (so to speak) methodological requirements of practical reasonableness (or modes of responsibility). He was aware that his first-level practical "first principles of natural law" are not moral principles, and he had enough philosophical acumen, and enough faith in the revealed word, not to fall for a consequentialist methodological norm (such as "maximize not premoral goods"); but he did not identify the intelligible links between the basic goods and the moral precepts that give definite guidance in particular cases.

Secondly, Aquinas (when he was doing meta-ethics, not when he was doing ethics) tried to force his account of natural law into a distinction (unhappily transposed from the distinction in Aristotelian physics between necessity and chance) between universals (*communia*) and particulars (*propria*). This led him to make those remarks of his (quoted everywhere today, as authoritative, by people who, however, disbelieve the greater part of Aquinas's philosophy and theology) to the effect that the precepts of natural law apply to particular cases not universally but only "in most cases" (*ut in pluribus*) (*Summa Theologiae* I-II, q. 94, a. 4). This is false to his own ethical reasonings, which everywhere (and rightly) presuppose (i) that the morality of particular acts is not affected by the "accidental" features of the case (such as that it is *Bert* who is killing and *Bill* who is being killed), and, correspondingly, (ii) that there are valid moral precepts that apply determinatively to *all* particular intentional performances that are instances of the class of acts to which the relevant precept relates, e.g., "Innocent people are not to be intentionally and directly killed," or "Sexual intercourse outside marriage is always wrong."

Some neo-scholastics, of course, were more or less aware that precepts of such specificity are not primary and self-authenticating, and so were unwilling to account for them by appeal to intuition (or to such equivalents of intuition as moral consensus, or the "[consensus of] Christian conscience"). Building on some rather unclear argumentation of Aquinas about sexual vice and about lying (*Summa Theologiae* II-II, q. 153, a. 2; q. 110, a. 3), they developed the thesis that it is a primary principle of natural law that natural human functions be respected and, more particularly, be not deflected from their "natural ends." This supposed principle was then employed to explicate the rational (i.e., natural law) character of the Church's constant proclamation of that divine command, which is fairly obviously implicit in the scripturally expressed divine commands about the use and abuse of sex: I mean the implicit command not to engage in sexual acts in themselves inapt for procreation, acts that do not "preserve the full sense of... human procreation..." (*Gaudium et Spes,* 51). When that command came under hedonist and consequentialist pressure, first in relation to contraception and then, logically enough, in relation to other forms of heterosexual, homosexual, or solitary masturbation, the supposed higher principle of natural law proved to be far from self-authenticating.

That is not to say that the principle about respect for natural functions is simply false. At least in relation to some human capacities, the principle amounts to something true, namely, that the exercise of those capacities is so structured that it will involve one willy-nilly in either respecting or choosing against a basic form of human good (such as the good of human-life-in-its-transmission, i.e., the good of procreation). And this fact is relevant morally, since there is a truly primary and self-authenticating requirement of practical reasonableness (i.e., of natural law) viz., the requirement that every basic human good be respected in every act. This requirement is the intelligible core (perhaps only dimly perceived by its author) in the version of Kant's categorical imperative that I recited before ("... treat humanity in oneself and others as an end not a means"); for every basic human good (such as life, knowledge, play, aesthetic experience, friendship, practical reasonableness, and religion) is an aspect of human personhood or, in Kant's word, of the *humanity* of a human individual.

The basic requirement of practical reasonableness that I have mentioned affords an "explanation" of many of the strict negative commands known to us in faith through Christ's revelation of himself and of the will of the Father. With this explanation we have a more than sufficient rebuttal of the charge that the authentically and infallibly[38] proclaimed Catholic moral teaching is legalistic. That is to say, we have a demonstration that our observance of those commandments of God is a reasonable service, a *rationabile obsequium*,[39] objectively and really adequately related to the goods-of-persons that God loves. And I say that this rebuts the charge of legalism "more than sufficiently" because that charge is, in my view, quite sufficiently rebutted by establishing the *possibility* that there is some explanatory principle that supplies the desired link between material moral norms and real human good. In other words, the charge of legalism could only be made out, in the face of God's word, by a demonstration that no such explanatory principle is possible, e.g., because consequentialism is true. But, of course, no such demonstration is forthcoming. And as for consequentialism, it is not merely undemonstrated; it is demonstrably untrue.

Well, the requirement that basic goods be not turned against in any act is not at all the only fundamental requirement of practical reasonableness; seven or eight others can be identified, including the requirement of impartiality, and the requirement of efficiency, i.e., of concern to secure maximum net good consequences within those limited contexts (defined by one's nonconsequentialist commitments) in which such a computation is in principle feasible. Together these eight or nine requirements supply the missing link in Aquinas's theory of natural law, the link between the first, premoral practical principles (in which we grasp the basic forms of human good as "to-be-pursued-and-realized") and the specific moral precepts that structure the virtues of justice, chastity, religion, and so on—the moral precepts (or *objectiva criteria ex personae eiusdemque actuum natura desumpta*) that express the discerning demands of the love of the Christian. For love of God and neighbor, which fulfills (Rom. 13:8, 10) and keeps (James 2:8-12) all the commandments of God, makes Christians unwilling to usurp the role of God's providential concern for the ultimate consequences of actions (cf. Gen. 50:20; Rom. 8:28; Mt. 6:25-34), or to treat their fellows as building blocks in the construction of some imagined "optimal" future, or to regard themselves as consistent consequentialists must regard themselves, as tools in that construction holding themselves ready to do *anything* to themselves or their hostages to avert the bad consequences threatened by nature, chance, or the opportunism of the wicked.[40]

Natural Law and "Historicity"

I began this paper by quoting Vatican II's affirmation of profound and rapid changes amounting to a true social and cultural transformation, of a shift from static to dynamic and evolutionary conceptions of things, and the need for new analyses and syntheses. What, then, should we be saying about the "historicity" of human nature and the possibility of "changes in the natural law"?

The first thing to say is that the philosophico-theological literature on this matter is of little value. Even very substantial writers fall into a cloudy rhetoric about the significance of cultural change,[41] or become entangled in an inadequately thought-out metaphysics in which "nature" is sometimes interchangeable, but at other times contrasted, with "essence," sometimes by definition unchangeable while at other times capable of change, and sometimes equated with the "transcendental" (epistemologically conceived, so that it includes only those human elements that are inevitably "affirmed" in any affirmation whatsoever).[42]

The second thing to say is that, so far as it is directed toward ethics and the natural law, the existing theological literature that proclaims the significance of historicity and changeable nature seems to *presuppose* an indefensible conception of practical reasoning, i.e., an indefensible conception of method in ethics. In the case of English-speaking theologians such as Fr. Timothy O'Connell or Fr. Gerard Hughes, the presupposition is typically of consequentialist ethical method—about which I will say no more here. In the case of continental theologians, the presupposition seems often enough to be neo-Suarezian: that one by speculative (metaphysical/descriptive) reasoning establishes first what is human nature, and then what is "in accordance with" (*conveniens*) that nature and thus a matter of "natural law." But this is a misconception of practical (including ethical) reason, which (as is emphasized both in Aquinas and in the recent developments I have spoken of) begins with a practical grasp of basic forms of human (personal) good as "goods to-be-pursued and realized and done," and continues through the discernment of the requirements of one of those basic goods (the good of practical reasonableness)— requirements that structure the pursuit of the other aspects of human well-being.

In short, general discourses about the changeability of human nature need not be taken seriously unless and until they get down to the serious business of considering someone for whom life (bodily life, including bodily health), or the transmission of life, or play, or aesthetic enjoyment, or speculative knowledge, or friendship, or religion, or authenticity, or self-integration, or practical reasonableness are not really good. Not surprisingly, such considerations are not to be found in the literature.

Beyond this, there is the more practicable task of evaluating the real changes in human culture, including not only such relatively superficial changes as have affected, say, human economics and thus the rights and wrongs of interest-bearing loans but also such relatively profound cultural changes as are effected by humans as makers of their own symbols, including the symbols (e.g., the Platonic dialogues, or the prophetic proclamation of personal responsibility) which bear and transmit changes in self-consciousness and which thus could (I suppose) affect, say, the rights and wrongs of penal servitude in its extension to dependents and descendants. All this is a necessary but immensely delicate task, threatened always by the too easy assumption that our forebears (Plato! Aristotle! St. John! St. Paul! . . .) lived in some *infancy* of human personality.

Against such easy assumptions, and indeed against much loose talk about changing human nature, we should set the Christology affirmed by Vatican II: "Christ fully manifests man to man" (*Gaudium et Spes,* 22, the last paragraph in the chapter on human dignity). He is the "perfect man" (*Gaudium et Spes,* 22, 38, 41, 45; and this perfection of his human nature is not affirmed merely in the eschatological sense). "In Him, human nature is assumed, not annulled" (*Gaudium et Spes,* 22). "By His incarnation He has somehow united Himself with every human being" (*Gaudium et Spes,* 22; *Redemptor Hominis* 13, 18). For "*all* human beings . . . have the same nature and the same origin" (*Gaudium et Spes,* 29; *Lumen Gentium,* 19), a single nature (*Lumen Gentium,* 13) which is "more fully manifested by the experience of past ages, the advance of the sciences and the treasures hidden in the various forms of human culture" (*Gaudium et Spes,* 44); and all have the "same calling and divine destiny" and so, fundamentally equal both in nature and in supernatural calling (*Gaudium et Spes,* 29), can be citizens of the one People of God regardless of race or place or time (*Lumen Gentium,* 13).

So the Council did not forbid us to accept, if we choose, such apparently *ad hoc* and certainly simplifying categorizations as that which contrasts "the classicist" with "the historical-minded world-view." But it did remind us that, if we want to be "historical-minded," we had better recognize that human history has a structure that is not straightforwardly "linear": Jesus Christ is the *center* of history (as well as its key and goal); see *Gaudium et Spes,* 10 and 45, the end of Part I; and also *Redemptor Hominis,* 1. And no one has given us intelligible reason to doubt those further affirmations of the Council, each given a certain solemnity and formality of wording:

> The Church affirms that underlying all changes
> there are many things that do not change, and which
> have their ultimate foundation in Christ who is the
> same yesterday, today, and forever (*Gaudium et
> Spes*, 10).
>
> The Council seeks to recall before all else the un-
> changing [*permanens*] force of the natural law of
> peoples and of its universal principles (*Gaudium et
> Spes*, 79)—the law that the Council had not hesi-
> tated to call "natural and gospel" [*lex naturalis et
> evangelica*]: (*Gaudium et Spes*, 74).

So "the Church proclaims the rights of man, *by virtue of the gospel committed to her*" (*Gaudium et Spes*, 49) those rights which are a principal component (*Dignitatis Humanae*, 6) of the common good of the human race as directed by the eternal law (*Gaudium et Spes*, 79). For "the fundamental law of the Christian dispensation" is this: "... the God who is Savior is the same God who is also Creator, the same too who is Lord both of human history and of the history of salvation" (*Gaudium et Spes*, 79). For "the fundamental law of the Christian dispensation" is this: "... the God who is Savior is the same God who is also Creator, the same too who is Lord both of human history and of the history of salvation" (*Gaudium et Spes*, 41). Christ restored our dignity (*Gaudium et Spes*, 41, 22) by taking our nature (*Gaudium et Spes*, 22), and so, reflecting surely on these teachings, Paul VI could say that the divine and natural law of right reason (*Humanae Vitae*, 27, 22), one fragment of which he had to proclaim again in *Humanae Vitae,* is "the law which is truly proper to human life restored [by Christ] to its own authentic truth" (*Humanae Vitae*, 19; cf. also 7)

Notes

1. All translations of Vatican II documents are my own, and are intended to be as close as possible to the literal structure of the Latin

texts. All emphases throughout the paper are mine, unless the contrary is indicated.

2. Cf. the passage from St. Thomas quoted in *Pacem in Terris* (1963) (Denz-Schön. 3573): *Summa Theologiae* I-II, q. 19, a. 4.

3. *Suaviter disponente*: a covert reference to Wisdom 8.1: "Adtingit enim a fine usque ad finem fortiter et disponit omnia *suaviter*— "Wisdom deploys her strength from world's end to world's end, and orders all things sweetly." There is thus a further covert reference, viz. to Vatican i's dogmatic Constitution *Dei Filius,* c. I: "God protects and governs by His providence all things which He has made, 'reaching from end to end mightily, and ordering all things sweetly' (cf. Wisdom 8. 1)."

4. *Summa Theologiae* I-II, q. 93, a. 2; the other texts are q. 91, a. 1 and q. 93, a. 1 (both concerning the eternal law).

5. Ibid., I-II, q. 91, a. 2.

6. Ibid.

7. Josef Fuchs S.J., *Natural Law: A Theological Investigation* (Gill & Son: Dublin, 1965), p. 10: ". . . the natural law itself is divine. This is made plain in Canon 27 of the Code of Canon Law"; p. 9: "The Code of Canon Law understands the revealed positive law, with the natural law, as being divine law (CIC, can. 6, 6° and can. 27; Cf. can 1038 § 1; can 1529; can 1926)." See also Denz.-Schön. 3272, and generally J-M. Aubert, *Loi de Dieu loi des hommes* (Tournai: Desclée, 1964).

8. *Acta Concilii Vaticani* ii, Vol. IV, pars VII, p. 443.

9. In "works" is included, of course, contemplation; see *Gaudium et Spes,* 38 and the *relatio ad* n. 38 (G) in *Acta Concilii Vaticani* ii, vol. IV, pars VII, p. 463 ("aspectus contemplativus et renuniationis huic mundo").

10. Clearly an echo of *Pacem in Terris* (1963) (Denz.-Schön. 3957): " . . . every human being has the character of a person i.e. is a nature endowed with intelligence and free will; and so, as such, each has rights and duties which flow, directly and together from his nature: rights and duties which, moreover, are general and inviolable and therefore cannot be alienated in any way. Now when we consider the dignity of the human person as conveyed in the truths of divine revelation. . . ." John XXIII and Vatican II both refer explicitly at this point to Pius XII's Christmas Broadcast of 24 December 1942 for this careful interrelating of dignity with responsibility and fundamental rights.

11. Karl Rahner expresses the common teaching of theologians at the

time of Vatican II: "It is right that there should be a 'conscience' which tells the individual man what he must do *as* an individual. That is to say: that the individual is not just one member of the human race with a common human nature (he is this too), but also unique and irreplaceable, he has a sphere of moral choices which cannot be clearly decided by universal norms and laws alone, but needs a special individual function of his conscience.... But because the individual does not take away the universal, but by God's will lies within what is universally human in him" [not a happy way of putting it: J. M. F.] "there is an individual morality only within a universal normative morality ... maturity of the Christian conscience is not an emancipation from and casting off of the universal norms preached by the Gospel and the Church ... it is the ability to apply these norms oneself to a concrete situation without needing help in every case ... A moral norm is by nature universal but, precisely as a universal law, is intended to be the rule for the individual case. And so when it is fully grasped and rightly understood and interpreted (that is, understood as the magisterium means it, not just as an individual thinks fit to interpret it), and bears on an individual case, then this unique individual concrete case is bound by the norm and obliged to abide by it. When, for example, the Church teaches that *every* directly induced abortion is morally wrong... then this applies to every individual case quite regardless of the circumstances": Karl Rahner, *Nature and Grace* (London and New York: Sheed and Ward, 1963), pp. 96, 97, 98, 99, 100.

12. See, e.g., Timothy E. O'Connell, *Principles for a Catholic Morality* (New York: Seabury Press, 1978), pp. 145-146; Gerard J. Hughes S.J., *Authority in Morals: An Essay in Christian Ethics* (London: Heythrop Monographs, 1978), pp. vii, 63.

13. Thus for O'Connell, the experienced facts include "values" ("independent of our wishes and our needs") such as beauty, honesty, compassion, etc.: O'Connell, pp. 118, 221. But for Hughes, the relevant facts are the "wants" of particular persons and the ordinary nonmoral knowledge of human nature and the world in which we live: Hughes, pp. 60-63.

14. O'Connell, p. 168; see also pp. 169, 146.

15. Hughes, pp. 10, 24.

16. Vatican I, *Dei Filius,* c. 2 (Denz.-Schön. 3003, 3004, 3005).

17. See E. Hamel, "La théologie morale entre L'Ecriture et la raison" (1975) 56, *Gregorianum* 273 at 282.

18. How? It is easy to forget, when one is discussing the consequen-

tialist theologians, that one is doing theology, not apologetics. But since we *are* doing theology, suffice it to recall Vatican II's *Dei Verbum* 19: "Holy mother Church firmly and most constantly has held and holds that *the four Gospels* just mentioned, whose historical character she unhesitatingly affirms, *faithfully convey what Jesus the Son of God, while living among men, really did and taught for their eternal salvation...*" (emphasis added). This does not, of course, foreclose exegetical and hermeneutical questions.

19. These verses are amazingly neglected: C. Spicq, *Theologie morale du Nouveau Testament* (J. Gabalda Paris: 1970) does not even mention them; R. Schnackenburg, *The Moral Teaching of the New Testament* (New York: Herder, 1965) gives them no discussion. The treatment in Irenaeus, *Adversus Haereses* IV, 12, 5, is as fresh and helpful as it was eighteen hundred years ago. See also Kittel's *Theological Dictionary of the New Testament*, vol. 2, pp. 548-49 (s.v. *entole*). For Christ's attitude to the Decalog, see also Mt. 5. 17, 19; Josef Fuchs S.J., *Natural Law: a Theological Investigation* (Dublin: Gill, 1965), pp. 33-37.

20. O'Connell, pp. 129-130.

21. Hughes, p. 18. The suggestion is advanced tentatively, but recurs in later argument: see, e.g., p. 95.

22. R. A. McCormick, "Notes on Moral Theology" *Theological Studies* 36 (1975): 77 at 84-85. It must be said that McCormick et al. use a rather simplified notion of parenesis; E. Hamel, "La théologie morale entre l'Ecriture et la raison" *Gregorianum* 56 (1975): 273 at 317 distinguishes between *pareclesis* (an urgent reminder or restatement of fundamental duties, made with considerable authority) and *parenesis* (more gentle and orientative, appealing more to generosity).

23. O'Connell, p. 220.

24. McCormick, p. 98.

25. O'Connell, pp. 147, 152-54. See also Hughes, p. 75; "Bert killed Bill... Perhaps... he thereby *obtained a great deal of money* on which he lived happily ever after. Perhaps the doctor who performed an abortion thereby *saved a marriage?* Clearly enough, the additional information about the relationship between the behaviour and human needs will not in every case lead us to change our moral judgment about whether the behaviour was right or wrong. *What cannot be said in advance*, however, *is that these features need not even be considered* before we make a moral judgment on what was done" (emphasis added). What Fr. Hughes says "cannot be said" is, of course, said (and "in advance"!) by Scripture and the whole tradition.

26. Hughes, p. 8; also p. 5.

27. Hughes, p. 19. Hughes adds: "This hermeneutical problem is quite a general one, and does not apply only to ethics, but to the interpretation and translation of any text from a different language or culture."

28. See B. J. F. Lonergan, *Method in Theology* (London: Darton, Longman and Todd, 1972), pp. 159, 208-209.

29. Irenaeus, *Adversus Haereses* IV, 13, 1 and 4; Aquinas, *Summa Theologiae* I-II, q. 100, aa. 1,3.

30. See Joseph Jensen, "Does *porneia* mean Fornication? A Critique of Bruce Malina" *Novum Testamentum* 20 (1978): 161, esp. 179-184.

31. "Proportionate reason," when used "at large", is a highly obscure phrase: see e.g. R. McCormick, "Notes on Moral Theology" *Theological Studies* 39 (1978): 76 at pp. 110-115 (where "inherent" or "essential" links are contrasted with empirical probabilities ranging up to practical certainties, and *this* contrast is then said to be "in other words" a matter of "proportionality," i.e., of finding the "lesser evil"). "Maximizing good and minimizing evil" *seems* relatively clear, until one asks (a) how one is supposed to measure incommensurable goods, and (b) whether one is to prefer a large surplus of "good" (at the cost of much evil) to a very small amount of "evil" (at the cost of foregoing much good), or *vice versa*. Question (b) shows that T. E. O'Connell has not begun to think through the logic of utilitarianism; the aphorism "Maximize the good and minimize the evil," which (O'Connell, p. 223) he says "has come to be known as 'Schüller's Preference Principle,'" is *flagrantly* absurd; competent philosophical utilitarians have been formulating their principle in terms of the "greatest possible *surplus*" of good over evil since, at the latest, H. Sidgwick, *The Methods of Ethics* (1st ed., 1874; see 7th ed., 1907, p. 413); and the problem of whether to prefer "much good" or "little evil" was vigorously explored by Cicero, *De finibus* II, 6-25, esp. 17

32. O'Connell, p. 161; see also p. 162.

33. Consequentialists sometimes think that they can give some sense to the Pauline dictum: e.g. "*moral* evil is not to be done for the sake of *premoral* good." But since, on their view, moral evil consists in not doing what is required to maximize net premoral good, they have to attribute to St. Paul the absurdly empty dictum "Do not fail to maximize premoral good for the sake of premoral good."

34. *Summa Theologiae* I-II, q. 71, a. 5 ad 3; II-II, q. 33, a. 2c; q. 3, a. 2c; Supp. q. 6, a. 5 ad 3; etc.

35. Immanuel Kant, *Foundations of the Metaphysics of Morals,* trans. Beck, (Indianapolis: Bobbs-Merrill, 1959), p. 47.

36. See Germain Grisez, "Against Consequentialism" *American Journal of Jurisprudence* 23 (1978): 21-41, 48-49.

37. (a) *Summa Theologiae* I-II, q. 94, a. 6c; also a. 2c; q. 99, a. 2 ad 2; q. 100, a. 5 ad 1, a. 11c; q. 58, a. 5c; q. 77q a. 2c; (b) *Summa Theologiae* I-II, q. 100, a. 3c, a. 11c.

38. O'Connell, pp. 95, 202, takes it for granted that there are no infallible moral teachings; he simply overlooks the infallibility of the ordinary magisterium, clearly taught by Vatican II, *Lumen Gentium,* 25. See Karl Rahner, *Nature and Grace and other essays* (London and New York: Sheed and Ward, 1963), pp. 98-99: "The fulfillment of the Commandments is an essential part of Christianity as such. ... Furthermore, the Church teaches these commandments with divine authority exactly as she teaches the other 'truths of the Faith' ... also through her *ordinary* magisterium, there is in the normal teaching of the Faith to the faithful in schools, sermons and all the other kinds of instruction ... binding on the faithful in conscience just as the teaching through the extraordinary magisterium is. ... When the whole Church in her everyday teaching does in fact teach a moral rule everywhere in the world *as* a commandment of God, she is preserved from error by the assistance of the Holy Ghost, and this rule is therefore really the will of God and is binding on the faithful in conscience, even before it has been expressly confirmed by a *solemn definition*". (Rahmer's Emphasis). Note that because of his dubious distinction between transcendental and concrete human nature, Rahner now thinks that "hardly any particular or individual norms" could be infallibly proclaimed; but he still affirms that such a proclamation can be by the ordinary magisterium: *Theological Investigations*, vol. 14 (New York: Seabury Press, 1976), p. 14. On the infallibility of the ordinary magisterium, see John C. Ford and Germain Grisez, "Contraception and the Infallibility of the Ordinary Magisterium" *Theological Studies* 39 (1978): 258-312; J. M. Finnis, "Conscience, Infallibility and Contraception" *The Month* (1978) 410-417 (N.B. The remarks on p. 415, attributing to Fr. T. Higgins a change of view about contraception are wholly mistaken: see my letter in [1979] *The Month*).

39. See Romans 12. 1; Vatican I, *Dei Filius,* c. 3 (Denz.-Schön. 3009); Karol Wojtyla, *The Acting Person* (Boston and London: Reidel, Dordrecht, 1979), p. 166; *Redemptor Hominis,* 19 at n. 144.

40. Thus O'Connell, p. 162, prepares us to "drop a bomb that will kill a million people." He "prays" that the need to do this will not arise, neglecting the fact that preparations for doing so are well advanced, and that this *sort* of action regularly took place in World War II and that (*qua* indiscriminate) it is solemnly condemned by *Gaudium et Spes,* 80 as a crime against God. McCormick is aware that, in the consequentialists' numbers game, willingness to kill one million to save two million is no different from willingness to kill one million to save one million and ten (i.e., to "save ten"): cf. *Theological Studies* 39 (1978): 76 at p. 109; he seeks to reconcile Christian teaching about indiscriminate bombing with his "mixed teleological" method by arguing that by such actions "one equivalently denies the freedom" of those whom one wishes to deter or dissuade from their hostile actions since "one supposes by his action that the cessation of others from wrongdoing is necessarily dependent on my doing harm" (p. 113). This argument fails completely; one's supposition is not about "*necessary* dependence" but about extremely *probable* correlation; nor is the supposition of continuance (otherwise) in wrongdoing a denial of freedom (sin is free). (Moreover—*ad hominem*—on pp. 112-13 McCormick treats contraception as justified where lack of intercourse "can easily harm the communicative good and *thereby* the procreative good itself"—as if acting on the basis of this fear were not a radical denial of the freedom of spouses!). The failure of the theological consequentialists (after sustained attempts) to integrate into their ethics even the most elementary Christian norms about direct killing of the innocent should be borne in mind when one is evaluating their incessant references to the marginal *quaestiones disputatae* of traditional Catholic ethics (e.g., Abraham and Isaac; "masturbation" to obtain semen; evacuation of the uterus to enable life-saving surgery).

41. E.g. Bernard Lonergan, "The Transition from a Classicist World-View to Historical-Mindedness." in *Second Collection* (ed. W. F. J. Ryan and B. J. Tyrrell; (London: Darton, Longman and Todd, 1974), pp. 1-9.

42. See, e.g., Karl Rahner, *Theological Investigations,* vol. 14 (London: Darton, Longman and Todd, 1976), pp. 15-16 (contrast between "transcendental necessity of human nature" and "concrete human nature"); K. Rahner and H. Vorgrimler, *Concise Theological Dictionary* (Freiburg: Herder, and London: Burns and Oates, 1965), p. 305, s.v. "Natural Moral Law" (natural law flows from "the objective structures of human nature which ... are implicitly affirmed by a transcendental necessity even in the act of this denial ... [and which]

objectify the will of God, their Creator . . ."); *Lexicon für Theologie und Kirche,* Bd. 7 (1962), col. 827 (distinction between essence and nature); cf. *Theological Investigations,* vol. 9 (London: Darton, Longman and Todd, 1972), pp. 214-17, 230-34. The criticisms in Donal J. Dorr, "Karl Rahner's 'Formal Existential Ethics,'" *Irish Theological Quarterly* 36 (1969): 211-29, are not superseded by Rahner's later work.

The Natural Law and Objective Morality: A Thomistic Perspective

William E. May
The Catholic University of America
Washington, D.C.

The teaching of Thomas Aquinas on the natural law has been the subject of extensive research. Many excellent books and articles are available to help anyone who is interested to investigate this topic in depth.[1] Why, then, one more essay devoted to this question?

In reply I can say, first, that the thought of St. Thomas on this subject is so rich that it merits renewed study. Even more important, however, in my judgment is the help that a study of Aquinas will bring to assessing critically recent developments in Roman Catholic moral theology. Thus before having recourse to the thought of St. Thomas, it will be worthwhile to review briefly these developments so that we can come to Aquinas with specific questions in mind.

Some Recent Developments in Roman Catholic Moral Theology

Today a significant number of Roman Catholic moral theologians find it necessary to dissent from authoritative teachings of the Roman Catholic Church on moral questions. The magisterium of the Church teaches that some specifiable sorts of human acts are wicked and contrary to the principles of the natural law. Among these are abortion, infanticide, euthanasia, willful self-destruction or suicide, genocide, the devastation of entire cities with their inhabitants, contraceptive intercourse, fornication, adultery, and sodomy.[2] A great many contemporary Roman Catholic moral theologians believe that contraceptive intercourse can be morally good,[3] even for unmarried persons[4]; several have explicitly affirmed the possibility that abortion, fornication, adultery, and sodomy can at times be virtuous[5]; and a few have written that infanticide,[6] euthanasia, and suicide[7] can at times be morally good choices. No contemporary Catholic moral theologian has as yet, to my knowledge, explicitly affirmed that genocide or the devastation of entire cities with their inhabitants might, under certain circumstances, be a morally good act. Still, as we will see, even these sorts of human acts cannot be excluded *in principle* by the kind of natural-law thinking advanced by some of these theologians.

The theologians supporting these positions claim that the natural-law thinking embodied in recent magisterial documents such as the encyclicals of Pius XII, Paul VI's *Humanae Vitae,* and the *Vatican Declaration on Certain Questions of Sexual Ethics* is ahistorical and physicalistic. Thus Charles E. Curran, commenting on the *Vatican Declaration,* says that the moral methodology found in it describes the fundamental principles of the moral order as "eternal, objective, and universal,"[8] and by so doing does not give "enough importance" "to developing historical and cultural realities."[9] Thus, too, Daniel C. Maguire can write, in an essay advocating the view that it can be morally good for a human person to intervene creatively and choose the time of his own demise rather than "await in awe the dispositions of organic tissue," as follows:

> Birth control was, for a very long time, impeded by
> the physicalistic ethic that left moral man at the

mercy of his biology. He had no choice but to conform
to the rhythms of his physical nature and to accept
its determinations obediently. Only gradually did
technological man discover that he was morally free
to intervene creatively and to achieve birth control
by choice.[10]

In place of this physicalistic, ahistorical natural law, these
theologians propose a different model of the natural law. This
has recently been developed at some length in a work by
Timothy E. O'Connell that has won the praise of Curran, John
F. Dedek, Josef Fuchs, and Agnes Cunningham as a significant
articulation of the best in contemporary Roman Catholic moral
thought.[11] A presentation of its leading ideas will therefore
give us an understanding of the natural-law theory shared, to
considerable degree, by those Catholic moralists who find the
teachings of the magisterium flawed by physicalism and an
ahistorical perspective.[12]

O'Connell notes that "the traditional moral maxim, do good
and avoid evil, may have some colloquial significance, but as a
precise description of the living of our lives it is simply and
inevitably impossible."[13] Because of our finitude and the limitations imposed upon us by the sociotemporal world in which
we live, "our best hope is to do as much good as possible and as
little evil as necessary."[14] The natural law proposed by
O'Connell—and in advancing it, he draws together in a syn-
thetic manner the thought of such writers as Josef Fuchs,
Bruno Schüller, Louis Janssens, and Richard A.
McCormick[15]—is described by him as "real, experiential, consequential, and proportional."[16] The characteristics of consequentialism and proportionalism are critically important,
because in the final analysis, as O'Connell observes, "specific
actions are to be evaluated from a moral point of view by considering their actual effects, or consequences."[17] In developing
this insight of contemporary theologians into the nature of the

natural law, O'Connell says that we discover the right thing to do "by balancing the various 'goods' and 'bads' that are part of the situation and by trying to achieve the greatest proportion of goods to bads."[18] In keeping with this consequentialist and proportionalistic natural law, O'Connell holds that the principle of double effect as traditionally understood must be rejected. It must be rejected because it held that one could not rightfully choose to do a deed having evil effects if those evil effects were directly intended or willed. But the direct intention of evil[19] is not, according to the consequential-proportional natural law of O'Connell and other modern theologians, morally significant, since it is precisely the consequences of an act that make it to be *morally* good,[20] however much "premoral" evil must be intended. Thus O'Connell argues that the maxim, " 'The end does not justify the means' must be rejected if by 'end' one means the consequences of one's act, for it is these consequences precisely that justify the means."[21]

This theory of the natural law rejects the view that there can be any specifiable sorts of human acts that are *always* wrong.[22] Thus the acts of deliberately willed abortion, directly intended infanticide, and even genocide and the deliberate devastation of entire cities with their inhabitants are, *in theory* at least, morally justifiable. They are *morally* wicked, as Richard A. McCormick explains, in the absence of a proportionate good, but they become morally good, despite the massive "premoral" evil they entail, in the presence of a proportionate good.[23] Since it is, however, hardly possible that there can ever be any good proportionate enough to justify the choice to destroy an entire race (genocide) or to perform acts entailing similar "premoral" evil, there are some sorts of acts that can be regarded practically as "disproportionate" to any realizable good.[24] Therefore, these moralists concede that there are some specifiable sorts of moral precepts or norms that are "virtually" exceptionless or "practically" absolute.[25] However, and this is very important, these moralists do not believe that these norms are truly unexceptional. In their theory one cannot claim, for instance, that it is *always* wrong to destroy an entire city with its inhabitants because this act could become morally good were its execution necessary to achieve a proportionate good.

In advancing this model of natural law, contemporary Roman Catholic moral theologians manifest an ambiguity to St. Thomas, or rather claim that his thought on natural law is ambiguous. On the one hand, some complain that his understanding of natural law is too physicalistic. Curran, for example, asserts that St. Thomas, by accommodating within his thought Ulpian's definition of natural law as "that which nature has taught all animals," definitely tends "to identify the demands of natural law with physical and biological processes."[26] Similarly O'Connell holds that St. Thomas includes "the demand to conform to animal facticity under the rubric of natural law."[27] Both writers regard this as a serious defect in St. Thomas's thought; it is precisely the flaw that makes many magisterial teachings untenable.

On the other hand, several of these theologians appeal to St. Thomas to support their positions. Thus Curran also writes that "Thomas's own understanding of the natural law does not seem to justify the insistence on universally valid, absolute norms of human behavior."[28] To support this claim Curran cites the teaching of St. Thomas that the more remote or particular precepts of natural law are valid "for the most part," but can be deficient in "particular instances."[29] Daniel Maguire does likewise. In arguing against a "taboo" mentality that would claim that there are unexceptional rules designating in advance of actual performance whether specific human acts are right or wrong, Maguire appeals both to this teaching of St. Thomas on the deficiency of the more remote precepts of natural law and to his teaching that "human actions are good or bad according to their circumstances."[30] Finally, Maguire,

Franz Scholz and others[31] claim that St. Thomas's interpretation of certain events in the Old Testament (e.g., Abraham's willingness to sacrifice his son Isaac) can best be understood as acknowledging that we can directly intend evil for the sake of a proportionate good.[32]

With this background of contemporary Roman Catholic moral theology in mind, I shall examine the teaching of St. Thomas on natural law and objective morality. Three central issues will merit consideration: (1) the meaning of natural law for St. Thomas and the significance of Ulpian's definition; (2) the development of our knowledge of natural law; and (3) "exceptions" to natural-law precepts.

The Meaning of Natural Law in St. Thomas

St. Thomas dealt with the subject of natural law formally and at some length in his *Summa Theologiae,* and references to natural law and to such allied notions as conscience, synderesis, providence, and divine law are found throughout his works, from his early *Scriptum super IV libros Sententiarum* onwards.[33]

In the *Summa Theologiae* Thomas prefaces his discussion of natural law with a consideration of law in general and of God's eternal law, and it is important for us, if we are to understand his notion of natural law, to understand the meaning that he gives to law in general and to the eternal law.

Law in General

Thomas considers law as an extrinsic principle of human actions, as distinguished from virtue, which is an intrinsic principle. Initially he describes it as a "rule or measure of actions whereby one is induced to act or is restrained from acting." It then follows that law pertains to reason because "reason, which is the first principle of human acts, is the rule and measure of human acts."[34] Law as such is thus, for

Thomas, something brought into being by reason; it is an *or-dinatio rationis*. That law as such belongs to reason and is indeed constituted by or brought into existence by an act of reason is made quite clear by Thomas in his reply to some objections. One objection had claimed that law cannot pertain to reason because St. Paul had spoken of a "law" that he dis-covered in his members (Rom. 7:23). In replying to this, Thomas observes that a law can be said to be "in something" in two ways:

> In one way [law is said to be in something] as in that which rules and measures. And because this is proper to reason, it follows that in this way law exists in reason exclusively.

He continues by saying that law can be said to exist in some-thing in another way as in that which is ruled and measured:

> And it is in this way that law is in all those things that are inclined toward something in virtue of some law; thus any inclination arising from some law can be called a law not *essentially,* but as it were in a participative sense.[35]

Another objection had contended that law cannot belong to reason inasmuch as it can be neither the power of reason itself, nor one of its habits or facilities, nor one of its acts. In replying to this, Aquinas states that the practical reason, or intelligence as ordered to action, in deliberating about what is to be done brings into being "universal propositions directed to action." These universal propositions of the practical reason play a role in deliberative inquiry about what is to be done comparable to that played by the universal propositions of the speculative reason relative to the conclusions that it establishes. "Universal propositions of this kind," Aquinas writes, "of the practical reason as bearing on what is to be done possess the meaning of law."[36] From this it is clear that for St. Thomas *law as such not only pertains to reason but consists of propositions or precepts that are brought into existence by reason as "practical," that is, as directed to action, to deliberation about the deeds that can be done by self-determining agents.* Here Aquinas clearly indicates that these actions can be judged "good" or "bad" in terms of propositions or precepts brought into existence by "practical reason."

Eternal Law

In considering the eternal law, St. Thomas first notes that the entire community of the universe is governed by God's mind. The eternal law is the "*ratio*" or "ruling idea of things that exists in God as the ruler of the universe."[37] Eternal law directs the entire created universe and the activity of all created things. The eternal law is, therefore, the "*ratio* or exemplar of divine wisdom insofar as it is directive of all acts and movements."[38] Eternal law has as its end the good of the whole created universe, and it is promulgated to those subject to it by the act of creation.[39]

Natural Law

Thomas teaches that all creatures are subject to and thus participate in this eternal law of God. But the manner of their participation differs because of their different modes of being.[40] Nonintelligent, nonrational beings participate passively in the eternal law because from it they receive an "impression" by virtue of which they "have tendencies to their proper acts and ends."[41] The eternal law and, thus, *law,* is found in them in a purely passively participated manner; *it exists in them as in beings that are regulated and measured by law.*[42] Intelligent, rational creatures, on the other hand, participate in the eternal law in a more noble manner because they are capable of providing for themselves and for others. Their active, intelligent participation in the eternal law, making it possible for this law to be found in them as in beings who rule and measure what is to be done, is precisely what is meant by natural law.[43]

It is very important, if we are to understand properly the teaching of St. Thomas, to bear in mind that natural law, as the actively intelligent participation by the rational creature in the eternal law, exists in the rational creature not as in that which is ruled and measured by law but as in that which rules and measures. The natural law of St. Thomas meets his own criterion for the meaning of law in its proper, formal sense. By this Thomas means that natural law, like all law in the proper sense and like the eternal law of God, is a work of reason. Natural law as it exists in the rational creature is distinct from the eternal law that exists in God the superintelligent Creator, but it is not separate from this eternal law. It is this eternal law itself mediated to or shared by the rational creature.[44] It marks both the nobility of the rational creature as the being created in the image of God and the great love that God has for the rational creature, whom he wills to share actively in his own provident wisdom.

St. Thomas makes this quite clear when he rejects the views, held by many of his medieval predecessors, that natural law is a power or a habit, in particular the habit of synderesis or of first principles of the moral order.[45] St. Thomas grants that the natural law may, in a secondary or derivative sense, be regarded as a habit insofar as the judgments of practical reason that together go to constitute it may be habitually kept in mind, but in the proper sense of the term natural law is *not* a habit, nor is it a power. Rather it is a reality brought into existence (*constitutum*) through reason; it is a work of human intelligence as ordered to action (*ratio practica*), just as a proposition or judgment of the speculative intellect is an achievement of human intelligence as ordered to knowing for the sake of knowing. The natural law, therefore, is something that we ourselves bring into existence through our own intelligent activity—it is *quod quis agit*—not something enabling us to bring things into existence through our practically oriented intelligent activity—*quo quis agit*.[46]

As such and properly, then, natural law is for St. Thomas an achievement of practical reason. It consists of a body of propositions or precepts—true judgments—made by the human intelligence as ordered to action and as ruling and measuring action, that is, as determining whether a proposed act is morally good or morally wicked.[47] As law, natural law is not in St. Thomas's judgment innate. What is innate is the God-given ability of the rational creature to come to know the body of true practical judgments, that is, judgments having to do with the moral meaning of the actions that the human person can freely choose to do. These judgments together go to make up or constitute natural law.

Also innate are "natural inclinations" orienting the human person to basic or fundamental goods perfective of his or her being. According to St. Thomas, "natural inclinations" or tendencies are those inclinations possessed by all beings in their own distinctive way whereby they are directed toward the realization of the end for which they were created.[48] The natural inclinations of a being orient it to the end(s), that is, good(s) for which it was made.[49] Rational creatures—human beings—like all beings, have natural inclinations, and these inclinations have a role to play in the way that human persons come to know the natural law. We shall soon look into this matter, but prior to doing so it is pertinent to examine briefly St. Thomas's accommodation into his teaching of Ulpian's famous definition of natural law as that which nature has taught all animals.

Ulpian's Definition and Natural Law

It will be recalled that some contemporary Catholic moral theologians, for example, Curran and O'Connell, lament St. Thomas's use of Ulpian's definition. According to them, his doing so clearly shows a physicalistic understanding of natural law, a requirement to submit passively to brute facticity. The preceding analysis of St. Thomas's teaching on natural law should be sufficient to falsify this contention. St. Thomas insists throughout his writings that law, properly and formally speaking, is something that belongs to reason. It is *aliquid rationis,* an *ordinatio rationis.* Law as such, and this includes natural law, can be predicated properly and formally *only* of reason, either divine reason or created reason. It may, however, be predicated in a derivative, secondary sense of what is ruled and measured and is therefore subject to law and to the rule of reason.[50]

St. Thomas certainly did make use of Ulpian's definition, both in his early *Scriptum super IV Libros Sententiarum* of Peter Lombard and in such later writings as the *Summa Theologiae.* Moreover, Thomistic scholars disagree over the significance to be given to his use of Ulpian. The great historian of twelfth- and thirteenth-century moral theology, Dom Odon Lottin, while insisting (*pace* Curran and O'Connell) that St. Thomas, in making room within his thought for Ulpian's definition, "in no way intended to withdraw from reason the mastery that it exercises over all the tendencies of man,"[51] nonetheless believes that at the heart of Aquinas's notion of natural law lies a "secret sympathy" for Ulpian's definition,[52] and he also believes that "the truly personal thought of St. Thomas" on the natural law is found in his early *Commentary on Lombard's Sentences* rather than in the *Summa Theologiae.*[53] Some observations on Lottin's position will be given at the end of this section; it is necessary now to look at St. Thomas's use of Ulpian's definition.

St. Thomas provides his most extensive analysis of natural law in his Lombard *Commentary* in connection with his discussion of a problem that had plagued his predecessors in their attempts to relate natural law to Scripture. How could the polygyny of the Old Testament patriarchs be reconciled with natural law?[54] This issue itself is not our concern here but rather St. Thomas's thought on natural law.

In his analysis St. Thomas insists on humanity's difference

from other animals. Since they lack intelligence, brute animals are impelled by a force of nature to perform actions proper to them; they are incapable of regulating their actions by any kind of judgment properly so-called, by law in its proper sense. There is, St. Thomas says, in brute animals a natural *aestimatio* leading them to perform actions appropriate to them, but no rational principle of activity. Rational animals, on the contrary, can know the end and relationship of means to end. They can therefore direct their own actions and govern themselves. In this early work St. Thomas teaches that the natural law exists in the rational creature as a "natural concept" whereby the human person "is directed to acting suitably with respect to actions proper to him, whether these belong to his generic nature, such as generating life, eating, and so forth, or whether they belong to his specific nature as man, such as thinking and things of this kind."[55]

What is most instructive about this passage is that in it St. Thomas explicitly holds that natural law is related to human intelligence, not to brute animality. The thought expressed here and elsewhere in this early writing[56] is thus of a piece with the thought of St. Thomas on natural law that we have already examined: Natural law is proper to rational creatures alone.

In the course of his discussion of the polygyny of the fathers, St. Thomas makes it quite obvious that he judges polygyny to be *contrary* to natural law, although in a way not so contrary to natural law as polyandry is.[57] One of the objections to this teaching had urged that a plurality of wives is in no way opposed to natural law because natural law, as Ulpian said, is "that which nature has taught all animals," and it is obvious that in the animal kingdom it is by no means unnatural for one male animal to mate with several females. It is in replying to this objection that St. Thomas takes up the celebrated definition of Ulpian, along with the definitions of Cicero and

Gratian.[58] St. Thomas says that natural law can refer to something that is natural *by reason of its principle or source*. This is the way Cicero understood it, because he said that it was something not generated by opinion but rather by a kind of innate power (*ius naturae est quod non opinio genuit, sed quaedam vis inseruit*). He then notes that the principle from which natural law springs may be extrinsic to the being ruled by the natural law, and in this sense St. Thomas understands the definition given by Gratian that the natural law is everything that is contained in law and gospel (*ius naturale est quod in lege et in Evangelio continetur*). Finally, he says that natural law may be understood not as referring to what is natural by reason of its principle or source but by reason of "nature," that is, *by reason of the subject matter with which the natural law is concerned* (*tertio dicitur ius naturale non solum a principio, sed a natura, quia de naturalibus est*). If natural law is taken in this sense, it is opposed to reason or set off vis-à-vis reason. Consequently:

> ... understood in this very limited sense, those things that belong *only* to men, although they are commanded by reason, are *not* said to be of the natural law; rather only those things that natural reason commands about matters common to man and other animals belong to the natural law in this sense.[59]

It is very important to understand St. Thomas here. He is surely *not* saying that the natural law, properly and formally as law, is something infrarational, an instinct that humanity shares with other animals, brute animal facticity. For he has stressed in the body of the article that natural law as such pertains only to human beings. In brutes there is no natural law, only a natural *aestimatio,* a power or force of nature impelling them to act in ways appropriate to achieve their ends. Thus in this celebrated passage St. Thomas is by no means repudiating what he had to say in the body of the article (or what he shall subsequently affirm in later writings) about the intrinsic rational character of natural law. He accepts Ulpian's definition of the natural law *only in the sense that it refers to the* subject matter with which natural law is concerned. The natural tendencies or inclinations that human beings share with other animals are fit matter to be brought under the rule of law, that is, under natural law as an achievement of human intelligence. This is evident from the text in question, for St. Thomas explicitly states that the natural law, understood even in this limited sense,[60] has to do with those things that "*natural reason commands* with respect to matters common to man and other animals" (*illa tantum quae naturalis ratio dictat de his quae sunt homini aliisque communia*).[61]

St. Thomas also makes room for Ulpian's definition in his later works, in the *Summa Theologiae*[62] and in his Commentary on the *Nicomachean Ethics*.[63] But in all these places the room given by St. Thomas to Ulpian's definition of natural law as the law that nature has taught all animals is quite intelligible and in accord with his own teaching on the natural law. Natural law as defined by Ulpian never has the meaning of the *ordinatio rationis* or *dictamen rationis,* the achievement of practical reason, that St. Thomas considers to be the essential element of law and of natural law in the formal sense.[64] Ulpian's definition can never be used in reference to natural law as that which is in something *sicut in mensurante et regulante*. It uniformly refers to natural law only in an accommodated sense, as found in something only "participatively, as it were" (*quasi participative*).[65] In brief, Ulpian's definition of natural law has pertinence to the tendencies or inclinations that human beings possess by virtue of being, in truth, animals, albeit animals of a special kind—tendencies that can be grasped by practical reason along with the real goods toward which they incline the human person. Once these tendencies and the goods correlative to them are understood by practical reason, the human person can make the judgment (articulate the proposition) that these are goods to be pursued and done. It is only when such propositions are articulated by practical reason that natural law in its formal sense is operative.[66]

From all this it is clear that Ulpian's definition did have an influence on St. Thomas. But it is in my judgment necessary to dissent from Lottin's contention that his more personal thought on natural law is present in the Lombard *Commentary* and that St. Thomas had a secret sympathy for Ulpian's definition, as though he preferred it to other definitions of natural law. Aquinas is quite clear throughout his writings, and particularly insistent in the *Summa Theologiae,* that natural law is formally and properly something that belongs to human practical reason. Thus with D. O'Donoghue and others I believe that Lottin's interpretation of St. Thomas's use of Ulpian is misleading.[67]

The Development of Our Knowledge of Natural Law

Formally and properly natural law is an achievement of human practical reason, consisting of a set or body of principles or precepts about what is and what is not to be done. Since St. Thomas rejects any kind of innate knowledge,[68] it is evident that he considers our knowledge of natural law and its precepts to be something that we acquire in life and that he recognizes a development in our knowledge of natural law both as individual persons and as members of the human community. The purpose of this section of this essay is to give the basic outlines of St. Thomas's thought on this subject.

The Role of Natural Inclinations and First Principles of Natural Law

Reference has already been made to innate natural inclinations. These are *not* to be identified with natural law, because natural law is an achievement of human reason, not something given. Nor are these natural inclinations innately known, as should be obvious from St. Thomas's position on innate knowledge. Still they function as dynamic sources of our cognitive struggle to come to know what we are to do if we are to be the beings we are meant to be, if we are to act rightly. Correlative to these inclinations[69] are fundamental or basic goods of the human person—goods we need if we are to be fully ourselves, if we are to be the beings God wills us to be. These goods likewise are not innately known, but St. Thomas affirms that we "naturally apprehend" the goods to which our natural inclinations direct us.[70] By this he means that there is no need for discursive, syllogistic reasoning in order for us to know these goods. To know them we need experience of life, but given this experience, we know these goods spontaneously, and in knowing them we make true practical judgments about what we are to do and not to do. These judgments of the practical reason are self-evidently true[71] and are articulated in propositions or precepts that serve as starting points or principles for intelligent deliberation about human action.

Among our natural inclinations are our inclination, as intelligent beings, toward being and truth and the fullness of being and of truth, and our inclination, as beings with an intelligent appetite or will, toward the good. Thus the absolutely primordial principle of natural law, brought into existence by the activity of practical reason, is that *good is to be done and pursued and evil is to be avoided.*[72] This is absolutely primordial because it is the basis for any kind of freely chosen intelligent human act and likewise the basis for any further *ordinatio* or command of practical reason. This precept needs no proof nor can it have any. Its truth is evident immediately to the human mind on understanding what "good" means.

Here it is very important to note that for, St. Thomas, the very first principle of natural law is a proposition of practical reason ordering us to pursue and do good and avoid evil. The good that we are to do and pursue through our free and intelligent activity is by no means limited by him to the moral good; it includes the full range of good, embracing everything that is judged truly to be a good of the human person. Naturally, moral good is within the scope of the good that we are to do and pursue and moral evil within the scope of the evil we are to avoid. The important thing for us to realize is that St. Thomas teaches that the very first principle of natural law requires that the whole range of human good is to be done and pursued and that all human evil is to be avoided.[73] His thought on this subject is, therefore, quite different from that of the contemporary theologians whose opinions were surveyed at the beginning of this essay. They drive a wedge between the moral good and what is variously termed "premoral," "nonmoral," or "ontic" good and hold that we can rightly intend deliberately "premoral" evil for the sake of proportionately greater "premoral" good. They hold that we are to do evil for the sake of a greater good.

That St. Thomas includes the full range of good achievable through human action within the scope of this primary precept of natural law is made abundantly clear from the fact that he teaches that there are in fact several "first" principles of natural law, and there are several "first" principles precisely because the good that we are to do and pursue includes the full range of good to which we are naturally inclined. The principle that good is to be done and pursued and evil is to be avoided is absolutely first, because it is implicit in all the other primary or first precepts of the natural law, so that a denial of them would entail the absurdity of denying it.[74] But the other primary precepts are not deduced from the precept that good is to be done and pursued and evil is to be avoided in any rationalistic manner. They too are self-evidently true and need no proof.

In other words, when St. Thomas says that there are several first or primary principles or precepts of natural law, he means that we can know, in a nondiscursive way, not only that good is to be done and pursued and that evil is to be avoided but also that there are generic kinds of goods that we ought to pursue in our lives through freely chosen and intelligent deeds, and that the evils destructive of these goods are to be avoided. He affirms this because there does exist within the human person a set of ordered natural inclinations directing us to all the goods corresponding to real but diverse dimensions or levels of our being. Because we are beings who subsist in ourselves— substantial beings—continuation in being is a good that we naturally seek, and thus life itself is a basic human good worthy of human choice and pursuit. Because we are living animals, bodied beings, who can share our lives with a new generation, procreation and human sexuality are goods that need to be pursued intelligently and protected. Because we are animals of a very special kind, human animals, with the inclinations or tendencies of intelligent and self-determining beings, we are inclined to live in communities and together with others to pursue the goods of truth and justice, friendship and peace, and we thirst for union with God. We are naturally inclined to these goods because we are the kind of beings we are, and these goods, consciously known, form the basis for true propositions of practical reason.

Note that all these primary or basic precepts of natural law are directive principles of human activity. They inwardly shape human choice and action so that without them it is impossible to act humanly at all, no matter whether the act chosen is *morally* good or not. These precepts are generic in nature and point us in a direction. They do not give us *a priori* knowledge of which specific human acts are good or bad, nor from them can we deduce rationalistically, precinding from experience, specific rules of conduct. They are directives or starting points for intelligent human activity.

Secondary and More Remote Precepts of Natural Law

St. Thomas teaches that more specific judgments or precepts about what is good or bad do belong to the natural law and are related to these basic, primary nondiscursively known precepts. He holds that more specific precepts of natural law can be "derived" from these more common precepts in two general ways. One is "after the manner of conclusions from the common principles of natural law" (*a principiis communibus legis naturae per modum conclusionum*); the other is "after the manner of a determination" (*per modum determinationis*) of what natural law means in more particular human situations. He gives, as an example of a precept derived in the first way from the more common precepts of natural law, the precept that *one ought not to kill,* holding that it is, as it were, a conclusion drawn from the more fundamental precept that *evil ought not to be done to anyone.* As an illustration of a determination of natural law, he suggests that the *way* an evildoer is to be punished is something to be settled by particular human societies, and settled, of course, in a just way, in accordance with a more basic precept that *one who sins or does evil ought to be punished.* St. Thomas says that precepts or judgments of the first kind, although belonging in one way to human positive law, nonetheless belong to natural law because they carry its force. Precepts of the second type are more properly the work of human positive law, but still, in order for such determinations to be just, they need to be in accord with the more common and fundamental precepts of natural law.[75]

When St. Thomas says that more specific natural law precepts—sometimes called secondary precepts—are derived from the more common or primary precepts, he in no way means that these precepts are known in a rationalistic, *a priori* manner. As R. A. Armstrong observes in an important study of natural law in Aquinas, the more specific natural-law precepts are "more deeply involved with the varying circumstances and details which surround any and every moral act."[76] Knowledge of these circumstances and details can only be achieved through experience and the discovery, by human intelligence, of the reality or truth-making factors that give to human acts their intelligibility or meaning. Judgments made on the basis of this knowledge require a "consideration" or "reflection," and some of these judgments can be made more easily than others. There is in other words, a gradual progression from the more general, direction-giving principles of natural law to its more specific directives of action or rules of action.

Here a key text to understand the thought of St. Thomas is that in which he argues that *all* moral precepts belong to natural law but do so in different ways. Aquinas writes:

> Every judgement of practical reason proceeds from certain principles that are known naturally ... and from these it is possible to make progress in diverse ways in making judgments about different things that are to be done. For there are some things that are so explicit in human acts that at once, with only a little consideration, they can be given approval or disproval in terms of those common and first principles (*quaedam ... possunt approbari vel reprobari per illa communia et prima principia*). But there are other things for whose judgment a good deal of consideration of the diverse circumstances is required; and to consider them diligently is simply not the task of just anyone but of the wise ... thus these things belong to natural law but nonetheless they require the discipline whereby those of less capacity (*minores*) are instructed by the wise.[77]

As this text shows, St. Thomas teaches that more specific precepts of natural law become known only by an intelligent "consideration" of human experience. Some more specific precepts (for instance, the precepts found in the Decalog) can become known after only a little consideration because they are closely connected with the primary precepts. Others can be known only with considerable difficulty and after much reflection simply because the relevant moral considerations or factors contributing to the moral meaning of the acts to be judged are much more difficult to discover, so that only the "wise," that is, persons who have the virtue of prudence,[78] are capable of making good moral judgments with regard to them.

Natural law, for St. Thomas, is an achievement of practical reason endeavoring to bring intelligent order into actions that human persons can freely choose. It is the participation of the human person in the eternal law of God, and it is a participation that deepens and develops both in the individual person and in the human community. It begins in precepts made "naturally," nondiscursively—precepts that give direction to human action while leaving undetermined the meaning of specific sorts of human acts; it proceeds to make more and more specific judgments concerned with more and more specific sorts or kinds of human acts and the conditions in which human beings act. Secondary precepts and those even more remote (from primary) precepts dependent upon both primary and secondary precepts are more specific than the basic or primary and generic precepts of natural law. They provide directives for human action by prescribing or proscribing specifiable sorts of human deeds. This leads us to a consideration of the question of "exceptions" to natural-law precepts.

"Exceptions" to Natural-Law Precepts

St. Thomas teaches that natural law is absolutely unalterable so far as its primary precepts are concerned. But he says that its secondary precepts, which are like particular conclusions from the primary precepts, although unchangeable "in the majority of cases," can nonetheless experience change "on some particular and rare occasions."[79]

How is his teaching here to be understood? Earlier in this essay I noted that some contemporary Roman Catholic moral theologians appeal to this and similar passages in St. Thomas to support their claim that there are no moral absolutes in the sense of universal negative prohibitions, such as the prohibition taught by the magisterium of the Church against directly intended abortion. The thought of St. Thomas, as I intend to show here, provides no support for this claim.

The Difference Between Speculative and Practical Knowledge

St. Thomas certainly recognizes that it is unrealistic and hence foolish to expect the same kind of precision in moral judgments that is possible in speculative matters. Speculative knowledge is concerned with what actually exists, not with what-is-to-be-done through human actions; therefore there is a necessity in speculative judgments lacking in practical judgments. He puts it this way: "Speculative or theoretic reason is occupied with natural truths that cannot be other than they are, and so without mistake it discovers truth in the premises from which it starts." Practical reason, on the other hand, is concerned with "contingent matters with which human acts deal, and although there is some necessity in common precepts, the more we get down to particular cases the more we can be mistaken." Because of this difference in the subject matter of the conclusions of speculative and practical reason St. Thomas says that "in matters of action truth or practical rectitude is not the same for everyone with respect to specifics but only with respect to common principles."[80] He illustrates this point by observing that we can conclude (by using as our starting point for deliberative or practical inquiry the precept that we

ought to act intelligently) that we should return to their rightful owners goods that we hold in trust. Nonetheless, this very
good and true conclusion of practical reason is not universally
applicable and admits of exceptions. For instance, it would be
irrational and therefore contrary to a basic natural-law precept
to act automatically in accord with this conclusion were the
rightful owner to demand return of his property in order to use
it for a wicked purpose such as attacking the common good.[81]

Contingencies and the Specification of Human Acts

St. Thomas's teaching on this matter is eminently intelligible and in accord with his whole thought on the morality
of human acts and the meaning of natural law and its precepts.
Still we must understand his thought properly. To do so, it is
necessary to recall that the reality ruled and measured by
natural-law precepts is the reality of freely chosen human acts.
Natural-law precepts are, as St. Thomas says, "universal propositions of practical reason."[82] The human acts ruled and measured by these precepts are particulars, and these particular
human acts must also be known if we are to determine whether
or not they conform to natural-law precepts. Particular, individual human acts can, of course, be known to be *instances of
specific sorts or kinds* of human action, and St. Thomas makes
it abundantly clear that there are certain specifiable sorts or
kinds of human acts that are morally wicked and therefore
unworthy of human choice and contrary to precepts of natural
law.[83] Among the sorts of human acts that are always morally
wicked are stealing,[84] lying,[85] fornicating,[86] commiting adultery,[87] and intending to kill a fellow human being on one's own
authority.[88] This list is illustrative, not taxative.

However, and this is the important consideration, St.
Thomas teaches that the determination of the moral species of
a human act differs from the determination of the species of a
natural object or physical action because of the contingent na-

ture of a human act. A natural object or physical action, which is the subject matter of speculative inquiry, is determined in its species by a naturally given form. A human act, which is the subject matter to be known in practical deliberative inquiry, is not determined to be an instance of a specific class by reason of any natural form but rather by a form that is determined by practical reason itself.[89] But in order for practical reason to make this determination, it must take into account the various contingencies or circumstances in which the act is done.

A human act, St. Thomas teaches, is determined to be the sort or kind of act that it is by reason of its object,[90] which is entitatively one and the same with the proximate end[91] that the moral agent must intend.[92] Nonetheless, and this is the precise point that St. Thomas makes, and which Maguire misunderstands, in the question in which he asks whether any circumstance or contingency can determine the moral goodness or wickedness of an act, a contingency can inwardly change the moral object that the agent must intend as the proximate end of his act. In other words, a circumstance that enters into the very condition of the objective act and thus specifies it can be morally determinative.[93] Thus the contingency that the rightful owner may seek his or her property for an evil purpose or may seek it while drunk can make all the difference in the world in determining whether one ought to act in accord with the remote precept of natural law that *one ought to restore goods held in trust to their rightful owners*. This contingency, which was not included in the articulation of the precept—and, St. Thomas says, it would be impossible to include every morally relevant contingency in the articulation of such precepts—changes the species of the human act that is to be done. It changes it from one ruled and measured by this precept to one that is *not* ruled and measured by it. This particular remote precept of natural law is "defective" to the extent that it does not nor cannot include within its articulation those contingencies that can inwardly change the moral species of the act toward which it directs us.

These observations should be of help to us in assessing the claims of some contemporary Roman Catholic theologians that St. Thomas's teaching on the natural law affords no reason for holding that there are moral absolutes. Since he does unequivocally teach that there are such absolutes, as has already been indicated, his teaching on the matter of "exceptions" to remote conclusions of natural law needs to be understood properly and not misused to support the view that on occasion acts such as adultery, fornication, the directly intended destruction of fetal life, etc. can be morally good.

Finally, it is necessary to say something about the claim made by some authors, for example, John Dedek, Daniel Maguire, Franz Scholz, and Richard A. McCormick, that the best way to understand St. Thomas's teaching on certain Old Testament events, such as Abraham's willingness to sacrifice his son Isaac, is to say that he subscribes to the view that we can directly intend a "premoral" evil for the sake of a higher good (itself premoral). In other words, these authors invoke the teaching of St. Thomas in interpreting certain Old Testament events as authoritative support of their view that it can sometimes be morally good to intend evil directly so that good may come about.[94]

God and Natural-Law Precepts

I submit that this is a wholly inaccurate and misleading interpretation of relevant Thomistic texts and the thought of St. Thomas. Aquinas did, of course, teach that Abraham did not act wrongly in choosing to sacrifice his son Isaac at the command of God.[95] He does not, however, argue that Abraham was intending to do an evil for the sake of some proportionate or higher good. Rather he teaches that the act Abraham intended was not, in truth, an act of homicide because of the very relevant contingency that God, the Lord of life, had intervened and by so doing had inwardly changed the species of the act in question so that it was not an act of homicide but one of obedience and hence of virtue.[96] Here it is important to realize that for St. Thomas evil is the deprivation of a *due* good.[97] Life is a basic, fundamental good of human persons, a good to be respected and indeed reverenced in them by their fellow beings, because it is a good gift from God. But God, in the thought of St. Thomas, owes no one anything. Life is a free gift from him, one that he can also take away.[98] Thus Abraham's choice to obey God was not a choice entailing the direct intent of what was known by him to be evil.

In other words, in offering an interpretation of the Genesis account of Abraham's willingness to sacrifice Isaac in obedience to a divine command, St. Thomas teaches that the act in question is one that is not contrary to the natural-law precept enjoining us not to slay the innocent *precisely because* the act in question is not an act of homicide. His whole point is that God, as supreme Lord of creation and author of the moral order, can inwardly change the moral species of the act (and thus the object of the act and the proximate end intended by the agent) through his free and intelligent activity so that the "form" of the act discovered by practical reason is different from the "form" of act prohibited by precepts of natural law.[99] In the very same question of the *Summa Theologiae* in which he discusses this problem, St. Thomas insists that the moral precepts of the Decalog, which follow with necessity and with only a modicum of consideration from the primary precepts of natural law,[100] are absolutely indispensable, even to God.[101] Moreover, St. Thomas makes it abundantly clear that God, and God alone, can act in such a way that an act lethal to an innocent human person can be inwardly changed in its species so that it is not in truth an act, morally, of homicide but one of obedience.[102] It is, therefore, in my opinion a serious misuse of

St. Thomas's teaching on this matter to infer that it supports the position that one can rightly intend evil directly for the sake of a good end. That position—that one can directly intend evil for a good end—is explicitly repudiated by St. Thomas[103] and no wonder, for it is a direct violation of the very first precept of natural law, which directs that *good is to be done and pursued and evil is to be avoided.* Far from regarding this as an unrealizable "maxim," as O'Connell and those whose views O'Connell so ably summarizes believe, St. Thomas considers this an absolutely universal and binding precept in terms of which all others are to be understood.

Conclusion

This analysis of St. Thomas's teaching on natural law and objective morality has, I hope, been of some help in assessing the meaning of our moral lives and in providing a basis for critically appraising recent developments in Roman Catholic moral theology. The natural law of St. Thomas is by no means a static conformity to physical or biological laws. It is, rather, a dynamic and ever growing participation of the human subject, whose personal life is profoundly influenced by the communities in which he or she lives, in the eternal law of God. It is a work of intelligence, an intelligence that respects the self-determining freedom of the human person, but an intelligence that nonetheless recognizes that evil is not to be done for the sake of good. It is the work of an intelligence that is capable of determining objectively the meaning of moral or human acts, and of persons who are summoned to a life of unspeakable bliss with God. We answer the summons to that life by our willingness to do good and by our unwillingness to choose to do what we come to know as evil.

In conclusion, I would like to note that advocates of dissent from magisterial teaching will find little support in St. Thomas. He is a humble advocate of papal authority, and affirms quite clearly that the teaching of the Roman Pontiff is to be accepted over that of any theologian, however learned.[104]

Notes

1. The following studies are helpful for understanding St. Thomas's teaching on natural law: R. A. Armstrong, *Primary and Secondary Precepts in Thomistic Natural Law Teaching* (The Hague: Martinus Nijhoff, 1965); M. B. Crowe, *The Changing Profile of the Natural Law* (The Hague: Martinus Nijhoff, 1977), pp. 136–91; Walter Farrell, *The Natural Moral Law According to S. Thomas and Suarez* (Dichtling: St. Dominic's Press, 1930); Germain G. Grisez, "The First Principle of Practical Reason: A Commentary on the *Summa Theologiae* 1–2, Q. 94, A. 2," *Natural Law Forum* 10 (1965) pp. 168–96, reprinted with abridgments in *Aquinas: Critical Essays*, ed. A. Kenny (New York: Anchor, 1976). Dom Odon Lottin, *Le droit naturel chez Saint Thomas d'Aquin et ses predécésseurs* (Bruges: Beyaert, 1931); Lottin, "La valeur des formules de saint Thomas d'Aquin concernant la loi naturelle," *Mélanges Joseph Maréchal* 2 (Bruxelles: L'Edition universelle, 1950), pp. 346–77; William E. May, "The Meaning and Nature of the Natural Law in Thomas Aquinas," *American Journal of Jurisprudence* 22 (1977) 168–89; D. O'Donoghue, "The Thomist Concept of Natural Law," *Irish Theological Quarterly* 22 (1955) 89–109; Paul Overbeke, "La loi naturelle et le droit naturel selon S. Thomas," *Revue Thomiste* 57 (1957) 53–78, 450–95.

2. For abortion, infanticide, euthanasia, genocide, willful self-destruction, and the devastation of entire cities with their inhabitants, see Vatican Council II, *Gaudium et Spes* 27, 51, 79, 80. For abortion, see also Pius XII, "Address to the Italian Doctors," November 12, 1944 in *Discorsi e Radiomessaggi* ⅞ (1945): 191; John XXIII, *Mater et Magistra*, 194; Paul VI, Allocution, "Salutiamo con paterne effusione," December 9, 1972, *AAS* 64 (1972): 1777; Sacred Congregation for the Doctrine of the Faith, *Declaration on Procured Abortion*, November 18, 1974.

For contraception, see, for instance, Paul VI, *Humanae Vitae* (1968).

For fornication, adultery, and sodomy, see Sacred Congregation for the Doctrine of the Faith, *Declaration on Certain Questions of Sexual Ethics (Persona Humana)*, December 29, 1975 (Washington, D.C.: United States Catholic Conference, 1976).

3. A sampling of contemporary Roman Catholic authors who take this position can be found in *Contraception: Authority and Dissent,*

Charles E. Curran, ed., (New York: Herder and Herder, 1969) and in *The Catholic Case for Contraception,* Daniel Callahan, ed., (New York: Macmillan, 1969). This view is also represented in a work commissioned by the Catholic Theological Society of America, Anthony Kosnik et al., *Human Sexuality: New Directions in American Catholic Thought* (New York: Paulist Press, 1977).

4. This, for instance, is the position taken by Philip S. Keane, *Sexual Morality: A Catholic Perspective* (New York: Paulist Press, 1977), p. 109.

5. On abortion, see, for example, Daniel Callahan, *Abortion: Law, Choice, and Morality* (New York: Macmillan, 1970); Daniel C. Maguire, *Death by Choice* (Garden City, N.Y.: Doubleday & Company, 1974), pp. 199-202, and also *The Moral Choice* (Garden City, N.Y.: Doubleday & Company, 1978), p. 448; John F. Dedek, *Contemporary Medical Ethics* (New York: Sheed and Ward, 1975), pp. 109-36; Richard A. McCormick, "Abortion: A Changing Morality and Policy?" *Hospital Progress* 60, no. 2 (February 1979): 36-44. It should be noted that none of these authors would hold that abortion on demand is morally good. Yet they all agree that directly intended abortion can be, in some instances, the morally justifiable choice.

On fornication and adultery, see Michael Valente, *Sex: The Radical View of a Catholic Theologian* (New York: Bruce, 1970); Kosnik et al., pp. 151-65.

On sodomy, see John McNeill, *The Church and the Homosexual* (Kansas City: Sheed, Andrews and McMeel, 1976); Charles E. Curran, "Dialogue with the Homophile Movement," in his *Catholic Moral Theology in Dialogue* (Notre Dame, Ind.: Fides, 1972); Kosnik et al., pp. 208-15. McNeill holds that sodomitic acts between adult, homosexually constituted persons in a relatively stable relationship are completely good, with no trace of evil. Curran believes that a degree of evil is present insofar as heterosexuality remains the ideal, but he sees sodomitic behavior as morally justifiable. Kosnik et al. are somewhat undecided whether to follow McNeill or Curran, but they agree that homosexual behavior is not necessarily immoral.

6. On infanticide, see Maguire, *Death by Choice,* pp. 7 and 12-13. On p. 7 Maguire cites Millard S. Everett to the effect that "no child should be admitted into the society of the living" who suffers "any physical or mental defect that would prevent marriage or would make others tolerate his company from a sense of mercy." As Paul Ramsey points out, Maguire "indicates no disagreement with such criteria." Paul Ramsey, *Ethics at the Edges of Life* (New Haven: Yale University Press, 1978), p. 206, n. 30.

In addition to Maguire, Albert Jonsen, a former Jesuit, finds it possible to defend infanticide as morally permissible in some instances. See *Ethics of Newborn Intensive Care,* Albert Jonsen and Michael J. Garland, eds., (Berkeley, Calif.: Institute of Governmental Studies, University of California, 1976), and an article co-authored by Jonsen, "Critical Issues in Newborn Intensive Care: A Conference Report and Policy Proposal," *Pediatrics* 55, no. 6 (June 1975): 756-68.

7. On euthanasia and willful self-destruction, see various writings by Maguire. In addition to his *Death by Choice* (see note 5) Maguire has defended mercy killing and deliberate suicide in "The Freedom to Die," originally published in the August 11, 1972 issue of *Commonweal* and reprinted in *New Theology 10,* edited by Martin Marty and Dean Peerman (New York: Macmillan, 1973), pp. 186-99, and in "A Catholic View of Mercy Killing," in *Beneficient Euthanasia,* Marvin Kohl, ed. (Buffalo: Prometheus Books, 1975), pp. 34-43.

8. It is very necessary, I believe, to note that the passage in the *Vatican Declaration* to which Curran objects so strongly is in fact an internal citation by that document of Vatican Council II, *Dignitatis Humanae,* 2, 3. Ironically Curran continues in his essay to contrast the approach to moral questions taken by the *Declaration* to what one finds in the documents of Vatican II!

9. Charles E. Curran, "Sexual Ethics: A Critique," in his *Issues in Sexual and Medical Ethics* (Notre Dame, Ind.: University of Notre Dame Press, 1978), pp. 38-39.

10. Maguire, "The Freedom to Die," in *New Theology 10,* p. 189.

11. Timothy E. O'Connell, *Principles for a Catholic Morality* (New York: Seabury Press, 1978). Curran's praise is contained in the Foreword that he contributed to the book. The encomia of Dedek, Cunningham, and Fuchs are printed on the book jacket.

12. I say "to considerable degree" because the theologians who basically agree to the positions developed by O'Connell differ among themselves in many ways.

13. O'Connell, p. 152. Although O'Connell's work is heavily in debt to the work of Richard A. McCormick, I believe that McCormick may have significantly modified his position. In "A Commentary on the Commentaries," an essay that he contributed to *Doing Evil to Achieve Good,* Richard McCormick and Paul Ramsey, eds. (Chicago: Loyola University Press, 1978), McCormick now frankly admits that it is impossible to weigh the human goods and to balance off good effects and evil effects (see in particular pp. 229 ff.). It would thus appear that McCormick now would repudiate the way O'Connell expresses matters as utilitarian.

14. O'Connell. The sentence is thrice repeated on pp. 152-53.

15. The pertinent literature here is extensive. McCormick has surveyed it quite thoroughly both in his *Ambiguity in Moral Choice* (Milwaukee: Marquette University Theology Department, 1973), in his "Notes on Moral Theology," for *Theological Studies* 33 (1972): 68-86; 36 (1975) 85-100; 38 (1977) 70-84; and 40 (1979) 59-80, and in the essay noted above in note 13. These works should be consulted for bibliographies. I have addressed this movement and the literature involved in several places. See, for instance, my *Becoming Human: An Invitation to Christian Ethics* (Dayton: Pflaum, 1974), chap. 4; "Modern Catholic Ethics: The New Situationism," *Faith and Reason* 4 (Fall 1978): 21-38; and "The Moral Meaning of Human Acts," *Homiletic and Pastoral Review* 79, no. 1 (October 1978): 10-21. Perhaps the most compelling essays criticizing the movement reflected in this literature are those of Paul Ramsey, "Incommensurability and Indeterminancy in Moral Choice," in *Doing Evil to Achieve Good*, pp. 69-144, and of Germain G. Grisez, "Against Consequentialism," *American Journal of Jurisprudence* 23 (1978): 21-72. Recently McCormick and Curran edited an anthology entitled *Readings in Moral Theology, No. 1: Moral Norms and the Catholic Tradition* (New York: Paulist Press, 1979). The anthology reprints important essays by Fuchs, Schüller, Janssens, and other contemporary Catholic theologians in which the consequentialist approach is set forth. Included are only two essays opposing this trend, namely, those of John R. Connery S.J. and Paul Quay S.J. It is my opinion that McCormick and Curran chose *not* to include the strongest articles opposing this trend, namely, articles by Paul Ramsey, Germain Grisez, and others.

16. O'Connell, p. 148.

17. Ibid., p. 147.

18. Ibid., p. 153.

19. Here it is necessary to observe that these contemporary writers sharply distinguish between "moral" evil and what they variously term as "premoral," "nonmoral," "ontic" evil. See the literature referred to in note 15 for the development of this distinction.

20. McCormick provides a Latin equivalent of this proposition when he holds that it is morally proper to intend directly a "premoral" evil *in ordine ad finem proportionatum*. See McCormick, "Notes on Moral Theology," *Theological Studies* 33 (1972): 74-75.

21. O'Connell, p. 172.

22. Those who support this view agree that it would always be wrong directly to intend what they call *moral* evil, e.g., the sin of another person. They also hold that it would always be wrong to intend to

murder someone. But they maintain that *murder* is a moral term, not a purely descriptive term, and that it means an "unjust" killing deliberately and intentionally of another. Their point is that it is impossible to use nonmoral terms to describe an act that would *always* be morally wicked. When I suggested that it would always be wrong to use public funds to pay one's mistress or that it would always be wrong to torture a person (cf. "The Moral Meaning of Human Acts," p. 13), McCormick responded that the words *mistress* and *torture* are not descriptive terms but morally evaluative terms ("Notes on Moral Theology," *Theological Studies* 40 (1979): 78-79). It is instructive that he ignored another example given, namely, that "it is always wrong to have coition with a brute animal." I hold that *mistress* and *torture* are not morally evaluative but simply descriptive, and I find it illuminating that McCormick chose to ignore the other example. It is absurd to consider *coition with a cow* as a *moral* phase; it is descriptive.

23. McCormick, *Ambiguity in Moral Choice,* p. 53: "... it is the presence or absence of a proportionate reason (good) which determines whether my action—be it direct or indirect psychologically or causally—involves me in turning against a basic good in a way which is morally reprehensible."

24. In "A Commentary on the Commentaries," McCormick seems to me to be coming to the position that there are some sorts or kinds of deeds, such as devastating entire cities with their populations, that are as it were intrinsically *disproportionate,* a shift in his position to some extent. See pp. 250-51. Nonetheless, in this essay McCormick still insists on the telelogical, i.e., consequential, nature of all concrete moral norms and must admit that, in principle at any rate, even the devastation of an entire city with its inhabitants could be morally good.

25. On this point, see McCormick, "Notes on Moral Theology," *Theological Studies* 32 (1972): 68-86, particularly at pp. 77 ff. In his *The Moral Choice,* Maguire speaks of concrete norms, such as a norm not to rape, as having "unimaginable exceptions," p. 162. By this he means that the justification of a rape of a mentally retarded girl, for instance, is almost unimaginable. Nonetheless, on his own principles it could be morally good. Perhaps there is a lack of imagination in Maguire, for it is not too difficult to conclude that many people might well imagine instances in which this sort of deed might be quite justifiable.

26. Curran, "Natural Law and Contemporary Moral Theology," in his *Contemporary Problems in Moral Theology* (Notre Dame, Ind.: Fides,

1970), p. 106. See also his "Absolute Norms in Moral Theology," in his *A New Look at Christian Morality* (Notre Dame, Ind.: Fides, 1968), pp. 75-89.
27. O'Connell, p. 138.
28. Curran, "Absolute Norms in Moral Theology," p. 83.
29. Ibid., pp. 82-83, citing *Summa Theologiae* 1-2, 94, 4.
30. Maguire, *The Moral Choice*, pp. 117-18, citing *Summa Theologiae* 1-2, 18, 3, *sed contra*.
31. Ibid., pp. 250-52. See also F. Scholz, "Durch ethische Grenzsituationen aufgeworfene Normenproblemen," *Theologischpraktische Quartalschrift* 123 (1975): 341-55; McCormick, "Notes on Moral Theology," *Theological Studies* 40 (1979): 79-80; John Giles Milhaven, "Moral Absolutes and Thomas Aquinas," in *Absolutes in Moral Theology?*, Charles E. Curran, ed. (Washington: Corpus, 1968), pp. 154-85. Of these articles Milhaven's is quite important and in many ways very helpful. Milhaven acknowledges quite frankly that St. Thomas definitely does teach that there are moral absolutes in the sense of universal negative prohibitions (cf. pp. 158, 169). Still his argument, and that of the other authors cited in this note, is that Aquinas was inconsistent in doing so and that the logic of his thought concerning the justifiability of the deeds attributed to the Old Testament patriarchs commits him to the position that a proportionately good end can justify intending evil.
    N. B. The article by F. Scholz referred to above has now been translated and printed in McCormick and Curran's anthology mentioned in note 15 above, *Readings in Moral Theology, No. 1: Moral Norms and the Catholic Tradition*.
32. The texts from St. Thomas pertinent to this matter are well presented in Milhaven's article.
33. For the historical development of St. Thomas's thought on natural law see Crowe and Lottin. Lottin and Crowe, in an earlier article ("St. Thomas and the Natural Law," *Irish Ecclesiastical Record* 76 (1951): 293-305) follow the chronology of Aquinas's works proposed by Grabmann and Mandonnet, and consequently consider the discussion of natural law in the *Commentary on the Nicomachean Ethics* (written, according to Grabmann, *c.* 1261-64 and, according to Mandonnet, *c.* 1266) chronologically prior to the presentation in the *Prima Secundae* of the *Summa Theologiae*. In his *Changing Profile of the Natural Law*, Crowe adopts the more accurate chronology proposed by R. A. Gauthier ("La date du commentaire de saint Thomas sur l'éthique à nicomaque," *Recherches de théologie ancienne et médièvale* 18 (1951):

66-105 and *Sententia Libri Ethicorum (Sancti Thomae de Aquino Opera Omnia* t. xlvii, Romae, 1969) praefatio, p. 201), who suggests the years 1271-72 for the composition of the *Commentary on the Nicomachean Ethics,* making it either contemporary with or perhaps a little after the composition of the *Primae Secundae.*

34. *Summa Theologiae* 1-2, 90, 1.

35. Ibid., ad 1.

36. Ibid., ad 2.

37. Ibid., 1-2, 91, 1. On the innovative character of St. Thomas's discussion of eternal law and the relationship between the eternal law and natural law, see Crowe, "St. Thomas and the Natural Law," pp. 302-3; Lottin, "Les Premiers Exposés scholastiques sur la loi éternelle," *Ephemerides Theologicae Lovanienses* (1937): 287-301; Walter Farrell, *The Natural Moral Law,* pp. 25-33.

38. *Summa Theologiae* 1-2, 93, 1.

39. Ibid., 91, 1, ad 1 and ad 2; 93, 1, ad 2.

40. This is an instance of a universal metaphysical principle of St. Thomas: *Quidquid recipitur ad modum recipientis recipitur.*

41. *Summa Theologiae* 1-2, 91, 2.

42. Ibid., 91, 2, and ad 3.

43. Ibid., 91, 2. On this matter it is worth noting what O'Donoghue has to say. He observes: "... there are two ways of understanding rational participation. We might see it as *receptive* participation: created reason is receptive of Eternal Law just as irrational nature is ... though in a higher way.... Or we might see rational participation as *legislative,* as participation in the very activity of legislating.... That we must understand rational participation in the second sense, seeing human reason as regulative rather than regulated, is clear from the fact that St. Thomas identifies the Natural Law with the 'propositions' or 'precepts' of natural reason. The matter is put beyond doubt by the discussion in Q. 93, a. 6, where a sharp distinction is drawn between participation in Eternal Law by way of *inclinatio naturalis ad id quod est consonum legi aeternae* and *ipsa naturalis cognitio boni....* That which differentiates Natural Law from natural inclination, and makes it law in the proper sense, is the fact that it is the work of reason, expression rather than impression. It comes from God, as all human things ... but the mind receives it, not as itself an object which is revealed by it, but as becoming a source of light, discerning and declaring the truth for human activity (cf. 1-2, 91, 2)." In O'Donoghue, pp. 93-94.

44. On this it is instructive to consult Appendices 2 and 3 (pp. 162-71)

by Thomas Gilby, the editor and translator of vol. 28 of the new Dominican Translation of the *Summa Theologiae* (New York: McGraw-Hill, 1966).

45. On the views of Thomas's predecessors see Lottin, and Crowe, *The Changing Profile of the Natural Law,* pp. 111-35.

46. *Summa Theologiae* 1-2, 94, 1.

47. Here it important to stress the role that practical reason plays for St. Thomas and the significance of the difference between speculative and practical reason. On this point, see Germain G. Grisez, *Contraception and the Natural Law* (Milwaukee: Bruce Publishing Company, 1964), chap. 3, and the literature cited there.

48. *Summa Theologiae* 1-2, 91, 2; 94, 2.

49. See ibid. 1-2, 8, 1; *De Veritate* 25, 1. See Armstrong, pp. 32-33, 46-48.

50. *Summa Theologiae* 1-2, 90, 1, ad 1 and ad 2.

51. Lottin, *Le droit naturel chez Saint Thomas* ... , p. 62: "Saint Thomas n'entend toutefois aucunement par là retirer à la raison la maitrise sur toutes les tendances de l'homme et il accepte tout ce qu'Albert le Grand avait dit à ce sujet."

52. Ibid., p. 66: "Mais cette habilitè même trahit le fond de la pensée de saint Thomas, je veux dire: ses sympathies sécrètes pour les formules du droit romain."

53. Lottin, "La valeur des formules de saint Thomas d'Aquin concernant la loi naturelle," pp. 368-69; cf. pp. 375-76. In *Le droit naturel* Lottin says: "La définition la plus stricte du droit naturel est donc celle d'Ulpianus, le juriste romain: '*ius naturae est quod natura omnia animalia docuit.*'" (p. 62).

54. *In IV Sententiarum* d. 33, q. 1, a. 1.

55. Ibid.: "Lex ergo naturalis nihil est aliud quam conceptio homini naturaliter indita, qua dirigitur ad convenienter agendum in actionibus propriis, sive competunt ei ex natura generis, ut generare, comedere, et huiusmodi; sive ex natura speciei, ut rationari, et similia."

56. See *In 1 Sententiarum* d. 39, q. 2, a. 2.

57. In the body of the article of *In IV Sententiarum* d. 33, q. 1, a. 1, St. Thomas asserts that polygyny is indeed against the natural law in the sense that it at least impedes partially the marital good of fidelity and the peace and harmony that ought to reign in the family. He notes that it totally destroys the good of the sacrament of marriage, but he concedes that it is not totally destructive of the good of procreation and in this sense is not contrary to natural law in the same way that

polyandry is, inasmuch as polyandry is destructive of the good of procreation.

58. In the text of his article St. Thomas erroneously attributes to Isidore the definition of the natural law given by Gratian, namely, as *that which is contained in the law and the gospel*. Cicero had defined it as *that which is not generated by opinion but by a certain innately given power*.

59. *In IV Sententiarum* d. 33, q. 1, a. 1: "ius naturale multipliciter accipitur. Primo enim ius aliquod dicitur naturale ex principio, quia a natura est inditum; et sic definit Tullius ... dicens: Ius naturae est quod non opinio genuit, sed quaedam innata vis inseruit. Et quia etiam in rebus naturalibus dicuntur aliqui motus naturales, non quia sint ex principio intrinseco, sed quia sunt a principio superiori movente ... ideo ea quae sunt de iure divino dicuntur esse de iure naturali, cum sint ex impressione et infusione superioris principii, scilicet Dei; et sic accipitur ab Isidoro ... qui dicit, quod ius naturale est quod in lege et in Evangelio continetur. Tertio dicitur ius naturale non solum a principio, sed a natura, quia de naturalibus est. Et quia natura contra rationem dicitur, a qua homo est homo; ideo strictissimo modo accipiendo ius naturale, illa quae ad homines tantum pertinent, etsi sint de dictamine rationis naturalis, non dicuntur esse de iure naturali; sed illa tantum quae naturalis ratio dictat de his quae sunt homini aliisque communia; et sic datur dicta definitio, scilicet, Ius naturale est quod natura omnia animalia docuit."

60. I believe that it is proper to translate, "strictissimo modo accipiendo ... illa tantum [esse de iure naturali] quae naturalis ratio dictat de his quae sunt homini aliisque communia" as follows: "in a *very restricted and limited sense* ... those things [are of natural law] which natural reason commands about matters that are common to men and other animals." This ought not to be translated as "in the most strict and precise sense," for in the most precise and formal sense this is *not* the meaning of natural law. For *strictissimus* as having the meaning of "most limited and restricted," see Roy J. Deferrari et al., *A Lexicon of St. Thomas Aquinas based on the Summa Theologica and Selected Passages of His Other Works* (Washington, D.C.: Catholic University of America Press, 1949) 5:1055, where this precise text (cited as *Summa Theologica* III, Supplement, 65, 1) is used to illustrate the meaning of "most rigid in interpretation." On this whole subject see my essay, "The Meaning and Nature of the Natural Law in Thomas Aquinas."

61. See text cited in note 59, particularly *in fine*.

62. In the *Summa Theologiae* St. Thomas refers (at least by implication) to the definition of Ulpian in 1-2, 94, 2; 95, 4, ad 1.

63. *In V Ethicorum*, lect. 12, n. 1019.

64. *Summa Theologiae* 1-2, 90, 1; 90, 1, ad 1 and ad 2; 91, 2.

65. Ibid., 1-2, 90, 1, ad 1; 91, 2, ad 3.

66. On this see Germain Grisez, "A Commentary on the First Principle of Natural Law ..."

67. O'Donoghue, p. 91. In my judgment, Aquinas retained Ulpian's definition, in a limited way, in his thought precisely because he held that the inclinations we share with other animals are truly substantive human inclinations, not a part of a nature subhuman in character. The goods to which they direct us are, moreover, truly substantive goods of the human person, goods that are to be loved and pursued through human action. For further development of this matter see my "The Meaning and Nature of the Natural Law in Thomas Aquinas," pp. 180-81.

68. *Summa Theologiae* 1, 85, 1.

69. Perhaps these inclinations can be even more fittingly called "needs" of the human person. On this matter see Mortimer Adler, *The Time of Our Lives: The Ethics of Common Sense* (New York: Holt, Rinehart and Winston, 1970), pp. 84-97. See also my "Natural Law, Conscience, and Developmental Psychology," *Communio* 2 (1975): 3-31.

70. *Summa Theologiae* 1-2, 94, 2.

71. On this subject see Armstrong, pp. 24-55.

72. *Summa Theologiae* 1-2, 94, 2. This text is so central that it should be cited at length. After first drawing an analogy between practical and speculative inquiry in which he affirms that we need principles or starting points for both, St. Thomas writes: "Sicut autem ens est primum quod cadit in apprehensione simpliciter, ita bonum est primum quod cadit in apprehensione practicae rationis, quae ordinatur ad opus: omne enim agens agit propter finem, qui habet rationem boni. Et ideo primum principium in ratione practica est quod fundatur supra rationem boni, quae est, *Bonum est quod omnia appetunt*. Hoc est ergo primum praeceptum legis, quod bonum est faciendum et prosequendum, et malum vitandum. Et super hoc fundantur omnia alia praecepta legis naturae: ut scilicet omnia illa facienda vel vitanda pertineant ad praecepta legis naturae, quae ratio practica naturaliter apprehendit esse bona humana." Note that here St. Thomas insists that the good that is to be done includes everything that practical reason naturally grasps as humanly good. He does not

restrict the good that is to be done or the evil that is to be avoided to moral good or evil.

73. This is clear from the text cited in the previous note. On this subject one of the finest commentaries is provided by Grisez in the article to which reference has already been made.

74. This aspect of St. Thomas's thought is well expressed by Armstrong, pp. 38-41 and by Eric D'Arcy, *Conscience and Its Right to Freedom* (New York: Sheed and Ward, 1965), pp. 56-64.

75. *Summa Theologiae* 1-2, 95, 2.

76. Armstrong, p. 93.

77. *Summa Theologiae* 1-2, 100, 1.

78. On the meaning of prudence in St. Thomas, see ibid., 2-2, questions 47-51.

79. Ibid., 1-2, 94, 5.

80. Ibid., 94, 4.

81. Ibid.

82. Ibid., 90, 1, ad 2.

83. St. Thomas is no legalist in the sense that he teaches that something is wrong because it is forbidden or good because it is commanded. Rather his notion of law is grounded on intelligence, ultimately the intelligence of God and proximately the intelligence or practical reason of God's rational creature. His point is that because something really is good it is in accord both with God's eternal law and the rational creature's active participation in it and that because something is really evil and opposed to the *bona humana* (cf. *Summa Theologiae* 1-2, 94, 2, text cited in note 72), it is contrary to both eternal law and natural law.

84. Cf., e.g., *Summa Theologiae* 2-2, 66, 5 and 6. In 66, 7 Thomas teaches that in cases of necessity a person has the right to the superfluous goods of another so that their appropriation is *not* theft. The moral object of the act has been inwardly changed.

85. Cf., e.g., ibid., 2-2, 110, 1 and 2.

86. Cf., e.g., ibid., 2-2, 154, 2.

87. Cf., e.g., ibid., 2-2, 154, 8.

88. Cf., e.g., ibid., 2-2, 64, 7. The entire point of this important article is to highlight the centrality of intent in moral action. St. Thomas expressly teaches here that it is wicked for a private person, in defending his or her own life against attack, to intend directly the death of the assailant. This article contains the essential elements of what later became known as the "principle of double effect." For more detailed analyses of this text and its significance in assessing the

thought of St. Thomas, see Joseph T. Mangan, "An Historical Analysis of the Principle of Double Effect," *Theological Studies* 10 (1949): 41-49; Germain G. Grisez, "Toward a Consistent Natural Law Ethics of Killing," *American Journal of Jurisprudence* 15 (1970): 64-96. The centrality of intent for St. Thomas in this text is badly mis understood by Louis Janssens in an influential article "Ontic Evil and Moral Evil"; *Louvain Studies* 4 (1974): 114-56. Janssens's essay is now found in *Readings in Moral Theology, No. 1* (see note 15 above).

89. *Summa Theologiae* 1-2, 18, 5.

90. Ibid., 18, 2 (on the specification of the human act by its object) and 18, 4 (on the specification of the human act by its end). An excellent exegesis of these and parallel passages is provided by Augustine Joseph Brennan C.SS.R., *Moral Action in Aristotle and Aquinas* (Canberra, Canberra, Province of the Redemptorist Fathers, n.d.), pp. 47-50, 64-72. See also Theo G. Belmans, "La spécification de l'agir humain par son object chez Saint Thomas d'Aquin (Art. II)," *Divinitas* 23 (1979): 7-61.

91. It is important to note the difference between the proximate end of the human act, one that must be intentionally present to and willed by the agent, and the remote end. For instance, the proximate end of the act of stealing, an end that this act itself realizes and an end objectively one and the same with the act of stealing, is the usurping of goods that rightfully belong to another. One might do this deed for some ulterior or remote end, say, almsgiving, but the act would remain an act of theft and would therefore be contrary to natural-law precepts. The centrality of the distinction between proximate and remote ends is luminously explained by St. Thomas in *Summa Theologiae* 1-2, 1, 3, and ad 3. His whole point is that human acts are morally specified by the proximate end intended by the agent and realized objectively in and through the deed. The contemporary Roman Catholic theologians who propose a consequentialistic natural law (*do evil for the sake of a greater good*) attempt to justify acts by the remote or ulterior ends to which they are ordered.

92. On this point, cf. Brennan, pp. 22-26 and the texts of St. Thomas cited there.

93. *Summa Theologiae* 1-2, 18, 10.

94. For Maguire, Scholz, and McCormick, see note 31. Dedek has appealed to the same teaching of St. Thomas for the same purpose in his article "Intrinsically Evil Acts in St. Thomas," scheduled for publication in *The Thomist*. It is instructive to observe that in this article Dedek never alludes to or attempts to incorporate the teaching of St.

Thomas on the objective determinants of the morality of human acts (*Summa Theologiae* 1-2, pp. 18-21) in seeking to analyze his teaching on the behavior of Abraham, Hosea, and the Israelites in "taking" the goods of the Egyptians.

95. The pertinent texts from St. Thomas on this matter are provided by Milhaven. Among the principal Thomistic texts are *Summa Theologiae* 1-2, 100, 8, ad 3; 2-2, 104, ad 2; *De Malo* 3, 1, ad 17; 15, 1, ad 8; *In I Sententiarum* d. 47, q. 1, a. 4 and ad 2.

96. *Summa Theologiae* 1-2, 100, 8, ad 3. In his Lombard Commentary, *In I Sententiarum* d. 47, q. 1, a. 4, and ad 2, St. Thomas even holds that God's action here is "quasi-miraculous."

97. *Summa Theologiae* 1, 48, 3.

98. For St. Thomas "the aliveness of living things is their very being (*esse*)" (*Summa Contra Gentes* 1, 98), and *esse* is the gift of God's free act of creation (*Summa Theologiae* 1, 45, 5).

99. Ibid., 1-2, 100, 8 and ad 3.

100. Ibid., 1-2, 100, 1.

101. Ibid., 100, 8.

102. Ibid., ad 3.

103. Among the texts in which St. Thomas expressly rejects the view that one can do evil to attain good are: *Summa Theologiae* 2-2, 64, 6 and 7; 154, 2; *De Malo* 15, 1, ad 3.

104. *Quodlibetal Questions* 9, 8 c, in *Quaestiones Quodlibetales*, Raymond Spiazzi, ed. (Romae: Marietti, 1949): "we must rather abide by the Pope's judgment than by the opinion of any of the theologians." Cf. *Summa Theologiae* 2-2, 1, 10; 11, 2, ad 3.

Part Three
Freedom, Sin, and Grace

The Love of God and Mortal Sin

Ronald Lawler, O.F.M. Cap.
Center for Thomistic Studies
University of St. Thomas
Houston, Texas

Introduction: The Importance of Human Beings and Their Free Decisions

Christian faith has always confidently proclaimed the importance of each human person, and the tremendous significance of his or her free personal actions.

The unbelieving world has been inclined to mock the seriousness with which faith views individual moral actions, partly because it does not see human beings, as individual persons, as transcendently important. Thus Bertrand Russell ridiculed the importance believers give to the law of nature, and pointed out that from the broader view of things human beings are no more than "tiny parasites of this insignificant planet."[1] David Hume took a similar stance in denying the importance of any alleged malice in an act of suicide: "The life of man is of no greater importance to the universe than that of an oyster."[2]

When a human person is counted as a fundamentally determined being, radically a creature of passion, whose real motivation is largely unconscious, one can hardly expect much of him or her. Thus Freud, in a famous passage, speaks of the inappropriateness of the high ideals of Christian love.[3]

The Christian expectations of humanity, that it should do no evil, and love God with its whole heart, and love its neighbor as itself, are founded on another vision of human beings and their God. Though faith knows that humanity is flawed and in many ways captive to the elements of this world, it knows there is greatness too in humanity. Faith sees the human person not merely as the image of God, "having free will and master over his own action,"[4] but as one called to friendship with God himself, and called even to draw upon divine resources for power to lead a worthy life. Of such a person great things can be asked. The gospels are not ashamed to tell us humans that our own free responses to divine invitations are decisive (under God's grace) for our attaining, or failing to attain, everlasting life.[5]

In this paper we shall discuss the love of God and mortal sin. In our broken world the love of God can hardly be understood without some grasp of the reality of grave sin; and sin cannot be understood at all without reference to the love of God.

A leading American scriptural scholar has remarked: "The more at ease we are with a personal God the more readily we can accept the reality of sin."[6] Conversely, the more we acknowledge the reality of sin, the more at ease we are with a personal and loving God. "It might even be said that the greatest sin is not to accept sin, because not to accept sin is to reject the One because of whom sin is possible."[7] This means that not to acknowledge sin (and grave sin, one might add) is not to acknowledge the kind of God Scripture proclaims: a God who can be saluted coherently as infinitely good and infinitely loving in a world saturated in pain; a God whose word in Scripture and tradition speaks so eloquently of the reality, seriousness, and significance of human sin.

The Love of God

The Mysteries of Faith: Context of the Command to Love

Freud had reasons to be astonished as the soaring idealism of the gospel moral teaching. Not only are we commanded to do no evil whatever, we are commanded to love God with our whole heart and mind and strength, and to love each neighbor with great generosity.

The moral teaching of the New Testament can only be grasped as credible in the context of the great mysteries of faith.

God is love. He is the eternal, interpersonal love that binds together the persons of the Trinity in the unity that is the supreme exemplar for every society of persons. In perfectly free love he created humanity and its world. He did not simply make us images of himself: He called us to share his life and to be his friends. When we sinned, God did not abandon us: The eternal Son himself became our brother. He, our God, died for us in the great mystery of saving love that gives. Thus he enabled us who dwell in a sinful world to share his divine life, to be called and to be children of God. This is the astonishing faith of Christians. These are the doctrinal roots of the plausibility of the sublime gospel law.

The New Law: Grace of the Holy Spirit

Thomas Aquinas's celebrated tract on the liberating "Law of the Gospel"[8] sums up splendidly the tradition of the fathers on the core of gospel life. The gospel law indeed commands us to love God and neighbor. But the new covenant is not fundamentally a moral system, not even a pair of commandments of love. It is newness of life in Christ. "The New Law is chiefly the grace itself from the Holy Spirit, who is given to those who believe in Christ."[9] Through this grace God's love is poured into our hearts, giving us the desire and the power to love him and one another. It liberates us from the multitude of unnecessarily burdensome and weary precepts of the old law; but it calls us toward a more perfect love.

Paradox: The Difficulty and Ease of the New Law.

Essentially the new law is far less burdensome than the old.[10] This is true even though the new law commands more

difficult things. Christ's "But I say this to you ... " utterances
in the sermon on the Mount proclaim the obligation to a better
life. (Mt. 5:21-48). Christ does not hesitate to teach that love
requires more of us (even in specific matters) than people had
realized before he illumined our lives with the fullness of divine revelation. The exclusion of even lustful thoughts, for
example, is more difficult than the exclusion of lustful deeds.
But God remedies this difficulty by the very fact that he does
pour his love into our hearts. Thomas Aquinas quotes Augustine: "Love makes light and nothing of things that seem arduous and beyond our power."[11] By giving his love into our hearts
he makes it possible and easy for us to do those things which
love itself requires.

Moral Law: The Law of Love

Now the moral law itself is essentially a law of love. Christ
taught people to observe the Decalog (Mt. 19:17-19; Mk.
10:17-19; and Lk. 18:18-20). He also taught them that loving
God and loving one's neighbor are the fulfillment of the law
and the prophets (Mt. 22:40).

While the gospel liberates us from wearying legalism and
the massive 613 precepts of the law, it does not excuse us from
the moral law. For the moral law unfolds the requirements of
love.[12]

In his treatment of the logic of moral precepts, Aquinas
points out that the first principles of the moral law itself are
those of love: Thou shalt love the Lord thy God; thou shalt love
thy neighbor.[13] And the negative precept inseparable from
them: "That one should do evil to no one."[14] For no one does
harm to one whom he or she truly loves. These first precepts
are self-evident to reason or to faith, Aquinas notes. From
them flow "with but slight reflection,"[15] the principles expressed in the Decalog. These are the clearly necessary requirements of love, when they are understood properly

(Aquinas's own explanation of them is a masterpiece).[16] For
the precepts of the Decalog do not point out to us simply certain
ways by which we might choose to serve the ends of love. Instead, they direct us immediately to care for the personal goods
which *are* ends that all the activities of loving are to be concerned with. Hence, the precepts of the Decalog properly understood are entirely unexceptionable.[17] They are moral absolutes, precisely because they require only what love necessarily guards. Other requirements of the moral law flow from
these, but all are contained in these as in their principles; and
the Decalog itself is contained in the command of love as its
principle.[18] "Love is the fulfillment of the law" (Rom. 13:9; cf.
Gal. 5:13). The fuller logic of the commandments of love is
explicated in the papers of this symposium that treat of consequentialism and the morality of principles. These papers
show how love never does any evil for the sake of any hoped-for
advantages whatever. If we love God and one another, we must
not do evil that good may come of it.

Universal Call to Perfection: Degrees of Perfection

Vatican II made it clear again that all Christians—not
merely religious or some special elite—are called to the heights
of perfection.[19] Christian perfection consists essentially in love,
and therefore essentially in keeping the commandments.[20] The
founding commandments of the new law are the commandments of love, which are true precepts. (Clearly the gospel
maintains that love can be commanded, as it is; this is far
different from saying that love can be compelled.) And they are
sufficient. Whatever else is required of us as obedience to the
commands of the Decalog is contained in the commands of love,
just as conclusions are contained in their principles.

The commandments of the gospel call us to the peak of perfection. Hence, Aquinas says that Christian perfection does not
consist in observing the counsels but in keeping the com-

mandments. This means *all* the commandments: those of love, and the commandments of the Decalog that follow from them. To observe the gospel counsels (such as poverty, chastity, and obedience) helps us keep these commandments, and thus helps us toward perfection.[21] These counsels help us by liberating us from the impediments to love, and in this way they help us to keep the commandments. To keep the counsels is not to be perfect; it simply frees us from lesser loves that may impede what is better. But the fulfillment of Christ's commands is doing that which is perfect.

Can the gospel commandments be kept? The precepts of love command not a measure of love, but command us to love without measure[22]; that is to love with the whole heart . . . to love our neighbor as Christ loves us. Though we are supported by gifts of grace, we never fulfill these commands utterly in our earthly life, but we can observe them essentially. Aquinas gives the example of a soldier in battle who is commanded to do specific things and to struggle all the way to victory. He cannot fulfill the total command until victory is in fact achieved, but he does not violate the total command as long as he remains a faithful soldier. In the same way we do not violate the precept of total love if we accept it, observe it essentially, and so remain open to continuing growth toward fuller love and toward its final completion in beatitude.[23] Even in the early stages of Christian life, when the intensity of love may be weak, there must be a certain mode of loving God "with the whole heart, the whole mind, the whole soul, and the whole strength." Any degree of true love requires (and is not possible without) a firm will to do *all* that love entirely *demands* (e.g., to believe Christ's Word proclaimed in the family of faith) and to avoid all that is incompatible with love (e.g., to keep the commandments of the Decalog). People who would be ready to violate a divine commandment for any reason whatever simply do not love God with their whole heart in any sense at all.[24] (In accord with tradition, Aquinas sees only what binds us gravely as a strict commandment.)

Requirements of Love

It is not possible for people to love God truly or to enter the kingdom of God simply by saying, "Lord, Lord!" (Mt. 7:21). It is not possible to tell ourselves that we love God radically if we do not do the will of the Father. This will is not expressed in extrinsic, arbitrary commands, but in the directives of One who is boundlessly wise and who requires only what is required by love. Thus it is not possible for us to do deliberate harm to our brothers and sisters, and still remain devoted to God in our hearts. As Jesus put it, "What I say to you is: everyone who grows angry with his brother shall be liable to judgment..." (Mt. 5:22).

Faithful love must grow beyond the minimal manner of loving God. The precepts and the grace of the gospel call us to perfection. But there is no perfection whatever, however full-souled our sigh of "Father!" may be, if we do not actually do the Father's will (Mt. 7:21). If we do not keep the commandments of friendship, love, and the Decalog, we do not love God. If we disregard the infinite love of God and despise the gifts that he has extended to us to make it possible for us to act in accord with love, we do not truly love him.[25] We are here speaking, of course, of deliberate disobedience to God's commandments in persons who act with sufficient knowledge and with full freedom.

For such reasons as these, it has never been possible to speak adequately of the love of God in our broken world without also speaking of that faithfulness to love that keeps us from grave sin. In the understanding of sin we come to an understanding of some of the requirements of love.

Mortal Sin

"The Bible," Fr. Léon-Dufour says, "speaks of sin often, almost on every page."[26] It has a rich vocabulary for sin: It employs many terms that speak of different facets of sin's reality—words that might rightly be rendered as missing the mark, rebellion, iniquity, and omission. But always its context for sin is religious: A relationship to God is implied. In speaking of sin, Scripture instructs on the love of God to which sin is opposed.

The Sense of Sin

Catholic theology uses the word *sin* in a variety of related senses (we shall note only a few distinctions).[27] Basic is the *act of sin* (and principally the act of mortal sin to which venial sin is but analogous). To sin mortally in this sense is to do deliberately a *deed* incompatible with the love of God. There are also *personal states of sin.* Through moral deeds of a serious nature we structure our inner dispositions and attitudes. When we commit *grave sins*—acts incompatible with God's love—we alter our relationship to God.[28] Moreover, we are born into a condition of sin that is not a fruit of our own personal sin; this condition is called *original sin.*

In addition, we use the word sin to refer also to concupiscence, the *inclination to sin* that remains in us fallen (but redeemed) people even after justification. Even though our hearts are ordered to God in friendship, there remains a weakness and a recurrent inclination to sin. In broader stances, we speak of the *sin of the world,* which can be interpreted in many ways and mean many things. Always it refers to the condition of social human beings who see much sin about them, feel within themselves an inclination to sin, and live in a world whose institutions are flawed because they are largely structured by individual and collective acts lacking justice and love; therefore, these institutions themselves further social inclinations to sin.

We are concerned chiefly with mortally sinful acts, that is, serious moral acts committed with understanding and freedom that are incompatible with the love of God. Faith teaches that we cannot simultaneously actually love God *and* actually offend him gravely.[29] We cannot actually offend love with a deliberate will, actually affront what friendship with God requires, and still retain a relationship of friendship or grace.

For human beings nothing is more important than that love should order their relationship to God. Hence, it is intensely important that we not commit mortal sins or remain in a state of alienation from God, in a state of mortal sin. Faith has had a very legitimate concern to identify carefully what is mortally sinful.

Today there is a certain inclination to fudge over a decisive borderline. Some would distinguish not simply mortal and venial sins, but mortal, grave, and venial sins. Fr. McCormick rightly notes that this threefold distinction can create confusion.[30] Surely it does; it raises confusion in a matter of central importance to the spiritual life. Clearly a modification of vocabulary does not justify a substantial departure from the normative moral tradition of the Church. Thus the Church has constantly spoken of some sins as *mortal* or *grave* (the words are regularly synonymous in classical literature, though both have other meanings). To concede that a sin like adultery is grave (as all tradition has said and therefore proclaimed it to be a mortal sin), but to mean that adultery is a grave, nonmortal sin (that one who does such a deed deliberately is not acting decisively against God's will and love) is to use a new conceptual framework to contradict the received teaching. A language change like this is more than a linguistic matter. It is a drastic departure from the received Church teaching in a matter of immense personal importance.

The received teaching of the Church on the elements constituting a mortal sin is well known. To sin mortally is to do a

gravely evil kind of deed, a deed incompatible with actual love
of God (and there are kinds of deeds that are thus incompatible); and to do the deed with full understanding and freedom.
This means that the acts must be done in accord with the
substantial requirement for a free choice. It is not necessary to
have perfect freedom (which only God has), but it is necessary
to have the freedom that makes the act truly and substantially
one's own. The agent must be the one who chose to act in this
way. The act was not that of a person mastered by alien compulsions and pressures but it was substantially that individual's own choice.[31]

The Church has always taught that there are acts so disor-
dered and alien to what love demands that to commit them
freely means separating oneself from the divine friendship and
the kingdom of God.

Theologians have long been aware of their responsibility to
declare no kind of action mortally sinful unless sacred Scripture, sacred tradition, or the clear teaching of the magisterium
make it evident that this is clearly the case, or unless theological reflection, rooted in these sacred sources, manifests the
point certainly.[32] But when such sources reveal that certain
kinds of deeds, freely done, "would engage the will in a kind of
choice incompatible with the love of God above all,"[33] this evidence must be taken into account.

Lists of Grave Sins

From the earliest days of Christianity, lists of sins have been
formulated for pastoral purposes. Thus St. Paul wrote to the
Corinthians: "Do not be deceived; neither the immoral, nor
idolaters, nor homosexuals, nor thieves, nor the greedy, nor
revilers, nor robbers will inherit the kingdom of God" (I Cor.
6:9).[34] In the patristic period there was a famous, small list of
sins so grave that they could not be forgiven unless one had
done public penance for them: the sins of apostasy, murder, and
adultery.[35]

Later the Irish sacramentaries provided longer lists of sins, the nature of which is in need of additional study. Even in the official documents of our own time, we find lists of grave sins. In *Gaudium et Spes,* for example, we read:

> All offenses against life itself, such as murder, genocide, abortion, euthanasia, and wilful suicide; all violations of the integrity of the human person, such as mutilation, physical and mental torture, undue psychological pressures; all offense against human dignity, such as subhuman living conditions, arbitrary imprisonment, deportation, slavery, prostitution, the selling of women and children... all these and the like are infamies indeed (*Gaudium et Spes,* 27; see also nn. 51, 79, and 80.)

Some comment is needed on these lists. Eugene Maly notes "The scriptural lists of sin are surely not intended as an exhaustive guide to the moral life. The Gospel can use no new set of 613 precepts pretending to be a complete moral code. Our fullness lies elsewhere: 'Love is the fulfillment of the law.'" Fr. Maly adds that the scriptural example has convinced the Church that a "catechesis of sin, specifying certain actions as morally reprehensible, is a necessary aspect of the presentation of Christianity."[36] Christianity is a new life, not a moral code. But the new life has moral requirements, and Scripture points to Christ himself precisely as the teacher of some of these specific moral requirements.

Bernard Häring insists that these lists are tinged with cultural relativity.[37] That is true, but the point must be nuanced very carefully. These lists are relative because they are pastoral documents suited to the needs of each age. Each period and place wishes to warn the faithful against the sins toward which the times are most inclined. (The Church must resist what C. S. Lewis noted as the inclination of the world, which is to do precisely the opposite of what the Church recommends. Thus ages of militancy and cruelty are likely to warn youngsters against weakness and effeminacy; licentious ages like ours are likely to caution people chiefly against prudery). Some relativity is present in the sense that both words and human institutions change with time; when the meaning of money and its function changes, the taking of interest can become something morally different in different contexts. But this relativity does not extend to the point that actions directly against the enduring values celebrated in Scripture and known to all cultures could ever in any culture be compatible with love. Thus murder, adultery, apostasy, rape, and abortion are temptations to the weaknesses of every age; they are always condemned by Christian moral teaching.

It is important to distinguish two ways of describing what a mortal sin is, and what we do in committing such a sin. First, there is the question of the focus of the human choice; what we wish to achieve in and by our actions and in and by our deliberate omissions. Second, there is the question of what we know that we are accomplishing through our actions or omissions.[38] Thus people who steal a Social Security check from an aged neighbor do so in the hope of a benefit to be enjoyed. Normally, or frequently, they do not desire an evil as such, that is, the injury to their neighbor. Far less do they desire the evil that they do to themselves in becoming unjust. This is the normal path for grave sins. We normally do not focus our concern on the will to dissociate ourselves from God or to change our fundamental orientation. Our desire is not to lose the life of love and grace that orders ourselves in relationship to the Father. Surely we do not wish the "second death" to which unrepented mortal sin leads. Mortal sin does not only involve what we wish to reap from it but it also involves what faith teaches it to be, and what the very nature of love reveals it to be. We do not normally separate ourselves from the Lord because we choose to reorient our lives in a mysterious, almost ineffable act. We separate ourselves from the Lord by deliberately and knowingly pursuing an attractive good in a way incompatible with the love of the Lord.

Senses of Fundamental Option and Fundamental Stance

The moderate view. Many contemporary moralists speak of mortal sin in the context of fundamental stances and fundamental options. The fundamental-option theory can be expressed in a moderate way that is fully compatible with the received teaching on mortal sin. Sin and acts of conversion are surely not fragmentary episodes in the spiritual life. They induce orientations into our inner life that are by their very nature enduring and dynamic. Serious *acts of charity* (to use Fr. McCormick's phrase,[39] which is far more felicitous than Fr. O'Connell's inept phrase—"*mortal acts of virtue*"[40]—are not only good acts. They establish within the former sinner a relationship of friendship with God—the state of grace—that is of its nature enduring. Aquinas even says of this relationship that it is "not easily lost."[41] Similarly, an act of mortal sin induces a state of alienation from God that we of ourselves have no power to terminate—a state of mortal sin.

The concept of fundamental stance stresses this important point. We should not imagine that acts of conversion and mortal sin are casual and rootless, so that we might frequently and easily pass to and from a loving relationship with God and mortal sin. Serious moral acts—acts of conversion, and mortal sins—have roots in prior acts that dispose us to them.

A moderate fundamental-option position would acknowledge the following situation:

> Human lives tend to have a basic orientation, that is, to become established in a rooted loyalty to God or to become more set in the selfishness that turns one from God. But this does not mean that those who would wish to serve God simply cannot commit mortal sins.... (Through deliberate unfaithfulness)

in small things we can drift toward (grave sin). It
would be presumptious to claim that one's life has
been so steadfastly turned toward God that it would
not be possible for a single act of lust or abortion or
blasphemy to change the direction of one's life. For if
one is prepared to do, and does, an action that is
gravely evil, and known to be opposed to the demanding will of God, and does this with sufficient
awareness and freedom, one reveals that one is not
firmly devoted to God, and expresses the spirit of one
who does not love him.[42]

The radical view. The moderate form of the fundamental-
option theory clearly has deep roots in Catholic tradition. But
the radical view of the fundamental option introduces a key
element discontinuous with the received teaching. It holds that
all human actions are "peripheral," except for those that have
a "core" or "radical" or "fundamental" aspect. The concept of
core action is difficult to grasp. Reality is said to be "very
obscure" to us.[43] For that reason we do not easily know if we
have really elicited such an action. Peripheral acts are concrete
acts with ordinary objective goals, like the act of adultery. A
core act can occur in and through such a concrete act. But
despite the fact that we perform an adulterous deed with all
the knowledge and freedom traditionally required for a serious
moral act—a mortal sin—of itself such an act would not be
mortally sinful *unless* it had also the core aspect.[44] In the core
of ourselves there must be a "free determination of oneself with
regard to the totality of existence, a fundamental self-
determination or choice between love or selfishness, between
the self and the God of salvation."[45]

Let us now consider what takes place in a homicide. The
radical view holds that we could perform an act of this sort—an
act that has always been held gravely wrong in the Church—
and perform it with the full ordinary freedom and understand-

ing, and still not turn aside from our continuing love of God. We must, it seems, not merely freely do something that faith has called incompatible with divine love, but we must, in some obscure inner facet of the act of slaying, precisely decide also to turn from divine love to selfishness; if murderers avoid doing that, they have not lost grace. It is this aspect that the magisterium objects to, and rightly so. The Sacred Congregation for the Faith in December 1975 declared:

> According to the Church's teaching, mortal sin, which is opposed to God, does not consist only in formal and direct resistance to the commandment of charity.... A person sins mortally not only when his action comes from direct contempt for love of God and neighbor, but also when he consciously and freely, for whatever reason, chooses something that is seriously disordered.[46]

The Bishops of the United States, in the National Catechetical Directory, made their own this position of the Holy See.[47]

We have indicated above the reasons why the radical view of mortal sin is defective. Radical theorists, in the usual expansive manner of contemporary revisionists, suggest grandly that "contemporary psychology" reveals this deeper form of freedom. The unwary reader might suppose that in psychology manuals generally we can find under "freedom, human" a new entry labeled "core freedom." We will not find this in many books of psychologists, I fear. This idea is to be found in the pages of a few people who belong to the interesting group of Thomists most affected by Kantian theory. That one should urge confidently such a radical change in ecclesial practice in the light of such an appeal to authority is astounding. The obscure, poorly elaborated views of a small set of scholars have been presented as more authoritative than the morally universal voice of tradition. We have much to do to relate theology with contemporary psychology, but this is no helpful step in that direction.[48]

Let us note a popular objection to the received view that a single deliberate mortal sin done with ordinary "full freedom and understanding," may change our fundamental relationship with God. What we are over a long period of time, what penetrates our being, what shapes our attitudes and dispositions—all this is said to reveal what we are far more adequately than a single action. For example, if we have practiced justice and honesty over many years, we may, under the pressure of difficult circumstances or in weakness, freely decide to do a gravely unjust deed. But this one act does not annul our history or change our fundamental stance. So a single gravely wrong deed could hardly change our long relationship of friendship with God.[49]

Sometimes this position has been presented as a discovery of the new personalism of our times. Actually it is an ancient objection to the received view; and those who raise it now seldom reveal awareness of the common response to it. In his recent commentary on Aquinas's treatment of the general problem in the *Summa* T. C. O'Brien notes that the Catholic tradition holds that a single mortal sin alters the fundamental stance of a person who had been in grace precisely because the center of Christian morality is the personal love of God, not human virtue or habits. This means that personalism of a Christian kind supports the received view, not the modern suggestion that we may have occasional moral holidays without altering much in our relationship to God. What the popular objection suggests is true on a certain level; the natural virtues we have remain intact even when we have done a single, gravely wrong deed. St. Thomas, following Aristotle, holds that the natural virtues are not normally lost by one act.[50] But the existential situation of human beings is different. There is a basic *theological fact* that Thomas respected: the teaching of faith that God has given us power to overcome every inclination to sin gravely, and that he requires us to do so. The heart of the supernatural life is not a set of natural habits but personal love. A serious, free, deliberate choice against love is as serious and decisive as a free, deliberate choice in favor of love. Deliberate actions that offend the infinite love calling us to faithfulness are not trivial episodes in a personalist theology.[51]

The objective element in mortal sin. There is a strong tendency today to deny the received teaching on the objective element of mortal sin. The objective element is only an element, of course; however grave the kind of deed we might do, our action would not formally be gravely sinful if we did not act with sufficient understanding and freedom.[52] It is granted, however, that the Church has constantly taught that there are such kinds of deeds that those who would do them with deliberate freedom are turning away from the love of God. For example, those who slay the innocent are attacking and gravely harming persons whom they ought to love if they are to love God. Should they do such things with understanding and freedom of choice, they would sin mortally.

Some fundamental-option theorists deny this teaching. They do not concede that freely doing any special kind of deed *implies* a turning aside from the orientation to love. Rather, they say, such deeds are occasions when human beings are more likely to order themselves (by the mysterious core act of freedom) away from love of God.[53] We might commit adultery (knowing that it is the sort of sin faith has declared a mortal sin) with full freedom of choice; but if we do not also reorient ourselves away from the former direction of our lives, we have not sinned mortally. And the reorientation is an added facet of the act, not necessarily implied by deliberately doing a deed that has so clearly been taught to be opposed to love. It is difficult not to see how great an opening such a teaching gives to every kind of self-deception.

The Church has taught that some kinds of sins are always grave of their very nature. To deny the faith, to slay the innocent, to commit adultery: these and other kinds of acts are *objectively* always grave.[54] There is a certain indivisibility to the object in such sins; we cannot murder "a little bit"; we can deny more or less of the faith, but to deny at all is to do a kind of deed essentially incompatible with love. Many other kinds of sins are not always objectively grave, because they do not so directly attack persons and their fundamental goods, and something morally different is done in various degrees of such deeds.[55] We all are familiar with the commandment "Thou shalt not steal." Taking a trifle from a wealthy person, however, is not related to love precisely in the same way as taking a large amount from the poor would be.

Surely there are some difficulties in this ancient and continuing ordinary teaching of the Church about the kinds of sins that are always or only sometimes objectively grave. But Fr. Häring seems excessively casual in his preparedness to dismiss certain aspects of this teaching. He holds that this received teaching of the Church cannot be infallible, because some have denied it.[56] The few (and entirely uninfluential) denials over the centuries, of course, need careful study. (We abstract from contemporary rejections, for the very question is whether these denials are legitimate in the face of the morally unanimous tradition of the Church.) But the weight of constant testimony in the Church by every kind of teacher—bishops, councils, theologians, doctors, saints, catechists, preachers, and parents—in a matter of such importance for salvation is so great that we can hardly flee the Church's teaching on the objective gravity of some sins without also denying that the Church is not infallible at all in matters of morals in its ordinary teaching.[57]

The objective seriousness of individual acts. The received teaching on the objective seriousness of certain kinds of acts needs to be studied also in the light of the received teaching on the morality of individual actions. No two acts are likely to be absolutely identical morally; we not only do various kinds of deeds but we also do them with a great variety of intentions and in a vast diversity of circumstances. The kinds of acts, our motives, and our circumstances—all these factors are said to be the determinants of the morality of individual acts.[58] Some have been tempted to feel that it is absurd simply to label every act of fornication a mortal sin, for there are clearly greater and lesser degrees of malice in diverse acts of fornication. Motives and circumstances also affect the morality of individual acts. Subjective reasons, the lack of freedom, or ignorance, might, as we know, remove all grave guilt. Even *objectively* the deed could in the concrete have various degrees of malice. If the deed is done with full freedom, it is seriously sinful because faith teaches that implicit in any objectively grave sin is a rejection of what love requires, a serious harm to persons or a great damage to their personal goods. But different motives and different circumstances would still distinguish different levels of malice in distinct acts of the same kind. Not all grave sins are equal.

For the same reason, some deeds that are of their nature only venial sins might concretely become serious. Fundamental-option theorists at times observe that a sin like a small theft or a small act of irreverence could be a grave sin. There is some truth in this; a very evil will can be expressed in an apparently trivial deed. They explain this by saying that even such deeds may be done in a serious (core) free act that alters the fundamental orientation of the person.[59] But Aquinas and the tradition of the Church had a better and more intelligible explanation. A small act of theft could be done with, for example, a motive of hatred; the small act of irreverence could be done in circumstances that made it an act of denial of faith. It is not the free doing of a slightly evil act as such that is gravely wrong. But circumstances and motives can give a different nature to the kind of act we concretely accomplish. The small theft done in real hatred is not objectively only a theft; it is a deed of hatred, and hatred is a gravely wrong kind of deed.[60]

Subjective morality: How common are mortal sins? A formal mortal sin—a personal act with all the consequences of a mortal sin—does not occur unless we perform an act that we understand to be a gravely evil kind of act with full freedom of the will. How common actually are mortal sins? Fr. Curran confidently assures us, "Mortal sin is a comparatively rare occurrence in the Christian life."[61] Unfortunately, he does not explain: compared to what? Compared to the number of acts of love? Compared to the number of sins people used to think? Which people? Mortal sin is certainly a terrible evil whenever it occurs. The writings of the doctors and saints, the public law of the Church, and the practices of Catholic life have certainly not assumed that mortal sin is so rare that people generally should not have much fear that they could really fall into it. In a parish of several hundred families, are many mortal sins likely to be committed in a year? Should we answer no, and begin to phase out opportunities for confession, it would be good to be in a position to offer splendid reasons in defence of this position.

Church law and practice over many centuries have commanded the faithful to confess at least once a year and whenever they are in mortal sin, and to mention in confession all grave sins, specifying their kinds and their number.[62] Moreover, Church law and practice has forbidden (with an injunction having scriptural foundations) people to receive communion when they are in a state of mortal sin.[63] In doing this, the teaching of the Church has supposed that we can have a reasonably sure awareness of the fact that we have committed a grave sin. Recently there has been a certain exaggeration about the difficulty of knowing whether one has sinned gravely. The most basic Church document used to fortify an agnostic reply is one from Trent which teaches that we cannot know *with the certainty of faith* that we are in grace.[64] But one hardly needs such certainty in the guidance of life. There are many circumstances that can justify doubt about our state. But from this we should not conclude that persons who have freely and deliberately acted in ways that are gravely wrong are not able to have a prudent moral certainty in the matter. Similarly, those who seek earnestly to serve God have a prudent certainty that they seriously love him.

Certainly, it seems clear (as pastoral theology has always recognized) that formal mortal sins are rarer than material mortal sins. Faith takes seriously the subjective conditions for the possibility of mortal sin. Modern psychology confirms what traditional pastoral wisdom knew; many evil deeds of human beings, especially those motivated by pleasure or fear, are not sufficiently free to be grave sins. But modern studies reveal in much greater depth the mechanisms by which understanding and freedom are blocked by wide varieties of unconscious motivations, compulsions, and the like.[65] While there have always been some who denied the practical possibility or the serious danger of mortal sin, excellent contemporary theologians are in accord with the teaching of the magisterium and Christian tradition that mortal sin is a real possibility. Since it is the worst evil we could do or suffer, we must acknowledge responsibly its possibility for ourselves and those for whom we have pastoral care.[66] Thus, in speaking of sexual sins, the Sacred Congregation for the Faith in its December 1975 decree restated the traditional teaching of the Church.

> [in certain kinds of sins, including sexual sins] it more easily happens that free consent is not fully given; this is a fact which calls for caution in all judgment as to the subject's responsibility.... However, although prudence is recommended in judging the subjective seriousness of a particular sinful act,

it in no way follows that in the sexual field mortal
sins are not committed.[67]

Certainly we cannot ignore the ordinary Church teaching
that sins of weakness (and not only sins of malice) can be
mortal sins.[68] Weakness can, of course, at times make a sin
that is of its nature grave become formally and subjectively
only a venial sin. We might be so moved by an overwhelming
passion to a sin of lust that there would be no substantial
freedom in the act, and, formally, no grave sin. But this is not
always the case. We might also choose freely to do evil deeds
toward which we are inclined by weakness.

Father Häring, in his new study of fundamental moral
theology, speaks of the "sinful talk of sin."[69] His remarks there
are of a very uneven quality, but the concept is not a bad one.
We can speak of sin sinfully, and we can speak of it lovingly.
There is a terrible responsibility for teachers in the faith when
they speak of so tremendous a subject or remain silent about it.
Fr. Curran remarks that some have applied to the contemporary theologian the text "Behold him who takes away the sins
of the world."[70] Alas, theologians cannot take away sins by
suggesting that the Church's ordinary teaching on mortal sin
is not true. Nor do they wish to pretend they can. But in the
way teachers of faith speak of sin they can profoundly help or
gravely harm their brothers and sisters in Christ.

To speak of sin lovingly is not to say that grave sin is unlikely for us or for those we love in Christ. This was never the
view of the saints or doctors of the Church. As Paul vi taught,
"This is an eminent form of charity for souls: to diminish in no
way the saving teaching of Christ."[71] He spoke of this in the
very context of noting the gravity of sins that people were not
likely to think grave. The Lord himself found it in accord with
love to proclaim what love demands when he said, "Anyone
who looks lustfully at a woman has already committed adul-

tery with her in his thoughts" (Mt. 5:28). Those who remind us that mortal sin is a fearful possibility in our sinful state need not be pessimists. Only when people are reminded of the tremendous importance of their personal decisions can they muster the decisive will to live as Christian people in a fallen world.

Those who continue to teach what faith has always taught about mortal sin do not forget that Christ has redeemed us. It is very true that we are sinners. It is very true that we are inclined toward sin in the most basic sense of the term—to mortal sin incompatible with the love of God. But God's love is strong. He wills to free us from our sin, and he has the power to do so. Many have not yet the power to resist even the sins of weakness and the material sins. All these temptations can yield to the saving power of him who died for us. But Jesus calls free people to faithful love and to everlasting life; and he teaches them the tremendous importance of their personal response to his mighty love. "Before man are life and death, whichever he chooses shall be given him" (Sir. 15:17). Happily God's strong grace is present to assist us to choose life.

Notes

1. B. Russell, *Why I Am Not a Christian* (New York: Simon and Schuster, 1957), p. 55.
2. D. Hume, "On Suicide," in R. Beck and J. Orr, eds., *Ethical Choice* (New York: Free Press, 1970), p. 73.
3. S. Freud, *Civilization and Its Discontents,* ch. 5 in the *Great Books,* vol. 54, pp. 786 ff.
4. Thomas Aquinas, *Summa Theologiae* I-II, Prol.
5. See R. Schnackenburg, *The Moral Teaching of the New Testament* (New York: Herder and Herder, 1965), pp. 329-39, for a forceful treatment of the decisions Christ demands of human beings.
6. E. Maly, *Sin: Biblical Perspectives* (Dayton: Pflaum/Standard, 1973), p. 2.
7. Ibid., p. 6.
8. *Summa Theologiae* I-II, qq. 106-8.

9. Ibid., I–II, q. 106, a.l,c.
10. Cf. Mt. 11:30; *Summa Theologiae* I–II, q. 107, a.4.
11. *Summa Theologiae* I–II, q. 107, a.4, ad 3; see also c.
12. Jn. 14:15; see *Summa Theologiae* I–II, q. 108, a.2,c, and q. 100, obj. 1 and ad 1.
13. *Summa Theologiae* I–II, q. 100, a.3, ad 1.
14. Ibid., q. 100, a.3,c.
15. Ibid.
16. Ibid., q. 100, esp. aa. 3,5, and 8.
17. Ibid., q. 100, a.8.
18. Ibid., q. 100, a.3,c.; Rom. 13:9
19. Vatican II, *Dogmatic Constitution on the Church (Lumen Gentium)* n. 40.
20. *Summa Theologiae* II–II, q. 184, a.3.
21. Ibid.
22. Ibid.
23. *Summa Theologiae* II–II, q. 44, a.6,c.
24. "Such perfection as this can be had in this world in two ways. First, by the removal from man's affections of all that is contrary to charity, such as mortal sin; and there can be no charity apart from this, wherefore it is necessary for salvation." *Summa Theologiae* II–II, q. 184, a.2,c.
25. *Summa Theologiae* II–II, 184,3. Cf. ad 2: "The lowest degree of divine love is to love nothing more than God, or equally with God, and whoever fails from this degree of perfection nowise fulfills the precept."
26. X. Léon-Dufour, *Dictionary of Biblical Theology,* 2nd ed. (New York: Seabury Press, 1973), p. 550.
27. Cf. I. McGuiness, "Sin, Theology of" in *New Catholic Encyclopedia* (New York: McGraw-Hill, 1966), vol. 13, pp. 241–45.
28. On the nature of mortal sin, see *Summa Theologiae* I–II, q. 88, a.1 and 2. Mortal sin is sin in the fullest sense; venial sins are called sins by analogy (q. 88, a.1, ad 1).
29. Cf. Council of Trent, Session 6, *Decree on Justification,* ch. 15, DS 1544.
30. Cf. R. McCormick, "Personal Conscience," in *An American Catechism, III Moral Theology. (Chicago Studies* 13 (1974)), p. 250.
31. Cf. J. Ford and G. Kelly, *Contemporary Moral Theology,* vol. 1, *Questions in Fundamental Moral Theology* (Westminster, Md.: Newman, 1958), pp. 205–33.
32. For an account of the traditional stance of caution in declaring

any kind of deed mortally sinful, see Ford and Kelly, pp. 447-49. An argument from the sources of revelation will follow the principles noted in Vatican II, *Dogmatic Constitution on Sacred Revelation (Dei Verbum)*, 10: Each of these sources is intimately interrelated with the others. Thus a scriptural study on the gravity of a kind of sin would not be theologically complete without reflection on the way the Church has understood the scriptural word in its tradition and in its magisterial guidance.

33. T. O'Brien, tr. and ed., *Summa Theologiae*, vol. 27 (I-II, qq. 86-89) (New York: McGraw-Hill, 1974), p. 115. Cf. I-II, q. 88, a.2, in which Aquinas declares that some kinds of deeds are always mortal because in doing such deeds freely "the will fixes itself upon something that in its nature is incompatible with the charity by which a person is directed toward the final end."

34. Cf. also Gal 5:19-21; Eph. 5:5; I Tm. 1:9-11; Rv. 21:8 and 22; 22:15.

35. Cf. *Oxford Dictionary of the Catholic Church*, 2nd ed. (Oxford: Oxford University Press, 1974), s.v. "apostasy," p. 74.

36. E. Maly, p. 31.

37. B. Häring, *Free and Faithful in Christ* (New York: Seabury Press, 1978), p. 393.

38. No one wills evil as such, Aquinas insists. But "when the will is directed to a thing that is in itself contrary to charity, the sin is mortal by reason of its object." *Summa Theologiae* I-II, q. 88, a.2. By turning to a good in a way that involves a choice contrary to charity, one turns away from God.

39. R. McCormick, p. 249.

40. T. O'Connell, *Principles for a Catholic Morality*, (New York: Seabury, 1978), p. 71.

41. *De Veritate*, q. 27, a.9, ad 1.

42. R. Lawler et al., eds., *The Teaching of Christ* (Huntington, Ind.: Our Sunday Visitor, 1976), p. 306.

43. R. McCormick, p. 249.

44. Some free acts involve "categorical freedom," freely doing this or that, as opposed to core freedom, in which one determines not a special act but the orientation of one's being, according to T. O'Connell, p. 62. Ordinary actions are said to be fairly superficial, an outer ring of the "onion" of a human being, p. 59.

45. R. McCormick, pp. 248-49.

46. Sacred Congregation for the Doctrine of the Faith, *Declaration on Certain Questions Concerning Sexual Ethics (Persona Humana)*, 10. Quoted in *Catholic Mind* (April 1976): 59.

47. National Conference of Catholic Bishops, *Sharing the Light of Faith: National Catechetical Directory for Catholics of the United States.* (Washington, D.C.: N.C.C.B., 1979) Ch. 5, fn. 33, p. 165.

48. Far more work is needed in the more substantial ways that J. Ford and G. Kelly handle such questions in *Contemporary Moral Theology,* cited above.

49. T. O'Brien, tr. and ed., *Summa Theologiae,* vol. 27, (I-II, qq. 86-89), (New York: McGraw-Hill, 1974), p. 112.

50. *Summa Theologiae* I-II, q. 71, a.4.

51. O'Brien, p. 112.

52. Cf. *Summa Theologiae* I-II, q. 88.

53. O'Connell, p. 72. Here Fr. O'Connell is saying that the doing of, e.g., an act of adultery with the ordinary free will is not necessarily a mortal sin, but an occasion of sin. Only if one on this occasion happens to have also the mysterious core act is a mortal sin committed.

54. *Summa Theologiae* I-II, q. 88, q.2.

55. Lottin, pp. 490-91.

56. Häring, p. 408. His hesitations focus on some sexual sins. But some of his remarks on pp. 406-7 also appear highly questionable.

57. J. Ford and G. Grisez point out how massive is the testimony of the Church in favor of its ordinary moral teaching in one specific point that has many parallels. Any model of the Church and any ecclesiology appealed to would have to respect this evidence if one is going to defend the common thesis that Christ and his Spirit teach in the Church. See "Contraception and the Infallibility of the Ordinary Magisterium," *Theological Studies* 39 (1978): 258-312.

58. *Summa Theologiae* I-II, q. 18. One can only be astonished at the surprising interpretation of this teaching given by T. O'Connell, pp. 78-81.

59. R. McCormick, p. 231, even claims that the received teaching that there can be a fully deliberate venial sin "is a contradiction in terms."

60. *Summa Theologiae* I-II, q. 88, a.2, c.

61. C. Curran, *Contemporary Problems in Moral Theology* (Notre Dame: University of Notre Dame Press, 1970), p. 22. This is a common claim among revisionist theologians. Compare this with the sober remarks of Ford and Kelly, p. 216, and their contention that "there are a great many mortal sins in the world."

62. Cf. Lateran Council IV (1215), cap. 21 (DS 812); Trent (1551), sess. 14, cap. 5, on penance, (DS 1683); *Code of Canon Law,* canon 906. See also Sacred Congregation for Divine Worship, *Rite of Penance* (1973), Introduction, n. 7.

63. Trent (1551) sees. 13, cap. 7 (DS 1647), and canon 11 (DS 1661).
64. Trent (1547), sess. 6, cap. 9 (DS 1534). See Aquinas's treatment of the problem in *Summa Theologiae* I-II, q. 112, a.5. In obj. 3 and ad 3 Thomas shows the difference between knowing one is in grace and knowing one is in sin. Certainty is possible for the latter.
65. Cf. J. Ford and G. Kelly, chs. 10-14.
66. Ford and Kelly, pp. 214 ff.: "We must start with the presumption that the normal individual is ordinarily capable of that degree of psychological freedom which is necessary to incur grave responsibility." Important Church documents are studied carefully here, and found in agreement with modern findings.
67. *Persona Humana,* 10. Quoted in *Catholic Mind* (April 1976): 59.
68. *Summa Theologiae* I-II, q. 77, a.8. See Ford and Kelly, ch. 11.
69. Häring, ch. 8, I, 1: "Sinful Talk of Sin," pp. 378 ff.
70. Curran, p. 22.
71. Paul VI, *Humanae Vitae,* 29.

"Deliver Us From Evil": The Meaning of Venial Sin

Rev. John R. Connery, S.J.
Loyola University
Chicago, Illinois

The distinction between mortal and venial sin goes back to the early Church and has its origin in the Scriptures themselves. The terms *mortal* and *venial* are of later vintage, but the underlying distinction is expressed in the New Testament, for instance, in such analogies as the speck versus the plank in the eye (Mt. 7:3) and the gnat versus the camel (Mt. 23:24), implying a vast difference between the corresponding sins. It is also expressed in terms of frequency and effects. The Scriptures speak of the daily sins of which we are all guilty, and tell us that if anyone tries to deny that he is a sinner, the truth is not in him (1 Jn. 1:8). Other sins are graver and call for "excommunication" (1 Cor. 5:1-3), or exclusion from the kingdom (1 Cor. 6:9). They separate us from Christ (1 Cor. 6:12), do not permit people to remain united with God (1 Jn. 2:24) and bring death with them (Phil. 3:9).

That the distinction is not just between moral species, but has theological implications is insinuated in the statements that these greater sins are not compatible with life in Christ, that they separate from Christ and cause death. The death of which the New Testament speaks is not the death of the body. In the Old Testament the death penalty was imposed for certain sins or crimes according to the *lex talionis,* but in the New Testament the kind of death related to serious sin was not of the body but of the soul. Sin was contrary to eternal life rather than to temporal life. Actually, as long as temporal life remained, those who were dead in this way could be vivified in Christ. The lesser sins, however, were also found in the just. They could coexist with life in the soul and did not exclude one from the kingdom. There was more then than just a specific difference between these sins and the greater sins mentioned above.

In the early Church a distinction was made between sins on the basis of the need for public penance and reconciliation. Lesser sins did not have to be submitted to public penance. Nor does it seem that private penance was available for such sins, at least in patristic times. By the time of Augustine, the terms *mortal* and *venial* were in use, and the distinction between these sins became more and more clear. Sins that were minor either because of the matter or because of a lack of sufficient consent could be removed by prayer, almsgiving and penance. Greater sins, which brought about separation from Christ and the kingdom, had to be submitted to public penance. They carried with them an "excommunication"—that is, a separation from communion with the faithful that could last for many years. The Church maintained this distinction of sins in opposition to the Stoics, and later to the Jovinians and Pelagians who held that all sins were equal.

With the advent of private penance, even lesser sins began to be submitted to confession and penance. In this discipline, although the theological and juridical aspect of sin was not neglected, confession and penance became more of an ascetical practice; more attention was given to the moral species of sins. Sin was looked upon as a disease of the soul, and it was thought that, like different diseases of the body, the different species of sin called for different remedies. Often enough, the theories of healing that prevailed in medicine were applied to spiritual healing.

Unfortunately, the distinction between mortal and venial sin is not as neat and exclusive as we would like, at least if we look at the terms themselves. We can even be misled. For instance, if we approach the distinction from the meaning of the term *venial,* we might arrive at the conclusion that mortal sin is not pardonable. It seems quite true that in the second and third centuries of the Christian Era, ecclesiastical pardon was not granted for some sins. Some may even have thought that the Church did not have the power to pardon these sins if they were committed after baptism. Generally speaking, however, the refusal to pardon these sins was only part of the discipline of some local churches, and was not based on any conscious limitation of the power of forgiveness. So it would be a mistake to conclude from the use of the term *venial* that the distinction was based on pardonability, at least in the above sense.

For the true meaning of the distinction, it is safer to approach it from the term *mortal;* some sins are mortal, others are not. But even this approach may not immediately lead us to the basic meaning of the distinction. It can refer, for instance, to the punishment merited by different sins; mortal sin merits eternal punishment, venial sin only temporal punishment. This is quite true, but it is not really basic. Sins are not mortal because they merit eternal punishment; they merit eternal punishment because they are mortal. So the difference in punishment cannot be the fundamental difference between the sins.

The distinction between mortal and venial sin can also refer to their different effects; mortal sin deprives the soul of supernatural life, or life with Christ. Venial sin neither takes away nor diminishes the supernatural life of the soul; it is therefore reparable and venial. St. Thomas compares sin in this respect to bodily diseases.[1] Some diseases are incurable, and hence are called mortal; others are curable. So some sins are called mortal since they are incurable of themselves; only God can cure them by restoring grace. Others are curable of themselves; hence they are called venial.

But even this difference is not basic. The loss of grace, or the supernatural life, is an effect of sin; it is not the sin itself. Theologians have put the basic difference in terms of the deordination of the act.[2] There are two kinds of deordination—regarding the end, and regarding the means to the end. In mortal sin the deordination regards the end itself. People choose themselves (at least in the form of some creature) rather than God as their ultimate end. In venial sin they remain faithful to God as their last end, but show an inordinate attachment to some creature and pursue it beyond its purpose. The act does not lead people away from God, but it cannot be directed toward God. This is the fundamental difference between mortal and venial sin.

Sometimes the distinction is put more concretely in terms of an *aversio a Deo* and a *conversio ad creaturam*. In both mortal and venial sin there is an unwarranted turning toward creatures. In this sense it can be said that both belong to the same species. But in mortal sin people substitute some creature for God as their ultimate end. It becomes their god, and the act therefore involves an *aversio a Deo*. In venial sin there is no *aversio a Deo*. People do not make a creature their ultimate end, but simply use it in a way that cannot be directed to God. So the basic distinction between mortal and venial sin is in the presence or absence of an *aversio a Deo*. In terms of the loss of sanctifying grace mentioned above, the relationship is one of cause and effect. The privation of grace can be called a habitual *aversio,* but it is still an effect of the actual *aversio* that constitutes the sin itself as mortal.

On the basis of the above analysis, it is maintained that the notion of sin is not univocal but analogous.[3] What this means is that the notion of sin cannot be applied equally to all sin. It is verified fully only in mortal sin, which contains both the *aversio* and the *conversio.* Venial sin, which is nothing more than a *conversio,* cannot be considered sin in the full sense of the term. But it is sin in an analogous sense, although it must be admitted that medieval theologians had difficulty explaining it.

When the claim is made that mortal sins have to do with the end of humanity, and venial sins with means to that end, it must not be inferred that the proximate object of mortal sin is God nor that it requires an explicit rejection of God. It should also not be concluded correspondingly that when the proximate object of the act is some creature or means to our last end, only venial sin is present. It is generally accepted that mortal sin can be present even though the explicit act deals with some creature or means to our last end, e.g., homicide, stealing, etc. Merkelbach offers as a reason for this the fact that some means are necessary to the last end, so that a deordination regarding these involves the last end. While no one disputes the general position that damage to or misuse of a creature can be mortally sinful, I am not sure whether this reason explains or complicates the question. But we will go into this issue more deeply later.

As I stated initially, the theological distinction of sins goes back to the New Testament itself, where it finds ample support. Theologians often made comparisons between sin and physical disease by way of argument. Just as not every disease is mortal or destructive of human life, so not every sin is destructive of the supernatural life. Comparison has also been made with human friendship. Not every offense terminates a friendship. It would seem reasonable on this basis to conclude that friendship with God is compatible with minor offenses.

Throughout its history the Church has defended the existence of venial sin and its distinction from mortal sin against specific attack. Against the Pelagians it asserted that even the just sin (DS 228-30). Pius v condemned the opinion of Baius that no sin is of its nature venial, but that all merit eternal punishment (DS 1920). Against the Protestant reformers the Council of Trent stated that not all sins take away justice, and that therefore there are venial sins (DS 1537). That the ordinary just can and do sin venially is established in the canon that even the just cannot avoid all venial sin without a special privilege (DS 1573).

The distinction of sins on the basis of subjective requirements, at least in recent times, has not been a matter of dispute. In the discipline of public penance in the early Church, very little was said about such requirements, and the emphasis was on the external act. A number of medieval theologians, including Thomas Aquinas, even thought that venial sin was present in the first movements of sensuality antecedent to any rational consent.[4] But in general for many centuries it has been agreed that even venial sin requires some consent, and that mortal sin demands adequate reflection and full consent of the will. If either is lacking, even though the matter may be serious, the sin is venial *ex imperfectione actus*. It may not always be easy to decide that an act is only venially sinful on this score, but at least the principle is undisputed. The question today revolves around the need for any further requirement, more specifically for serious matter, to commit a serious sin. In other words, can mortal and venial sins be distinguished not only by reason of the imperfection of the act but also by reason of matter?

For many centuries theologians have distinguished between sins that were always mortal, those that were generally mortal but might be venial by reason of the parvity of matter, and those that were always venial. These distinctions seemed to be clearly on the basis of matter, and it is this kind of distinction that is in question. Does the presence or absence of serious matter make the difference between mortal and venial sin?

The problem is this: Since all sins violate the divine order, which is what makes them sinful, why are not all sins against the divine charity, and hence mortal? Some who maintain that all sins are alike in this respect attribute the distinction to the divine decree. God had decreed that some sins rupture the divine friendship, while others do not. This was the position Baius took, and as we have already seen, the Church has condemned it. As we have also seen, theologians have accepted a distinction based on the matter of the sin. To them lesser violations do not involve a substantial violation of the divine order; hence they do not destroy or lessen our friendship with God. Some recent theologians, although they accept the theological distinction of sins, are not satisfied with the explanation that depends solely on the matter of the sin. To them this does not explain why a negative answer to God does not involve a complete perversion of the relation between Creator and creature. Comparison with human friendships does not help since the relationship is between Creator and creature.

One of the authors who espouses this approach is Josef Fuchs. In order to understand his position, it will be necessary to study his analysis of the moral act.[5] Fuchs sees in the perfectly human moral act a double dimension. There is a choice of a particular act as well as a disposition of the person. These are not two acts but two dimensions of one and the same act, the one explicit, the other implicit. Of these the second dimension is really the more important; this is what makes the person good. Some theologians have illustrated this dimension with the example of a mother and her child. The mother has a multiplicity of particular acts to perform in reference to the care of her child. Somewhere along the line, in one of these acts, she commits herself to the care of the child; she puts herself at the disposal of the child, and gives the child's needs precedence over her own comfort or convenience. Theoretically, her care for the child might remain on a superficial level of isolated acts unrelated to each other. But this is not the way it usually happens. She opts not only to perform individual acts but to put herself at the disposal of the child and this founds an habitual intention toward the care of the child which influences and directs future acts and decisions. Similarly in the moral life there occurs a commitment of self which grounds future moral choices. St. Thomas claims that the child makes this at the beginning of his moral life ... a commitment to God or self.[6] Put in more theological terms, the commitment to God is an act of fundamental charity ... love of God above all things. Since the love must be *effective* as well as *affective,* it calls for the exclusion at least of mortal sin. This will call for grace, since it is the teaching of the Church that mortal sin cannot be avoided for a long period of time without such grace.

So the perfectly moral act, according to these authors, contains a double dimension; the choice of a particular act and a free disposition of self. Sometimes the latter is referred to as a fundamental choice or option since it goes beyond the particular choice and represents a free disposition of self in regard to one's final end. This disposition of self can (and must) take place at the beginning of one's moral life, or it can be a repetition of such a choice, or it can be a change of this choice. If it is a change, it will be mortal sin, as will be seen. Not every moral act, however, will be perfect, or go this deep. There will be superficial or peripheral acts which for one reason or another will not involve a personal commitment. They may be morally good acts which will be seen in relation to one's last end, but they will not penetrate to one's basic commitment. They will not be perfectly human acts.

For a perfectly human moral act one needs the usual knowledge and consent. This refers not only to the particular act, but also to its implicit content, the disposition of the person in relation to his last end. But speculative knowledge will not suffice; a degree of realization, or what is called estimative knowledge, is needed. Fuchs admits that there are degrees of intensity and depth to this knowledge not only in reference to the particular act but also regarding the disposition of the person toward his or her last end. This knowledge and perception must, of course, be followed by full consent. The act will not be perfect if the knowledge and perception are deficient, e.g., if it is superficial (as in young people), or if the consent is not free.

Fuchs then relates all this to a distinction that some theologians have been making recently between grave and slight human acts. Traditionally, the distinction had been applied to mortal and venial sins. More recently, it is being applied to good acts, and these authors see in good acts the same theological distinction they see in sin. Good acts, just as sin, can be grave or slight. Fuchs asks whether the perfectly human act, as already described, can be considered a grave human act, i.e., whether it involves a disposition of ourselves in relation to our final end (*conversio* or *aversio*).[7] His response is that if it is an explicit act of love of God, it will be a grave human act as long as it fulfills all the requirements of the perfectly human act. But if it is a human act involving some other object, he says rightly that there is a difference of opinion. Some require besides a perfectly human act *grave* matter. In other words the fact that the act is perfectly human is not enough. His own opinion is that serious matter is not a requirement, although he concedes that generally if the matter is slight, the act will not be perfectly human, and therefore a slight act.

As we have already hinted, this opinion is relevant to the distinction between mortal and venial sin, and the whole question of the relation of venial sin to slight matter. To Fuchs whether charity is refused or not does not depend on the matter of the act but on the disposition of ourselves in relation to God. This disposition of ourselves is not formally an act of free will about this or that object, but an act of fundamental liberty in which we dispose of ourselves. So according to this approach, a negative moral act will be grave or mortal, if the opposition to God present in all sin penetrates to our commitment. If the opposition does not penetrate to this commitment, the sin is venial. Fuchs traces this inability of human beings always to dispose of themselves in particular acts to original sin. So in this opinion sin is grave if the act is perfectly human; it is slight if it is not perfectly human.

What this means, at least theoretically, is that grave matter is not a determining factor in grave sin; nor is slight matter a determining factor in slight sin. The determining factor is the presence or absence of a change in fundamental option. If there is no change in the option, even though sin would be present, it would not be mortal, but venial.

Briefly, then, it is the presence or absence of a change in the fundamental option that will determine whether a sin be mortal or venial. But this raises a further question: How do we determine whether such a change has been made? In other words, how do we determine in practice whether we have committed mortal or venial sin? There are two ways of making such a determination, depending on the circumstances. If we have had some experience, i.e., if we find ourselves regularly committing sin in a serious matter, we can conclude that we have made a fundamental option in the direction of sin. Habitual sin is hardly consistent with a fundamental option or commitment to Christ. Even though the particular sin might not, at least initially, constitute a change in the fundamental option, the frequent repetition could hardly occur without such a change. The frequency would clearly be a sign of a habitual orientation in the direction of sin. But what if we have no such experience, and there is question of a judgment of a particular act? Can we make a judgment in such circumstances? Fuchs argues that such a judgment can be made by having recourse to the matter of the sin itself. If the matter is serious or grave, the agents can at least make a presumption that their whole persons and orientation are involved. They will know that the choice or decision they are making go beyond the particular act and reflect a deeper level of their personalities. On the other hand, if the matter is slight, their deeper personality may not be engaged. They will sin, but they can presume that their sin will not alter their basic orientation. They may still be habitually committed to God as their goal. Even in the particular act, then, we can make a presumption about our option and hence about the gravity of the sin.

To some this may look like bringing matter in by the back door after throwing it out the front door. To Fuchs the difference between his position and the traditional position is that the matter of the act is not the determining factor in making the distinction, but only the sign. The determining factor is the disposition of the self, and the emphasis is on this. But the matter is still relevant. Even though the disposition of the self is not the same as the explicit act, it does occur in connection with this choice; it is only in making such a choice that the fundamental option is ordinarily changed. Theoretically, an explicit choice of God might be made that would involve an explicit disposition of the self, but usually it does not happen this way. So ordinarily a fundamental option is made or changed in a decision regarding some other act. Since this is true, even though the disposition goes beyond a particular choice, it is not independent of it. The more serious the matter of the choice, the more likely are the agents to be aware that their whole persons and the direction of their lives are involved. On the other hand, the less serious the matter is, the less likely are they to be aware of this phenomenon. So although the difference between mortal and venial sin is not determined by the seriousness of the matter, the latter is a sign that grounds a presumption regarding the nature of the sin. It is conceivable that people would not dispose of themselves in a particular choice where the matter was serious. It is also possible that they would dispose of themselves in a choice where the matter was slight, but the ordinary presumption will be that the presence of a disposition of self or a change in such a disposition will be related to the matter of the act. And this will be as true of a good act as of a bad act.

Fuchs considers this explanation of the difference between mortal and venial sin more probable than the one that sees it in the matter of the sin. To him it puts the difference where it should be: in refusing or not refusing charity to God. The seriousness of the matter is important as a sign but not as a determining factor. One may or may not agree with this position, but if it is properly understood, there seems to be nothing in it contrary to the official Church teaching. The Church has never given an official explanation of the reason underlying the distinction between mortal and venial sin. It has condemned only the opinion that it depends on the divine decree.

In summary, then, if an act is perfectly human, it includes besides its explicit content a disposition of ourselves. If the act is morally good, the disposition or commitment will be to God or our last end; if it is morally bad, the commitment will be to ourselves (or some created object) and will constitute mortal sin. If the act is not perfectly human, it may still be good or bad and sinful, but it will not engage our whole self, and the good or bad will be slight or venially sinful. The requirements for a perfectly human act, then, become all-important in determining whether an act will be gravely or slightly sinful.

It would be impossible in a paper of this length to go into all these requirements, but one of them perhaps should be singled out—the requirement that the knowledge of the morality of the act be evaluative. This is not the kind of speculative knowledge we can get from a catechism about the rightness or wrongness or seriousness of an act, but a personal grasp or realization of these aspects of a particular act. There are, of course, degrees of realization, but a certain minimum is necessary to call into play our commitment. This is particularly relevant to the role that the matter of the act might play in the distinction between mortal and venial sin. Even though the matter of some act may be grave or serious, it may not be perceived as serious, and hence may not evoke a fundamental commitment. It will be a slight moral act, and if it is evil, a venial sin.

The question of evaluative knowledge comes up often in connection with juvenile or adolescent masturbation. It is not easy, especially in our culture, for a youngster to grasp or appreciate the seriousness of this act. It was easier perhaps to do this in the days when this whole subject was surrounded with awe and fear. Many or most of these fears were false, and have since been dissipated, but as long as they prevailed, they generated an atmosphere of serious concern that no longer exists. We are certainly better off without false fears, but it must be admitted that without them it is more difficult, particularly for adolescents, to grasp the seriousness of this particular sin. We know that many in our culture conclude from the fact that these fears are no longer founded that there is nothing wrong with masturbation. Some would even want to consider it a legitimate stage in the sexual development of youngsters. I do not think we have to accept either of these conclusions, but I do feel that in the type of unconcerned atmosphere we live in today, it may be very difficult for adolescents to grasp the seriousness of masturbation.

The recent declaration of the Sacred Congregation on the Doctrine on faith explicitly recognizes many of the above problems but advises that they offer no reason to call into doubt traditional teaching about the morality of masturbation.[8] On the level of fault or sin, the declaration is opposed to any general presumption of the absence of serious responsibility. This would not do justice to the moral capacity of human beings. But it does recognize the fact that in sexual matters it more easily happens that free consent is not fully given, and it calls for caution in all judgement of responsibility in individual cases. In the case of adolescent masturbation, the immaturity of the individuals may well be a consideration. It may keep them from really perceiving the seriousness of the matter, and hence from placing a perfectly human act.

Even when we can conclude that only venial sin is present because of the immaturity of the adolescents in question, there is no reason for complacency. We cannot be satisfied with anything less than sexual maturity and chastity. The importance of sexual maturity hardly needs proof or argument. And the importance of chastity not only as the way to maturity but as a particular expression of our Christian commitment seems equally clear. Venial sin may be compatible with a good fundamental option, but a life committed to Christ is not a life of venial sin.

This brings us to the final question, the relation of venial sin to the fundamental option. As we have already seen, it will not involve a change in a good fundamental option. But it will certainly not strengthen it, and may well weaken it. It will not strengthen a good option because it cannot be directed to God. It may well weaken it because it represents a pursuit of creatures that may ultimately result in substituting some creature for our final end.

A good fundamental option and the resulting intention—an act of love of God above all things, and the continuing intention of this in our moral lives—are fostered first of all by acts which evoke and deepen this option (grave moral acts) and to a lesser degree by good moral acts which, even though they may not call this option into play, are still directed toward the last end of human beings. Even these acts protect a good fundamental option. The Christian life springs from a basic commitment to charity (founded on faith and hope) which, as it develops, expresses itself through the other virtues of prudence, justice, temperance, and fortitude. It is through these virtues that charity is actuated and expressed in the daily life of the Christian. Venial sin may be unavoidable, but it will not contribute to the Christian life. The serious Christian cannot be complacent about it.

Notes

1. *Summa Theologiae* 1-2, q. 88, a. 1
2. Ibid.
3. Ibid., 1-2, q. 88, a. 1, ad 1
4. Ibid., 1-2, q. 74, a. 3
5. Josef Fuchs, *Theologia moralis generalis, Pars altera* (Roma 1967/ 68), pp. 1-18
6. *Summa Theologiae* 1-2, q. 89, a. 6
7. Fuchs, pp. 137-57
8. *Declaration on Certain Questions Concerning Sexual Ethics,* 9-10 (Vatican City, 1975).

Freedom, the Human Person, and Human Action

Joseph Boyle, Jr.
St. Thomas College
St. Paul, Minnesota

Introduction

The title of this presentation indicates three large and complex areas of inquiry: freedom, human action, and the human person. Clearly it is impossible in this presentation to say all that must be said about these notions in order to give an adequate ethical or theological account of them. I will deal with these notions insofar as they are important for an understanding of the rich but opaque concept of moral responsibility and for an understanding of the nature of human agency.

Talk about human agency and moral responsibility leads very directly to thought about free choice and its role in human life. Indeed, for most Christians free choice is the locus of moral responsibility, and actions done by free choice provide the paradigm of human agency. Of course, there are many non-Christian thinkers who deny the reality of free choice and consequently assign meanings to the words *moral responsibility* and *human agency* that do not involve reference to free choice. It is perhaps more surprising—but not all that surprising—to find that Catholic theologians deny the seemingly obvious connections between free choice and moral responsibility and human agency. Such theologians do not deny that human beings are free moral agents. Instead, they *relocate* the source of moral responsibility. The moral responsibility of human beings is located in what they call *fundamental freedom* or *transcendental freedom,* an aspect of the self that is distinct from free choice. I think that this relocation effort is misguided; there is no theoretical justification for the effort. Moreover, if this relocation effort succeeds, the moral seriousness of Christian life will be undercut because serious sin will be excluded as a viable option, and voluntary behavior will have no determinable relationship to a person's moral self. By contrast, I will argue that the locus of moral responsibility is free choice. One might state a good deal of my view bluntly in the following terms: It is within the power of each of us to choose going to hell; no cosmic option and no metaphysical stance are required, but merely the choice to do or not do some more or less simple thing.

Freedom

One of the great advances achieved in recent philosophical work on freedom is the clear articulation of the fact that *freedom* has a number of distinct meanings.[1] Several of these meanings are very important for Christian moral life. The freedom of the children of God and the freedom from the bondage of sin, for example, are important realities effected by grace and central values in the Christian life.[2] In one sense of *freedom,* however, it does not refer to a value or a reality established by grace but rather to a fact about human nature, namely, to the fact that human beings can themselves determine the actions they do, the lives they live, and the kinds of person they are. That human beings are self-determining is not a judgment about what is good for human beings or about what they can or should become. Instead, it is a judgment about what human beings *are,* that is, about human nature. The truth of this judgment is not a practical truth about what is to be done, but a theoretical truth about human nature that is both explicitly and implicitly taught by revelation, and that can be established by philosophical reasoning.[3] The failure to distinguish the sense of *freedom* that refers to a fact about human nature from those senses of the word that designate values can obviously lead to considerable confusion.[4] I shall be concerned only with freedom of self-determination in this presentation. Although the judgment that human beings can freely determine themselves by their own agency is not a judgment whose truth is established by moral theology or moral philosophy, its truth is an essential presupposition of these disciplines, as indeed it is of the moral life itself as understood in the Christian tradition. It is because human beings are free agents that they are beings governed by moral norms. St. Thomas suggested this dependence of morality on humanity's free self-determination in the Prologue to the second part of the *Summa Theologiae:*

> Because, as Damascene says, man is said to be made in the image of God inasmuch as by "image" is meant one who has intellect, is free in choosing and through oneself able to act ... it remains for us to consider this image—namely, man—insofar as he is the principle of his acts as having free will and control of his acts.[5]

In a word St. Thomas said that because human beings are intelligent, free, and self-moving—because they are in this way images of God—their actions must be studied in the special way that characterizes moral theology. This presupposes that it is only because human beings are self-determining that human actions are within, as it were, the moral ball park. This is not to say that the human person establishes moral norms by self-determination; instead, the human person needs moral direction because he or she is self-determining and can determine himself well or ill. Thus the freedom of self-determination does not settle what is right and wrong, but it makes it possible and necessary for human beings to be guided by moral norms.

If people were not self-determining, moral norms would have no use. Unless it is within our power to live in accord with a moral norm, the norm is useless. If we are determined by factors other than our own free agency to live in accord with the norm, it no longer functions as a moral norm but as a prediction that states what a person will do, not what he or she *should* do.

Thus it is not the case, as is frequently assumed, that the connection between freedom of self-determination and morality lies only in the fact that self-determination is required if an agent is to be held accountable, responsible, or, in the case of bad acts, culpable for his or her behavior. Important as this connection is, it is a consequence of the fundamental connection between morality and self-determination, namely, that moral rules are primarily directives for a person's free self-determination. Moral life as understood in the Christian tradition would make no sense at all if human beings were not self-determining.[6]

The importance of the connection between self-determination and the moral life in the Judeo-Christian tradition is suggested by the fact that the affirmation of self-determination is a distinctive feature of Judeo-Christian anthropology. Virtually all believers affirm that humanity is self-determining, and virtually no one else does so. The ancient Greek philosophers did not deny self-determination, but they did not clearly affirm it. This affirmation was first clearly made in the Old Testament, and self-determination did not enter philosophical discussion until the era of the Fathers of the Church. Self-determination was taken for granted in medieval discussions and was explicitly denied only when the Judeo-Christian conception of reality was questioned and denied. The rejection of self-determination was first developed by philosophers like Spinoza and Hobbes. The case for the rejection of self-determination was carried forth by the intellectual heirs of these philosophers—Hume, the utilitarians, Hegel, Marx, Nietszsche; and so on. The denial of self-determination has been one of the foundational doctrines of modern secular humanism and, not surprisingly, it has been challeged only by those who wish to defend some form of Judeo-Christian orthodoxy.

Given the distinctively biblical character of the emphasis on self-determination, it is not surprising that this emphasis is absolutely foundational to the scriptural view of reality. As St. Thomas suggested, it is through human self-determination that human beings are in the image of God. God himself is to be understood as a free agent; nothing determines God but God himself. If it did, he would not be the first principle of all reality. Moreover, creation proceeds from God not because of any inherent necessity of God's nature—this would be emanationism. God freely creates. Likewise human beings must also be in some way self-determining if they are to be God's images. What is more, it is no accident that God has made us in his image. He loves us and desires a kind of fellowship and community with us. This community requires free self-determination on God's part and on the part of human beings. The covenant must be freely offered and freely accepted. Our cooperation with the redemptive work of Christ must be freely given. If freedom of self-determination is denied or even overlooked, God's revelation concerning the meaning of human life will be fundamentally distorted.

Many philosophers and theologians have identified free choice and freedom of self-determination. However, I have made no mention of free choice so far. This omission has been intentional. I believe that what I have called freedom of self-determination simply *is* free choice. But since proponents of the doctrine of fundamental freedom deny that human basic self-determination is effected by free choices, it is important not to *assume* at the outset what I intend to show, namely, that freedom of self-determination is simply free choice.

Free Choice

A person makes a choice when he or she selects one of a set of practical options, that is, a person chooses when faced with alternatives for action. We see that we could do this, or that we could do that—but not both, and consequently we select one or the other. A choice is free, in the relevant sense, when the person's own choosing determines which of the available options is selected. In other words all the factors determining the outcome of the act of choosing other than the agent's very choosing itself are not sufficient to determine the selection that is made. In short, a free choice occurs when a person might select this or that, and that person himself or herself determines which he or she will select.[7]

Understood in this way, free choice is an act of the will. The selection of one of a set of options is the person's determination to realize that option. Thus the preference involved in choosing is not a matter of finding or rating one option as more attractive than the others. Choice is not an approving or disapproving of an object or a projected course of action, but it is a person's commitment to *do* the act. Thus one's own doing is necessarily a part of what it is that one chooses.[8]

This brief account of free choice will be developed as we proceed. At this point it is necessary to turn from considerations about what free choice is to the question of whether human beings can make free choices. Modern nonbelievers answer this question with a resounding and often scornful no! The doctrine of determinism is a received truth in the contemporary secular orthodoxy. For believing Jews and Christians, and for Catholics in particular, however, there is no doubt that free choice is real.

The reality of free choice is explicitly affirmed in Scripture:

> He himself made man in the beginning, and then left him free to make his own decisions. If you wish, you can keep the commandments, to behave faithfully is within your power. He has set fire and water before you; put out your hand to whichever you prefer. Man has life and death before him; whichever a man like better will be given him (Si. 15:14-18).

The author of Sirach echoes Deuteronomy: "I set before you life or death, blessing or curse. Chose life... " (Dt. 30: 19). Moreover, the Church has solemnly defined that human beings can make free choices,[9] and the magisterium of the Church has affirmed the reality of free choice down through the centuries.[10] Moreover, what Scripture and the Church teach about free choice is consistent with common human experience: Most people have the experience of facing options, that is, the experience of situations where spontaneous action based on desire, habit, or the judgment that something is worth doing has been blocked by the fact that several things suggest themselves as worth doing. Most people are aware that, in some such situations, it is within their power to carry out either of the alternative courses of action that present themselves in deliberation, and that there is no experienced factor that determines them to do one or the other. Furthermore, many people would judge reflectively that, when one of the options was selected, it was they themselves, by their own choices, who selected the option. The array of arguments that seek to overturn this experience or to establish that it is necessarily illusory are very weak.[11] In fact, the affirmation of the deterministic conclusions of these arguments is necessarily self-defeating.[12]

Free choice, therefore, is the form of self-determination which revelation affirms, which common human experience reports, and which the antideterminist polemics of Christian apologists defend. Perhaps theological analysis will show that these affirmations, reports, and arguments do no more than "point the way to a deeper grasp of freedom."[13] Nevertheless, it is free choice that has been affirmed, and those who wish to locate self-determination elsewhere than in free choice must show why this move is necessary.

Since free choice is a kind of self-determination, and is the only kind that has been affirmed in the tradition, it is not surprising that it has been regarded as the locus of moral responsibility. St. Thomas was not atypical when he said, "It must be said that man has free choice; otherwise counsels, exhortations, precepts, prohibitions, rewards, and punishments would be in vain."[14]

The connection between free choice and moral responsibility can be stated as follows. First, if one is to be responsible for one's acts in the way Christian morality supposes, one must truly be the principle of these acts; this responsibility requires that one be the cause of one's act in a special way. Not all causal responsibility is moral responsibility; one is causally responsible for what one unknowingly brings about, but in many cases one is not morally responsible for such events. Likewise, the voluntary behavior of animals and small children, which is free in the sense of being uncoerced, is behavior for which they are causally but not morally responsible. Moral responsibility requires that the agent be a kind of unmoved mover—that the agent initiate the act by his or her own initiative. The possibility of hell shows that this type of initiative is required for moral responsibility. This punishment would not be appropriate unless the act that got one into this state were truly one's own. Free choice involves this kind of self-initiation; if a choice is free, then one determines oneself to act one way rather than another, and the causal factors outside of one's choosing are not sufficient to determine the choice. One truly does it oneself.

Second, morality is concerned with the orientation of human beings to what is good. Moral obligations are the requirements of human goodness; they are the demands of human flourishing or of human well-being or happiness.[15] Human beings are existentially related to what is good by acts of the will. When human beings recognize that something is good, they necessarily will it in some way. However, it is by making choices that people establish a definite relationship between themselves and what is good. Here it is not simply a matter of spontaneously loving what they see to be good, but a choice to realize some action that is seen to be good in preference to some other action that is also seen to be good. Such preferences establish a definite relationship between the human self and the goods, and it is in establishing this relationship that people constitute themselves as moral or immoral persons. In short, free choices are acts for which human persons are fully responsible and in which they determine themselves in morally relevant ways; it is in this sense that free choices are said to be the locus of moral responsibility. Proponents of fundamental freedom do not deny that one's self-initiation of acts and one's constituting of oneself in relationship to the good are essential for moral responsibility. What they deny is that these features of moral responsibility are ultimately based on free choices.

Before examining the reasons for the rejection of free choice as the locus of moral responsibility, it is necessary to consider briefly the relationship between free choice and human action, since this connection figures importantly in the discontent of the proponents of fundamental freedom.

A human action is not simply a piece of behavior ascribable to a human person. It is a voluntary act, that is, an act involving human reason and will.[16] The distinction between human

actions and human behavior that is not voluntary is marked in
the scholastic tradition by the distinction between human acts
and acts of humanity. The former are characterized by the role
of intellect and will; such acts are sometimes called "intentional" or "purposeful" (or "done on purpose") or "deliberate."
Acts of humanity are not voluntary; they include such things
as reflex actions and conditioned responses.

Human acts, then, are acts of which, as St. Thomas says,
human beings are the masters. Such acts are performed on the
basis of human knowledge and will. Human beings are masters
of their acts in the most proper sense when the acts are freely
chosen.

It is tempting to think that the relationship between one's
freely chosen acts and the act of free choice is merely a causal
or instrumental relationship; this supposition is mistaken. As I
noted above, what one chooses is to do something in such a way
that the action done, together with one's doing of it, constitutes
what one chooses.[17] Of course, it is not the case that one
chooses every human action that one performs. We do many
things without choosing to do them. Habitual patterns of behavior, for example, contain many human acts that are not
individually chosen. It is frequently the case that such patterns
of behavior are originally initiated by free choices, and it is
often the case that they should and could become matters for
deliberation and choice, so that these human acts almost always have some relationship to free choice.

It is also important to note that what one chooses is not each
and every known aspect of a physical act. One chooses to do
something insofar as one judges it to be good, and not everything that one recognizes to be part of a physical act or its
consequent effects is contained in what it is that one judges to
be good and is committed to realizing in action. There is much
in any free act that is *praeter intentionem agentis*.

One's human action and one's choice to perform that action

are essentially related: Actions are part of what one chooses. Moreover, one's choice constitutes part of the definition of the act as a human act. When St. Thomas asserted that moral acts receive their species according to what is intended,[18] part of what he meant is that human acts cannot be specified for purposes of moral evaluation, independently of what the agent in acting is committed to realizing. In morally significant acts, what one is committed to realizing is what one chooses, or is a line of action one chose to initiate, or is something one could and should have chosen to realize or not to realize. We can say therefore, without too much oversimplification, that human acts are defined as what human beings choose.

In more traditional language what I am saying is this: The object of an act or the *finis operis* of an act insofar as it is a human act is the person's doing of what the person in choosing committed himself or herself to realizing.

This tight connection between the choice and intention, on the one hand, and human actions, on the other, shows clearly that the relevance of choice and intention to moral evaluation is not simply as determinants of the imputability of human actions. Thus the simple picture that human acts as events in the world are the object of moral evaluation, and that intentions and choices are relevant only for determining the imputability of those acts, is mistaken. One's choices and intentions and one's actions insofar as they are chosen and intended are the primary object of moral evaluation because it is in them that a person establishes a relationship to the goods. "Subjective" questions about imputability concern whether or not a choice was free, or whether or not a person understood what was at stake in the choice he or she made, or whether or not a given action was chosen, or other such questions.

The distinction between what is often loosely called the "objective" and the "subjective" factors for determining respectively the morality of an act and the moral status of an agent is usually thought to be a distinction between what one evaluates by moral rules and what is required to determine the ascription or imputability of what is so evaluated to the one who did it. However, if one who is a Christian comes to believe that the objects to which moral norms apply are actions taken in abstraction from the choices or intentions they embody,[19] then one is stuck with an entire domain of morally relevant considerations which are not part of what objective morality bears on and which cannot be simply a part of the determination of an agent's imputability. A person's self-determination is plainly central in the Christian understanding of moral life, but it does not fall on this account into the category of objective moral evaluation—the objects in this category are actions regarded as events. Nor is self-determination relevant to morality only as part of the determination of whether an act is fully voluntary and imputable: A person's self-determination has a specific character; one can determine oneself one way or another. Thus it would seem that some moral norms must be brought to bear on it. If this self-determination must be part of "subjective morality," then subjective morality must contain a certain type of moral norm, but not the ordinary "objective" norms that apply to actions. Since the person's self-determination is what is central from the point of view of Christian living, the "subjective" norms that bear upon a person's self-determination are where the moral action really is. The objective norms become secondary.

The point is this: If actions are defined independently of choices, and if intentions are still regarded as objects for moral evaluation, the Christian moralist will have to construct another level of moral norms to guide one's self-determination insofar as it does not fall under the norms that guide actions. Thus we have a twofold system of moral evaluation and consequently of moral responsibility. Given the importance of self-determination, it is plain that the responsibility for one's actions will be downplayed. What's more, the responsibility at the level of actions is not—in this conception of action—related in any clear way to the moral domain: What do the merely "ontic" goods at stake in action have to do with a person's self-constitution in relation to human goods and God? This question is difficult to answer; and this difficulty may be some of what is behind the plea for a more person-oriented and a less action-oriented moral theology. If actions are mere events, then the charge that traditional moral is too act-oriented would be correct. It seems, however, that human actions are not mere pieces of behavior, but are defined by the choices or intentions that they embody. Of course, one might admit that actions are defined by choices and intentions, but still maintain that responsibility for actions is not the basic responsibility associated with self-determination. If self-determination is not free choice but something else, like the exercise of fundamental freedom, then our moral responsibility for our acts will be relegated to a secondary status.

Fundamental Freedom

Fundamental freedom is difficult to define in a precise way; it does not correspond to any experience—or at least not to any readily articulable experience. Moreover, the language used to describe it is often metaphorical. It will be helpful, therefore, to consider how some of its proponents describe it:

> Basic freedom, on the other hand [as contrasted with freedom of choice], denotes a still more fundamental, deeper-rooted freedom, not immediately accessible to psychological investigation. This is the freedom that enables us not only to decide freely on particular acts and aims, but also, by means of these to determine ourselves totally as persons and not merely in any particular area of behavior.[20]

But there is another dimension to freedom. It is not the freedom of choice to do a particular thing or not, a choice of specific objects. It is rather the free determination of oneself with regard to the totality of existence and its direction. It is a fundamental choice between love and selfishness, between self and God our destiny. This is often called by recent theologians the fundamental option, an act of fundamental liberty.[21]

According to this theory, man is structured in a series of concentric circles or various levels. On the deepest level of the individual, at the personal center, man's freedom decides, loves, commits itself in the fullest sense of these terms. On this level man constitutes self as lover or selfish sinner. This is the center of grave morality where man makes himself and his total existence good or evil.[22]

Several characteristic features of fundamental freedom emerge from these descriptions. First of all, it is exercised at the very core of the human person; thus it is the locus of self-determination, and hence of basic moral responsibility. Second, it does not have as its object any particular action or set of actions but rather its object is the entire self in its relationship to God. Third, the exercise of fundamental freedom is not an action in any normal sense of the word. Something like an option or preference is involved, but this preference is more like a stance or attitude than an act of choosing. Furthermore, there is no explicit awareness of a time when one took one's fundamental stance.[23] Both the second and third of these features imply that the exercise of fundamental freedom is not identical with free choice. This nonidentity is clearly affirmed by all the proponents of fundamental freedom. It is none too clear exactly what the relationship between free choice and the exercise of fundamental freedom is, [24] but it is clear that one can choose freely in a way inconsistent with the exercise of one's fundamental freedom without altering the fundamental stance established by this freedom.[25]

This account of fundamental freedom gives rise to the question of why so many contemporary moralists and theologians believe fundamental freedom to be a reality. Fundamental freedom is not part of experience in any ordinary sense; consequently, its affirmation is not based on experience. Moreover, there does not appear to be any philosophical argument that seeks to show the unavoidability of the affirmation of fundamental freedom.[26] What does seem to be the basis for the assertion of fundamental freedom is the conviction that free choice cannot adequately explain certain aspects of the Christian understanding of self-determination and moral responsibility. Free choice is believed to have several essential features that are inconsistent with essential features of self-determination as the *total* self-disposition of the person. Total self-disposition is said to be inconsistent with free choice in two ways. First, free choice is an object of human self-consciousness whereas one's total self-disposition cannot be objectified and must remain transcendental, that is, the knowledge of one's self-determination must remain unthematic and prereflexive. Second, free choice is limited in a variety of ways insofar as what is chosen is always in some way limited. By contrast, a person's total self-disposition must bear upon the whole of his or her existence in relation to God and thus cannot be limited in this way.

There are several considerations supporting each of these claims. The view that the total self-disposition of the human self cannot be an object for consciousness is based on the idea that an object is necessarily an object for a subject; if there is an object known, then there must be, distinct from the object known, a subject who knows. The argument is developed from this point by the observation that if a person's disposition were an object for consciousness, then it could not be *total,* for there would have to be a subject disposing itself toward this object. So total self-disposition cannot be objectified and must remain prereflexively and nonthematically grasped. Fuchs has stated this argument clearly:

> Conversely there can be no particular, categorical act of basic freedom—for a person can never grasp and engage the totality of himself categorically as an object. As soon as the self, as subject, grasps at the self as object, the subjective self that acts is no longer to be found within the self confronting it as object.[27]

Free choice, the argument continues, is an object of consciousness. It is the freedom we can experience and study psychologically. In short, total self-dispostion cannot be an object; free choice is an object. Therefore, free choice cannot be what disposes us totally.

A more properly theological consideration is adduced in support of this conclusion: Since free choices are objects of consciousness, they can be known with considerable certainty. Thus, if free choices were the basic locus of a person's self-determination, then one could know one's moral condition with considerable certainty, and therefore one could know with considerable certainty whether or not one was in the state of grace. The Council of Trent denied that human beings could have this certainty (DS 1534). If one's self-determination is at the transcendental level of fundamental freedom, no one such problem arises.[28]

I turn now to the second way in which free choice is said to have properties inconsistent with those of the total self-disposition of human beings, namely, the limitations of the former and the unlimited character of the latter. Free choices have certain particular acts or things as their objects; these objects are limited in a variety of ways. First, the object of choice is always a limitation in any act of selecting. One chooses to do one thing and thus leaves something else undone.[29] Second, the choices one makes are of objects spread over one's existence; they are choices of different things at different times. Thus there is no principle of unity in the various choices a person makes.[30] By contrast one's fundamental self-determination is not limited in these ways. It is not primarily directed toward particular actions and projects but rather toward one's total self as related to God. Furthermore, one's fundamental self-disposition organizes and structures one's life as a whole and constitutes oneself as a certain kind of person.[31]

This last point introduces another way in which one's self-determination is not limited as choices are. One's total self-disposition establishes a stable and enduring self whereas free choices are transitory. As O'Connell says:

> Thirdly, agents, by definition, are changeable beings. As actions change the doers of actions change. It follows from this, then, that agents are preeminently "do-ers," while persons are more clearly understood as *"be-ers."* Human beings, inasmuch as they are agents, exercise their existence through actions. But humans-as-person exercise their reality precisely by being.[32]

These arguments constitute the case for fundamental freedom as I understand it. I turn now to a criticism of these arguments that, in my view, are not successful. The point of my criticism is to show that free choice does not, in fact, lack the features required of the locus of human self-determination. It has most of the features that the proponents of fundamental freedom claim it lacks. The features it does lack are only disputably genuine properties of self-determination.

I will consider the arguments for fundamental freedom in

the order in which I presented them. First is the argument that free choice, because objective, cannot be total. To begin with, one might wonder exactly how total one's self-determination really is. Presumably one can determine oneself only with respect to what is somehow within one's power. It is by no means clear that the human self, as given subject of conscious experience and action, is among the things about which a person can determine himself or herself. Despite this difficulty, the argument does bring out one important fact: One's self-determination cannot be a datum of experience in the way that, say, feeling a pain is a datum of self-awareness; nor can one's self-determination be a proposition one affirms about oneself. Self-determination is some sort of action—something one does, and not something that is *given*. Thus the self-consciousness of one's determining oneself in those acts by which one does determine oneself is not like the self-consciousness that a person often has of pains or pleasures or memories. These things are often presented to consciousness as objects given in a way not all that different from the way experience of objects external to the self is given. The self-awareness of determining oneself is more like the unthematic awareness one has of one's act of knowing when one is knowing.

However, it is important to note that what is known unthematically in one intentional act can itself become thematically known as the object of another intentional act. One can form propositions about one's prereflexive awareness, thus making this prereflexive awareness to be an object of consciousness. Moreover, it is possible to form universal propositions about human consciousness, including the transcendental, prereflexive aspects of it. The writings of proponents of fundamental freedom contain many such propositions. These general propositions can refer to all acts of awareness, including the very acts by which these propositions are formed and asserted. Thus the range of propositions cannot be limited so as to exclude propositional knowledge of the transcendental self as known. Surely, this is a type of objective knowledge. The price of such a limitation would be very high since the very statement of the limitation would make reference to what the statement itself claims cannot be referred to. It is hard to see, therefore, why self-determination—even if "total" in some sense—cannot be the object of propositional knowledge. So it seems that one's self-determination need not be as unknowable as the proponents of fundamental freedom suppose.

This conclusion is completely consistent with the teaching of Trent on the awareness of one's justification (DS 1534). Trent stated that one cannot know with certitude that one is justified. This is logically consistent with a person's knowing with certainty that he or she is *not* in the state of grace. This logical possibility is important to consider since one's own free self determination is sufficient to exclude oneself from God's grace, whereas it is plainly not sufficient for having grace.

Furthermore, there are epistemic difficulties involved in knowing that on a particular occasion one has made a free choice. These difficulties are such that one cannot know with certainty that one has made a free choice. This is not to say that there are not situations in which a person has very good reason to believe that he or she has made a free choice.[33]

These difficulties are glossed over by the characterization of free choices as objects of consciousness accessible to psychological investigation. The person does not experience something *happening* that the person can identify as his or her choice. One does not encounter one's choices; one makes them. The experience is an experience of doing something, not of being given something. In this sense choice is not a *datum*.[34] In sum, free choice is not an object in the way it would have to be to be excluded as the act in which a person determines himself.

I turn now to the criticism of the argument that free choice is too limited to be the locus of self-determination. First of all, choice is limited by being a selection—one chooses to do one thing and not another—but this is not incompatible with its being an act that determines the self. One could not determine oneself at all unless there were some options and some selecting as is suggested by the fact that fundamental freedom also involves option between God and the self. So the limitation of choice cannot be the mere fact that it is a selecting—it must rather lie in what is selected. The objects of choice are acts, and these are said to be un-unified, not capable of constituting an abiding self and sometimes merely "peripheral," and springing "from a superficial level of the personality."[35]

This argument is based on a view of free choice that is altogether inadequate. As I pointed out above, free choice is the choice to do an action; what one chooses is to do something. Thus what one chooses includes both the action done and one's doing of it. This is part of the reason why free choice may properly be called *self*-determination: One determines oneself to be a person who does the action in question.[36]

Furthermore, not all the actions one chooses to do are discrete behavioral performances. People choose their careers, life-styles, and vocations. My choice to marry my wife, for example, was not simply a choice to say certain words to my wife long ago but to be a husband. The overarching commitment involved in this type of choice makes reference to a multitude of actions including further choices, and other acts of the will. Many of these are not foreseen in any clear way at the time of the basic commitment. Still such a commitment is a choice—one is determining oneself to do a number of more or less specified things.

In basic commitments of this type, moreover, the focus on the self is clear and explicit because of the very indeterminacy of the particular acts involved. In such choices one focuses primarily on the self one comes to be in making this or that commitment. The particular actions that will realize the goods on which one's commitment is based are part of what one chooses, but because one recognizes that the realization of these goods requires development and further choices, one focuses on the self one is committed to be.

Just as in these fundamental choices there is focus on self, there are many choices in which the focus is on the actions done. In cases where the action chosen is a particular performance or nonperformance, and where the choice is not a radical change in one's commitments, the focus will often be on the specific content chosen. Likewise, in sinful choices there is some motive for ignoring one's self-involvement in the bad act. Nevertheless, whether the focus in any given choice is upon the particular action or upon the self's constitution, both are involved in every choice. One chooses that one shall do some more or less specified thing. Thus the argument that free choice is limited to objects and to particular actions seems to be based on the mistaken supposition that the two aspects of what is chosen must be the objects of two distinct exercises of freedom—free choice for the action, and fundamental freedom for the self.

This discussion of overarching choices suggests that the choices in a person's life can fit into a kind of unified whole. Such commitments require that one make further choices as the commitment unfolds. To the extent that one is faithful to the overarching commitment, the more particular choices one makes will creatively develop a person's life in ways that will realize the goods that ground the fundamental choice. To the extent that a person integrates all of his or her personality—not just the choosing self but the person's desires, understanding and all the dimensions of the personality with the choosing self—one has an integrated life which, if it is based on upright choices, will be a virtuous life.

So far I have been emphasizing that there are choices that

can be a stable, integrating factor in a person's life because of their long-term, overarching character. But there is another way in which all choices have a nontransitory character. One chooses to do something because one sees that action as somehow good; in a choice one constitutes oneself with respect to the good or goods one chooses and toward other goods as well—indeed, in some way toward all the goods. While the action one chooses to do is in many cases transitory, the relation one constitutes toward the goods is not transitory. Unless or until one makes a contrary choice, one's relation to the goods established by the choice of the action remains. The nontransitory character of one's self-constitution follows from the fact that activity of the will is not a physical process. Free choice as an act of the will is a spiritual operation; the very fact that it is free demands that it be such.

To sum up, what is chosen in free choices is not only actions but the self's doing of the actions. Free choices are thus self-constituting, and this self-constitution is not transient in the way a physical act is. What's more, choices can organize and structure a person's life into a meaningful whole. Thus the fact that self-determination is in some ways a total disposition of the self is not inconsistent with self-determination's being established by free choices. Free choice is not limited in the ways this argument suggests.

Even at this point in the argument, however, we are likely to feel the force of the objection that some free choices are merely peripheral and spring from a superficial level of the personality. In a way the observation is correct and could be understood as a part of the pastoral wisdom of the Church. But the correctness of the observation does not require the abandonment of free choice as the locus of moral responsibility.

A free choice can be peripheral if what is chosen is light matter; it can also be peripheral if in some way the freedom or knowledge is seriously limited. One who sins through weakness *can* be making a free choice—and such sins can be formal mortal sins—but the imputability of the sin is often qualified, and it is often unclear exactly what one chose to do in such situations. To suppose, however, that peripheral choices must be contrasted with a person's true self-determination at the level of fundamental freedom is simply to assume what must be shown. It is question-begging to suppose that this phenomenon of peripheral choices must be explained by the twofold level of freedom.

To sum up the argument to this point, fundamental freedom is postulated because free choice is alleged to be incapable of explaining human self-determination. The arguments supporting this allegation have been found to be wanting, so there seems to be no warrant for affirming that there is such a thing. Occam's razor can be used to shave some very fuzzy theological beards.

In addition to the lack of any warrant for affirming the reality of fundamental freedom, the notion has consequences that are simply acceptable. I will mention just two of these.

One who accepts fundamental freedom posits two levels of moral responsibility: the responsibility one has for particular acts and choices, and the fundamental responsibility one has for one's self-determination at the level of fundamental freedom. It is obvious that it is the latter type of responsibility that really counts; that's where we make or break ourselves morally. The most obvious difficulty with this view of moral responsibility is that it downplays the person's responsibility for his or her freely chosen behavior: Thus one can freely choose to contracept, masturbate, abort, or whatever, and *still not necessarily* alter one's fundamental stance toward God. Other speakers have emphasized that God's revelation clearly excludes such acts as inconsistent with the love of God and neighbor. I simply want to add that the double-decker view of moral responsibility has the same type of difficulty that

plagues all dualisms: How does one get the two realities together? Are we to suppose that there are two selves? Or should
we say that there is only one source of true self-determination?
If we suppose that this source is fundamental freedom, then
what happens to the freedom—the self-initiation—of free
choices? Is this merely a participation in the freedom of the
fundamental self? If so, what about those choices that are contrary to one's fundamental option? This is a semantic morass.

The second unacceptable implication of the doctrine of fundamental freedom is that it makes mortal sin—a bad exercise
of fundamental freedom—to be an unintelligible possibility, an
option that is really no option at all because there is no good
that could move the will to opt for it.

Fundamental freedom is said to have for its object oneself in
relation to God.

The option is to say yes or no to God. What this option
amounts to is very unclear. In the first place yes and no are
primarily cognitive terms, and how one would determine oneself by saying yes or no independently of choosing to do something is very unclear. Perhaps we should take *yes* to mean *I
will serve* and *no* to mean *I will not serve,* but then we have
what looks like options for choices. It is worth noting that the
blessed who see God as he is, say *yes* to him in a very clear
sense. Seeing the infinite goodness of God, they cannot but love
him; with respect to loving God there is no free choice for the
saints. Their choices on earth and, in particular, the obedient
choice involved in the act of faith, determined them—insofar as
it was within their power—as servants and lovers of God. But
that choice to obey the revealing God with the assent of faith
seemed to be a choice. *I will serve* means that I choose to do
certain things.

In any case, the affirmative option—saying yes to God—is an
option that has an intelligible ground—the understood goodness of the human good of religion. What about the option

against God on the account of the proponents of fundamental freedom?

O'Connell has described this option as rooted in some perversity, as a rejection of one's opportunities for action and the possibilities of one's own being.[37] For Fuchs this option is a "withdrawal into oneself."[38] For McCormick it is an option for selfishness.[39]

The problem with these descriptions is that they provide no ground for the bad option. Why should anyone perversely reject one's possibilities, withdraw into oneself, or opt for selfishness? What in other words is the intelligible good involved in such options? Unless there is *some* such good, the option is irrational in a way inconsistent with the option's being in any way a rational human option. Of course, one could specify a certain real or apparent good that one might selfishly choose, but then one's option would be to pursue these goods. Such an option would seem to be a mere free choice.

If a fundamental option is not to be a free choice, and if it is to be a human act of some sort, then perhaps it should be looked at as simply a turning away from God—a formal rejection of God that is not specified by any other option. But then the question is why one should turn away from God. God is good; serving him is good. Surely the rejection of God or his service is not based on the goodness we can see in these options. Thus there must be something one regards as evil in the act of serving of God; of course, there is difficulty in serving God, and this might be grounds for refusing to serve Him. But if difficulty is token to an evil, the ease and comfort involved in a life without the difficulty must be regarded as good. To refuse to serve God because it's hard, is to turn away from God as a means to a life of ease; this kind of rejection is clearly a choice.

My point is this: If one's rejection of God is not a free choice based on some other mutable good then it is simply unintelligible; it cannot be a human act, but is the rejection of good as good or the embracing of evil as evil. As St. Thomas showed, one cannot choose evil as such; sin is both an aversion from God and a conversion toward a mutable good. Remove the conversion, and sin becomes unintelligible as a human act.

The Annunciation provided an example of a fundamental option that was in many ways typical of the fundamental commitments described in Scripture. Surely, Our Lady's *fiat* was the commitment that shaped her entire life. The act of obedience established what Mary was and always will be—the Mother of God. But equally obviously it was a choice; possibilities were presented, and spontaneous acceptance was blocked by difficulties—she was a committed virgin. As Pope John Paul II said, the angel's direction was:

> difficult to reconcile with the choice she had made "according to the Spirit."
>
> Then the angel explains: "The Holy Spirit will come upon you, and the power of the most high will cover you with its shadow" (Lk. 1,35). Mary still does not know how this will come about, but she does know one thing very clearly: that everything is bound to be consistent with her own choice made at the right moment according to the Spirit. So she says: "Behold the handmaid of the Lord; may it come about according to your word" (Lk. 1, 38)[40]

It was a mere choice to obey.

As always, Our Lady's example is instructive. The pastoral and theological difficulties surrounding the notion of moral responsibility are real. We theologians and philosophers have work to do in this area. But we must do it obediently in faith. This requires that we affirm the responsibility that human persons have for their freely chosen acts, and that we avoid theorizing that will undercut the moral seriousness of the Christian concern for the actions human beings freely do.

Notes

1. See Mortimer J. Adler, *The Idea of Freedom*, 2 vols. (Garden City, N.Y.: Doubleday, 1958, 1961); for a brief treatment, see Joseph M. Boyle Jr., Germain Grisez, and Olaf Tollefsen, *Free Choice: A Self-Referential Argument* (Notre Dame, Ind.: University of Notre Dame Press, 1976), pp. 8-10.

2. See Xavier Léon-Dufour, ed., *Dictionary of Biblical Theology*, 2nd ed. (New York: Desclée, 1973), "Liberation/Liberty," pp. 308-11; Ronald D. Lawler O.F.M. Cap. et al., eds., *The Teaching of Christ: A Catholic Catechism for Adults* (Huntington, Ind.: Our Sunday Visitor Press, 1976), pp. 291-92.

3. The evidence for these claims is cited below and in notes 4-12 where free choice is discussed.

4. This type of confusion plagues both philosophical and theological discussions of freedom. For example, many people believe that because persons are in a situation where they are not free to do as they please, they cannot make a free choice; in a theological context this confusion appears in the perplexity felt by many people over the fact that the act of faith involves a free choice to assent and is an act of obedience.

5. *Summa Theologiae* I-II, Prologue; the translation is mine.

6. The Church's condemnation of Michel du Bay, who was an early proponent of what is now called "soft determinism," are instructive here. Du Bay held that "what comes about voluntarily comes about freely even if it comes about necessarily." This necessity is obviously inconsistent with self-determination, though it is consistent with "freedom" in one of its senses. See D.S. 1939, 1941, 1966.

7. See *Free Choice*, pp. 11-12, for a more formal definition and an explication of some of the properties of free choice.

8. See *Free Choice*, pp. 13-23, for a fuller clarification of free choice; it is important to note that not everything that is called a *choice* in ordinary language is a free choice in the sense of "free" and "choice" used here. See Cardinal Karol Wojtyla, *The Acting Person*, trans. A. Potocki and ed. A. T. Tymieniecka (Dordrecht: Brill, 1979), pp. 149-51, for an account of the self-constitution involved in human action: "When we speak of 'performing an action' we see the person as the subject and the agent while the action itself appears as a consequence of the efficacy of the agent. This consequence is external with regard to the person, but it is also internal to, or immanent in, the person. . . . What was said previously about the dynamism of the will explains why actions which are the effect of the person's efficacy, namely those

actions "proceeding" from actual existing, have simultaneously the traits of outerness and innerness, of transitiveness and intransitiveness; for every action contains within itself an intentional orientation; each action is directed toward definite objects or sets of objects, and is aimed outward and beyond itself. On the other hand, because of self-determination, an action reaches and penetrates into the subject, into the ego, which is its primary and principal object."

9. Cf. Council of Trent, Session 6, January 13, 1547, *Decree on Justification*, ch 1, (DS 1521): " ... though free will *(librium arbitrum)* ... was no means extinguished in them" (the antecedent of *them* is the Jews and Gentiles).

10. A detailed list of magisterial pronouncements on free choice is found in K. Rahner, "Freedom, III. Theological," *Sacramentum Mundi*, 2. 361. Fr. Rahner comments: "In the documents of the magisterium, freedom is usually understood as man's psychological and moral freedom of choice in general, but with particular attention to matters of sin and justification where it is regarded as the ground of responsibility before God. The precise nature of this freedom is not described but presupposed as known. The documents stress, however, that freedom does not merely mean absence of external coercion, but also absence of inner compulsion."

11. For a short critical discussion of these arguments, see *Free Choice*, pp. 48-103.

12. For a detailed argument that determinism is self-defeating, see *Free Choice*, pp. 139-85.

13. Karl Rahner S.J., "Freedom, III Theological."

14. *Summa Theologiae* I, q. 83, a 1.

15. Although the Christian moral tradition is nonconsequentialist in its approach to moral thinking, this tradition is with few exceptions teleological. Aquinas is perhaps the best example. His discussion of moral theology begins with a consideration of the end of human life, and it is this end that ultimately establishes moral norms. This emphasis is founded in Scripture: The Commandments are the rules for a full human life; the work of the Christian is to contribute to the *pleroma*—the fullness of all things in Christ.

16. See *Summa Theologiae* I-II, q. 1, a 1; q. 6 aa. 1,2.

17. I refrain from calling "what one chooses" the formal object of choice because the formal object of choosing involves reference to the preference of one means over another. See *De Veritate* q. 22, a. 13, ad 16. The object chosen—as distinct from the object of the act of choice—is more like the formal object of the act of intention, which does not involve the disjunctive object of choice but rather a good that

one is committed to realizing. The difference between choice and intention is not important for our present purposes except that it is possible to intend an act that one did not choose. For the relationship between choice and intention in Aquinas see my "Aquinas on *Praeter Intentionem*," *The Thomist* 42 (1978): 650-57.

18. See *Summa Theologiae* II-II q 64, a.7; I-II, q 72, a.1; q 109, a 2 ad 2.

19. Timothy E. O'Connell, *Principles for a Catholic Morality* (New York: Seabury, 1978), pp. 79, 169-171, holds a position close to this; he denies that intentions or motives are part of the objective evaluation of acts, but allows that what he calls the "purpose of the action" is part of the objective evaluation of the act. But apparently the *finis operis* of the act is in no way defined by reference to the agent's will. Motive in this sense is simply one of the circumstances of the act to be evaluated by consequentialist considerations. Agents' intentions or motives are for O'Connell not a part of objective morality. Consequently he objects to the traditional principle of the three fonts of morality and to the double-effect principle. These principles, he claims, confuse the objective and the subjective side of morality. Of course, these objections come to nothing if O'Connell's distinction between subjective and objective is mistaken. Likewise, it is not entirely clear what O'Connell means by subjective morality; it is "central to the actual pursuit of Christian life" and is outside of the domain where objective, consequentialist considerations apply. Moreover, this area seems to be one where some moral evaluation is needed; it's not simply a matter of determing the imputability of the act to the agent.

20. Josef Fuchs S.J., *Human Values and Christian Morality* (Dublin: Gill, 1970), p. 93.

21. See Richard A. McCormick S.J., "The Moral Theology of Vatican II" in *The Future of Ethics and Moral Theology* (Chicago, Argus, 1968), p. 12.

22. John W. Glaser S.J., "Transition between Grace and Sin: Fresh Perspectives," *Theological Studies* 29 (1968): 261-62. There are many other accounts that differ only in detail. Karl Rahner's is perhaps the most influential. See especially, "Theology of Freedom," in *Theological Investigations,* vol. 6 (London and New York: Herder and Herder, 1969), pp. 178-196. A critical survey of much of this literature is found in Theodore Hall O.P., "That Mysterious Fundamental Option," *Homiletic and Pastoral Review* 78 (1978): 12-20, 29-32, 44-50. Fr. Hall's analysis is one of the few critical discussions of fundamental freedom of which I am aware.

23. See Rahner, p. 202.

24. For McCormick, one's acts can share in the orientation of one's fundamental option but they need not; for O'Connell, pp. 63-64, fundamental freedom is an informing principle that unifies one's choices and acts. He also speaks as if acts are signs of one's fundamental option. Fuchs speaks as if free choices are means used by one's fundamental freedom.

25. See Glaser, pp. 263-65.

26. Given the background of the doctrine of transcendental freedom in German idealism, it would not be surprising if there is a transcendental deduction of it. I have not seen such an argument and sum up in what follows what might be the elements of such an argument. The affinities of fundamental freedom with German idealism are clear. The distinction between fundamental freedom and free choice is reminiscent of the Kantian distinction between phenomenal and noumenal reality. Schopenhauer uses this Kantian distinction to articulate a doctrine of transcendental freedom, which is stated in terms very similar to those used by Catholic moralists in stating the doctrine of fundamental freedom. See Vernon J. Bourke, *The Will in Western Thought* (Garden City, N.Y.: Doubleday, 1966), p. 93.

27. Fuchs, p. 99; see also O'Connell, p. 62.

28. See Rahner, pp. 191-92; Fuchs, p. 105.

29. See O'Connell, p. 62.

30. See Rahner, p. 184.

31. Ibid; see also McCormick, p. 15, Fuchs, p. 100.

32. O'Connell, p. 60.

33. See *Free Choice,* pp. 175-76.

34. This paragraph is adapted from *Free Choice,* p. 20.

35. Fuchs, p. 99; see also Glaser p. 265.

36. See Wojtyla in note 8 above, for a clear exposition of this point.

37. O'Connell, p. 62.

38. Fuchs, p. 95.

39. McCormick, p. 12.

40. Cardinal Karol Wojtyla, *Sign of Contradiction* (New York, 1979), p. 38.

Part Four
Moral Methodology

Loyalty to God

Frederick S. Carney
Southern Methodist University
Dallas Texas

I appreciate more than I can express in words the invitation
to participate in this workshop on the principles of Catholic
moral life. Many of you have better credentials on this subject
than I have, and much more experience with the everyday
workings of Catholic morality. So I shall understand this invitation to be part of the spirit of the times, so beautifully
expressed by Pope John XXIII and so impressively supported by
each of his successors, in which Catholics and Protestants are
asked to participate in each others' forums. Even so, I wish to
tell you of my profound respect for the rich tradition of Catholic
moral reflection as I have come to know it, and to acknowledge
how greatly I have been personally benefited by the writings of
Catholic moral theologians from the apostolic age to the present. The list of particular Catholic authors to whom I am
intellectually and practically indebted is far too long to mention. Nevertheless I do want to acknowledge the many gifts
and graces I have encountered during extended periods of
residence with the Jesuits at Georgetown University in Washington and with the Benedictine monks at St. John's Abbey
in Minnesota, and also to indicate to you the sense of ex-
citement and satisfaction I have experienced during almost
fifteen years of teaching Thomas Aquinas to Methodist semi-

nary students in Dallas, Texas. Although I am not a Catholic, I have been greatly fed and nourished by your distinguished moral tradition, and have often found myself very thankful for it.

When Professor May invited me to contribute to this workshop on the topic printed in your programs ("Fidelity to God, not Calculation"), I had some reservations about its wording. So he kindly agreed that I could modify the topic somewhat. Although there are clearly times when one wants to say "loyalty or fidelity to God, not calculation," it is not always the case in Catholic morality, as I shall attempt to demonstrate later, that calculation is inconsistent with loyalty to God. Indeed, in some instances calculation would seem to be required by loyalty to God. This is especially so if the word *calculation* is used as a shorthand expression, as it often is, for a wide range of teleological procedures in obligation theory. If, then, the relation of calculation to loyalty is neither one of necessary disjunction (as pure deontologists might hold) nor one of necessary conjunction (as pure teleologists might contend), the exact relation between them needs to be investigated. Thus I shall take it as my task to explore this relation in Catholic moral thought. And because loyalty to God is the superior principle of the two—since there are no instances of moral action when we should not be loyal to God while there are instances when we should forgo calculation—the new title of this address is simply "Loyalty to God." In the first part I shall examine the concept of loyalty to God, in the second the relation of calculation, and more generally of teleological procedures, to such loyalty, and in the third the bearing of this analysis on what has been called *conflict situations* in several recent writings in Catholic moral theology.

I

It is a striking fact that very little attention has been given in the historic literature of Catholic morality to the term *loy-*

alty to God or to its near cognates. References abound in this literature to such moral terms as love, justice, faith, hope, good, evil, righteousness, wickedness, humility, truthfulness, and a number of other such expressions of moral duty, virtue, and value. But loyalty, either to God or to human beings, is not a common expression in Scripture. Nor is it very often to be found as a basic term in the major ethical writings of the early, medieval, or modern church. Nevertheless, the concept of loyalty is there all the time, and has performed a major role in the moral life and thought of the church. For it is imbedded in the notion of faith, not as the entire scope of faith, but as one essential component of it. Thus someone who is not loyal to God is understood to be seriously lacking faith in him.

The faith of which I am speaking is, of course, New Testament faith, not the exclusively cognitive notion of it sometimes employed, for example, by St. Thomas Aquinas, who wrote that faith is "the act of intellect when it asserts to divine truth under the influence of will moved by God through grace."[1] Of course, New Testament faith includes a truth component. But it is also much more than cognitive. This can be explained by first identifying generic faith, or the faith that is an aspect of all human experience, and then clarifying New Testament faith by means of it. Faith generically is a response to objects of trust and/or commitment. In its complete form it involves both the passive movement of confidence or trust in valued objects and the active movement of loyalty or commitment to such objects. These objects can be things, persons, or states of affairs. Thus we can have faith generically, for example, in gold or airplanes, in a loved one or a leader, in physical fitness or political freedom. Such objects of faith call us forth into life. If we are not responding to something, we are, as it were, "not living" or "dying on the vine." In this sense everyone either faiths or dies.

These objects of trust and loyalty can be conceived as gods, as

H. R. Niebuhr points out, and faith in them thus understood as one or another form of theistic faith.[2] For what is a god other than that in which our hearts place their trust and/or that to which we offer ourselves up in loyalty? If there is a plurality of objects in which we faith with no ultimate order among them, the form of our theistic faith is polytheism, or the worship of several gods. If there is a single object of our faithing activity whose relevance is affirmed for only a particular group of persons, such as a nation or a class, the theistic form is henotheism, or tribal religion. It is only when there is just one ultimate object of trust and commitment, although without the denial of lesser and subservient loyalties, and this ultimate object is understood to be relevant to all persons and experiences, that the theistic form is monotheism.

The theistic form of New Testament faith is a monotheism oriented not only to the god of Abraham, Isaac, and Jacob, but also and more decisively to the god revealed in and through Jesus Christ. This god, whom we understand to be the author of our creation, redemption, and spiritual guidance, is the one whom we are called to trust above all other objects of trust and to whom we are called to be loyal above all other objects of loyalty.

Thus far I have been speaking of faith in this god more or less as one might speak of faith in any other god, that is, generically. But New Testament faith also involves the assent of the mind that the god it proclaims is the *true* God, not one god among many gods, nor one understanding of God among many understandings of God, but the One who *rightfully* claims our ultimate trust and loyalty, and indeed the trust and loyalty of all persons everywhere. It is in this sense and for this reason that St. Thomas Aquinas was undoubtedly right when he wrote of faith as involving the assent of the intellect to divine truth. This cognitive element of faith is also what St. Augustine had in mind when he wrote that "the first and chief function of faith is to give men belief in the true God."[3] Without New Testament faith's cognitive element of truth, in addition to its fiducial elements of trust and loyalty, it is hard to see why we should choose its God rather than some other god or gods as the ultimate object of our responses and the shaper of our moral experiences. This is to say, it deeply matters whether we live the truth or a lie, whether our trust and loyalty are ultimately offered up to the true God or to idols, whether we properly perceive the fullness of the reality we encounter or allow ourselves to be self-deceived about this reality and the consequent shape our lives should take in response to it. For this reason, loyalty to God as faith's active movement of commitment, together with trust in God as faith's passive movement, depend upon a true understanding of this God as known through faith's cognitive component.

Moreover, to know this God is to know his causes, and to be loyal to this God is to be loyal to his causes. For there can be no loyalty to God that is not also a loyalty to what he wills for his world, a loyalty to what he is doing for and through his world. This is the starting point of Christian morality. From it all else derives.

Thus there can be only a limited sense in which the concepts of love and justice can be rightly considered in Christian morality as independent principles, that is, principles separated out from this context of loyalty to God, indeed from the even fuller dimensions of faith in God. This limited sense of love and justice as independent principles is one in which we can disengage the core content of these principles from its larger context, can point to the implications of this core content for moral dispositions and behavior, and can acknowledge that these principles, so far as their core content is concerned, can be a part of ethical systems other than Christian. Nevertheless, for the Christian, acting as Christian, a disposition or act of love or justice toward the neighbor is also a disposition or act of loyalty to God, and thus of loyalty to his causes in and through the world. For such a Christian, loyalty to God is not merely a motive for the act or disposition of love or justice defined independently of such loyalty but is also a constituent feature of the act or disposition. For example, visiting the neighbor in need is not only a loving response to the neighbor, but also a loyal response to God. And the disposition to treat persons with fairness is also a disposition of loyalty to God. There is more taking place in such acts and dispositions than can be expressed by independent notions of love or justice.

Another reason why Christians should be somewhat cautious of treating love and justice as independent moral principles is that there are variant meanings of these terms in our secular culture, and when love and justice are divorced from their context of loyalty to God, their core content can be defined in ways not appropriate to what is meant by them in Christian morality. It is all too easy to interchange one of these secular meanings of love or justice for Christian love or justice, and not to realize that something of importance may be lost in the process. For example, John Stuart Mill proposed to identify Christian love with utilitarianism,[4] an identification that badly distorts the meaning of Christian love, though this has not prevented some moral theologians, such as Joseph Fletcher, from enthusiastically adopting and recommending it.[5] As another example, William Frankena, who cautions students of philosophy about accepting the equation of Christian love with utilitarianism, nevertheless proposes that "the clearest and most plausible view" is to identify love with the philosophical principle of beneficence, that is, of doing good.[6] This is an improvement over the utilitarian interpretation of Christian love, but it has its problems also. I suggested in a recent, and basically appreciative, essay on Frankena's ethics that the beneficent translation somewhat misconstrues the substantive content of Christian love because it does not conceive such love against its proper background in faith and hope, and because it does not grasp the sense in which this love is, for the Christian, a response to grace in which the loving response is partly structured by the nature of God's graceful activity in and through his world.[7]

Now this God and his causes, together with our loyalty to this God and his causes, bring into existence a moral relationship, or more precisely a covenant, between God and us, and between our neighbors and us. This covenant is not only the bond morally uniting us with God and our neighbors but also the litmus test as to whether or to what degree popular and philosophical notions of love and justice are properly expressive of Christian morality. For this covenant has certain discriminate features that are determinative of Christian morality, features that can help us to decide the meaning of love and justice, and the extent to which Christian love and justice, so far as they are obligation notions, are to be understood teleologically in Christian morality as distinguished from the extent to which they are more properly therein to be interpreted deontologically. I shall discuss this issue at some length in the second part of this essay, where I examine the role of calculation in loyalty to God.

Such loyalty, however, orients and determines not only the obligation element of our moral lives but also the virtue and value elements. These three elements (obligation, virtue, and value) jointly constitute the full range of our moral accountability, although some writers and epochs have neglected or deemphasized one or another of them. The obligation element of Christian morality focuses upon the principles and rules of human acts, and responds to the question "What morally ought to be done?" The virtue element emphasizes moral ideals about human personhood or character, and responds to the question "What qualities or dispositions of a person, for which the person can be held accountable, are commendable or reprehensible?" The value element pertains to the moral assessment of objects or states of affairs, and responds to the questions "What objects or states of affairs are good or bad?" and "In what sense and to what degree are particular objects or states of affairs good or bad?" The distinction among these moral elements can also be observed by inquiring what it would mean to default regarding each of them, and what psychological state is appropriate to each of them. If one defaults on an obligation, one violates or transgresses a norm or standard, the fitting psychological response to which is a sense of guilt. If one defaults regarding what is genuinely held to be virtuous, one falls short of one's ideal, places a bad mark on one's character or uncovers one's moral nakedness, and one would ordinarily respond with the feeling of shame. If one defaults in the selection of one's values or in one's loyalty to one's values, one is disoriented or self-deceived, the appropriate response to which is probably remorse.

All three of these elements have been heavily involved in the rich tradition of Catholic morality, and each can be seen as making its special contribution to loyalty to God. Nevertheless, in early eastern Christianity (the Christianity of the Alexandrian theologians and the Cappadocian fathers, among others) the emphasis is largely on virtue theory, with some attention to value theory, and an almost total neglect of obligation theory. St. Athanasius, for example, interpreted the Christian moral life not as an obedience to commandments nor a fidelity to moral law, but as, what he called, a "journey to virtue," and set before his readers the life of St. Antony as the ideal exemplification of this journey.[8] This same theme was picked up by St. Gregory of Nyssa, who employed the image of a "journey of virtue" in commending the life of Moses as the Christian moral ideal.[9] St. Athanasius provided further insight into his virtue-predominant interpretation of Christian morality in the following quotation:

> We must further bear in mind that if we do not give
> up these things [material goods] for virtue's sake,
> later we must leave them behind and often, too, as
> Ecclesiastes reminds us, even to persons to whom we
> do not wish to leave them. Then why not give them
> up for virtue's sake so that we may inherit a king-
> dom besides? Therefore, let none of us have even the
> desire to possess riches. For what does it avail us to
> possess what we cannot take with us? Why not
> rather possess those things which we can take along
> with us—prudence, justice, temperance, fortitude,
> understanding, charity, love of the poor, faith in
> Christ, meekness, hospitality?[10]

Evagrius Ponticus, who is closely related in outlook and temp-
erament to the Cappadocians, even went so far as to say that
after a certain stage in life obligations are no longer of much
importance.

> A man who has established the Christian virtues in
> himself and is entirely permeated with them no
> longer remembers the law or commandments. . . .
> Rather he says and does what excellent habit
> suggests.[11]

In early western Christianity, however, under the influence
of such theologians as Tertullian, St. Cyprian, St. Ambrose,
and above all St. Augustine, obligation notions achieved a new
importance and joined virtue and value notions as component
elements of loyalty to God. In this regard Old Testament ideas
of divinely given law and commandments were taken more
seriously than in the East, and the Pauline and Ciceronian
notion of natural or moral law written in human hearts and
discernible by human reason began its long and important development in the Christian morality of the West. The precise
combinations that are possible in joining virtue, value, and
obligation notions are numerous, depending upon the exact

meaning and function given by an author to each of these moral elements and upon whether an author's interests center largely around human dispositions (as with St. Augustine) or around human acts (as with St. Thomas Aquinas). In fact, a wide variety of combinations was articulated by different western theologians from the early through the medieval and Reformation periods.

In the modern world, however, the emphasis has definitely switched away from one or another combination in which all three elements played important roles to an obligation-dominant interpretation of Christian morality. In the process, virtue theory came to be neglected, or at least minimized, and value theory took on a different role under the banner of obligations from what it had in the virtue-centered theory of early eastern Christianity and in the various tripartite theories of western Christianity throughout most of its history. This development in moral theology rather closely paralleled a development in secular moral philosophy. I am referring to the rise at approximately the same time of both Kantianism and utilitarianism, these two mutually antagonistic systems of moral obligation that together, until recently, had all but conquered the moral sensibilities of the modern western world, the one system deontological (deriving the good from the right) and the other teleological (deriving the right from the good), and each system relegating to virtue, when it discussed it at all, the extremely limited role of nurturing such human dispositions as would enable persons to perform more dependably what obligation is understood to require.

Recently, however, dissatisfaction has been growing among some moral theologians with obligation-dominant theories of Christian ethics, and new attempts are being made by them to recover the role of virtue in the interpretation and practice of the Christian life. The efforts of such ethicists as James Gustafson, Stanley Hauerwas, and Enda McDonagh are promising in this regard.[12] Not much attention has yet been paid, however, to the revitalization of the notion of value and to its role in moral theology. This also needs to be done. For all three elements of moral accountability—virtue, value, and obligation—are properly to be understood as elements of the Christian's loyalty to God, and the conjoining of them in such a manner as to acknowledge an important role for each makes for a richer understanding of such loyalty.

What are the grounds of loyalty to God? Why should we be loyal to him? The primary answer is that loyalty to God represents the truth about our existence. We were created for loyalty to him. He has established the terms of reference for our lives, and invites us to be loyal to these terms as expressive of our loyalty to him. Not to do so is to deceive ourselves about who we fundamentally are. In this sense the failure to know and to orient our lives around these terms of reference—what covenant loyalty requires—is self-deception. So the primary answer to the question why we should be loyal to God is that we should live the truth, not a lie.

There may also be secondary reasons for such loyalty. One such reason is gratitude, the expression of thankfulness to a benefactor for benefits received in the past. Another is self-interest, the expression of desire that the benefactor will provide benefits in the future. Gratitude is backward-looking, while self-interest is forward-looking. But both pertain to benefits, which may be interpreted either as extrinsic or intrinsic to the loyalty offered. If extrinsic, the loyalty is a means to an end, namely, the benefits that lie outside and beyond the loyalty and are considered a reward for the loyalty. If intrinsic, the loyalty is not a means to some benefits external to it, but is its own reward, namely, that of becoming a person of loyalty through being loyal. If one believes benefits, either past or present, to be a necessary or desirable motive for being loyal to God, it is morally less risky to emphasize intrinsic rather than extrinsic benefits.

Nevertheless, there are problems with making either of

these secondary reasons for loyalty to God into the primary one, with the substitution of either gratitude or self-interest for the primary reason, that is, that loyalty to God represents the truth of our existence, enabling us to live the truth rather than a lie. If gratitude is made primary, then loyalty to God becomes a means of being grateful. And gratitude takes over as the highest principle of Christian morality in the place of loyalty to God. If self-interest is made primary, then loyalty to God becomes a means to the advancement of the self. And a form of egoism or, if enlightened by emphasizing intrinsic rather than extrinsic benefits, a form of eudaemonism becomes the highest principle of Christian morality in place of loyalty to God.

It would be an unnecessarily severe ethic that proposed to remove altogether any reference to benefits from the reasons for being loyal to God, either in gratitude regarding past benefits or in self-interest regarding future benefits. And Christian morality does not, I believe, require it. All that is needed is that there be a sufficient reason for being loyal to God that is not benefit-oriented, and that this reason actually be the primary reason for loyalty to God. Granted this, the other reasons may also be employed without doing violence to the Christian ethic or harm to the Christian soul.

It is interesting to note that an analysis very similar to this, but with some variations, is set forth by St. Bernard of Clairvaux on the reason why we should love God. If we change love for God in the following passage by St. Bernard to loyalty to God, we have an interpretation that has much in common with the preceding argument.

> You wish me to tell you why . . . God should be loved? My answer is that God himself is the reason why he is to be loved. . . . There are two reasons why God should be loved for his own sake: no one can be loved more righteously and no one can be loved with greater benefit. Indeed, when it is asked why God

should be loved, there are two meanings possible to the question. For it can be questioned which is rather the question: whether for what merit of his or for what advantage to us is God to be loved. My answer to both questions is assuredly the same, for I can see no other reason for loving him than himself.[13]

In summary, the major points that have been made in this discussion of the concept of loyalty to God are the following: (1) Such loyalty is a component of Christian faith, and more precisely its active fiducial component which, together with the passive fiducial component of trust and the cognitive component of truth, constitute the whole of such faith; (2) loyalty to God involves a loyalty to his causes, to what he is doing in and through his world, and only in a limited and often misinterpreted sense a commitment to independent principles of love and justice; (3) this loyalty pertains to our entire moral existence—to the values we hold, to the person we aspire to be, and to the obligations incumbent upon us; (4) the primary reason for being loyal to God is that doing so best expresses the truth rather than a falsehood about our existence, and that gratitude and self-interest may also be reasons, though secondary, for such loyalty.

II

What then is calculation? And how does it properly relate to loyalty to God in Christian morality? Calculation is a term that is employed both in a restricted sense and in an extended sense. In its restricted sense calculation involves quantification. Persons employing it in ethics first assign numerical quantities, both positive and negative, to various goods and evils, or to desirable and undesirable outcomes of human action. They must also calculate the probabilities that the relevant outcomes would actually result from this or that action, and build these probabilities into their matrices. They then assess that action to be morally right that can ordinarily be expected to bring about, all relevant outcomes included, the highest total of positive quantities or the lowest total of negative quantities. This was actually the method recommended by the utilitarian philosopher Jeremy Bentham, who thought we should use pleasure and pain as the measure of good and evil, and assign numerical values to pleasures and pains according to such indices as their intensity, duration, probability, proximity, fecundity, and purity.[14]

Such a quantifying method, even when divorced from a hedonistic interpretation of goods and evils, does not seem to be what most persons have in mind today when they speak of calculation in ethics. Rather they tend to emphasize qualitative rather than quantitative assessments of good and evil outcomes of human action, and thus employ the more extended sense of calculation in ethics. This is what St. Augustine had in mind when he wrote that we should prefer eternal or spiritual goods to temporal or worldly goods, although he did not call the assessment of human acts based on such a preference by the name of calculation. This qualitative choice of goods in human acts is also fundamental to the famous treatise on human ends in the *Summa Theologiae* of St. Thomas Aquinas, although St. Thomas likewise did not identify this choice as one of calculation. Nevertheless, the term is achieving an increasing vogue today among Catholic moral theologians. Father Richard McCormick, for example, although he objects to what he calls "a simple utilitarian calculus,"[15] indicates that it is nevertheless a calculus he has in mind at the heart of his own method in moral theology.[16] This method is a teleology of obligation. That is to say, it is a method that begins with a prior determination of what things or states of affairs are good or evil, and makes a determination of the moral rightness or wrongness of human acts on the basis of the extent to which such acts advance or serve these goods and evils. And most Catholic moral theologians who speak of calculation, whether with favor or disfavor, seem to assign approximately the same meaning to it.[17] Thus by calculation I shall henceforth intend a qualitative teleology of obligation.

Now it is a thesis of this essay that calculation, in the sense just indicated, is a necessary but far from sufficient expression of what is morally required by loyalty to God. Thus, I contend, calculation cannot be the entire subject matter of Christian morality, and indeed is actually corruptive of Christian morality when it is employed to preempt moral roles that are properly to be performed by other moral methods. An obvious area of its insufficiency is that neither calculation nor any other obligation method, nor even all obligation methods combined, is capable of doing justice to our accountability to God in the moral realms of virtue and value. But I shall not pursue that insufficiency here, turning rather to another of its limitations. This is its inability to be an adequate moral expression of loyalty to God even within the realm of moral obligation alone. For there are aspects of our loyalty to God that can only be given expression by noncalculation considerations that are more properly to be considered deontological. Thus I shall argue that loyalty to God requires an understanding of moral obligation that is partly deontological and partly teleological. A mixed theory of obligation in Christian morality is therefore indicated.

There is, I think, not much need to argue the case for some calculation in Christian morality. So I can be brief. The case is essentially that to be loyal to God is to be loyal to his causes, and to be loyal to his causes is, among other things, to help our neighbors in need when we are able to do so and when the manner of doing so does not violate some other and preemptive duty. For example, we are called by loyalty to God to calculate what distribution of our charitable contributions will provide the most help to those in need and to follow through with the conclusions of our calculation, provided that we have not stolen the money with which we are proposing to help our neighbors nor previously promised the money as repayment of a debt nor made some other commitment for its use. Likewise in our use of force in the defense of others against aggression, we need to calculate the proportionate good and evil of attacking alternate legitimate targets so that we do not do more harm thereby than would be done by the evil we are attempting to restrain, provided of course that we were initially justified in taking up arms against the aggressors and that we are not violating some other and preemptive moral obligation in the target we attack in the defense of others. Further examples are readily available but these should suffice to indicate that there are circumstances in which calculation is not only morally permissible but also morally required by loyalty to God and to his causes in and through the world.*

The noncalculation obligations of loyalty to God are less obvious to some persons, including a number of rather prominent Catholic moral theologians. I will therefore give more attention to their explication. There would seem to be essentially three arguments for such noncalculation or deontological aspects of moral obligation: the conceptual argument, the historical argument, and the practical argument. The conceptual argument holds that there are some duties that are constitutive

---

Editor's note. The need for calculation *within* the framework provided by loyalty to God, of which Professor Carney speaks here, is clearly recognized by Catholic moral theologians who oppose the movement within Catholic thought that seeks to determine the rightness or wrongness of acts in terms of their consequences. For an analysis similar to that of Professor Carney regarding legitimate use of calculation, see Germain G. Grisez, "Against Consequentialism," *American Journal of Jurisprudence* 23 (1978): 21-72, at 49-50. W. E. May

of our relation in trust and loyalty with God. Their right-making qualities are not dependent upon their outcomes, but upon the very nature of the acts themselves. They are part of what it means to be involved in a fiduciary relation with God, and by extension a fiduciary relation with his people. If he and they and we are jointly participants in a covenant relationship, it behooves us to know what are the membership terms, as it were, of this covenant and to abide by these terms in the course of serving our neighbor in need, of promoting good in the world, or of doing whatever it is that calculation calls us to do.

These membership terms, or deontological duties, are ordinarily the prior obligations incumbent upon us before we set about our teleological activities. What are these membership terms or covenant duties? Obviously one of them is truthfulness. Another is promise-keeping. Still another is respect for persons, that is, refraining from violations of the life, body, or property of others. They can be given a teleological interpretation, and even defended in large part on teleological grounds. But to do so is to miss their essential nature. It is to treat them as morally important only in terms of their outcomes rather than to consider them as human acts that are morally important in themselves, whatever their outcomes, in that they are expressive of the covenant binding human being to human being in trust and loyalty, indeed expressive of the covenant binding humanity to God.

The historical argument for noncalculation or deontological components of moral obligation is that they constitute an irreducible part of the rich tradition of Catholic morality. Consider, for example, truthfulness. Catholic literature most of its centuries, including writings of the major theologians, is quite clear that lying is wrong whatever the consequences, and that the reason it is wrong does not depend on calculation but on the very nature of the act itself.[18] By way of illustration, I call attention to the positions of three major theologians on the wrongfulness of lying. The first is a passage from St. Clement of Alexandria.

> Being then persuaded that God is always present everywhere, and being ashamed not to tell the truth, and knowing that ... even a lie is unworthy of himself, ... he [the Christian] neither lies nor does anything contrary to his agreements, ... nor denies what he has done, being resolute to be clear of lying, even though he should die under torture.[19]

That certainly is a strong defense of truthfulness that does not rely on calculation for its justification.

The second illustration is provided by St. Augustine. He wrote in many places throughout his works against lying, and devoted two treatises entirely to this issue.[20] His basic position was that to lie is intentionally to tell a falsehood, or intentionally to tell the truth believing it to be a falsehood, and that the act of lying is wrong, whatever the consequences, because God in his Scriptures has always disapproved of lies. Nevertheless, St. Augustine believed that some lies, though morally wrong, are less blameworthy than others, especially lies told with a benevolent motive. Lies were classified by St. Augustine along a scale of more to less blameworthiness, depending upon the ends they were designed to serve. But at no point in his writings did he justify lies. For him, the wrongness of lies was absolute, as contrasted with their relative blameworthiness. In this more basic sense lies are nonscalar. Their intended ends, other than intending to lie or not to lie, do not count.

St. Thomas Aquinas, who provides the third illustration, was also rather emphatic about the negative moral status of lies, although not primarily on the ground of revelation, as with St. Augustine, but of reason. He held that there are three components ordinarily present in lies, the telling of a falsehood, the intention that a falsehood be told, and the intention to deceive others by means of the falsehood. He further believed that it was the second of these two components that makes the falsehood into a lie, and that "every lie is sinful," whatever the outcomes.[21]

The historical argument I am making here is not one of claiming from tradition that all lies are always wrong, although St. Clement of Alexandria, St. Augustine, and St. Thomas Aquinas apparently believed they are. Rather it is that major theologians of the rich Catholic moral tradition have employed deontological, and not merely teleological, analyses of the rightness and wrongness of acts. Furthermore, even if there are valid arguments that a lie in very rare circumstances may be morally justifiable in Christian morality, it is not clear that such arguments need be teleological. Indeed, they could well involve the moral priority of one deontological norm over another.

The practical argument for recognizing limits in the employment of calculation or teleological methods in Christian morality pertains to the very great difficulty we often experience in knowing what the future outcomes of particular acts will actually be, and therefore in making moral decisions exclusively on the basis of our assessment of the goods and/or evils in expected outcomes. Surely the very great difficulties, indeed gross errors, being made today by our best economists in making accurate predictions about the near future in the American economy should give us pause about any method that relies exclusively on calculation. If highly placed economists, with the most advanced computers available, with elaborate economic models of the American society, and with large staffs to assist them are so often wrong in their calculations, how can we expect the average Christian, or even the best of moral theologians, to be right in his or her expectations of the effects of an act?

Furthermore, human attempts to influence the future in

order to promote good and mitigate evil often go awry, and produce outcomes far worse than would occur under deontological procedures. Stuart Hampshire wrote very movingly a few years ago of this unintended effect of calculation, supposedly for good ends, in the Vietnam War in an essay entitled "Morality and Pessimism." He observed that the:

> implicit optimism [involved in teleology] has been lost, not so much because of philosophical arguments but perhaps because of the hideous face of political events. Persecutions, massacres, and wars have been coolly justified by calculations of long-range benefit to mankind; and political pragmatists in the advanced countries, using cost-benefit analyses prepared for them by gifted professors, continue to burn and destroy. The utilitarian habit of mind has brought with it a new abstract cruelty in politics, a dull, destructive political righteousness: mechanical, quantitative thinking, leaden academic minds setting out their moral calculations in leaden abstract prose, and more civilized and more superstitious people alike destroyed because of enlightened calculations that have been proved wrong.[22]

I am not, however, suggesting that teleologically oriented morality always has this kind of outcomes, only that it sometimes does. And when it does, it is worth asking the question "By what alternative moral method should we live before God and in transactions with our neighbors?" We can at least faithfully try to meet those obligations that are constitutive of our covenant relationship with God and our neighbors. We can tell them the truth, fulfill our promises, and respect their lives and property. In this practical sense also deontological considerations have a bearing and validity that stand over against calculation as teleological considerations.

III

In the final section of this essay I wish to discuss briefly what is to be done in loyalty to God in what some Catholic ethicists call *conflict situations,* especially when an aspect of the conflict is a disagreement between teleological and deontological analyses. One proposal is to use a weighting or balancing procedure in such conflicts, with alternative courses of action compared in terms of their teleologically determined weights or overall goods and evils, and with moral preference to be given to the course of action that is proportionately better. This procedure is actually one of calculation. When it is used to adjudicate conflicts between teleologically constrained courses of possible action, there would seem to be no harm in its employment. Indeed, it is the appropriate method to employ when only the principle of proportion is relevant. But when deontological issues are involved, either solely or in combination with teleological ones, then it would seem to be quite inappropriate. For it is to use calculation or teleology to adjudicate nonteleological issues or conflicts between teleology and deontology. Yet some Catholic writers, for example, Richard McCormick, seem to think there is no other way of adjudicating such conflict situations.[23]

But surely they are wrong on this point. For a lexical ordering of obligation principles or rules can also be employed in such situations. A lexical ordering is one in which the full requirements of one principle or rule are to be met before moving on to a second one. Indeed, such a lexical resolution of conflicts is ordinarily much more appropriate to instances in which deontological aspects of loyalty to God are involved than any kind of calculation. This is because if we adequately understand the constituent features of covenant loyalty, we know that they are not to be compromised, except perhaps in very rare instances, in the process of promoting good and mitigating evil. But in suggesting the appropriateness of lexical ordering in conflict situations involving both deontological and teleological considerations, I am not so much attempting to impose a lexical imperialism, although I obviously prefer such a method, as to resist an imperialism of calculation, proportionate good, or whatever a purely teleological method is called.

Another procedure has been advanced by Albert Di Ianni.[24] This is one in which all right actions are called teleological ones and justified in terms of their contribution to the promotion of good, but in which a distinction is made between dignity values and welfare values. Dignity values cover the territory ordinarily assigned to deontological considerations, and are ordinarily given preference over welfare values, which are the usual concerns of calculation. This is an intriguing proposal, for it seems to provide a means of reconciling conflicts between deontological and teleological expressions of loyalty to God by making the entire matrix of obligation teleological. But the cash value of this proposed procedure is to leave the issues just about where they were, though with a different vocabulary. There is, however, a significant break in it with more customary teleological procedures in that it adopts a lexical ordering of dignity values (the usual deontological considerations) over welfare values.

Still again we can resolve the conflict between deontological and teleological considerations in loyalty to God by redefining human acts in such a way that we do not know whether they are lies, promise-breakings, stealings, etc., until we first know whether they are teleologically justified. McCormick, for example, asks whether for St. Thomas Aquinas "every falsehood is necessarily a lie?"[25] The answer, of course, is no. Only an intended falsehood is a lie. But McCormick would seem to go a step further and suggest that an intended falsehood is not a lie if it is teleologically justified. It would be a strange moral universe indeed if he could get away with that bit of verbal legislation!

In summary, my argument with some expressions of Catholic morality today is that they have taken a rich moral tradition with great breadth and depth and subtlety and complexity, and reduced it to a very restricted moral theory. My argument is for letting our moral thinking be as broad and comprehensive as the great tradition of Catholic morality truly is.

Notes

1. *Summa Theologiae*, 2a, 2ae, Q. 2, a. 9.
2. This entire analysis of generic faith and of types of theistic faith is extensively indebted to H. R. Niebuhr, *Radical Monotheism and Western Culture* (New York: Harper and Brothers, 1943).
3. Augustine, *City of God*, 20. 2.
4. John Stuart Mill, *Utilitarianism,* Library of Liberal Arts (New York: Bobbs-Merrill Co., 1957) chap. 2, pp. 22 and 28.
5. Joseph Fletcher, *Situation Ethics* (Philadelphia: Westminster Press, 1966).
6. William Frankena, *Ethics,* 2nd Ed. (Englewood Cliffs, N.J.: Prentice-Hall, 1973), pp. 56-59.
7. Frederick S. Carney, "On Frankena and Religious Ethics," *Journal of Religious Ethics* 3, no. 1 (1975): 18-22.
8. Athanasius, *The Life of St. Antony,* Ancient Christian Writers (Westminster, Md.: Newman, 1950), sec. 3, p. 20.
9. Gregory of Nyssa, *The Life of Moses,* Classics of Western Spirituality (New York: Paulist Press, 1978), sec. 290, pp. 128-29.
10. Athanasius, sec. 17, p. 35.
11. *Praktikos,* chap. 70 in Cistercian Studies Series *Praktikos and Chapters on Prayer* (Kalamazoo, Mich.: Cistercian Publications, 1972), p. 35.
12. See also my essay "The Virtue-Obligation Controversy," *Journal of Religious Ethics* (Fall 1973): 5-19.
13. Bernard of Clairvaux, *On Loving God* in *The Works of Bernard of Clairvaux,* vol. 5 (Washington, D.C.: Cistercian Publications, 1973), sec. 1, p. 93.
14. Jeremy Bentham, *An Introduction to the Principles of Morals and Legislation,* in *A Fragment on Government and an Introduction to the Principles of Morals and Legislation* (Oxford: Basil Blackwell, 1960), chap. 4, pp. 151-63.
15. Richard McCormick, *Ambiguity in Moral Choice* (Milwaukee: Marquette University Theology Department, 1973), p. 97.

16. Ibid., pp. 60, 61, 62, 67, 85.

17. It is notable that Protestant moral theologians do not much use the term except when addressing themselves to recent developments in Catholic moral theology.

18. St. John Chrysostom's *On the Priesthood,* chap. 3 contains one of the very few exceptions to this judgment of which I am aware, asserting as it does an argument for deceit under a special set of circumstances. (Crestwood, N.Y.: St. Vladimir's Seminary Press, 1977), pp. 47-51.

19. Clement of Alexandria *Stromateis* 7 in *Alexandrian Christianity,* edited by Henry Chadwick (Philadelphia: Westminster Press, 1954), chap. 8, p. 126.

20. Augustine *On Lying* in *The Nicene and Post-Nicene Fathers: St. Augustine,* vol. 3 (Grand Rapids: Wm. B. Eerdmans Publishing Company, 1974), pp. 457-77; *To Consentius: Against Lying* in the same volume, pp. 481-500.

21. *Summa Theologiae* 2a, 2ae, Q. 110, aa. 1 and 3.

22. Stuart Hampshire *New York Review: A Special Supplement,* 25 January 1973, p. 26.

23. Richard McCormick *Ambiguity in Moral Choice,* p. 76; and again in "Notes on Moral Theology: 1978," *Theological Studies* 4, no. 1 (March 1979): 73.

24. Albert Di Ianni, "The Direct/Indirect Distinction in Morals," *Thomist* 4, no. 3 (July 1977): 350-80.

25. McCormick, "Notes on Moral Theology: 1978," p. 75.

Christian Moral Theology and Consequentialism

Germain G. Grisez
Mt. St. Mary's Seminary
Emmitsburg, Maryland

In his theological reflections, St. Augustine sharply distinguished between the disposition of an upright will toward God and its disposition toward everything else. God alone is to be enjoyed; everything else is to be used. The one thing necessary for human fulfillment is union with God in the beatific vision; every thing else is only a means to this.

Augustine's theology can be criticized, but it ought not to be oversimplified. Augustine's universe is not godless. Creatures are creatures of God; this world is a stage on which the drama of redemption takes place; and at least some human acts have a sacramental significance. Hence, Augustine's view that everything but God is to be used did not have all the negative implications one might expect it should have had for created goods and human life in this world.

However, in the modern western world, many people imbued with Augustinian ways of thinking have lost their faith. God is removed, and only utensils remain. This situation, of course, is absurd. However, an apparent order will be restored and life will find a new meaning if something within the remaining reality is elected to fill the role formerly played by God. Quite naturally, something human seems most appropriate. So secular humanism is produced.

No matter what each form of secular humanism takes to be the proper object of enjoyment, it takes everything else to be a mere means. In Augustine, various relationships to God preserved the dignity of persons; somehow the goods of the human person could ground moral absolutes in matters such as killing the innocent, adultery, lying, and so on. In any secular humanism, there are no absolutes in such matters. No good of the human person is sacred if its destruction is required to attain the one thing necessary.

For example, the British utilitarians treated preferred states of human consciousness as the only self-validating value. In this theory moral norms that are generally valid must yield in situations where their violation is required to promote the enjoyment or lessen the misery of most people. Too bad if one is in the minority. Even worse if one is a nonperson.

Secular humanists, whether they accept a utilitarian theory of enjoyment or whether they hold a different view, uniformly consider many received Christian moral norms to be arbitrary, irrational constraints on life. Pressed to argue against those who still hold traditional views, humanists have uniformly rejected such constraints as obstacles to the fullest attainment of whatever is taken to be the self-validating value. And when Christians and others object that a secular humanist program will destroy or damage certain goods of human persons, the answer is that even if certain goods are lost, greater goods will be achieved. As Lenin said, "One cannot make an omelet without breaking eggs." Similarly, individual liberty and the reduction of public welfare costs are considered greater goods than the lives of the unborn. But the weighing is facilitated by arbitrarily declaring the unborn nonpersons.

Here we see the historical source of consequentialism. Bad trees sometimes by accident bear a good fruit, and so the origin of consequentialism does not prove it to be a bad method of moral judgment. However, as we shall see, there is no fortunate accident in the present case.

For any consequentialist, the morality of at least certain choices is settled by their effects. If one is able to adopt a proposal that promises only good consequences, one has no problem. In such cases no choice is necessary. Choice becomes necessary when there are diverse proposals that promise more or less appealing good effects, but each of which also involves at least the bad effect of forgoing what the alternative proposal promises. To tell whether a choice is right or wrong, one must look at the effects of the choice. The consequentialist says one ought to choose the proposal that seems most likely to maximize good effects and minimize bad effects.

Some might object that arguments of this form can be found in the writings of people of all times and places. Even many Christian writers seem to argue at times that a choice that would otherwise be wrong ought to be made because of the bad consequences of choosing otherwise. To some extent I will dissolve this objection later in this paper by distinguishing between consequentialist reasoning and other reasoning easily confused with it.

But to some extent the point is sound. People of all times and places sometimes do offer consequentialist justifications for some of their choices. But if, as I am convinced, this form of argument is faulty, its widespread use must be regarded much as we regard the widespread use of an invalid form of the syllogism. It is one thing to use an argument of a faulty type. It is quite another thing to articulate and systematically employ a faulty form of reasoning. It is systematic consequentialism that is a modern, western, and initially secular humanist development.

When a form of reasoning has been articulated and is being criticized, the fact that arguments of this form have been used in an unsystematic way by honest and well-intentioned persons is very weak evidence in favor of the validity of the form of reasoning under examination. Therefore, even if contemporary theologians who adopt consequentialism find some genuine examples of consequentialist reasoning in the writings of saints and the teachings of the Church, this does not show the method to be valid. The whole point of critical reflection is to make less likely mistakes that are quite likely without such reflection.

Thinkers who agree in being consequentialists differ on many closely related points. For example, some urge that consequentialism can be used to determine the morality of every choice, while others wish to restrict the use of consequentialism. It might be restricted to cases in which some other accepted norm or set of norms fails to yield a definite result or leads to perplexity. It might be limited to the choices by which one adopts one's life-style as a whole, or the rules of society, or something else that will serve as a standard for subsequent choices. Some wish to limit consequentialism whenever it is used by requiring that tests of fairness or of piety be met by proposals before they are allowed to become options for choice governed by consequentialism. Consequentialists also differ in their views about whose interests are to be taken into account when good and bad effects are appraised.

Consequentialists, to the extent that they are such, consider ethics an art of living. Moral goodness becomes a technical-esthetic quality of human acts, a quality they have insofar as they are effective means to whatever is taken to be the end. In other words, the good or goods that are the ends transcend moral goodness. Whether the end is enjoyment, freedom, public welfare, or something else, the end is a self-validating good, while moral goodness is important because of its effectiveness in promoting the end. To mark the distinction between moral good and evil and the goodness and badness of terminal values and disvalues, the latter are sometimes called "nonmoral," "premoral," "ontic," or "basic human" values and disvalues.

Philosophers and others who attack consequentialism often begin by proposing examples which they think the particular theory they are confronting will have trouble in handling. For instance: What if the happiness of all the rest of humankind could be secured by subjecting one innocent person to endless torment? This procedure is not usually very effective, for a consequentialist always can argue that his or her theory can deal with the example, either in accord with existing moral norms ("People could not really be happy on that basis") or by revising them into a more rational scheme ("If it truly were possible, it would be right"). At best, working with examples leads a consequentialist to restrict the scope of the application of the method ("Consequentialism only applies to a choice among options that do not involve injustice to anyone").

There are many philosophical arguments against consequentialism. In appraising good and bad consequences of proposed choices, whose interests are to be considered? To what extent must one try to think up other possible courses of action? How far must consequences be investigated? How is the weighing of the various values and disvalues to be done? Cogent answers to none of these questions have been forthcoming, although the questions have been around for a long time. Still, many consequentialists cling to their faith in the method. They hope that someone will find solutions to all these difficulties.[1]

If consequentialism were put forth as a mystery of faith, this dogmatic attitude would be understandable. The odd thing is that consequentialism claims to be knowledge.

To see what is essentially wrong with consequentialism, one need not worry about whether it is limited in one or another way. In any case there is no consequentialism unless some judgments as to what choice one ought to make are held to be properly grounded upon the comparison of the good and bad effects of choosing one or another alternative. (A consequentialist can allow that other conditions also must be satisfied for right choice.) Just insofar as consequentialism applies in reaching the judgment, the alternative promising greater good (or lesser evil) should be judged morally right.

The most central trouble with this attempted theory, it seems to me, is that it requires two incompatible conditions to be fulfilled simultaneously. First, the choice to be made must be between alternatives that really are morally significant. Second, the person about to make the choice must have reached a definite conclusion, by consequentialist weighing, as to which alternative promises the greater good (or less evil).

The first condition—that the alternatives really be morally significant—entails that the one choosing be able to choose the morally evil possibility. There is no moral significance in a choice between right and wrong proposals unless one is in danger of making the wrong choice. By itself, this first condition poses no problem. However, the second condition—that the one about to choose has reached a definite conclusion as to which alternative is preferable in consequentialist terms—requires a knowledge that would preclude a wrong choice.

Why is this so? Because nothing is chosen except insofar as it seems good. If one alternative is seen to promise definitely greater good or lesser evil, the other hardly could be deliberately chosen. What reason or motive could there be to choose the lesser good or the greater evil? In a consequentialist's view of things: None. For in this view, the premoral goodness of the outcome determines the moral rightness of the choice that is a means to it, and the method excludes any other intelligible factor that might tempt a rational agent to choose wrongly.

In recent publications I have extensively articulated the preceding argument. Therefore, although this argument is central, I offer here no more than this brief sketch of it.[2] The point is that if one knew *in the way consequentialism requires* what one ought (on its account of "ought") to choose, one could not choose otherwise.

If the argument against consequentialism just summarized is sound, then consequentialism is *not* a false theory. A theory that requires that two incompatible conditions be met is not false, but absurd. It is literally meaningless. It is like telling someone to prove a point, but to be careful not to try to prove any but the most obvious point.

Richard A. McCormick S.J., in arguing for consequentialism, nearly perceived its inherent inconsistency:

> ... the rule of Christian reason, if we are governed by the *ordo bonorum,* is to choose the lesser evil. This general statement is, it would seem, beyond debate; for the only alternative is that in conflict situations we should choose the greater evil, which is patently absurd.[3]

McCormick is speaking of a theoretical alternative, while consequentialism is concerned with the practical alternative. But the two levels are isomorphic in the respects that are relevant, and had McCormick realized this, he would have seen that if a consequentialist judgment were possible, choice against it also would be absurd.

Incidentally, the answer to McCormick's argument is that in any morally significance choice, there are at least some aspects of good and evil that cannot be measured by any available standard. So one is not reduced, as he mistakenly supposes, to having to choose between the lesser *measurable* evil and the greater *measurable* evil.

Someone who accepts consequentialism will object that if consequentialism is meaningless, then it is hard to see how expressions such as the *greater good* can be used meaningfully, as they undoubtedly are, in many judgments bearing upon action. For these legitimate uses also involve some sort of measuring of values.

For example, the Church characterizes one individual as holier than most others when it canonizes a saint. A judgment is made that someone has died in heroic sanctity, and this judgment leads to the act of canonization.

The answer to this objection is that, while the Church appraises holiness in making this judgment, it does not weigh the premoral good and premoral bad consequences of various options open to it. Rather, assuming the Lord Jesus as a standard, the Church judges the lives of those it canonizes to be so like his that they can be proposed as models for us. A morally specified standard is applied to moral data to reach a moral appraisal. Something similar is done when the law applies an accepted rule of justice to a crime or controversy to reach a just judgment on a case. The scales of justice weigh, but not in terms of premoral goods and bads.

Nor is this the only way in which we talk meaningfully of the *greater good* when we make judgments bearing upon actions. Often when we have decided what to do, technical questions remain about how to do it. If various approaches are possible, and if they do not seem to differ in any morally significant way, the alternatives can be appraised in terms of efficiency. For example, a Christian trying to meet a neighbor's need will calculate with care how best to meet this need. That approach is adopted which meets the need at a minimal cost.

Consequentialists often seem to be confusing such technical reasoning with the moral reflection required to reach a judgment of conscience. But the two sorts of practical reasoning differ, since technicians ignore moral issues or proceed only after they have been resolved. The technicians draw their practical conclusion as a nonmoral normative judgment from nonmoral goods and bads, namely, the costs of each alternative approach. Only if technical experts are muddled and irresponsible enough to exceed the bounds of their competence do they try to draw ethically and politically significant judgments by a method of cost-benefit analysis that necessarily leaves out of account nonmeasurable and intangible factors.

The preceding examples of some nonconsequentialist uses of the *greater good* and similar expressions in practical judgments make clear that when people articulate reasons for acting, they will often use language that sounds consequentialist. Moreover, in our secular humanist culture, even morally upright people are likely to talk like consequentialists when they defend judgments made on moral principle. A husband, for example, might repulse another woman's offer out of faithfulness to his wife, but in spurning the offer, he may plea a concern about the potential bad consequences by saying, "Of course, I find you attractive. But no, we all might wind up getting badly hurt." Such a reply is better form in our society than "I reject your sinful suggestion."

The various uses of language that sound consequentialist, but actually are not, lend consequentialism the specious appearance of a meaningful theory. Undoubtedly many examples of moral reasoning can be found in the Christian moral tradition that appear superficially to exemplify consequentialist method. Such examples must be interpreted very carefully. There is consequentialism only if the author is trying simultaneously to meet the two conditions that define consequentialism: to reach a judgment in a case of morally significant choice as to what ought to be done, and to base the judgment on a comparison of the premoral goods and bads that would be brought about by the execution of each choice.

Among Catholic moral theologians, Louis Janssens,[4] Josef Fuchs S.J.,[5] Timothy E. O'Connell,[6] Gerard J. Hughes S.J.,[7] and Philip S. Keane S.S.,[8] among others, seem to have adopted rather thoroughgoing forms of consequentialism. Charles E. Curran[9] and Richard A. McCormick S.J.[10] also defend con-

seqentialism, but they think its application should be limited
to conflict situations, and perhaps also by certain nonconsequentialist restraints.

I have been arguing against consequentialism for years.
Proponents of the new moral theology, with the exception of
McCormick, have been ignoring this criticism.

McCormick's most extensive consideration of any work of
mine bearing on consequentialism was in his 1973 Marquette
lecture "Ambiguity in Moral Choice." There he dealt with the
treatment of double effect included in my 1970 book *Abortion:
The Myths, the Realities, and the Arguments.* Although my
central argument against consequentialism was not fully articulated until later, it was stated briefly in that work.[11] But
instead of coming to grips with the argument against consequentialism, McCormick ignored it, and suggested that I am
fleeing comsequentialist calculation because of nervous fear.[12]

McCormick was quite right in thinking that consequentialist calculation frightens me. But I do not think that my
reaction is a nervous fear; it seems to me to be a reasonable
horror. Even though I consider consequentialism quite a meaningless development, I wish to explain why I regard it with
horror rather then with complacency (as would be the case if
consequentialism were only some piece of innocent nonsense).
In order to clarify my position on this point, I will now turn to
McCormick's most recent publication on this subject, which
takes the form of his contribution to a book entitled *Doing Evil
to Achieve Good: Moral Choice in Conflict Situations.*

In this work McCormick is confronted by Paul Ramsey, who
presses the objection that consequentialism demands the commensuration of the incommensurable. McCormick suggests
that the solution to the problem of how to measure goods and
bads, as consequentialism requires us to do when in judging
what we *ought to do,* is simply to choose what we *are going to
do.* McCormick says:

> What do we do? *Somehow or other,* in fear and trembling, we commensurate. In a sense we *adopt* a hierarchy. We go to war to protect our freedom. That means we are willing to sacrifice life to protect this good. If "give me liberty or give me death" does not involve *some* kind of commensuration, then I do not know what commensurating means.[13]

And he goes on to add several more examples similar to this one.

We must admit that the commensuration of goods and bads is accomplished in this way. The trouble is that the commensuration is in the choice, and the choice settles all the questions which, according to consequentialist theory, should have been settled rationally in reaching a judgment of conscience prior to choice. Choice does determine the limits of options to be considered, the consequences to be inquired about, and the persons to be taken into account; these boundaries are drawn automatically when choice cuts off deliberation. Moreover, choice does determine which good will henceforth be considered greater, and which evil lesser; the good with which we identify in choosing becomes part of our subjective measure of value.

In sum, McCormick in his most recent publication thinks he is explaining what consequentialism needs to explain and cannot explain: how we can know what is the lesser evil as a condition for choosing it. Instead he asserts something that is true but irrelevant to his purpose: that by choosing something, we can determine it to be the lesser evil for ourselves. (Choice can do this, not because it transforms the good and bad in what is chosen, but because it transforms the choosing self; in this way our choice settles what is a greater good or lesser evil for ourselves.)

While McCormick's assertion that we commensurate in choosing is useless for his purpose, it is not useless for mine. If consequentialism is meaningless, as I hold it to be, it obviously cannot serve as a method of moral judgment. But once we have made a choice, and all the variables that a consequentialist cannot settle rationally are settled by this choice, then the pattern of consequentialist reasoning can be used to articulate in a persuasive way our reasons for making the choice.

Inasmuch as morally significant choices are free, conclusive justifications for making them cannot be given by appealing to something that would have determined the choice, A person who holds nonconsequentialist moral principles, for example, a believing Christian, can justify choices by appealing to such principles. A consequentialist, just insofar as he or she is one, cannot appeal to nonconsequentialist moral principles. The only thing left to appeal to is the expected good and bad effects of the choice made and of the rejected alternatives. Every choice promises some benefits; this is true even of every choice that would be rejected by these adhering to nonconsequentialist moral principles. So people who think in practice as the consequentialists urge us to think, justify themselves before their own consciences and the criticism of others by means of an account given from the view reached through their choice.

What I have been describing is a process with which we all are familiar. Psychologists call it "rationalization." It is clear that consequentialism can and does serve this purpose. To take one example: The atomic bombing of Hiroshima and Nagasaki was done in execution of a terroristic policy. This policy was adopted partly out of revenge and partly in the hope that it would help hasten victory. The terrorism was carried out in the context of an unjust demand that Japan should surrender unconditionally. In the event, a surrender with certain conditions was accepted because the United States had no more atomic bombs on hand and wanted to get the war over with. The terrorism was rationalized with consequentialist arguments, for example, that it saved more lives not only of American soldiers but also of Japanese soldiers. However, Japanese peace feelers were ignored until after the atomic bombs had been dropped. And other ways to carry on the war without invading the Japanese home islands were never seriously considered.[14] Nor was serious consideration given to the possible future of world politics and terrorism, a future we now know included both the nuclear deterrent and Vietnam.

Please notice that I am not here attacking consequentialism by means of this example. A consequentialist probably would say that the architects of terror did not calculate as carefully as they should have. My central argument against consequentialism is that it is meaningless. What I am showing with this example is why a meaningless attempt at ethical theory still is appealing, why it shows itself protean in its ability to take on new forms, and why it displays remarkable endurance despite all the well-known and never answered arguments against it.[15] As a method of rationalization, consequentialism is serviceable, and even the most sophisticated people can become irrationally attached to what they find serviceable.

Thus far I have tried to make clear what consequentialism is and what it is not. I have sketched out the argument that consequentialism is literally meaningless. I then showed that there are various legitimate uses of language that sound consequentialist but are not. Finally, I have shown that, although consequentialism is a meaningless ethical theory, it is a serviceable method of rationalization.

Now I come to the second part of this paper. I believe that the adoption of consequentialism is having devastating effects on Catholic moral theology. I will try to show how these effects follow, not always as logically necessary conclusions but at least as likely consequences, given our present situation. Some might claim that in what follows I am trying to give a consequentialist argument against consequentialism. But that criticism misses my point. My argument against consequentialism is sketched out above and stated more fully in other publications. All I am going to try to do now is to clarify what has been and is happening in Catholic moral theology as the new approach takes over.

We are in a time when renewal in moral theology demands new insights and new initiatives. For this very reason there is a special need for discernment between insights and initiatives that will contribute to authentic Christian renewal and up-building and those that will not. What follows is an essay in aid of discernment. If consequentialism is what I think it is, if it is having the results I think it is having, I hope this essay will help those who have adopted consequentialism to see that they have made a mistake, and that it will help others to avoid and correct this mistake.

In previous writings I not only attacked consequentialism but also attacked other aspects of the new morality. In carrying on this polemic, I did not distinguish sufficiently between the consequentialism of the dissenting theologians and their dissent itself. If we make this distinction, we can and should take a less absolute stand against dissent as such than the one I have taken in the past.

In order to see clearly what effects the adoption of consequentialism is having, we must first see what dissent in moral theology might be like if consequentialism were not adopted. To show this, I apply to a view of my own—the view that capital punishment cannot be morally justified—as much of the rationale for theological dissent as does not require the adoption of consequentialism. This analysis will allow me to compare the effects that dissent without consequentialism would have with the effects that dissent with consequentialism is having. In this way, the proper effects of consequentialism will become clear.

The received Catholic teaching on capital punishment is that it can be morally justified and, under certain conditions, perhaps even required. It is written: "You shall not allow a sorcerer to live" (Ex. 22:18), and again with respect to capital punishment of the crime of homicide: "He who sheds man's blood, shall have his blood shed by man, for in the image of God man was made" (Gn. 9:6). Nevertheless, it seems to me that there probably can and should be a development of Christian moral teaching that would expand the traditional prohibition of the killing of the innocent into a prohibition of all direct killing. How can I justify this dissent from a received teaching?

Until now I have justified it as follows. The Old Testament must be understood in the light of the New, and both must be understood in the light of the Church's teaching as a whole. In the light of such consideration, I suspect that capital punishment was not enjoined any more than slavery, and that a legitimate development of the former can be made, just as a legitimate development on the latter has been made.

The expansion of the prohibition of killing would respond to our deepened awareness of the dignity of the person, who is not merely a part of the state, and to our increasing sensitivity to the sanctity of human life, which remains the personal good it is, even if it happens to be the life of a murderer. Moreover, I note that the teaching Church and the believing Church as a whole seem increasingly less eager to defend capital punishment as justifiable, let alone to propose it as a moral imperative.

To understand more perfectly the frame of mind underlying the preceding justification, it is helpful to consider the situation of sincere pagans who reach their moral judgments from some nonconsequentialist moral principles. For the most part conclusions will follow from these principles without trouble, but eventually—simply because the principles are not absolutely true and precise—an attempt to apply the principles will lead to perplexity: The same choice will be enjoined and forbidden.

Underlying the alternatives will be goods to which the person is committed—in other words, certain aspects of his or her own moral identity. Moreover, either choice by itself can be justified by a method arising from the principles themselves without any consequentialism. At this point some modification is needed in the principles hitherto held. This modification ideally will be based upon fresh insight into human goods and their rational implications, but it also will require a modification of the self established by prior choices to the extent that these choices were mistaken.

Christians usually are saved from perplexity because the teaching of the Church is very extensive and very wise, since it is based upon the Word of God and upon the experience of his people trying to live in friendship with him. The net of Christian morality extends over almost all the problems that are likely to arise. For Catholics in modern times, until recently the tight net of Christian morality was especially unlikely to generate perplexity because probabilism allowed the net to stretch at many points. Where others would have felt perplexity, Catholics were allowed by a probable opinion and a competent confessor to follow their own consciences, that is, blamelessly to do as they pleased.

Theologians, however, had to face up to new problems that would cause perplexity. It was their job to generate probable opinions. To do this, they had to work directly from the fundamental principles of Christian morality. In other words, they had to proceed much as sincere pagans do. A new probable opinion tried to express a new insight into the rational implications for life of human goods. The only difference was that the theologians understood these goods in the light of faith, and were helped by the same light to discern their rational implications.

My dissenting opinion on capital punishment, then, is not an attack upon the principles of Christian morality; rather it is an expression of these very principles. I became sensitized to the sanctity of life as I was studying the problem of abortion. My argument against abortion is that those choosing to kill the unborn are willing to destroy human lives in case the unborn are in fact human persons, and that such willingness is unjustifiable by any good consequences since the end does not justify the means (cf. Rm. 3:8). Theoretical coherence seems to demand the exclusion of all choices to kill persons, and so to demand the exclusion of capital punishment.

Moreover, many Christians formerly thought of the state as if its interests were those of a whole of which individuals were only parts, so that capital punishment could be justified in the same way as amputation. But this view surely is not Christian. Nor could I find any other Christian basis to justify capital punishment. In this situation, despite the received teaching, I think it probable that capital punishment is morally unjustifiable.

Of course, many secular humanists also reject capital punishment. They do so as a part of their rejection of retributive justice as such; their theory of punishment is consequentialist. Although I must admit that I doubt I would have reached my present position in respect to capital punishment if many others—and especially our chief opponents on the abortion issue—did not consider it unjustifiable, I do not share their reasons. I am not dissenting from this particular point of received Catholic teaching on the basis of a secular, rational principle but rather on the basis of the Church's teaching itself.

Dissent of this sort does not require any consequentialist calculation in which the obligation of submission to Church teaching is outweighed by the good effects of changing the teaching. This point can be clarified by an analogy. Sometimes a loved and honored parent makes unreasonable demands. An obedient child will fulfill such demands provided that there is not some serious conflicting duty. In case there is such a duty, the loving and obedient child will gently refuse to fulfill the unreasonable demand, confident that the parent's own deeper wish would be that the real duty be fulfilled in a virtuous way, rather than that the particular demand be satisfied. The underlying assumption is that the parent is not perfectly integrated, and that we must honor the parent's deeper self in case it conflicts with some superficial aspect of that self.

It is clear enough that the Church's moral teaching has developed in the past. We no longer burn heretics, and no one today tries to justify slavery of any sort. Vatican Council II accepted and proposed as Catholic teaching, for example, certain views on religious liberty that not long ago constituted a dissenting position on the subject. Since development in moral teaching clearly is legitimate and necessary, and since my views on capital punishment seem to me to be grounded in deeper Christian principles; I believe that my dissent on capital punishment is within the legitimate bounds of Christian moral reflection.

Having reached this point, I call attention to a fact about which I was not clear before I began preparing this paper. Some—perhaps most—of those who dissented from the received Catholic teaching on contraception between 1964 and the publication of *Humanae Vitae* in 1968 very likely did not go beyond this point. The suggestions of some of the fathers of Vatican II, which were partly incorporated into *Gaudium et Spes,* and which were subsequently endorsed by the majority of the Pontifical Commission of Paul VI, could fit as to their essentials into the framework of the argument given above. The proposal was to modify a particular teaching point in order to make the whole of Catholic moral teaching more coherent, and thus to remove a seeming perplexity of married couples, without doing violence to anything fundamental. The avoidance of violence was considered possible because the Christian conception of the goods of marriage itself was thought to have become clearer.

However, I do not think that my dissent on capital punishment can be assimilated so closely to the theological dissent on contraception after *Humanae Vitae* was published in 1968. There are two points of difference.

First, the reaffirmation of Paul VI of the received teaching ought to have been answered by a new and deeper theological reflection, not by the unthinking repetition of arguments the Pope had already studied and rejected. Such new reflections, I think, would have made clear that we must not argue, as the dissenters argued (and still argue), that nondefined teaching is noninfallible teaching. A more open consideration by theologians of the relevant evidence would, I think, have convincingly shown that the received Catholic teaching on contraception and many other matters has been infallibly proposed by the ordinary magisterium. I shall not pursue this point here, since John C. Ford S.J., and I have published a paper treating it at length.[16]

People who hold the dissenting view on contraception might argue that the received teaching on capital punishment can also be infallibly proposed by the ordinary magisterium. But I do not think this is so. Still I must admit that I have not carefully examined this question, which is especially difficult because of the scriptural foundation for the licitness of capital punishment. In response to this admission, objectors probably would reply that their attitude toward the teaching of the ordinary magisterium discussed in the Ford-Grisez article is similar to mine toward the troublesome scriptural texts.

This last reply will be allowed to stand, not because I concede the point at issue, but because it would take me too far afield to pursue it now. The exchange does point up one thing: Objectively, the categories of teaching infallibly proposed and teaching not infallibly proposed are neat and exclusive. But epistemically—that is, from the point of view of people who are trying to recognize to which category a particular point of teaching belongs—the situation is not so simple. We face a spectrum from what is certainly infallibly proposed through various grades of what is probably or possibly infallibly proposed down to what is certainly not infallibly proposed. This fuzziness renders possible dissent from an infallibly proposed teaching by a well-intentioned error—a possibility instanced by the material heresies of various Fathers and Doctors of the Church.

The second point of difference between my dissent on capital punishment and the dissent on contraception after *Humanae Vitae* is that the latter but not the former negated the norm as obligation, sought to displace it in pastoral practice, and so impugned the teaching and governing authority of the Pope and the bishops who stood with him. It was these aspects of the dissent that were reproved by the bishops of the United States in their November 1968 pastoral.[17]

And it still seems to me, as it did in 1968, that Catholic theologians or priests who cannot in good conscience accept, propose, and apply a point of moral teaching on which the Pope or local bishop are insisting ought to resign. We should not expect superiors to allow their own authority to be used by their subordinates in a way that the superiors cannot in conscience approve. If a conflict of judgments is irresolvable, the judgment of the superiors must prevail. This is simply part of what it means to have a hierarchy in the Church.

If what I have just said is correct, the dissent after *Humanae Vitae* went beyond a very important boundary. Some theologians had adopted consequentialist arguments for contraception before *Humanae Vitae*. Afterward, virtually the whole body of dissenting theologians came to understand the method and to use it or condone its use not only to justify contraception but to justify dissent itself. Such dissent, it was argued, was necessary to relieve married couples of an onerous burden of conscience. Moreover, dissent came to be regarded as a necessary means of transforming the relationship between the sacramental teaching authority of the bishops and the authority of the theologians as expert scholars.

Today we are in a position to begin to see the devastating effects of the adoption of consequentialism by many Catholic moral theologians.

The first point is that consequentialist reflection upon past action tends to create the illusion that we could not have done otherwise than we did. To have chosen the lesser good or the greater evil would simply have been absurd. This phenomenon leads directly to psychological determinism, at least with respect to choices that are thought to be shaped by consequentialist reasoning.

The point I am making is exemplified by the British utilitarians. They looked at action from the perspective of people who review it with consequentialist spectacles. They accepted psychological determinism, and denied the freedom of choice traditionally considered an essential condition for moral responsibility. They claimed that, to be morally responsible, freedom from external coercion is sufficient. But they never explained how anyone can do what is wrong. Their theories underlie contemporary views that no one ever does wrong. People only make mistakes, act immaturely, suffer from neuroses, are damaged by bad institutions, and so on.

Catholic theologians who adopt consequentialism are not likely to deny free choice altogether. On the one hand, a blanket denial might not seem necessary, especially if it is held that some choices or aspects of choices are not subject to consequentialist calculation. On the other hand, the exclusion of free choice from Christian life as a whole clearly destroys the Christian conception of the person and excludes the very possibility of the act of faith. In an earlier paper in this workshop, Joseph M. Boyle, Jr., discussed this last point at some length, so I need not expand upon it.

However, if we begin to look at choices in a consequentialist perspective, we are likely to begin to think of them as if they were not free, and yet as if they remain morally significant, for consequentialism implies this with respect to the choices to which it is applied. Please notice that this position, if it were articulated, also would clearly conflict with faith, for we believe that people do not incur guilt except by abusing their freedom of choice.

Nevertheless, many Catholic moralists seem to me to have begun drawing out the implications of a premise that they do not make explicit: Choices that they think are subject to consequentialist judgment are not free. There are many implications to this development.

First, no such choice can be the fundamental commitment of Christian life, for this commitment surely must be free. Thus it seems necessary to posit this commitment elsewhere than in the choices consequentialist reasoning is thought to regulate. Boyle also has analyzed at some length how proponents of fundamental option theory are trying to insulate the center of the Christian self from almost all sinful choices.

Second, if we cannot consistently consider choices regulated by consequentialist reasoning to be free, we cannot consistently consider mortal sin to be a possibility in matters of such choices. Consequentialism allows for sufficient reflection or for full consent, but never for both. In the sexual area, the exclusion of mortal sin seems especially plausible, since we also experience psychological compulsion in this area. This feeling, together with the half-formed thought that the apparently greater good compels acceptance of one alternative, easily seems to preclude moral responsibility. So we encounter arguments roughly like the following one: Everyone masturbates, and so it is natural and virtually inevitable; and besides it is better to release sexual tension than to be distracted by it from more important things such as sleep, study, and prayer. As a result, grave matter clearly is excluded from masturbation by such an argument.

My third point is more complex and even more important than the preceding two. The adoption of consequentialism transforms the way we look at our whole moral lives.

Christian faith teaches that the communion of our freedom with God's freedom and the conformity of our wills to his will are the heart of the Christian moral life. Everything else in Christian life is significant only insofar as it leads up to or flows from this central relationship. God freely reveals himself in Christ; we freely accept his offer of friendship. Since this communion of freedoms is central to Christian life, what is most important about our choices is how they share in and express this communion. In other words, what our choices do to ourselves, how their execution puts all parts of ourselves to work in the service of love, thus integrating our whole mind and heart and soul and strength with the love of God—this is by far more important than any consequences our choices bring about outside our self-determined selves. Thus Christian morality is a morality of the heart. The conformity of our hearts to the heart of Christ is what is more important.

I realize that theologians who accept consequentialism are likely to protest that they accept everything in the preceding paragraph. But consequentialists must take the consequences very seriously, not only because they think that the consequences determine the morality of the acts to which consequentialism is thought to apply but also because the theory implies that these acts cannot be freely chosen. If they are not freely chosen, they cannot either contribute to or destroy the moral self.

The diversion of attention away from the moral self toward the consequences of acts changes our whole conception of moral life. This change is reflected in a loss of interest in the quest for personal moral purification and sanctification. The idea of saving our soul begins to seem unreal. There is a decline in reflection upon the state of our soul and a withering of interest in the ministry of the cure of souls.

Moreover, this diversion of attention tends to make a limited consequentialism spread. For example, we begin by approving contraception for the contribution it is expected to make to preserving the goods of marriage. This initial move draws attention away from the marital relationship as an aspect of the moral selves of the spouses and turns attention upon their experienced or phenomenal relationship, which is what contraception serves. The relationship of marriage itself thus is withdrawn from the field of moral goods, where it is inviolable, and transferred into the area of nonmoral goods, where it must compete against other prospective goods. If a marriage seems to be broken down, divorce appears justified. And so the absoluteness of the commitments of Christian marriage, of religious vows, and of other aspects of the Christian personal vocation is negated.

When consequentialism has spread to commitments like those just mentioned, virtually nothing is left of Christian life. The act of faith establishes a personal, covenant relationship with God. But the common Christian vocation to share in this covenant is concretized in our personal vocation. Marriage, for example, not only symbolizes but in a real way concretely shares in the unity of Christ with the Church. The very meaning of faithfulness to such commitments is that we stand by them, for better and for worse, regardless of any apparent consequences in doing so. Ordinary promises sometimes can be rightly broken, but vows that incarnate our commitment to God cannot be. If we accept consequentialist justifications for breaking such commitments, faith itself will soon be tested by the quality of our religious experience and the other benefits it yields. To put faith to such a test is already to have abandoned it.

In sum, if what I have been saying is correct, the adoption of consequentialism in Catholic moral theology, even if initially with some limits, tends to undermine the moral self of the Christian; it ultimately threatens to subvert faith itself. I now turn from the subject matter of theology to the work of theology itself. Here too consequentialism has devastating effects.

The adoption of consequentialism by a moral theologian, even in a restricted form, sets off a dialectical movement of incursion of reason upon the claims of faith. As I explained previously, from the point of view of someone who is trying to judge whether a teaching is infallibly proposed or not, the neat categories become a sort of spectrum with many shades of what is probably and possibly infallibly proposed in between the extremes of the certainly infallibly proposed and the certainly not infallibly proposed. Thus there is a gradual shading in the claims that the obedience of faith makes upon a believer.

Dissent justified by a consideration of measurable consequences—as the dissent after *Humanae Vitae* was—seems to involve no fundamental disloyalty when the claims of obedience are perceived to be at the weak end of the spectrum. Yet such dissent weakens respect for authority and the disposition to conform our judgment to the received teaching. At the same time, the application of consequentialism to solve one problem disposes people to consider other problems from a new perspective. Some of these can be resolved by extending dissent only slightly—just far enough to override the weakest of the claims to obedience that we have hitherto respected. The deepening of dissent further intensifies the dispositions that dissent sets up, and so on. Thus rationalism waxes as obedience gradually wanes.

Dissent that does not involve the acceptance of consequentialism need not generate this vicious dialectic. What is different about consequentialism is that it implicitly involves a principle alien to faith. The proof is that Christian faith is clearly incompatible with the thesis, implicit in consequentialism, that there can be morally significant choices that are not free choices. Once a principle alien to faith is adopted as a standard for theological judgment, theology becomes alienated from itself. It ceases to be faith seeking understanding, and turns itself into unfaith seeking rationalization.

The dialectic I am describing is a new experience in the Catholic Church. But already a century and more ago, some Protestant theologians transformed their discipline into a sort of philosophy, often into a philosophy of religious experience.[18] Academic theologians of the time felt impelled to try to meet the criteria of rationality accepted by their academic, non-believing colleagues in philosophy, history, and the emerging disciplines of psychology and the social studies. Many of these theologians declared their autonomy from their ecclesial communities. The authority of these communities had already been rendered ambiguous by the Reformation's emphasis upon the normativity of Scripture at the expense of the normativity of the living Church handing on its faith under the leadership of a hierarchical magisterium.

Thus liberal Protestantism developed. Like their brethren of the last century, many Catholic theologians today are becoming converted to the priority of secular academic standards of responsible inquiry over anything specifically Christian and Catholic. If the effect of this conversion at first appears limited, this appearance only persists because at first much of what the Church believes and teaches seems rationally justified, and much more can be reinterpreted ingeniously so that the incompatibility between Catholic faith and nonsubmissive autonomous rationality can remain obscure.

From the analysis of possibly licit dissent that I provided earlier in this paper, it should be clear that I am not arguing for theological immobility—for a rigid adherence to everything that has ever been said with even the minimal degree of magisterial authority. Such a posture would constitute a sort of Catholic fundamentalism, and this would be untenable. But a theology essentially emancipated from the hierarchical magisterium is not the only alternative.

In theological dialectic, no matter how it is conducted, everything moves. But it makes a great difference whether certain truths of faith itself or some principles outside faith are accepted as the principles of the very possibility of the dialectic. Whichever principles are chosen to play this key role, they will develop in all sorts of ways, but they will never negate themselves, provided that they were a self-consistent set to begin with.

To hold the Catholic position that there is some definite content to faith and some definite truths that God has revealed is to hold precisely that the theological dialectic depends upon these truths for its very possibility. Faith itself embraces certain truths that can also be known by reason. But any beliefs absolutely outside faith must be regarded as less certain than it. The light of faith reduces all human science to opinion; the folly of God is wiser than the wisdom of human philosophy. It follows that any proposition that does not somehow fall within faith not only must be held tentatively as open to development but even be subject to negation if this is required by faith's unfolding implications.

I am asserting, not' denying, that the human mind as such, and therefore the Christian mind, always is on the move. But it makes a great difference what is considered to be immune from contradiction, although even it remains open to development.

A moral theology that emancipates itself from the hierarchical magisterium and that adheres to a method implicitly incompatible with the Christian conception of the person and of moral responsibility is no longer a Catholic moral theology. Those who have adopted consequentialism perhaps initially dissented on the peripheral matter of contraception by appealing to more central Christian norms. But when they adopted consequentialism, their whole project changed radically.

They began to criticize the Church's moral teaching by means of this and other extrinsic principles, and to state opinions in the form of consequentialist argumentation. Although consequentialism has been so effectively attacked and has shown itself so thoroughly indefensible that it can be held only as a nonrational conviction, they apparently think this method transforms their opinions into knowledge. Hence they seem to think they have moral science by which they can judge and condemn teaching efforts of the popes and bishops if these efforts are unsupported by fresh and rationally cogent arguments.

If the preceding analysis is correct, it has at least one extremely important practical implication. The Pope and the other bishops need not always regard theological dissent as a form of disloyalty that must be suppressed. However, when theologians adopt a methodology from outside faith, one even implicitly incompatible with faith, and withdraw this principle of their own reflection from criticism in the light of faith, then those who share in the apostolic office ought not to continue to condone dissent.

The bounds of legitimate dissent have been crossed long since. The new moral theology is not an option within the pluralism of Catholic theologies, but an option alternative to Catholic faith itself. What is needed now is a clarification so that those who have made this option in confusion and by mistake, but whose fundamental option remains that of Catholic faith, will be able to reconsider and retract.[19]

Christian moral theology is impossible without the obedience of faith. Christian moral life requires obedience to the received moral teaching. And the proper functioning of the hierarchical teaching office depends upon the courageous obedience of the Pope and the other bishops to Christ and the

Holy Spirit. But is not obedience a childish and servile virtue?

Christian morality that insists upon obedience is not childish; it is a guide to rational service. Such service requires mature choices, for Jesus wishes us to do what he did, and even greater things than he did. Moreover, this morality is not slavish, for the slave could understand what his master is about but is not given knowledge. By contrast, Christian morality guides us in conscious cooperation with Jesus in his work.

Yet obedience remains necessary. First, because there is still something both childish and slavish about us as we now are. We are God's children, but we are not yet mature members of his family, and so we do not know him as he knows us, and we must trust him in a way that he need not trust us. Furthermore, we are friends of Jesus, but imperfect ones. When we sin, the duties of friendship seem heteronomous. The New Law is written in our hearts, but our hearts are divided, not simple and pure.

Even so, the yoke of obedience need not be onerous. For God wishes to bring us up by helping us to understand his plans more perfectly and to share more maturely in carrying them out. God also is like a generous master whose slaves are prisoners serving a well-deserved sentence of hard labor. He wishes our work in his service to be transformed into a better relationship—one of mature friendship and equality.

At a deeper level, however, the obedience characteristic of Christian life never will be transcended. Every perfect and good gift comes from above, from the Father. Even within the Trinity, there is procession, there is hierarchy. The divine persons are an orderly family. As everything is, so it acts. Thus Jesus obeys the Father and the Spirit obeys both the Father and the Son (cf. Jn. 16.13).

If we are called to share in the divine nature, we also are called to share in the obedience of the divine family life. Even in heaven we shall have to know our place and fulfill it. But such obedience will no longer be in any way servile or childish. The freedom of the children of God will be perfect in eternal obedience.

One final objection, however, brings us down from the heights of this reflection. Surely obedience is acceptable if it means something so elevated. But to obey Paul VI? Clearly, that would have been another matter! A modern and responsible theologian has to draw the line somewhere between the obedience of faith due to God and obedience to particular, nondefinitive decisions of a pope.

In part, this objection points back to questions already touched upon. But there is a further element that lends to the objection plausibility, and this element needs to be answered. It is a fear that the obedience due to God will be given idolatrously to human beings. Many Christians faithful to the Reformation are deeply imbued with this fear. Some Catholics also share it.

I think that reflection on the principle of subsidiarity can help us meet this concern. According to subsidiarity, it is better for persons do for themselves what they can do, and for people to do in small communities what small communities can do, rather than to socialize and centralize. Those who adhere to consequentialism will have a hard time understanding the point of this principle, for it will seem to them a rule of inefficiency.

But from the point of view of an ethics that stresses the self-constituting aspect of human acts over their efficacy in getting results, subsidiarity makes good sense, for it subordinates efficiency to an active, conscious participation. And participation is good because it gives more people more chances to do more significant things—and so to be more, even if they do not bring about more.

It seems that God is more interested in giving us opportunities for self-realization in doing good than he is in getting results efficiently. God always could cause the results without us. But even God cannot make us agents who fulfill ourselves in our work without giving us the graces of abilities, norms, and acts that make possible and constitute our work.

All through the gospels it is obvious that the apostles are eager to share in the work of Jesus. They long for places in his kingdom. He accepts death when their formation is barely underway. And he explains that he must go so that the Spirit may come. A parable might clarify this point.

A certain retired rich man decided to start a new business. He instructed his son, gave him financing, and sent him to set up the enterprise. The task was difficult but fulfilling for the son. Once the business is launched, however, the son also must retire, for if he does not, his associates will never have a chance at leadership. If the business is to continue as a family business, the associates must be adopted by the father. To do this, the father must send an attorney with the power to carry out the adoption. And so, in a way, the natural son's retirement was necessary for the coming of the attorney.

If the central insight of this parable is sound, then God applies the principle of subsidiarity in his work of creation, redemption, and sanctification. The benefits of the Eucharist could have been caused without the priest, but the priest cannot exist without the Eucharist. People of sincere heart might come to God without the apostolate of the Church, but the Church cannot exist without the apostolate. And the coming to be of the Church is important because it is the earthly beginning, a beginning that also is our work; it is the beginning of the family of God, the pleroma of Christ, and the temple of the Spirit.

In short, we ought to have obeyed Paul vi, and we ought to obey John Paul ii, not because they are sometimes helpful functionaries but because they are sacraments. And this, finally, is the reason why there is a difference between theologians and bishops, even when both groups are faithful and moved by God's grace. In their professional capacity the former utter the words of people of faith; the latter utter the Word of God in whom we believe.

Notes

1. An important summary of the difficulties philosophers find in consequentialism is Dan W. Brock, "Recent Work in Utilitarianism," *American Philosophical Quarterly* 10 (1973): 241-69. Alan Donagan, *The Theory of Morality* (Chicago and London: University of Chicago Press, 1977), pp. 172-209, lays out some of the standard Kantian objections and argues against consequentialism generally, especially (pp. 199-209) on the way in which ignorance blocks utilitarian calculation. Germain Grisez, "Against Consequentialism," *American Journal of Jurisprudence* 23 (1978): 21-72, contains further references; note especially the admission by J. J. C. Smart quoted on p. 30 that calculation is impossible, and related admissions by Jeremy Bentham and Garrett Hardin (pp. 35-36) which make clear that "calculation" is determined by choice. An important clarification of the nonconsequentialist nature of moral norms is B. J. Diggs, "Rules and Utilitarianism," in Michael D. Bayles, ed., *Contemporary Utilitarianism* (Garden City, N.Y.: Doubleday & Company, 1968), pp. 203-38.

2. See "Against Consequentialism," pp. 41-49; Germain Grisez and Joseph M. Boyle, Jr., *Life and Death with Liberty and Justice: A Contribution to the Euthanasia Debate* (Notre Dame, Ind. and London: University of Notre Dame Press, 1979), pp. 346-55. Although these previous articulations of the argument are fuller, the present state of it contains two important refinements: (1) I now make it clear that none of the differences among forms of consequentialism are relevant to what is wrong with it, since all forms of consequentialism are intended to bear upon certain choices (whether of acts or of rules or of something else) and are supposed to settle the morality of such choices (whether after other conditions are met or not); (2) I now make explicit the formal contradiction implicit in the consequentialist conception of moral judgment and choice.

3. Richard A. McCormick S. J., "Ambiguity in Moral Choice," in Richard A. McCormick S. J., and Paul Ramsey, *Doing Evil to Achieve*

Good: Moral Choice in Conflict Situations (Chicago: Loyola University Press, 1979), p. 38.

4. Louis Janssens, "Norms and Priorities in a Love Ethics," *Louvain Studies* 6 (Spring 1977): 212-13 and passim.

5. Josef Fuchs S.J., "The Absoluteness of Moral Terms," *Gregorianum* 52 (1971): 436, 445, and 455.

6. Timothy E. O'Connell, *Principles for A Catholic Morality* (New York: Seabury Press, 1978), pp. 144-64. This book is important because, as a textbook, it makes clear the institutionalization of the moral theology of dissent. It also provides a more comprehensive and clearer statement than is found in the work of many others who share in the movement.

7. Gerard J. Hughes S.J., *Authority in Morals: An Essay in Christian Ethics* (London: Heythrop Monographs, 1978), pp. 64-90. At times (e.g., pp. 82 and 111) Hughes seems about to recognize noncommensurability, and to be about to slip into subjectivism. This slide is understandable, inasmuch as goods can be rendered commensurable as the consequentialist wishes only *in choosing*. The phenomena of deliberation and choice only lend consequentialism any plausibility at all if the process is regarded retrospectively, as J. S. Mill, for example, normally regards it.

8. Philip S. Keane S.S., *Sexual Morality: A Catholic Perspective* (New York, Ramsey, N.J., and Toronto: Paulist Press, 1977), pp. 46-51.

9. Charles E. Curran, *Themes in Fundamental Moral Theology* (Notre Dame and London: University of Notre Dame Press, 1977), pp. 133, 141. Because Curran's methodology is essentially rhetoric, he makes a great fuss over what various positions are called, and does not regard himself as a "consequentialist." But by definition he is. I think it odd he considers me a "deontologist," but do not object, except that he seems to think the name sufficient refutation.

10. Richard A. McCormick S.J., "A Commentary on the Commentaries," in McCormick and Ramsey, eds., pp. 193-267, and in many other recent publications.

11. Germain Grisez, *Abortion: The Myths, the Realities, and the Arguments* (New York and Cleveland: Corpus Books, 1970), pp. 310-311. In *Ambuiguity* (p. 26) McCormick challenges me to give a clearer account of "proportionate reason." I distinguish various modes of obligation (responsibility) of which only one is that one may not do evil that good might follow therefrom. One has a proportionate reason for doing what does not violate that mode of obligation, though it involves foreseen harm, if and only if it does not violate any other mode of

responsibility—e.g., universalizability (the golden rule). In the same work (p. 34) he finds difficulty in understanding what I mean by "to turn directly against these goods." Similarly, in "Current Theology: Notes on Moral Theology 1977: The Church in Dispute," *Theological Studies* 39 (March 1978): 95-96, in criticizing William E. May, McCormick still finds difficulty in understanding what is to count for such a turning. He quotes two passages from my works in which I talk of "acting directly against," and this is what I mean. One acts directly against a good if and only if one makes a choice by which one adopts a proposal such that the content of the proposal includes destroying or harming one or more instances of that good. For example, one acts directly against the good of life if one in deliberation considers a proposal to kill someone and by choice adopts this proposal. The execution of such a choice would be "direct killing." McCormick often writes as though he believed that offering a few criticisms against those who have made reasoned objections to his views dispensed him from the need to answer the objections (a little offense is the best defense).

12. "Ambiguity," p. 34; cf. p. 26. to analyze someone's psyche is *ad hominem.*

13. "A Commentary on the Commentaries," p. 227; cf. p. 225. McCormick here at last explicitly makes the move which I described and which he ignored in my attack on utilitarianism in *Abortion,* p. 310.

14. See Michael Walzer, *Just and Unjust Wars: A Moral Argument with Historical Illustrations* (New York: Basic Books, 1977), pp. 251-83, treats bombing in World War II, including the A-bombing of Japan, and the nuclear deterrent. The summary of the data is interesting, and many of Walzer's conclusions are sound, but his ethical theory is not wholly adequate. I personally first became sensitized to consequentialism when as a graduate student I became friends with a Japanese of my own age who had lived in Nagasaki, but was away for the day when it was destroyed. Almost everyone and everything he had ever known and cared about were obliterated that day. In the early 1960s, conferences on ethics and international politics at Georgetown University began to clarify the issue for me theoretically. The nuclear deterrent is a paradigmatic embodiment of this horrible pseudo theory.

15. I do not presume to judge the hearts of those who articulate and defend consequentialism at the theoretical level. When I first began to think about ethics (1959-60), it seemed to me a very plausible theory.

But I felt that the objections to it would have to be answered, and in trying to answer them, I discovered that they cannot be answered. If Richard McCormick or any of the other theologians I am criticizing thinks he can defend his theoretical position, I shall be pleased to meet in fair debate, oral or written. Unless and until those who hold this theory show a serious willingness to try to defend it, the impression that they hold it dogmatically can hardly be avoided.

16. John C. Ford S.J. and Germain Grisez, "Contraception and the Infallibility of the Ordinary Magisterium," *Theological Studies* 39 (June 1978): 258-312.

17. "Norms of Licit Theological Dissent," National Conference of Catholic Bishops, *Human Life in Our Day* (Washington, D.C.: November 15, 1968), pp. 18-19.

18. The experience did have a short run in the Catholic Church around the turn of the century in the modernism crisis. But not everything in the crisis of that time is essentially connected with the liberal movement in theology, which essentially amounts to the supposition that there is somehow or other a fixed place to stand in some sort of knowledge outside faith, and that this standpoint provides a more valid condition for dialectic than does faith itself (e.g., as articulated and defended by the living magisterium of the Catholic Church). The liberal theologian thinks he or she is a scientist, and that belief (as opinion) must not override science. A good example of the liberal theological view by a Catholic theologian is David Tracy, *Blessed Rage for Order: The New Pluralism in Theology* (New York: Seabury Press, 1975), pp. 6-7, and passim. The odd thing is that liberal theology, far from being science, simply is bad philosophy that is taken too seriously by theologians.

19. Some who sympathize with the Catholic dissenting theologians are quick to criticize as "uncharitable" any clear and forceful attack upon dissent such as I make here. I do pray that all the dissenting theologians to whom I make reference in this paper, as well as all who connive in dissent, and I will meet together in heaven. And I suggest that much light is shed upon the relationship between charity, truth, and dissent by a careful reading of the New Testament passages listed in any concordance under "teaching" and other words in its family. One need not examine every New Testament book to see several important points; one can start with the Second Epistle of John.

Making Moral Choices in Conflict Situations

Rev. Joseph T. Mangan S.J.
Loyola University
Chicago, Illinois

One of the most critical cases in which I have ever been involved occurred in the Archdiocese of Chicago in the 1950s. At that time I was professor of Moral Theology at the archdiocesan major seminary. I had been reading about the case in the daily papers before I was asked to get involved in the final moral decision making. The case was that of head-joined twin girls. They had been born by Caesarean section in one Catholic hospital and moved to another, where it was judged they could be better cared for. The question to be answered was whether it was good medicine and good morals to separate the twins from each other. If so, how was the separation to be accomplished?

Since the twins had been born into a Catholic family, and were being cared for in a Catholic hospital, the Cardinal Archbishop was asked to make sure that the moral decision would be a good one. He wrote and asked me to accept the responsibility for making that decision.

The first step, of course, in responsibly making any such decision—whether in the field of bioethics, justice, or whatever field—is to learn the facts and the proper interpretation of the facts. Basic as this step seems, it should not be presumed too easily. I always want to discuss medical cases with the doctors who are closest to the case, who know the facts, and who have the best judgments about their own proper interpretations of the facts.

Another important factor is knowing what questions to ask to uncover the relevant facts. On occasion, since I am not a medical doctor, I have asked a doctor I did not know or an individual patient to talk with a specific doctor—a specialist in the relevant field of medicine whose knowledge and judgment I was sure of. If in my judgment I need further consultation, say, with other moral theologians, I institute such consultations. Only after completing the necessary consultations do I help the patient or doctor make a good moral decision.

In the case of the head-joined twins, I visited the hospital where (on a lighted screen) the chief neurosurgeon explained with the aid of X-ray pictures what the various examinations had revealed, what procedures were contemplated, and what the dangers and hopes for success were. It seemed that the two babies were joined at the superior longitudinal sinus of the brain. Each girl seemed to have her own sinus, which for about a quarter of an inch was common to both.[1]

Curiously enough, two years before in the same city of Chicago, there was another case of head-joined twins, both boys, who were separated at a public nonsectarian hospital. These twins also had been joined at the superior longitudinal sinus, but in this case there was only one sinus shared by both. In separating the two, the sinus had to be taken from one boy and given to the other. The one from whom the sinus was taken never regained consciousness and died thirty-four days later. The other twin lived into boyhood. In the history of a number of head-joined twin operations, this one was judged to be the first in which even one twin had survived a surgical separation. The doctors reported, however, that at no time in their preparations or in the operation itself did they intend to sacrifice the life of one boy to save the other. The doctors' judgment was that the other blood vessels in the brain would compensate for the missing sinus, and the baby would continue to live.

Understandably, the experience of the doctors in the case of the boys provided valuable help in the case of the girls. One doctor from the first team even volunteered his services in the second case. It seemed a relatively simple decision to make in my case that a grave risk to the life and quality of life of the girls was warranted. For there was substantial hope that, through surgical separation, the girls would be able to lead normal lives. The critical question became whether the operation would necessarily inflict a lethal blow on either twin. In the doctors' judgment, barring unforeseen complications, there was a strong, well-founded hope that the operation could be performed without causing death or grave harm to the quality of life of either twin. The operation would certainly be less hazardous than the one performed on the boys. Each girl would retain her own longitudinal sinus, and the opening into each sinus where they were common could be covered with a gelatin sponge.

The surgical separation would be hazardous, but it certainly would not involve the direct intention to kill either twin. The hope of benefit to each twin warranted the risk of harm necessarily present. We came to the conclusion that the surgical separation would be an example both of good medicine and good morals. The examinations, study, preliminary preparations, and surgical separation extended over a period of about six months. Both twins survived the operation.

It seems elementary to add that without the help of the medical doctors, I could not have begun to make a responsible decision in this case. The Second Vatican Council mentioned the need of churchmen to rely more on the competency and experience of members of the laity in their academic and pastoral endeavors. I must confess in response that from the start of my apostolate as priest and theologian, even before Vatican II, I never could get along without the help of the laity. I have always felt free to call on others whose help I needed to understand and properly interpret the facts in any case. The members of the laity, whether Protestant, Jew, or Catholic, were always most generous with their assistance.

In making a moral decision in any situation—whether a situation of special conflict or not—I strive to arrive at a decision based on our heavenly Father's truth, as I understand it. Three witnesses are critical for me in assessing this truth. They are the living voice of our Father's creation, the living voice of our Father's revelation, and the living voice of our Father's Church founded by our Lord Jesus Christ. But since physical creation, divine revelation, and the living voice of the Church do not provide clear answers to all contemporary questions, scholars representing various disciplines, without contradicting any of these three witnesses, can be of tremendous auxiliary help with their discoveries and insights uncovering the truths of our heavenly Father. For as Vatican II so aptly stated:

> ... if methodical investigation within every branch of learning is carried out in a genuinely scientific manner and in accord with moral norms, it never truly conflicts with faith. For earthly matters and the concerns of faith derive from the same God. Indeed, whoever labors to penetrate the secrets of reality with a humble and steady mind, is, even unawares, being led by the hand of God, who holds all things in existence, and gives them their identity ... (*Pastoral Constitution on the Church in the Modern World,* n.36, Abbott edition, 1966).

For the past decade or so, unfortunately, we have been experiencing an era in which professedly Catholic scholars have been contradicting the living voice of the Church and the authentic Catholic doctrine expressed by that voice. It behooves those loyal to authentic Catholic doctrine, therefore, to deepen their understanding of and commitment to that doctrine as normative for the faithful. It also behooves the faithful to deepen their understanding of and commitment to the magisterium as the authentic voice of Christ in the world today. This brings me to the first conflict situation of my presentation, that between the Church's magisterium and the contemporary dissenting theologians and others. How should I and the Catholic faithful react to this conflict situation?

Vatican II stated:

> ... Bishops are preachers of the faith who lead new disciples to Christ. They are authentic teachers endowed with the authority of Christ, who preach to the people committed to them the faith they must believe and put in practice.... Bishops, teaching *in communion with the Roman Pontiff*, are to be respected by all as witnesses to divine and Catholic truth. *In matters of faith and morals, the Bishops speak in the name of Christ* and the faithful are to accept their teaching and adhere to it with a religious assent of soul... (*Dogmatic Constitution on the Church*, n.25, Abbott edition, emphasis added).

> *The task of authentically interpreting the Word of God* whether written or handed on, has been *entrusted exclusively to the living Magisterium* of the Church whose authority is exercised in the Name of Jesus Christ... (*Dogmatic Constitution on Divine Revelation*, n.10, Abbott edition, emphasis added).

> (Parents) must always be governed according to a conscience dutifully conformed to the divine law itself, and should be submissive toward the *Church's*

> *Magisterium, which authentically interprets that law*
> in the light of the Gospel. The divine law reveals and
> protects the integral meaning of conjugal love, and
> impels it toward a truly human fulfillment ... (*Pas-*
> *toral Constitution on the Church in the Modern*
> *World,* n.50, Abbott edition, emphasis added).

> As regards activities and institutions in the tem-
> poral order, *the role of the ecclesiastical hierarchy is*
> *to teach and authentically interpret the moral princi-*
> *ples* to be followed in temporal affairs. Furthermore,
> it has the right to judge, after careful consideration
> of all related matters and consultation with experts,
> whether or not such activities and institutions con-
> form to moral principles ... (*Decree on the Aposto-*
> *late of the Laity,* n.24, Abbott edition, emphasis
> added).

Clearly the teaching of the magisterium is normative of what
is morally acceptable behavior for the Catholic faithful.

Acknowledging this unique role of the living magisterium of
the Church, i.e., of the Bishops in union with the Pope, we must
also acknowledge that the theologians have a legitimate, special role in participatory relation to that magisterium. The
theologians have special competence in researching our
Father's truth. Their special role calls upon them to manifest
responsibly their particular insights to their peers, to the
members of the Church's authentic teaching body, and to the
people of God at large.

Again, as Vatican II stated:

> ... all the faithful, clerical and lay, possess a lawful
> freedom of inquiry and of thought, and the freedom
> to express their minds humbly and courageously
> about those matters in which they enjoy com-
> petence ... (*Pastoral Constitution on the Church in*
> *the Modern World,* n.62, Abbott edition).

With the help of the Holy Spirit, it is the task of the entire People of God, especially pastors and *theologians,* to hear, distinguish and interpret the many voices of our age, and to judge them in the light of the divine Word... (*Pastoral Constitution on the Church in the Modern World,* n.44, Abbott edition, emphasis added).

While adhering to the methods and requirements proper to theology, *theologians* are invited to seek continually for more suitable ways of communicating doctrine to the men of their times. For the deposit of faith or revealed truths are one thing; the manner in which they are formulated without violence to their meaning and significance is another... (*Pastoral Constitution on the Church in the Modern World,* n.62, Abbott edition, emphasis added).

It is the task of exegetes to work... toward a better understanding and explanation of the meaning of Sacred Scripture, so that through preparatory study the judgment of the Church may mature. For all of what has been said about the way of interpreting Scripture is subject finally to the judgment of the Church, which carries out the divine commission and ministry of guarding and interpreting the Word of God. (*Dogmatic Constitution on Divine Revelation,* n.12, Abbott edition).

Since Vatican II many theologians and others, striving to fulfill their vocations within the Church, have made attempts to contribute positively to the development of Catholic moral theology by rethinking fundamental principles, freedom and responsibility of conscience, the validity of absolutes, the importance of the person, etc. Many of these attempts have been very thoughtful and thought-provoking, and a significant contribution to the ongoing, positive development. In general, these published discussions are properly asking questions and making suggestions, but not giving answers reducible to practice. Some of the discussions, however, under the banner of academic freedom, pretend to offer valid answers reducible to practice, contrary to authentic Catholic doctrine promulgated by the one magisterium.

Especially today, some theologians in their quest for theological understanding are very jealous of their proper academic freedom theoretically to question magisterial statements of doctrine.[2] Proper academic freedom is one thing, but nowhere in the Documents of Vatican II do we find any indication that theologians may legitimately so express dissent as to instruct the faithful to behavior contrary to authentic Catholic doctrine, contending that such behavior is valid and morally acceptable for the Catholic faithful.

When a private theologian or a group of theologians proposes to their peers or to the public at large insights contrary to authentic Catholic doctrine, their views do not constitute a sufficiently solid base for implementation by the faithful in their daily lives. Lest there remain any doubt, just ten years after Vatican II the Sacred Congregation for the Doctrine of the Faith, speaking with papal authority explicitly affirmed this truth.

Responding to the American Bishops on the subject of sterilization under date of March 13, 1975, the Congregation declared:

> The Congregation, while it confirms this traditional doctrine of the Church (on sterilization), is not unaware of the dissent against this teaching from many theologians. The Congregation, however, denies that doctrinal significance can be attributed to this fact as such, so as to constitute a "theological source" which the faithful might invoke and thereby

abandon the authentic Magisterium, and follow the opinions of private theologians which dissent from it (Translation published by the Bishops of the United States, n.2).

On another occasion, a few months earlier, the same Congregation, speaking again with papal authority, issued a Declaration on Abortion under date of November 18, 1974, for the whole Catholic Church to "confirm certain fundamental truths of Catholic doctrine for all Christians." In that declaration the Congregation called attention to recent "controversies and new opinions, . . ." and added:

> it is not a question of opposing one opinion to another, but of transmitting to the faithful a constant teaching of the supreme Magisterium, which teaches moral norms in the light of faith. It is therefore clear that this Declaration necessarily entails a grave obligation for Christian consciences (*Declaration on Abortion* by Sacred Congregation for the Doctrine of the Faith, U.S.C.C., 1975, n.4, p.2).

Unfortunately we are faced today with examples of some theologians who on their own authority and dissatisfied with legitimate academic freedom, seem to offer specific guidelines to the faithful for behavior as morally acceptable in practice contrary to Catholic doctrine. How then should the faithful react to the conflict between the dissenting theologians and the magisterium of the Church? All members of the Church should be willing to listen to the responsibly expressed speculative insights of all theologians, but should at the same time acknowledge the real obligation of living their daily lives according to the norms promulgated by the magisterium of the Church, the authentic voice of Christ in the world today. The changing, speculative opinions of contemporary theologians in expressing dissent do not dislodge authentic Catholic doctrine.

Let me cite one example: I wish to affirm that in my judgment the argumentation and teaching of Pope Pius XII about
deliberately aborting an unborn baby are still decisive in the
behavior of the Catholic faithful. The authentic Roman
Catholic doctrine was clearly and succinctly expressed by Pope
Pius XII in two formal addresses delivered respectively on October 29, 1951, and November 26, 1951:

> 12. Every human being, even the infant in the
> mother's womb, has the right to life immediately
> from God, not from the parents or any human society
> or authority. Therefore, there is no man, no human
> authority, no science, no medical, eugenic, social,
> economic or moral "indication" that can show or give
> a valid juridical title for *direct* deliberate disposition
> concerning an innocent human life—which is to say,
> a disposition that aims at its destruction either as an
> end in itself or as the means of attaining another end
> that is perhaps in no way illicit in itself. Thus, for
> example, to save the life of the mother is a most
> noble end, but the direct killing of the child as a
> means to this end is not licit....
> The life of an innocent person is untouchable. Any
> direct attempt or aggression against it is a violation
> of one of the basic laws without which men cannot
> live together in safety ... (*Address to the Italian
> Catholic Union of Midwives,* Oct. 29, 1951).
> 10. Innocent human life, in whatsoever condition
> it is found, is withdrawn, from the very first moment
> of its existence, from any direct deliberate attack.
> This is a fundamental right of the human person,
> which is of general value in the Christian conception
> of life; hence as valid for the life still hidden within
> the womb of the mother, as for the life already born
> and developing outside of her; as much opposed to
> direct abortion as to the direct killing of the child

before, during or after its birth. Whatever foundation there may be for the distinction between these various phases of the development of life that is born or still unborn, in profane and ecclesiastical law, and as regards certain civil and penal consequences, all these cases involve a grave and unlawful attack upon the inviolability of human life.

11. This principle holds good both for the life of the child as well as for that of the mother. Never and in no case has the Church taught that the life of the child must be preferred to that of the mother.... No, neither the life of the mother nor that of the child can be subjected to an act of direct suppression. In the one case as in the other, there can be but one obligation: to make every effort to save the lives of both, of the mother and of the child.

19. On purpose We have always used the expression "direct attempt on the life of an innocent person," "direct killing." Because if, for example, the saving of the life of the future mother, independently of her pregnant state, should urgently require a surgical act or other therapeutic treatment which would have as an accessory consequence, in no way desired or intended but inevitable, the death of the foetus, such an act could no longer be called a direct attempt on an innocent life. Under these conditions the operation can be licit, like other similar medical interventions, granted always that a good of high worth is concerned, such as life, and that it is not possible to postpone the operation until after the birth of the child, nor to have recourse to other efficacious remedies... (*Address to the National Congress of the Family Front and the Association of Large Families,* Nov. 26, 1951).

This authentic Catholic doctrine has been explicitly reaf-

firmed in recent years after the Second Vatican Council by the
Sacred Congregation for the Doctrine of the Faith in its *Declaration on Abortion,* Nov. 18, 1974:

> 14. Divine law and natural reason, therefore,
> exclude all right to the direct killing of an innocent
> human person. However, if the reasons given to jus-
> tify an abortion were always manifestly evil and
> valueless the problem would not be so dramat-
> ic.... We proclaim only that none of these reasons
> can ever *objectively* confer the right to dispose of
> another's life, even when that life is only beginning.

In Footnote 15 of that same Declaration, the Congregation
affirms with strong approval the doctrinal teaching of Pope
Pius XII, and quotes explicitly one typical statement that for-
mulates Catholic doctrine on abortion:

> As long as a man is not guilty, his life is untoucha-
> ble, and therefore any act directly tending to destroy
> it is illicit, whether such destruction is intended as
> an end in itself or only as a means to an end,
> whether it is a question of life in the embryonic
> stage or in a stage of full development or already in
> its final stages (Nov. 12, 1944).

Any theologian today, therefore, who maintains that in any
circumstances, exceptional or not, it is objectively lawful for
the Catholic faithful to have or perform a direct abortion is
contradicting the authentic doctrine of the Church. Such a
theologian is not exercising his academic freedom properly and
no member of the Catholic faithful may in practice follow such
a theological view.

In the second half of this paper I intend to review the relevant truths and reasoning behind the principle of double effect.
This I agreed to do when I accepted the invitation to participate

in this workshop. Understandably, I shall be building on what has already been very effectively explained in some of the previous papers, which I shall now be taking for granted. Some repetition may be unavoidable, however, for clarity's sake, but I shall keep it to a minimum.

The principle of double effect is the first of two basic, interrelated insights of traditional moral theology. The second is the traditional analysis of the moral act. Both these insights have been accepted by the magisterium of the Church in its moral decision making. In this paper I wish to affirm my confidence in their continued validity, although both of them, as traditionally understood, are under attack today by some contemporary theologians. Since a proper understanding of the principle of double effect flows from proper understanding of the analysis of the moral act, I shall consider the latter first.

What the traditional moral theologian is doing in analyzing the moral act is discerning the objective morality of the act as a whole. This objective morality is determined by what are called the elements of the moral act or the fonts of morality, namely, the object in the strict sense, the circumstances or situation of the act, and the end or purpose of the act. To determine the total objective morality, all three elements need to be considered, not just one or more of them.

The object in the strict sense is what the agent primarily and proximately intends in the order of execution. Of its very nature it is always directly intended as a means to the accomplishing of the final purpose. What is included as part of this directly intended object is not only the physical element, i.e., the physical action and its physical effect, but also the moral element, i.e., the deliberate intending of that action and its physical effect. It is precisely because this moral element is included in the object that the object cannot be called simply "ontic," "premoral," or "nonmoral," as some modern theologians seem inclined to do. For the moral order is the order of willing, and the primary physical effect is not distinguishable from the moral object.

The object of the moral act, therefore, is either morally good, morally evil, or morally indifferent, depending on whether or not it conforms to the norm of morality.

The circumstances and the end of the moral act in the order of execution are understood to be added to the object in the strict sense. In the order of intention, however, the end or purpose is the element that penetrates both the object and the circumstances. For in the order of intention the end of the moral act is what is primarily intended.

Circumstances, therefore, that further determine the object in its moral aspect can determine the specific morality of the object in degree, in moral species, or in theological species. For example, the widow in the gospel story who gave from her poverty did a more virtuous act by that very fact than the rich man who gave from his abundance.

The end of the moral act, i.e., the purpose or motive why the agent is acting, even though it is what is primarily intended in the order of intention, cannot remove the morality of the object and the circumstances. A good end, therefore, does not justify the performance of an act that is evil by reason of the object and circumstances. But a good end makes for the total good of an act that is good by reason of object and circumstances. And an evil end makes a moral act evil in spite of good object and circumstances.

I want to emphasize this point: To determine the total objective morality of a moral act, all three elements—the object in the strict sense, circumstances, and end—must be assessed, not just one or the other element.

What this means for the moral act is as follows: First, if the object is good in itself, then the circumstances and/or the end can make the act evil or add additional goodness; second, if the object is morally indifferent in itself, the circumstances and/or the end will make the act good or evil; and third, if the object is evil in itself, the circumstances and/or the end, no matter how good they may be in themselves, cannot make the moral act totally good, since it continues to be morally evil by reason of its object.

With this understanding of the object of the moral act, I think we are ready to face what, in my judgment, is the core of the difference between the thinking of some modern theologians (i.e., the consequentialists and proportionalists) and the traditional theologians, both of the present and former times. According to traditional moral theology, some actions are so intrinsically evil that no circumstances or good purpose can possibly eliminate the objective moral evil if the actions are directly intended, e.g., actions of blasphemy, adultery, killing an innocent human person on human authority, etc. The modern consequentialists and proportionalists seem to deny that there is any such action that cannot, with sufficient reason, be performed lawfully. From this root error, it seems to me, these modern theologians have developed their present mode of thinking.[3] After maturely weighing the arguments and insights of these contemporary dissenting scholars, I find their argumentation unpersuasive.

Before entering into an explanation of the principle of double effect in today's market, I would like to make some introductory remarks. Thirty years ago in the March issue of *Theological Studies,* I published an article entitled "An Historical Analysis of the Principle of Double Effect." In doing the research preliminary to that article, I faced a major problem of interpreting the various terms with different meanings that were used by various authors. Sometimes, too, I noticed that within the same author's writings the same term would have different meanings in different contexts.

For example, St. Thomas Aquinas and practically all the

moralists up to the nineteenth century used the term *effect per se* in two different senses. One sense is that of the effect coming from a cause which of its very nature is ordained to produce that effect. The other sense is that of an effect intended directly by the will of the agent, whether it comes from a cause which of its very nature is ordained to produce that effect or not. Similarly they used the term *effect per accidens* to signify two kinds of effects. One sense is that of an effect coming from a cause which of its very nature is not ordained to produce that effect. The other sense is that of an effect which merely is not directly intended by the will of the agent.

Aquinas also used the terms *intentio* and *intendere* in different senses in different contexts. In one place he seems to restrict the meaning of *intentio* to intending only the ultimate end of the moral action. In other places he seems to mean intending proximate ends as distinct from the ultimate end, and intending the object of the moral act as distinct from the end.

This phenomenon has led to conflicting interpretations by modern scholars of theology texts of the past.

Some modern theologians, too, adding foundation for further confusion, have introduced their own meanings to terms fairly clear in general fifteen years ago. I refer especially to new meanings being given to the terms *direct* and *indirect*. But we read also of the new distinctions between intrinsic evil *in the strong sense* and *in the weak sense,* and of the principle of double effect *in the strict sense* and *in the broad sense.* We usually find this terminology in the writings of those disenchanted with the traditional understanding of the principle of double effect or of those completely rejecting it.

Among the published insights individual authors seemed to misidentify the focus of their attack or questioning. For example, the Reverend Peter Knauer S.J. seemed to be questioning the traditional analysis of the moral act rather than precisely the principle of double effect. Accepting his statement at its asserted value as an evaluation of "the principle of double effect," I do not think Fr. Knauer understood the principle.[4] Other commentators on Fr. Knauer's analysis have experienced similar misgivings. Knauer makes the principle so much into something it is not that Dr. Germain Grisez accuses him of "carrying through a revolution in principle while pretending only a clarification of traditional ideas."[5] Fr. Richard McCormick S.J. "can only wonder why Knauer retained the terminology at all."[6]

With special personal interest I keep reading and studying the theological insights of these various disenchanted authors to discern, if I can, the validity of their insights. My educated reaction is that the principle of double effect retains its validity in spite of the modern onslaughts, and that the magisterium of the Church under the guidance and strengthening power of the Holy Spirit is well advised to continue using it in making moral decisions.

Now I would like to delineate with some precision the meaning of certain terms used again and again in the explanation of the principle of double effect.

To intend something directly is to intend something in itself either as an end of a moral act or as a means to the end. For example, when a surgeon intends to amputate an arm to save the patient's life, he directly intends to save the patient's life as the end of the moral act. He also directly intends to amputate the arm as a means to the end of saving the patient's life. The surgeon therefore directly intends both the amputation and the saving of the patient's life. The amputation clearly is approved and chosen as a means to the end.

To intend something indirectly is to intend something, not in itself, i.e., not directly, but only in its cause as a foreseen effect of that cause, i.e., as a side effect or by-product of one's action. The effect sincerely is not desired, not wanted, not approved, not chosen, i.e., neither as a means nor as an end. For example, a person with a common cold takes some cold medicine, foreseeing that the medicine will also cause unwanted drowsiness. The person directly intends to take the medicine as a means of getting rid of the cold; he or she directly intends getting rid of the cold as the end. But he or she does not directly intend the unwanted drowsiness either as a means or an end. Only indirectly does the person intend the drowsiness, i.e., only in directly intending the cause, the taking of the medicine.

Next, I want to clarify the meaning of the term *effect*. In general, an effect is that which the agent causes. In this general sense, an effect can be either part of the object or a circumstance or the end of the moral act. In the principle of double effect, the effect is identified as a *further result* of the object of the moral act complete in itself. This *further result* is called *further* because the complete object of the moral act is considered the first result. This *further* result, therefore, is distinct from the complete object in the strict sense of the moral act.

The complete object of the moral act, including the first result, is always directly intended by the agent. The *further result,* if directly intended, is the end of the moral act. If only indirectly intended, the *further result* sincerely is an unwanted circumstance or an unwanted effect. This means that in the valid application of the principle of double effect, the directly intended good effect is the end of the moral act, and the indirectly intended evil effect technically is an unwanted circumstance of the moral act.

The statement of the problem to which the principle of double effect responds is as follows: Is it ever morally lawful to perform an action that will produce two foreseen effects, one good and one evil, when the evil effect in the procedure contemplated still remains an evil effect to the extent that the agent may not directly intend the foreseen evil effect? In the context of the traditional analysis of the moral act, the principle of double effect gives an affirmative—but a qualified affirmative—answer to this problem question.

The traditional principle of double effect may be stated as follows: It is morally lawful to perform an action that will produce two foreseen effects, one good and one evil, if the following four conditions are verified at the same time:

1. The action performed (i.e., the object of the moral act) is either morally good or at least indifferent in itself;

2. The good effect is not produced through the evil effect (in other words, the evil effect is not directly intended as a means to the good effect);

3. The good effect and not the evil effect is directly intended as the end of the moral act;

4. There is a proportionately grave reason for permitting the foreseen evil effect to occur.

The first condition is that the action performed (i.e., the object of the moral act) is either morally good or indifferent in itself.

This condition refers to the action that the agent primarily and proximately intends in the order of execution, e.g., the action of deliberately excising a gravely pathological tube, or the action of administering a dilatation and curettage operation (a D & C) on a woman. The action is always directly intended.

If the action performed (i.e., the object of the moral act) is evil in itself, nothing can make it morally good or indifferent. In such a case evil would be chosen directly, either as an end in itself or as a means to some other end. There could be no question of merely permitting or tolerating the evil. An ordinary example is that of killing an innocent human person on human authority.

Some modern theologians consider that the direct killing of

an innocent human person on human authority can be merely an "ontic" or "premoral" or "nonmoral" evil, but not necessarily a moral evil. Abstractly, of course, the killing of an innocent human person can be considered a "nonmoral evil," but when it is done deliberately, directly, the human action of killing is a moral action of killing. In this sense, therefore, the object of the moral action can be said to include the nonmoral, physical evil of killing a human person. But the moral object includes more than that; it includes the deliberate, direct intention to kill an innocent human person, which is always objectively morally evil.

If this condition is fulfilled, it is clear that the object of the moral act is morally good or at least indifferent. From the aspect of the object of the moral act, therefore, there is no reason why the moral act may not be performed.

The second condition is that the good effect is not produced through the evil effect (in other words, the evil effect is not directly intended as a means to the good effect).

In this condition we are considering especially the causal relationship between the action as cause and the two effects. We pay special attention, therefore, to the way the two effects flow from the action as cause. The temporal relationship between the two effects is important, but it is possible for the evil effect to take place in time before the good effect without the good effect being produced through the bad effect.[7] The certainty with which the two effects will take place is also important, but again it is possible for us to be equally certain that the good and evil effects will be produced without the good effect being produced through the evil.[8]

If we analyze the physical structure of external actions with double effect, we shall see that these actions fall into three classes with regard to the causal relationship between the action as cause and the two effects:

1. In some cases the action primarily produces the good effect and then the evil effect is produced through the good effect. In these cases the good effect is not produced through the evil, but rather the evil is produced through the good. The physical structure of the action could be diagrammed as follows:

ACTION → GOOD EFFECT → EVIL EFFECT

2. In other cases the action primarily produces the evil effect, and then the good effect is produced through the evil effect. In these cases the good effect is produced through the evil. This signifies that the evil is the directly intended means to the good effect. The physical structure of such an action could be diagrammed as follows:

ACTION → EVIL EFFECT → GOOD EFFECT

3. Finally, in the third class of cases, the action does not primarily produce either the good or the evil effect. Rather it produces both effects independently of one another, so that neither effect is produced through the other. In these cases the good effect is not produced through the evil, and the evil effect is not produced through the good. Both effects are produced equally immediately. The physical structure could be diagrammed as follows:

$$\text{ACTION} \begin{cases} \nearrow \text{—GOOD EFFECT} \\ \searrow \text{—EVIL EFFECT} \end{cases}$$

This second condition indicates that the physical structure of the action may be of the first or third class but not of the second.

For many years, especially in the more recent years, some moral theologians and others have expressed difficulty with understanding this condition, its application to complex cases, and its relationship to the first condition. To help overcome this difficulty, theologians have suggested two practical tests or "rules of thumb." Each of these tests is simply a particular way of applying the condition that the good effect must not come through the evil effect. It is important to bear in mind, therefore, that they are applications of this condition, not substitutes for it. Since Fr. William Conway and Fr. Vermeersch have given such lucid explanations of these tests, I shall borrow their wording:

> The first of these tests could be stated as follows: "Is it possible to imagine a physically possible situation, however improbable, in which the evil effect would be prevented, but in which nevertheless the act would produce the good effect?" If it is, then the external act is *per se* lawful.
>
> As an illustration of the use of this test we may take the case of the Arctic explorer who leaves a companion in the tent and walks out into morally certain death in the snow, because he knows there is not sufficient food in the tent to keep both of them alive until a rescue party reaches them. The good effect is the saving of his companion's life; the evil effect is his own death. Now it is possible to imagine a situation—not very likely perhaps, but still physically possible—in which the evil effect would be prevented, say if the explorer, after walking for several hours were to come upon an abandoned tent with an adequate supply of food and equipment, and in which he too was subsequently picked up by the rescue party. In such a case the evil effect would not take place but the good would not thereby be prevented; the favorable position of the companion left in the first tent would not be lessened in any way by the discovery of the second tent. The test thus helps to throw into bolder relief that the evil effect in this

case is not the means through which the good effect is achieved.

The same test can be applied with advantage to well known moral cases, like that of the sailor who swims away from a life-boat in mid-Atlantic because it was clear that, while he was in it, the boat was overcrowded and slowly sinking; or the case of the soldier who raises himself into a prominent position in order to draw the fire of the enemy while his companions make a dash across an exposed piece of ground.

With regard to this first test, however, two points are worth noting. The first is that in imagining the situation in which the evil is prevented we must always keep within the bounds of physical possibility ... i.e. does not involve any suspension of the physical laws of matter. ...

The second point to be noted is that the test is positive and not negative in its application. In other words, if the act passes the test it may be inferred that the external act is *per se* lawful; it does not at all follow that if the act fails to pass the test the external act is unlawful. Thus it may be lawful for a surgeon to remove a cancerous womb containing a live non-viable foetus although it is physically impossible to remove the diseased organ without the death of the foetus necessarily resulting. ... The fact is that both effects of an act of two effects may be physically inseparable from the act and yet they may issue from it independently, neither coming through the other. In the traditional terminology of the theologians, the two effects may issue from the act equally immediately in the order of causality.[9]

With special clarity Vermeersch has expressed the second test as follows: Think of the action separated just from the

circumstances from which the evil effect flows. Would the
agent in that case want to perform the action? If he would, then
the good effect is not produced through the bad effect. If he
would not, then the good effect is produced through the bad
effect.[10] For example, a man leaps to his death from a ninth
floor window in a burning building to avoid death by fire.
Would he leap from a burning building if the window from
which he leaps were on the first floor? The answer, of course, is
in the affirmative. Therefore, in leaping from the ninth floor,
the man does not directly intend to kill himself to avoid death
by fire.

> Not all practical cases are amenable to the applica-
> tion of these tests and in the last resort we must
> always fall back on the fundamental issue—does the
> good effect come through the evil effect? In many
> cases it is not easy to see whether it does or not, but
> the difficulties are more of fact than of principle.[11]

The reason for this second condition of the principle of double
effect is as follows: If the condition is fulfilled, it is clear that
the evil effect is only a circumstance of the moral act, is only
permitted, and is not directly intended. If this condition is not
fulfilled, it is clear that the evil effect is the approved means of
producing the good effect and is directly intended in itself. That
is moral evil, and we may never do moral evil that good may
come of it. A good end does not justify the use of morally evil
means (cf. Rom. 3:8).

Examples

1. The excision of a pregnant gravely pathological fallopian
tube to save the life of the mother with the foreseen death of
the fetus is morally permissible as far as this condition is concerned. For the good effect, the saving of the mother's life, and
the evil effect, the death of the fetus, flow equally immediately

from the removal of the pathological fallopian tube. The mother's life is not saved through the death of the fetus, but through the removal of the pathological tube.

2. The D and C operation on an unmarried woman two months pregnant to save her reputation is not morally permissible, according to this condition. For it is through the evil effect, i.e., the direct killing of the fetus, that the good effect, the saving of the mother's reputation, is produced.

3. Another case now appearing in the literature is that of a pregnant woman with an aortic aneurysm ballooning threateningly behind the uterus. To get at the aneurysm, the doctors judge that they must evacuate the uterus, thus directly killing the fetus. This procedure would violate this second condition of the principle of double effect; it would therefore be morally objectionable.[12]

The third condition is that the good effect and not the evil effect is directly intended in itself as the end of the moral act.

This condition indicates that the end of the moral act must be good. Only the good effect may be directly intended as the motive for the moral act. The foreseen evil effect may not be directly intended nor approved, but only permitted or tolerated. For to the extent that the agent directly intends the evil, the act is morally objectionable.

The fourth condition is that there is a proportionately grave reason for permitting the foreseen evil to occur.

This condition indicates that, if a sufficiently grave reason is present, the law prohibiting the foreseen indirectly intended evil effect ceases. Once this law ceases in a concrete situation, the evil effect may be permitted. The obligation is satisfied by taking reasonable care lest the evil effect follow from the action performed.

This may be put briefly in another way: In pursuing our right to do good, morally we are unable to avoid the evil in a particular situation, if there is a proportionately grave reason for permitting it.

Furthermore, if the agent can reasonably produce the good effect in some way that does not produce the evil, he must accomplish the good that way. Otherwise he would reasonably be judged to directly intend the evil. Why else would the agent choose to produce the good effect in a way that includes the evil, when he or she can choose another way that does not include the evil effect. The agent certainly would not be taking reasonable care to avoid producing an evil effect.

The principles for judging whether there is a proportionately grave excusing cause for permitting an evil effect are as follows:

1. The greater the evil foreseen, the greater the reason must be for permitting it. For example, it would not be lawful indirectly to kill a fetus when the good to be accomplished is the avoidance of a slight illness to the mother. *Notate bene:* Comparative estimates must be qualitative as well as quantitative. For example, in applying the principle of double effect to conventional or nuclear bombing in a just war, we must pay attention not only to the numbers of innocent people who may be killed or prevented from being killed but also to the religious and civil liberty that may be preserved.

Here I would like to acknowledge a service provided by the consequentialists and proportionalists in recent years. By their emphasis on consequences, they have helped make the theological community more and more sensitive to quality-of-life factors in our comparative estimates.

2. The closer the cause to the evil effect, the greater the reason must be for permitting the evil. A greater reason, therefore, would be needed to excuse one who proximately, as compared to the one who only remotely, cooperates in the sin of another, e.g., in the sin of drunkenness.

3. The more certain the evil, the greater must be the reason for permitting it. A lesser reason, therefore, would be sufficient, in the case in which the good will most certainly be accomplished and the evil only more or less probably.

4. A greater reason would be required, if the agent by omitting the contemplated action would completely impede the evil effect, than if the agent knew the evil effect would take place anyway.

5. The greater the obligation to prevent the evil, the greater the reason must be for permitting it. A greater excusing cause is needed, therefore, in the one who is obliged *ex officio* to prevent the evil than in the one who is obliged only from charity.

6. A greater excusing reason is required for cooperation in the formal sin of one's neighbor than with a sin that remains only material.

Conclusion. If the four conditions of the principle of double effect are fulfilled at the same time in any concrete case, the lawfulness of the whole moral act is manifest and the evil effect is not imputable to the agent. For from the third condition it is clear that the end of the moral act is good. From the first condition it is clear that the object of the moral act is morally good, or at least indifferent. From the second condition it is clear that the evil effect is only permitted and not directly intended. And finally from the fourth condition it is clear that the obligation is satisfied of taking reasonable care lest the evil effect follow from the action performed. No reason remains, therefore, for imputing the evil effect to the agent.

Furthermore, as some theologians express it, the agent acting according to the principle of double effect is judged to be in a state of moral impossibility to avoid the evil effect. Hence, because of the moral impossibility, he or she is excused from the obligation of preventing the evil.

The conclusion can also be expressed as follows: *Per se* a

human person has the right to perform a good or indifferent action with a good effect or purpose. And under the valid application of the principle the agent does not lose that right even though he or she foresees an unintended evil effect will result.

After the formal presentation of my paper I was asked by one or other of my listeners to address myself to two well-known cases.

The first is that of a hunter who is hunting deer. Within range he sees a movement in the bush, but cannot discern whether it is a deer or another hunter moving about. May the hunter shoot to kill, hoping the moving object is a deer? True, in this case there is question of two effects, one good and one evil, the killing of the deer and the killing of a human person. But the case does not fit within the context of the principle of double effect. There is not here an example of an action that produces two effects; rather the action produces one or the other effect. The hunter, of course, must make sure that the moving object is not a human person before he shoots.

The second case is that of craniotomy or embryotomy of an unborn baby to save the life of a pregnant woman. Both Germain Grisez and Joseph Boyle in recent years have written suggesting that in such a case the killing of the unborn baby is not a direct killing.[13] Fortunately, in the light of medical and surgical advances today, this is not an acute problem. The dangers formerly judged to demand this operation today are eliminated by less radical measures. As I understand this case, cutting up the child and removing it piecemeal is clearly a lethal blow whose only *per se* immediate effect is killing the child. Every effect that is the only *per se* immediate effect of a deliberate action is necessarily directly intended. Killing the child, therefore, is directly intended. In this analysis the saving of the life of the mother takes place mediately through the direct killing of her child. Clearly in this analysis the principle of double effect cannot validly be applied to this case. This type of case was discussed vigorously toward the end of the nineteenth century and finally condemned as immoral by the Roman Catholic Church.[14]

Notes

1. Harold C. Voris M.D., Wayne B. Slaughter M.D., Joseph R. Christian M.D., and Edward R. Cayia M.D., "Successful Separation of Craniopagus Twins," *Journal of Neurosurgery* 14, no. 5 (1957): 545-60.

2. Walter J. Burghardt S.J., "Stone the Theologians! The Role of Theology in Today's Church, *Catholic Mind* (September 1977): 42-50; and Avery Dulles S.J., "The Magisterium in History: A Theological Reflection," *Chicago Studies* (Summer 1978): 264-81.

3. Richard A. McCormick S.J., "Notes on Moral Theology," *Theological Studies* (March 1978): 109. Note that McCormick is himself a proportionalist or consequentialist.

4. Peter Knauer S.J., "La Détermination du bien et du mal moral par le principe du double effet," *Nouvelle Revue Théologique* 87 (1965): 356-76. See also the English translation of this essay "The Hermeneutic Function of the Principle of Double Effect" in *Natural Law Forum* 12 (1965). The translation was reprinted in Charles E. Curran and Richard A. McCormick, eds., *Readings in Moral Theology, No. 1: Moral Norms and the Catholic Tradition* (New York: Paulist Press, 1979).

5. Germain Grisez, *Abortion: The Myths, the Realities, and the Arguments* (New York and Cleveland: Corpus Books, 1970), p. 331.

6. Richard A. McCormick S.J., *Ambiguity in Moral Choice,* Père Marquette Theology Lecture, 1973, pp. 7-12.

7. A. Vermeersch, "Avortement directe ou indirecte," *Nouvelle Revue Théologique* (1933): 605; also B. Merkelbach, *Quaes. de Embry. et de Steril.,* q. 3, art. 1, lv, p. 34.

8. A. Vermeersch, *Periodica* (1932): 109; and Wm. Conway, "The Act of Two Effects," *Irish Theological Quarterly* (April 1951): 131.

9. Conway, ibid., pp. 125-37.

10. A. Vermeersch, "Avortement directe ou indirecte," p. 605.

11. Wm. Conway, p. 136.

12. Richard A. McCormick S.J., "Notes on Moral Theology," p. 76.

13. Germain Grisez, p. 341; and Joseph Boyle, Jr., "Double-effect and a Certain Type of Embryotomy," *Irish Theological Quarterly* 44, no. 4,

(1977): 303–18. It needs to be said that both Grisez and Boyle still insist on the role of intentionality, and propose their position as illustrating the principle of double effect, not as one justified by the "proportionate good."

14. John Connery S.J., *Abortion: The Development of the Roman Catholic Perspective* (Chicago: Loyola University Press, 1977); see especially chaps. 12–15 on the controversy over craniotomy and its resolution.

Part Five
Conscience and the Moral Life

The Meaning of Conscience

Rev. William B. Smith
St. Joseph's Seminary
Dunwoodie, Yonkers, New York

The meaning, nature, place, and function of conscience in Catholic moral theology are much debated, important, and perhaps the most confused area of contemporary moral discussion.

American society is agreed on the crucial importance of conscience and conscience convictions, but that agreement bleeds away into ambiguity, and at times even into controversy, when one asks: What is conscience? What precisely does it mean? The fact that secular society has not yet succeeded in defining conscience in a way acceptable to all surely affects us, our society, and our discussion. In my judgment, it is then doubly important to present with precision the nature, function, and meaning of conscience in Catholic tradition lest further Catholic confusion only render general confusion that much more confusing.

I shall purposely limit this presentation to a few remarks about conscience terminology; the nature, function, and meaning of conscience; and some current misuses of conscience because, in fact, the possible applications are as extensive as moral theology itself.

The Meaning of Conscience: A Necessarily Nuanced Vocabulary

It is traditional and wise to begin with a definition of terms. In the English word *conscience,* we are blessed with a single noun, but we are bloated with different and differing adjectives based on it. In English the noun *conscience* (Latin *con+scientia*) is distinguished from the noun *consciousness*—the latter being a more psychological term of reference. Consciousness is an awareness, a remembering that is basically *retrospective* and *reflective.*

Moral theology is aware of this understanding and its importance, but like the language itself, the word *conscience* is and has been for centuries basically an act of judging: a *prospective* and *directive* act of judgment; a decision of conscience.

The conventional textbooks of Catholic moral theology explain the nature of conscience and its precise function at some length.[1] A reliable and closely reasoned treatment of this subject is presented in "Conscience in the Catholic Theological Tradition," an article by J. V. Dolan S.J. in an otherwise uneven collection.[2]

For locating the unity of Christian morality, the International Theological Commission has provided us all with a useful proposition with which to direct our study:

> The unity of Christian morality is based on unchanging principles, contained in Sacred Scripture, clarified by Sacred Tradition, and presented in each age by the Magisterium.[3]

These precisely sacred sources—Scripture tradition, and the magisterium—are a sound theological guide for our understanding of conscience and its place and meaning in Catholic tradition.

The word *conscience* (Greek συνείδεσις) appears some twenty-eight times in the singular and once in the plural in the New Testament. The equivalent term does not appear at all in the Hebrew Bible and but once in the Septuagint.

The New Testament usage, especially in St. Paul and his epistle to the Hebrews, of συνείδεσις is basically a *reflective* one. That is, human beings are understood to be so constituted by God that, should they go beyond the moral limts of their nature, they will sense the pain of conscience.[4] Some contemporary authors[5] have taken the term *heart* (Greek καρδία) to fill in this Old Testament void and to extend a New Testament blend. But this effort simply mistakes one facet of conscience for conscience itself; thus C. A. Pierce's classic work *Conscience in the New Testament* remains, I think, unchallenged.[6]

Aware of the biblical usage and background, and of continuing refinements in Catholic tradition,[7] we must admit quite frankly that the nature and meaning of conscience in contemporary moral theology is not simply a retrospective-reflective awareness or remembering.

Many metaphors in current coin describe conscience as the *voice of God,* as an *inner voice,* as a *still small voice* within one's so-called heart of hearts. Such expressions are useful only insofar as they are recognized and acknowledged as metaphors. Conscience is often described as a sense of guilt or of pangs, or as a system of values, feelings, and insights; conscience is said to sting, to blame, to accuse, to prompt, or to assuage. Moral theology knows these descriptions, but the precise nature and function of conscience in Catholic moral theology is that act of passing or making a personal judgment on the moral quality of a proposed and particular action—a judgment of mind on a particular moral issue that confronts it and must be resolved.[8]

It is this *prospective-directive* act of judgment—the technical name of which is *antecedent conscience*—that is the chief interest of the theologian and the moralist.[9] All properly moral questions touch this; all properly moral applications involve this.

Properly speaking, conscience neither invents law nor does it create objective value. Its function is to apply either general or particular moral knowledge to any prospective and particular action. Throughout the entire discussion of conscience, there will be an objective and a subjective referent. *Objectively,* moral knowledge or wisdom is based on some objective consideration, some norm other than myself, e.g., God's revelation, the teaching of the Church, the teaching of the Buddah, the teaching of Gandhi, etc. And, *subjectively,* it is the person subject (you, I, anyone) who applies that objective moral wisdom to concrete situations, and it is that concrete function of application that so concerns moral theology.

Indeed, moral law or moral wisdom would be rather useless unless each person had the power and ability to apply them to concrete situations. This focus on the "decision" or "judgment" of conscience is well established in ancient and recent Catholic theological tradition. Vatican Council II presented and presumed this understanding (*Gaudium et Spes,* nn.16, 17, 41). The Canadian Catholic Conference underscored this point in its closely reasoned *Statement On The Formation of Conscience* (December 1, 1973), which stated that conscience is the ultimate "judgment."[10]

Consistently the National Conference of Catholic Bishops has continued and maintained this same meaning. It stated in its *Basic Teachings for Catholic Religious Education:*

> Each person must have a right conscience and follow it. Conscience is not a feeling nor self-will, although these may affect the degree of culpability. Conscience is a personal *judgment* that something is right or wrong because of the will and law of God (n. 17).[11]

In the report of the Ad Hoc Committee entitled "On Moral Values in Society," it stated:

> The practical *judgment* by which we estimate the relationship of concrete acts to our value system is called the *decision of conscience*. Not a distinct faculty, conscience is a moral *judgment* by which we determine a concrete act or omission to be consistent or inconsistent with the ideals we espouse. (n. 4)[12]

In its moral pastoral *To Live in Christ Jesus,* the National Conference of Catholic Bishops stated:

> We still must decide how to realize and affirm them in the concrete circumstances of our lives. Such decisions are called *judgments of conscience.*[13]

Finally, in its publication entitled *Sharing The Light of Faith* (N.C.D.), it stated:

> Such decisions are called *judgments of conscience.... Decisions* of conscience must be based upon prayer, study, consultation, and an understanding of the teachings of the Church. One must have a rightly formed conscience and follow it (n. 103) (emphasis added).[14]

Since conscience is a judgment, two possibilities are always real: We can judge correctly (that is, have a correct conscience) or incorrectly (that is, have an erroneous conscience). Hugh L. Carey, the Catholic governor of New York State, has developed his own peculiar notion of conscience with respect to the death penalty and abortion, which the *New York Times* saw fit to print as the "Quotation of the Day." Mr. Carey stated, "My mind does not govern my conscience; my conscience governs my mind."[15] Whether the governor was advocating a mindless conscience or a conscienceless mind I do not know; what I do know is that any and every rational mind is capable of correct judgments and erroneous judgments.

With regard to objective morality of whatever kind, that objective judgment can be a correct one or an erroneous one. Subjectively, the subject—the person who judges correctly or incorrectly—can be certain or doubtful about a particular judgment, regardless of whether that judgment is correct or erroneous. I belabor this distinction somewhat, before considering the rules for practical action, because I fear that the possibility and actuality of objectively erroneous but subjectively certain judgments have mysteriously disappeared from discussion and consideration. Some people seem to think and write that the only consideration worth mentioning or writing about is personal certitude and certain personal conviction—as if it really did not matter whether that certain judgment was correct or erroneous.

True, there are classically two practical rules for action: (1) Always obey a certain conscience! and (2) Never act on a doubtful one! To this, all will nod in agreement. But it is often here that slogans and/or silence substitute for study. For some people it is now common practice and almost common parlance to say "Follow your conscience!" and say no more. But this is most incomplete and actually misleading. Here, much more must be said about the formation of a correct conscience in the first place.

It is here, in the proper formation of a correct Catholic conscience, that the sources of sacred theology (thus of Catholic morality) will loom largest. Sacred scripture, sacred tradition, and the magisterium will either be accorded primary place or be reduced in status, by various arrangements, to the level of "privileged" or even "precious" input among other competing sources of input in the formation of a correct Catholic conscience. The more one dissents from Catholic teaching, the less likely is it that the sacred sources (*loci theologici*) will be primary.

In fact, Vatican Council II had but one, *ex professo* statement on the formation of conscience:

> In the formation of their consciences, the Christian faithful ought carefully to attend to the sacred and certain doctrine of the Church (*Dignitatis Humanae,* 14).

The official footnote of the Council fathers (*Dignitatis Humanae,* 14, fn. 35) cited the *locus classicus* on the formation of a Catholic conscience, the discourse of Pope Pius XII of March 23, 1952, "On the Correct Formation of a Christian Conscience."[16]

Factor for factor, no single element looms so large in the formation of a Catholic conscience as does the "sacred and certain doctrine" of the Catholic Church. Some see our Spirit-guided teaching as a heavy burden on already overburdened intellects. I prefer to see such Spirit-guided guidance as a blessing—indeed, a necessary blessing, resting as it does on sacred sources.

At the start I announced my gratitude for the single English noun *conscience,* and cautioned about the bloated adjectives that often surround that noun in usage. In my judgment it is logically and pedagogically important to employ precise accurate terminology in this area; e.g., to say "a correct conscience" or "an erroneous conscience." I say that because such expressions as "sincere conscience" or "good conscience" are very much in vogue today. I would like to think that we can always presume that all parties to the discussion are "sincere"; if not, that's a different kind of problem—a problem of "bad" or "insincere" faith.

A whole literature and language of sincere conscience have emerged in our society; they can be doubly misleading, first, as to decisions of conscience and, second, as to the formation of conscience.

Obviously, sincere honesty will be paramount in the assessment of subjective culpability—the presence or absence of personal fault. But just as obviously, personal sincerity will not make or unmake reality.

Jane Fonda, who has a charism for selective moral outrage, once achieved the level of Charlie Brown on a national TV talk show by stating: "How can I be wrong when I'm so sincere?" Like myself and everyone else, she can be in her judgments sincerely correct or sincerely mistaken. Doesn't it strike you as odd that no one ever seems to be right or wrong anymore—either they mean well, or they are probably sick?

Thus too often the incomplete, unnuanced advice to "follow your conscience," while saying no more, is simply a half-truth that says nothing to the correctness of our decisions of conscience. Even though sincerity is a necessary quality of all conscience decisions and decision making, it is not the only relevant criterion. In coming to Washington, D.C., from New York City, one can take the Eastern Shuttle. In New York the shuttle has three aisles to the Washington plane and three more to the Boston plane. If I rushed down Aisle 6 in a hurry to get here, no one could question my sincerity, but neither could anyone question the fact that I would be going about four hundred miles per hour in the wrong direction—toward Boston!

Please do not misunderstand me. Sincerity is a vitally important subjective quality of every conscience decision. It is not the only quality, however, nor is it the only one worth mentioning.

Similarly, in a sincere formation of conscience and, in particular, in a correct formation of a correctly Catholic conscience, our search, and even our openness toward the authentic sources of Catholic morality should be honestly admitted. In the formation of a Catholic conscience, if one rejects any unwelcome messages from the magisterium of the Church, would it not be more honest and sincere to admit that faith problem instead of disguising it completely in conscience jargon?

After all, docility—teachability—is an integral part of prudence. Dolan is, I think, correct in asking if people are so much more adult and self-directed because they substitute their own favorite authority for another authority, say, for example, the authority of their favorite local theologian for that of the Pope?[17] Clearly, one would still be arguing from authority, but a good deal more than just credentials would be changing in that exchange.

Clearly, there is some confusion at present. Obviously, the winds of doctrine are blowing furiously in many directions, but confusion can also serve a rationalizing process already in motion. Conscience judgments are not disinterested decisions about room or body temperature. In deciding what's good, we are deciding what's good for ourselves. Cardinal Newman once made a point that I know I can't escape: "The aim of most conscientious and religious men is not how to please God; but how to please themselves without displeasing God."

No one dare trivialize this crucial effort of forming and informing a correct Catholic conscience. The prod of conscience only goes against the so-called better self for as long as there is a better self to go against. There is such a thing as a dead conscience: The disregard of our society for the moral judgments of the first chapter of St. Paul's epistle to the Romans is not just the result but the penalty of wrongdoing. We are all capable of coming to terms with a corrupt style, an installed habit, perhaps even in "good conscience" but, of course, in "bad faith." Again, Dolan provided a lasting axiom: If we fail to act as we really judge is right soon enough, we come in time to judge as we act and call it right.[18]

No one is exempt from rationalization in the effort at conscience formation, especially quiet rationalizations in the correct formation of a Catholic conscience. If people sincerely reject the teaching of Scripture, tradition, or the magisterium, they might be sincerely convinced, but they are judging still by norms that are different from mine and from anything the Church has taught on the matter. In some cases the sincerity claimed is a purely emotional one where the practical intellect is under the sway of appetite and swamped by desire. In many cases today it is sad to note that the sincere search of some has been derailed by uncertain guides blowing uncertain trumpets and leading sincere people not toward but away from the authentic sources of Catholic morality.

The Meaning of Conscience: Freedom of Conscience in Vatican II?

There has been no shortage of claims alleging the discovery of a doctrine of "freedom of conscience" in the documents of Vatican Council II. First, let us not confuse "religious freedom," which Vatican II certainly did teach (cf. *Dignitatis Humanae; The Declaration On Religious Freedom*), with a so-called freedom of conscience that the same Council did not teach and, in fact, took some pains to avoid.

As a first step, we should not confuse *physical* freedom with *moral* freedom, and then escalate that confusion to the status of an alleged "right." *Physical* freedom is the *physical ability* to do something, to act or not act, as in the physical ability to throw yourself in front of a moving car. *Moral* freedom is the *moral right* to perform an act. Clearly, one does have the physical *ability* to throw oneself before the car—presuming this is not a rescue—but no one has the moral *right* to do so suicidally.

In essence, no one has, nor can have, the *moral right* to do what is *morally wrong*. Let's recall that the "religious freedom" taught and expounded by the Council was a *freedom from coercion*—an external civil right in the civil order. On this point the Council document was explicit:

> Religious freedom, in turn, which men demand as necessary to fulfill their duty to worship God, has to

do with immunity from coercion in civil society. Therefore, it leaves untouched traditional Catholic doctrine on the moral duty of men and societies toward the true religion and toward the one Church of Christ (*Dignitatis Humanae,* 1).[19]

The religious freedom thus proclaimed is a freedom *from* coercion—a freedom *from,* not a freedom *for* doing whatever one wants. The required nuance and necessary precision about the meaning of this *Declaration* has been provided by John Courtney Murray, one of the contributors to the document who took great pains that this teaching not be confused with a non-Catholic understanding of freedom of conscience.

Fr. Murray wrote:

> It is worth noting that the Declaration does not base the right to free exercise of religion on "freedom of conscience." Nowhere does this phrase occur. And the Declaration nowhere lends its authority to the theory for which the phrase frequently stands, namely, that I have a right to do what my conscience tells me to do, simply because my conscience tells me to do it. This is a perilous theory. Its particular peril is subjectivism—the notion that, in the end, it is my conscience, and not the objective truth, which determines what is right or wrong, true or false.[20]

Commenting further on n.14 of the same Declaration, Fr. Murray stated:

> It might be noted here that the Council intended to make a clear distinction between religious freedom as a principle in the civil order and the Christian freedom which obtains even within the Church. These two freedoms are distinct in kind; and it would be perilous to confuse them. Nowhere does the Declaration touch the issue of freedom within the Church....[21]

Again Fr. Murray defined his terms with great care and precision. Religious freedom rises in the political and social order: relationships between people and government, and human beings and human beings. This is the order of human rights; here the principle of freedom is paramount. But, human beings also live in another order of reality—the spiritual order of the relationship of human beings to what is objectively true and morally good.

> This is the order of duty and obligation. In it a man acts freely indeed, but under moral imperatives, which bind in conscience. No man may plead "rights" in the face of the truth or claim "freedom" from the moral law. The distinction between these two orders of reality would be admitted by all men of good sense. The underlying intention of these two paragraphs of the Declaration is to make the distinction clear, lest religious freedom be made a pretext for moral anarchy.[22]

Classic and repeated Catholic doctrine has insisted that the so-called freedom of conscience is nothing other than the freedom to recognize the order designed by God and to adapt one's conduct to it. Thus the Council Declaration and one of its best-informed commentators took great pains to prevent misunderstanding and to preclude moral confusion. Anyone who fosters teaching contrary to the moral teaching of the Church under the name of "freedom of conscience" fosters a false claim.

After all, where I have a "moral right" to do good, and a "moral right" to do the opposite, I would then have a moral "right" to do anything I choose and simply call it "moral." That would be the moral nonsense that Murray insisted that we must avoid.

Vatican Council II employed the word *conscience* some seventy-two times.[23] Only once did the term *freedom of con-*

science ever appear in the texts of the Council (cf. *Declaration on Christian Education,* 8). That single use was in the sense accepted above, that the Church had a right to be free from coercion in the civil order in establishing its schools. All other seventy-one mentions of the word were with such conventional qualifications and nuanced adjectives, as "correct conscience," "rightly informed conscience," etc.

No doubt, this was a thin distinction, but a necessary one; it was also a distinction that Pope Paul VI saw the need to emphasize.[24] Indeed, this distinction between "religious freedom" and "freedom of conscience" is one that careful scholars have examined at some length,[25] but which popular writers and popular presentations regularly confuse.[26] A non-Catholic understanding of "freedom of conscience" cannot be foisted upon nor found in the documents of Vatican II. In fact, the Council made no small effort to avoid that particular confusion. It is also helpful to recall that the supposedly classic Reformation stance of the supreme autonomy of individual conscience has not been without its problems both in history and in contemporary discussion and application.[27]

Thus, for the sake of a sound theology and pedagogy, I think that it is necessary to avoid incomplete statements, e.g., "Follow your conscience" (*sine addito*), largely in the context of what is claimed and confirmed by individual sincerity. Such incompleteness is misleading and detrimental both for correct conscience decisions and a correct formation of conscience. (I have treated elsewhere an alleged "moral right" to dissent,[28] which has had the same deleterious effects on decisions and formation of conscience. Unfortunately, there have now appeared whole treatises on conscience whose method, presuppositions, thrust, and conclusions are structured—frankly—to enshrine a basically non-Catholic concept of "freedom of conscience" or an alleged "moral right" to dissent from Catholic teaching.[29] Such presentations normally involve a changed ecclesiology, especially regarding assent to the sources of sacred theology (Scripture, tradition, and the magisterium), rather than any radical revolution in the nature, function, and meaning of conscience.

The Meaning of Conscience: Internal-Forum and Good-Conscience Solutions?

A number of questions, especially those touching marital doctrine and morality, have created serious divergences in pastoral practice under the category of "internal-forum" and/or "good-conscience" solutions. Initial efforts seemed to be aimed at "regularizing" the irregular condition of divorced and remarried Catholics now living in invalid unions. The so-called good-conscience solution has never been limited to just that, however, since on the face of it, any difficult moral application can, in theory, be left to the "good conscience" of the person involved without mention or reference to whether that "good" (sincere) conscience is correct or erroneous. Thus the following consideration is more typical than unique, for the understanding of conscience involved obviously has wider, if not unlimited, application.

First, then, let us locate one point of discussion. In conventional reference, the external forum concerns actions of the faithful, clerical or lay, innocent or guilty, in the eyes of the Church; this forum is exercised publicly and has juridical effects. The internal forum is the forum of conscience regarding actions of the faithful, clerical or lay, innocent or guilty, before God; this is exercised privately and has no juridical effects unless specifically provided for. The internal forum is sacramental when it must be exercised in the sacrament of penance or in connection with it; it is extrasacramental when not subject to this limitation.[30]

An entire genre of literature has now appeared on "internal-forum solutions"—often called *pastoral solutions*—not because of any change in Church doctrine or Church law, but because of a changed and erroneous notion of the meaning and function of conscience.

The most common mention of so-called internal-forum solutions has to do with admitting divorced and remarried Catholics to the Eucharist without benefit of ecclesiastical annulment or dissolution.

A recent collection of differing but basically like-minded views, most of which lean away from accepted Catholic practice at the expense of authentic Catholic doctrine, has been gathered and presented by James J. Young C.S.P.[31] Similarly, J. T. Catoir, a former judge of the Paterson diocesan tribunal, has written that the presumption for the validity of the first marriage might be wrong. He then counseled the following questions to resolve the fact via the internal forum: Do you feel that you are living in sin? Do you understand your present marriage to be an adulterous one? He further counseled that if the concerned person has studied the statements of the Church, reviewed his life situation with a priest, struggled with the questions involved, and "still has no sense of sin, then he ought not be deprived of the Eucharist." What is the reason for this advice? "The benefit of doubt should favor the human conscience."[32]

Sound logic, doctrine, and practice demand that I, in turn, ask the following question: If the other spouse of the same first marriage has followed the same process, studied the same statements, reviewed her life situation, struggled with the same questions, and still had a sense of sin, then should she be deprived of the Eucharist on the basis of Catoir's reasoning since the "benefit of doubt should favor the human conscience"?

Surely it makes little sense to pretend that a personal, subjective conviction makes or unmakes reality. Were both husband and wife to proceed in all good conscience and in all sincerity to directly opposite conclusions, can one maintain that she is truly married to him, but that he is not married to her?

Piet Fransen, in one of his many studies[33] of the famous Canon 7 of Session 24 of the Council of Trent (regarding divorce on the ground of adultery, DS 1807), took great care in presenting just what the fathers of that Council did anathematize in that canon:

> The canon deals only with what the textbooks call the "intrinsic indissolubility" of marriage, namely that a marriage does not *ipso facto* break up because of adultery, or in terms that come closer to Luther's thought in his *De captivitate babylonica,* with the fact that the partners decide this question among themselves in their own conscience.[34]

It seems to me that what the fathers of Trent precisely anathematized is what so many authors and others are proselytizing—that marriage breaks up *ipso facto* when its partners, or a partner, decide(s) the question in his or her conscience or in their conscience.

Clearly, no reader can pretend that the problem I here mention is restricted to the realm of theory. I speak of a problem advocated in some literature, taught in some seminaries, and practiced in some dioceses with quasi-approval or semi-approval; at the very least, it enjoys benign neglect. This so-called pastoral solution of conscience will render consistent pastoral practice impossible, which alone will rightly trouble many consciences.

The next step, again the the name of "good conscience," has already been taken. Canon 12 of the same session of Trent (DS. 1812) teaches that matrimonial causes belong to ecclesiastical judges. Edward James, a practicing civil lawyer, wrote in *America* magazine about his own annulment proceeding:

> But while awaiting the tribunal decision, I was sud-
> denly overcome with the profound realization that
> my future marital life was not going to be deter-
> mined by the decision of that august group, but
> rather by the dictates of my own conscience. ... The
> point I am trying to make, since the reason for my
> placing myself before the tribunal was that of recon-
> ciliation of conscience, once that conscience had been
> made up, the decision of the tribunal had become
> academic.[35]

Mr. James was not alone in his understanding of the nature
and function of conscience.[36] It does not even surface in this
analysis whether one's conscience could be erroneous in decision or formation; the thrust is to the effect that whatever my
conscience decides to be right is, for that very reason, right.
Some have then apparently moved from the prayerful hope
"May my conscience ever be right!" to the nonnegotiable
statement "My conscience cannot be wrong."[37]

Perhaps I have overexemplified one particular misapplica-
tion of a conscience decision—the so-called internal-forum solution. But if I am not mistaken, the same umbrella term can
also be invoked for any possible conscience decision. Quite
often this will be in the language of "responsibility," especially
"responsibly" as in "responsibly decide." Thus we find such
suggestions as the following: "Responsibly consider Church
teaching (often called mere statements)"; "responsibly consider
your life situation"; and "responsibly decide in your conscience
what to do."

Apart from overworking a single adverb (responsibly) to the
point of effectively begging the question, the real moral task is
to think through what is the "responsible thing" to do, and
then do it. But to prescribe or predict antecedently that this is a
responsible decision, is simply to foreordain the success of one's
responsibility rhetoric, to describe in advance one quality of

decision making, while neatly avoiding or skipping completely the real task of determining what is or is not the responsible thing to do or avoid. The quality of decision making is relevant, but it is not a substitute for what is objectively correct or erroneous.

Thus, the "good-conscience" and "responsibly-decide" technique removes us effectively from the conventional notion of antecedent conscience, which is so crucial to Catholic moral reasoning. They have reached the point where an objective referent is not mentioned at all. One suspects that *what* one does is not important; instead, the frame of reference (or responsibility motif) in which you are deciding is all that is important enough to mention.

As above, whether it is a dissent from the teachings of *Humanae Vitae* concerning abortion, sterilization, and contraception, or whether it is an assent to something the Church does not offer (the Eucharist to persons who are living in a second or invalid marriage), the so-called good-conscience or internal-forum "solution" solves just about everything. This is because the possibility and reality of an objectively erroneous conscience are just not considered very much if at all.

Perhaps too many of my points have been about terminology and loose language. Nonetheless, it is my honest contention that, in the areas of conscience decisions and formation of conscience, we must attend carefully to the theological vocabulary employed, most especially the precise nature, function, and meaning of conscience in Catholic moral theology. I hope the importance of such precision is obvious; it should be obvious that I am not trying to defend some peculiar scruple of my own.

In a famous encyclical, the late Pope Paul VI made a similar appeal—one not well-listened to but well-worth repeating:

> You know, too, that it is of the utmost importance,
> for peace of consciences and for the unity of the
> Christian people, that in the field of morals as well

as in that of dogma, all should attend to the Magisterium of the Church, and all should speak the same
language (*Humanae Vitae,* 28).

Pope Paul closed that citation as I close this article with the
same appeal: "In the field of morals... all should speak the
same language"—renewing the plea of St. Paul the Apostle:

I appeal to you, brethren, by the name of our Lord
Jesus Christ, that all of you agree and that there be
no dissentions among you, but that you be united in
the same mind and the same judgment (1 Cor. 1:10).

Notes

1. For textbooks, see: Aertnys, Damen, Visser, *Theologia Moralis,*
vol. 1, 18th ed., (Rome: Marietti, 1967), nn.138-59, pp. 189-218; Nol-
din, Schmitt, Heinzel, *Summa Theologiae Moralis,* vol. 1 (33rd ed.)
(Innsbruck: Felizian Rauch, 1960), nn. 208-256, pp. 197-240;
M. Zalba, *Theologiae Moralis Compendium,* vol. 1 (Madrid: B.A.C.,
1958), nn. 640-734, pp. 355-419. E. D'Arcy, *Conscience and Its Right
to Freedom* (New York: Sheed and Ward, 1961). Ph. Delhaye, *The
Christian Conscience* (New York: Desclée Co., 1968). A. Fagothey,
Right and Reason (St. Louis: C.V. Mosby Co., 1976), pp. 39-49.
2. J. V. Dolan S.J., "Conscience in the Catholic Theological Tradi-
tion," in W. C. Bier, ed., *Conscience: Its Freedom and Limitations*
(New York: Fordham University Press, 1971) pp. 9-19.
3. International Theological Commission (October 4, 1972) in *La
Documentation Catholique* 70 (May 20, 1973), p. 460; Eng. trans. in
(London) *Tablet* 227 (July 7, 1973), p. 647.
4. J. C. Turro, "Conscience In the Bible," in Bier, ed. pp. 3-8 at p. 6.
5. T. E. O'Connell, *Principles for a Catholic Morality* (New York:
Seabury Press, 1978). Cf. ch. 8 "Conscience," pp. 83-97, esp. 85-88.
Perhaps in this O'Connell is following B. Häring, *Free and Faithful in
Christ* vol. I, (New York: Seabury Press, 1978), pp. 225-29, who offers
the same easy equivalence, namely, what Paul means by *heart* is
what we mean by *conscience;* or, in vintage Häring, for Paul,
suneidesis points out "the constructive, creative quality of the human
heart" (p. 228). In all probability, St. Paul meant no such thing, for it
is mildly anachronistic to "discover" so much Fromm and Maslow in
any New Testament author. Furthermore, Häring's treatment of St.

Thomas Aquinas on conscience is poor (pp. 230-31). Much preferred is the excellent, but very concise, summary of T. Gilby, O.P., in *Summa Theologiae*, vol. 18 (New York: McGraw-Hill, 1965), appendix 15— "Conscience," pp. 180-83.

6. C. A. Pierce, *Conscience in the New Testament* (London: S.C.M. Press, 1955).

7. For a concise summary of the nature of conscience and the essential role of prudence in St. Thomas, see Gilby, pp. 180-83.

8. Ibid. p. 182.

9. J. Dolan, p. 10.

10. Canadian Catholic Conference, *Statement on the Formation of Conscience* (December 1, 1973), n. 6; also in *Crux Special* January 4, 1974 4 pp.; *Catholic Mind* 72 (April 1974): 40-51; *Statement on the Formation of Conscience* (pamphlet) (Boston: Daughters of St. Paul, 1974), 29 pp.

11. NCCB, *Basic Teachings for Catholic Religious Education* (January 11, 1973) (Washington, D.C.: USCC, 1973), n. 17, p. 18.

12. NCCB, *On Moral Values in Society* (November 19, 1974) (Washington, D.C.: USCC, 1975) n. IV, p. 6.

13. NCCB, *To Live in Christ Jesus* (November 11, 1976) (Washington, D.C.: USCC, 1976), part 1, "Conscience," p. 10.

14. NCCB, *Sharing the Light of Faith* (National Catechetical Directory) (November 17, 1977) (Washington, D.C.: USCC, 1979), n. 103, p. 58.

15. *New York Times,* (April 6, 1978), p. B, I.

16. *A.A.S.* 44 (1952): 270-78.

17. J. Dolan, p. 17.

18. Ibid., p. 18.

19. W. M. Abbott S.J. ed., *The Documents of Vatican II,* (New York: Guild Press, 1965), p. 677.

20. Ibid., p. 679.

21. Ibid., pp. 694-95.

22. Ibid., p. 676.

23. Cf. X. Ochoa, *Index Verborum cum documentis Concilii Vaticani Secundi* (Roma: Commentarium Pro Religiosis, 1967), pp. 106-7.

24. Paul VI. "To the College of Cardinals" (December 29, 1976) in *The Pope Speaks* 22 (1977), p. 20.

25. P. Pavan, "Declaration on Religious Freedom," in H. Vorgrimler, ed., *Commentary on the Documents of Vatican II,* vol. 4, (New York: Herder and Herder, 1969), pp. 49-86; R. J. Regan S.J., *Conflict and Consensus* (New York: Macmillan, 1967); R. J. Regan S.J., "Con-

science in the Documents of Vatican II," in W. Bier, ed., pp. 29-36; M. Carter, "*Dignitatis Humanae*—Declaration on Religious Freedom," *The Jurist* 36 (1976): 338-52.

26. E.g., J. Deedy, "Troubled Vatican," *New York Times* (October 13, 1972), p. 39; D. J. Thorman, "Views and Reviews," *National Catholic Reporter* 13 (October 21, 1977), p. 6. H. Küng, *Freedom Today* (New York: Sheed and Ward, 1966), p. 60; C. Davis, A *Question of Conscience* (New York: Harper & Row, 1967). *Time* 113 (June 18, 1979), p. 35.

27. H. Shär, "Protestant Problems with Conscience," in C. E. Nelson, ed., *Conscience: Theological and Philosophical Perspectives* (New York: Newman Press, 1973), pp. 79-94; Also, M. G. Baylor, *Action and Person: Conscience in Late Scholasticism and the Young Luther* (Studies in Medieval and Reformation Thought 20) (Leiden: Brill, 1977).

28. W. B. Smith, "Catholic Theology, Catholic Morality and Catholic Conscience," *Proceedings of the Fellowship of Catholic Scholars* I (1978): 39-53, esp. 42-50.

29. T. O'Connell, pp. 83-97; B. Häring, pp. 265-84.

30. T. Bouscaren and A. Ellis, *Canon Law,* 3rd ed. (Milwaukee: Bruce Publishing Company, 1961), pp. 132-33.

31. J. J. Young, ed. *Ministering to the Divorced Catholic* (New York: Paulist Press, 1979); note esp. Young C. E. Curran, R. McCormick, A. McDevitt, F. Finnegan, B. Häring, J. Heagle, and CTSA—Study Commission, "The Problem of Second Marriages" (August 1972).

32. J. T. Catoir, *Catholics and Broken Marriage* (Notre Dame, Ind.: Ave Maria Press, 1979), p. 59.

33. P. Fransen, "Divorce on the Ground of Adultery—The Council of Trent (1563)," in F. Böckle, ed., *The Future of Marriage As Institution,* Concilium 55 (New York: Herder and Herder, 1970) pp. 89-100.

34. Ibid., p. 96.

35. E. James, "Marriage Tribunals: Another Viewpoint," *America* 140 (May 5, 1979), pp. 370-71 at p. 370.

36. S. J. Kelleher, "Looking Back, Looking Ahead," *America* 139 (November 18, 1978), pp. 355-57. Note: "The use of the internal forum solution, whereby divorced Catholics who remarry may responsibly conclude that they can in good conscience receive the Eucharist, is becoming more and more widespread" (p. 355).

37. T. O'Connell, pp. 91-93. O'Connell proposes a novel distinction that he entitles Conscience I, II, and III. The last he describes as an "infallible guide for our actions." He blends and then very much esca-

lates what he calls "the infallible obligation of conscience" into an infallible guide. There is obvious confusion here between the certainty of an obligation and moral certainty, further confused by insisting that what I should do, I may do, and I must do. If taken literally, this rigorizing maximization would eliminate the distinction between precept and counsel along with destroying the distinction between objectively correct and subjectively certain.

Moral Education and the Formation of Conscience

Paul J. Philibert O.P.
The Boys Town Center for the Study of Youth Development
The Catholic University of America
Washington, D.C.

Not infrequently, persons I meet, when they learn that I teach and research in the area of moral psychology and Christian ethics, express sincere condolences—as if they were talking to a condemned man who somehow must accept living with an uncomfortable burden that normal people would find intolerable. This reaction I attribute to some feeling on their part that they would hate to be responsible for having to tell other people what to do. "Imagine the consequences if you made a mistake! How could you live with the guilt and remorse?"

The topic of this presentation is one of the areas of moral studies that helps support the plausibility of the position that moral theologians don't tell other people what to do. Rather they try to assist others to recognize within themselves the God-given resources that allow them as humans, uniquely among the ranks of physical creation, to be self-actualized and responsible beings who generate values as they make choices in the pursuit of goodness and wholeness.[1]

Although it has been commonplace since the time of Aristotle to insist that a good bit of experience is necessary before one becomes a trustworthy judge in moral matters,[2] and although Kierkegaard in the last century laid down a structure of levels of moral adequacy,[3] it has only been within the last five decades that precise, scientific work has been done that attempts to chart the journey of moral stages and describe their characteristics. I place at the beginning of this endeavor the pioneering work of Jean Piaget, who studied the reactions and responses of children from birth to adolescence, and described a number of features of growth that we have come to accept as developmental stages. But the name most familiarly associated with theories of moral education in the United States is that of Lawrence Kohlberg, who for twenty-five years has been defending the hypothesis that all human persons pass through a sequence of types of moral reasoning that we have come to call *stages of moral development*.[4] (I am going to assume that my readers have some familiarity with Kohlberg's stages, and so will not attempt to expose them methodically— something that a large number of readily accessible writings have done already. I will, however, try to make my remarks here about the stages intelligible to those who are not previously acquainted with Kohlberg's theory.)

It may be another testimoney to the already noted uneasiness of many people with ethical issues, that Kohlberg's work has become, as one critic calls it, "an educational bandwagon."[5] To be honest, however, I must also remark from my own experience in speaking with adult groups that the popularity of Kohlberg's theory can be attributed as well to the way it matches important incidents in the life experience of those who hear about it. It sounds realistic. The exposition of the Kohlberg stages usually stirs up in the mind of hearers memories of situations where they found themselves reasoning according to the values described by the various stages. Perhaps most appealing of all, for educators and parents, the orderly presentation of levels and stages suggests two qualities that we are accustomed to accept as representative of dependability and efficiency: Kohlberg's theory comes dressed in the trappings of the *scientific,* and offers itself as a manageable *technology* or *technique.* The one quality (science) removes our fears of making mistakes; the other (technique) promises results!

It is not really quite as simple as all that, however; and for the next little while I will try to show why. Within the available space, I want to remark (a) about the limits that must exist in theological borrowing from the social sciences; (b) about the plausible or dependable conclusions of moral education theory within its own methodological framework; (c) about what Christian moral education can appropriate from that framework; and (d) about what other tasks of conscience formation remain outside the parameters of this dialogue with moral education theory.

Can Theology Borrow From the Social Sciences?

It requires more than a footnote to insist on the need to establish *if* and *how* moral theology and the social sciences might mutually collaborate in a common dialogue about human problems. One need not look back to Galileo or even to Darwin to find instances of embattled misunderstanding be tween churchmen and scientists. The present debate about what constitutes the real issues in the abortion question illustrates the kind of confusion that arises from not establishing foundational rules for dialogue.[6] A very large number of those who favor abortion-on-demand seem to find it completely unnecessary to distinguish between scientific opinions that view the fetus as an empirical object and moral arguments that view life-in-the-womb as a moral object.

As we turn toward the areas of sociology, psychology, and social psychology, we discover the same need for guidelines for mutual understanding as elsewhere in the arena of scientific-humanistic dialogue. One way of describing the differences in position and attitude that separate the two sides of the dialogue is to point out that the social sciences maintain a very low profile of assumptions about their scientific object, approaching it uniquely from an empirical curiosity (or so runs their claim), while theology, on the other hand, maintains a high profile of assumptions that include what believing theologians consider to be data that are certain because divinely revealed. In the words of a distinguished colleague: "It is poor moral methodology to simplistically reduce the moral norm to the findings of science, especially the empirical sciences which describe the present state of human existence."[7]

Distinct Methodological Profiles

The "scientific method" can mean a variety of things. As a point of view, it can be as broad as a philosophy of life or even, as Thomas Luckmann argues, an invisible religion underlying the pragmatic value orientations in our society.[8] Until very recently, when tragic incidents like the Three-Mile-Island accident or the Chicago DC-10 crash forced on us some drastic value revisions, the undoubted progress of scientific technology has represented the closest thing we Americans have had to unify us in a common set of social values. We all want progress, affluence, mobility, a free consumer market, and a variety of other values—which, however, because we are under their influence, we tend not to see as chosen values but simply as features of the way things are. Seldom do the values implicit in our social system come to light sufficiently for us to appreciate their rationalistic reductionism, which dismisses as irrelevant all individual qualities of a person save effective functioning within a predictable social *role* and a measureable *productivity* in the economic order.[9] It takes the eerie rationalism of government officials explaining that "one extra cancer fatality" and "one nonfatal cancer" will be caused by the Pennsylvania nuclear reactor accident—as if that explained away the danger and the protest—to appreciate the degree to which persons have been reduced to numbers within our social ethos at present.

When it comes to the methodology of the sciences, a few general broad observations can facilitate a better focus on their possible dialogue with theology. Within the perspective of the social sciences, the human person is perceived as an object *qua* object. Only empirically observable movements, products, and changes effected by persons are relevant for scientific observation. Questions of value or statements of goals and purposes are, with rare exception, considered off limits to scientists. Motivation is described scientifically only in terms of a description of observable external influences. Human subjects are of interest for the social sciences because it is taken for granted that they are essentially undifferentiated instances of a group or class of objects called *human beings*. A social scientist is embarrassed by a colleague who opines about the human condition without substantiating *data*—which means quantitatively expressed profiles, established in the language of statistics, of variances in human behavior.

The methodology of theology is quite different. Theology works with a corpus of texts and a tradition of beliefs that are unified in the inner life experience of faith in God and the encounter with divine love in prayer. Theology is value-laden: Its fundamental perspective is its affirmation about the trans-empirical derivation of all empirical phenomena from the personal benevolence of a divine Father. The most radical principle of verification of Christian theological claims is the inwardly perceived testimony of religous experience, with which are associated such typical Christian categories as vocation, conversion, faith, and the like.[10]

With this higher profile of assumptions, theology's perspective on the human as the object of investigation will be quite different from that of the social sciences. Unlike them, with their insistence upon the dependability of only empirical (extrinsic) data, theology will view the person not exclusively as an object among the objects of the world but also as a desiring subject or self-moving agent. The person's testimony to inner experience—introspection, reflection, and empathic communion—will play a privileged role in the work of theology. Motivation will engage, if it can, the interior influence of religious experience: "the obedience of faith"[11] and a fundamental sense of vocation. Furthermore, since theology deals with the story of all that is, theology will be concerned to make a coherent whole out of all the evidence for reflection that is available to its purview.

Theology: Eminence or Dialogue?

Given this characterization, we can easily be reminded of the days when theology readily assumed the mantle of the queen of the sciences, an eminence that shared with Christian philosophy the task of keeping the other sciences in their places. Since the empiricist revolution that has marked the post-Enlightenment period, however, it is theology and philosophy that are on the defensive within the context of learned people in our society. We should not forget that. For among other considerations, the dialogue with contemporary science will serve to keep theology honest by forcing theologians to relate their dogmatic assumptions to whatever empirical evidence may be relevant to their investigations.

The key to my position here, however, is merely to insist that when theology *borrows* from the social sciences, the theologian must perform the act of seeing the scientific conclusion within its own methodological framework, judge the matter within its own frame of reference, and only then appropriate it as a datum within theology's framework—which will include, of course, placing it alongside other data not available to the empiricist as well as receiving it on the terms of the very different methodology of theology.

An example of this is childhood confession. When one arrives at the psychological conclusion that confession, as it has been largely experienced in recent generations, evokes enormous psychological difficulties for children, there is the strong temptation to simply do away with confession for children! Some religious educators seem to have come to that conclusion simply by taking the psychological data within their own framework and applying them to the theological problem of childhood confession. Doing so, they left aside the steps mentioned above, namely, placing the psychological data alongside other, theological data, and receiving these data within the broader methodological framework of theology. To do these two steps is to introduce evidence—from Scripture about the action of the Spirit, from history about the origins of the sacrament—which modify the simple judgment that childhood fears are inevitable and that therefore the sacrament is to be avoided. With the revision of the rite of confession, placing it in a communal liturgical experience of the local community, many of the frightening aspects of "confession" as we knew it as children years ago have disappeared. As many authors have shown, this is still a "disputed question" in many ways. But at least I can insist that if we make a theological and pastoral judgment about childhood confession, it must include the relevant theological and religious-cultural data that would properly and adequately nuance the shape of the question.[12]

These very general observations take us as deeply into this question of methodologies as I can hope to go in this context. Some of the observations in the next section of this paper will illustrate better how the shift of methodologies works out in practice. I will say in summary, however, that while the social sciences do not aspire to discuss either the spiritual resources nor the ultimate destiny of humanity, theology on the contrary finds its integrity precisely by situating itself as honestly as it can within the context of interiority and finality.

Dependable Contributions of Moral Development Theory

In the application of Lawrence Kohlberg's stages of moral development to moral theology, we can find an illustration of the need for methodological understanding and care in the translation from social science to theology. Kohlberg's work borders on the frontiers of several disciplines: psychology, sociology, educational theory, and philosophy. (From the perspective of some decades hence, Kohlberg's chief contribution to the world of ideas may well prove to be the amazing result that his hypotheses and theory have generated debate on a common topic about roughly the same set of premises within such a wide array of disciplines.) In addition to methodological assumptions common to the social sciences (mentioned above), Kohlberg's point of departure can be characterized by the two following assumptions: (1) in the acquisition of advanced stages of moral reasoning, the only relevant resource of the personality is "autonomous moral rationality"[13]; and (2) the only relevant question in the form of moral analysis deals with the issue of justice.[14]

Kohlberg's understanding of the philosophy of moral obligation is largely identical with the perspective of the neo-Kantian moral philosophy that dominates contemporary academics and letters. *The* problem of moral philosophy in this tradition is achieving objectivity, making sure that one's judgment is not biased by an indulgent self-interest. Stanley Hauerwas describes some features of this position as follows:

> We are moral to the extent that we learn to view our desires, interests and passions as if they could belong to anyone. The moral point of view, whether it

> is construed in a deontological or teleological man-
> ner, requires that we view our own projects and life
> as if we were outside observers.... The self is often
> pictured as consisting of reason and desire, with the
> primary function of reason being to control desire. It
> is further assumed that desire or passion can give no
> clues to the nature of the good, for the good can only
> be determined in accordance with "reason."[15]

What such a position achieves is a sustained analytic focus on
how to arrive at justice as fairness—each individual having an
equal chance to make a claim for sharing in the limited resources of a common world. What the same position never man-
ages to achieve, however, is an explanation for the moral energy
or passion that is the point of departure for moral achievements
in the world of things, as opposed to moral thoughts in the
world of ideas.[16]

Kohlberg's focus on justice as the unique moral problem is
not as serious as his insistence upon reason as the unique resource to deal with this problem. For the problem of justice is
not, in my view, merely the issue of measuring mathematically
the precise limits of a fair distribution of disputed goods. Behind
that essentially quantitive judgment are several adjustments
of sensibility that control (to some degree) the reasonable judgment of fairness or equity. Among these adjustments of sensibility is the person's orientation to the world as "understood,"
"familiar," and "participated." Kohlberg's stages describe a
good bit about changing relations between the person and the
world according to these sensibilities, although he does not
make enough of that dimension of his own work, in my view.
Another area of adjustments of sensibility underlying justice
as fairness is one's self-appreciation in terms of the issues
of vocation, generativity, and world view.[17] Moving an individual from the sensibilities of unstructured hedonism characteristic of Kohlberg's Stage 2 to the sophisticated attitude

of Stage 5, which is generative of social values, requires more than restructuring "autonomous moral rationality." It implies realms of experience that, for the theologian, must entail questions of world view, ultimacy, and destiny or vocation.

My comments also argue for some appreciation of psychodynamic elements in the characteristics of moral growth. In addition to the restructuring of "autonomous moral rationality," as explained by Kohlberg, there are certainly events of importance that lie in the following areas: (a) the adjustment from infantile notions of the self as clumsy and ineffective to a healthy, worthy self-image; (b) the self-conscious experience of using one's gifts fruitfully and effectively within a social context; and (c) the structuring of peer relations with some dependable bonding in friendship as a skeleton for the values that underlie a world of shared meanings.

Elsewhere I have summarized much of the criticism that has been raised against Kohlberg's position, much of it within the psychological academy.[18] I will not repeat those complaints here, except to suggest in broad form where the problems seem to lie. A variety of scholars are finding that stage scoring on Kohlberg's moral-dilemma questions does not effectively predict moral action: People who think Stage 5 thoughts don't always (or predictably) perform equivalently mature actions. Others complain that Kohlberg's system is proving to demonstrate a definite cultural bias in its construction: Persons from other racial and cultural origins, on the one hand, and women within our own cultural matrix, on the other hand, both fail to show comparable stage advance scores with the scoring of male Americans.[19] Finally, a variety of complaints have been made about Kohlberg's rationalism, from the complaint about his conception of the realm of ethics to uneasiness about his understanding of personality theory.[20]

The Pluses

I have mentioned these various difficulties with Kohlberg's moral development theory because they illustrate in part my observations made above. Even though within his own schedule of assumptions and principles Kohlberg is contented to describe moral growth as the restructuring of moral reasoning, his conclusions have to be received within theology with an eye to the broader conception of the moral universe that abides there. For example, moral theology is concerned about the importance of appetites as indicators of needs and potentialities of the human organism,[21] about the openness of the human spirit to the influence of the Spirit of God, and about the human community as a nurturing matrix where values are communicated not just intellectually but also by the attitudes and taken-for-granted personal interests of the social environment.

Nonetheless, these difficulties with Kohlberg's assumptions do not vitiate completely the contribution of his research. Many aspects of his theory have been supported by a growing consensus in developmental psychology that a certain number of phenomena of human growth are characteristic of all persons. The continuing work of Piaget and his associates at Geneva, the work of Furth and Youniss and their associates at the Boys Town Center, and the efforts of Loevinger and Haan to reconstruct a developmental theory of ego development or moral development—all these projects have certain features in common, which I take to be the most stable contributions of the field at this time and which I will describe in psychological terms before suggesting how these ideas translate into theology.[22]

Dependable Contributions From the Developmentalists

1. *The relational environment.* The structure of social rela-

tions controls in very large part the development of moral understanding. Kohlberg's terms for his levels (preconventional, conventional, and postconventional) show that a major feature governing stage advance in his mind is the ability of persons to orientate themselves to a certain frame of reference. The preconventional person is someone who fails to understand *why* the customs of society work the way they do; the conventional person is at home in social understandings; and the postconventional person is able to go beyond the strict letter of the law to see how justice is better served by adjusting the letter of the law to an unusual situation. Although Kohlberg has not spelled out a further aspect of this relational environment, there is one (which I call the *transactional response*) that complements Kohlberg's theory.

Like the work of Eric Berne and transactional analysis, I believe that we tend (by reason of learned unconscious reactions) to structure our responses according to the way in which people address us. We never altogether get over being the way others ask us to be. We are inclined to respond spontaneously after the pattern that others set down.

If we are addressed in a strong parental tone, we are likely to respond with a sheepish child response. But transactional analysis also insists that we can *unlearn* this spontaneous response or, better, we can *learn* to respond in adult fashion even when we are addressed as children. It is important for us to keep in mind this transactional response (which of course is not the whole answer to how people behave) as one of the features in the moral landscape that provides context for the free choices that we are capable of making at our very best.[23]

This transactional response is ambivalent, however. It can be seen as a kind of *determinism:* This is particularly true when unconscious, repressed responses continue to influence our reactions to certain individuals. Some people have an authority problem (a hang-up with dealing matter-of-factly with persons in authority roles). This is a not infrequently found example of transactional response as a paralyzing determinism. The transactional response can also be seen as a *facilitating human environment*. Good leadership produces good leaders, not inveterate followers. Some of Kohlberg's writings on "the just community" are illustrative of this reality, even though his terminology and conceptualization are different from mine. Being treated as a responsible and capable person is the most positive contribution toward becoming such a person.

2. *Mutual relations*. The quality of social relations governs the onset and stabilization of independent and responsible thinking. Thirty-five years ago Piaget distinguished between "authority relations" and "mutual relations."[24] In authority relations, the reasons for things and the directions of action lie in the hands of another, to whom we defer because of an imposing personality—greater size, power, education, or intelligence. It is characteristic of early childhood to live within authority relations (and likewise characteristic to rebel in tantrums against the authority whose norms never engage fully with the child's understanding).

Mutual relations are the product of peer interactions. Piaget established his insights into this realm of behavior through observing children change in their relationship to one another and to the rules in common childhood games. The children's ability to argue out reasons for the accepted maneuvers they have been taught challenges them to understand why they are doing these acts as well as to recognize that a mutual consent is responsible for the concrete, lived-out experience of value that they discover in their activity with peers.

One way of phrasing the consequences of this perspective is to say that authoritarian institutions will inhibit not only the improvisation that may produce an original behavior, but will likewise inhibit the internalization of moral reasons for doing even socially conservative acts within the moral agent. The person in an authoritarian context is likely to respond to the question "Why did you do that?" with the answer "Because the boss said I had to," rather than with the answer "Because clearly it's the right thing to be done here, isn't it?" When psychologists talk about persons reaching the capacity for autonomy, they are not usually speaking of a capacity for doing something original or unforeseen, but rather of a capacity for doing whatever is done with a motivation that is cognitively clear and emotively comfortable to the person acting. In order for this to occur, the person acting will see himself or herself as somehow the peer of his or her companions in the relevant moral landscape of the act.[25]

3. *The gradual and integrated acquisition of moral capacities.* There is some order of sequential development whereby a person acquires first *this,* then *that.* . . . In Piaget's format, first muscular equilibrium, then language, then spontaneous but haphazard experimentation with causal explanations, then logical thinking. . . . In Kohlberg's stages, first fear and hesitancy, then bargaining, then cooperation, then critical insight. This is an important perspective, for even though all of Kohlberg's *stages* may not be exactly sequential as he describes them, no one would challenge that his *levels* are sequential in the sense in which we are speaking.

While a certain amount of caution is due here, still to some degree the claims of the developmentalists must be accepted that each person must visit each step or stage along the path to maturity, and that we cannot expect someone in a lower stage to appreciate the motivation characteristic of a higher stage situation. Certainly one dimension of moral experience where this seems generally true is in the realm of sorting out the differences between what society wants and what *I* (as a unique moral agent) really want. No one altogether escapes the childhood experience of feeling alien to new situations.

(Any child coming into a new schoolroom is going to need time for readjustment.) In some lives this alien feeling can be the basis for a deeply rooted incapacity to take initiatives or to contribute to the full capacity of one's gifts.

Kohlberg's theory claims that we need to make our educational interventions into carefully diagnosed strategies that are specific to the stage of reasoning in which we find our students.[26] Some critics have dismissed the efficacy of this claim since Kohlberg's interventions often result in people changing what they *say* they think should be done, but not what they *do* in actual behavior.[27] It would be wise to note this serious deficiency in the Kohlberg program, but likewise to note that the problem may well lie in the area of the *insufficiency* of Kohlberg's explanation rather than in its being in *error*. Elsewhere I have indicated that I believe that a number of other factors, such as moral intensity, experience, and practical training, control moral behavior—factors that go beyond the realm of "autonomous moral rationality" alone.[28]

4. *Advance through experience.* Developmental theorists talk about the phenomenon called *cognitive disequilibrium.*[29] By this they mean that persons are motivated to advance to new heights of moral reasoning because they are challenged by the experience of a situation they cannot make sense out of in their present understanding. An example would be the following: A law-and-order person who takes it for granted that social conventions and legal demands are morally right is confronted by a situation in which someone is treated unfairly by the law, as happened in the last decade in the Mississippi Delta where discriminatory voting laws made it next to impossible for blacks to register to vote. A Stage 4 person cannot at one and the same time think of moral right and wrong in stage four terms, viz., that whatever the law says is right, and assume the sensitivities of late Stage 4 thinking, viz., that all those who belong to the society have equal rights under the law. There is

a disequilibrium between the criteria of right and wrong and the behavior of the social authorities. This has to be resolved somehow. Through such instances persons are moved to remake their structures of interpretation. A Stage 4 person in such a situation is going to move to a new structure, Stage 5, which has among its characteristics an awareness of the time-bound and human derivation of human law. The unchange-ableness that Stage 4 invested in law and order yields now to a new sense of responsibility, and the person's moral reasoning moves forward.

As Bernard Häring observes with balance, Kohlberg has repeatedly insisted on a dynamic aspect indicated by the fact that each stage contains some horizon and some tendency toward the next stage.[30] One of the justifiable consequences of this position is the conviction that moral growth is a life-long phenomenon. Though we have been habituated to consider children in their preteens (wrongly, I think) as capable of a radically self-dispositive *actus humanus,* the cognitive dis-equilibrium perspective allows us to see that it is only through gradually acquired experiences of inadequacy that they find the pathway to their true resources. (This still leaves an opening for sin through laziness, ungenerous timidity, or selfish-ness.) But a good deal of childhood and adolescent moral life is exploratory in the sense of exploring with the contours of the moral world. And we cannot expect a dependable map from young adventurers newly out on their journey, at least in those areas that pertain to their knowledge and freedom vis-à-vis their own resources of imagination, ingenuity, determination, stamina, and the like.

Another consequence of this position is that we need to develop more intelligently what I would call a *philosophy of mistakes.* None of us avoids mistakes altogether. What is more important, mistakes teach us something essential to the moral task, viz., that a certain form of behavior or of thinking just doesn't work in a given situation. So much of the detailing of moral rules and regulations is very abstract for the life of an adolescent that I am persuaded that the most effective teacher of moral generosity and of responsible love for teenagers is going to be their peer experiences with other children. Thus supportive and creative association with people of responsible and benevolent values is one of the central instruments for the development of mature and loving persons in the Church, particularly among adolescents.

What Can Theology Appropriate and How?

In estimating the contributions of moral development theory so far, I have kept within the language and framework of psychology. Seeing things through the keyhole of social science gives us a view that we don't forget. Moving back into theology, we transform our description of what we have seen into something coherent with the broader reaches of a science based upon revealed (transempirical) premises that are integrated with the premises of reflective reason.

In attempting to assess the contribution of developmental moral theory to moral theology, I have raised a context germane to an important observation. I tried to show earlier that, within its own methodological framework, developmental psychology made certain assumptions that effectively pertain to the terrain of philosophy and theology. That is to say, the presupposition that reason alone undergoes the developing restructuring of stages that characterize moral advance is a philosophical assertion beyond the competence of psychology adequately to verify; and the supposition that the realm of the moral is limited to empirical behaviors motivated by empirically observable influences is a theological assertion of a kind, and an unacceptably restrictive one. We have dealt with these two presuppositions by indicating that when we arrive at the translation of the findings of developmental psychology into

theological conclusions, we will need to refocus our understanding of what is the relevant moral landscape of our discussion.

It is equally important to point out that certain streams of
theological thought have likewise made assumptions proper to
the competence of developmental psychology. Some theologians and religious educators appeal to a naive confidence in
the efficacy of repetition to educate, and to a conviction that
the articulation of logically ordered and linguistically correct
language communicates according to the intention of the
speaker.[31] They take these assumptions uncritically as premises into their theological and catechetical reflection. While I
have not made either of these assumptions a focus of my presentation, I believe that it ought to be clear from what I have
argued here that a good deal of communication never meets its
mark. When it fails to measure the cognitive and value context
of its audience, information is not the simple-minded communicative commerce many think it to be. While a responsible
developmentalist would refuse to say that *nothing happens*
when too advanced language is addressed to an audience, a
theologian who becomes informed of the research in communication and developmental psychology would likewise not expect that an adult can simply communicate in linguistically
correct formulas the moral experience that is pointed out in
theological and catechetical teaching.

Some Reference Points for Theology

Keeping in mind then that what theology borrows from psychology becomes formally a theological premise, i.e., enters
into the methodology and imaginative landscape of a transempirical discipline, I will offer a few conclusions that can enter
under these conditions into the work of ethical reflection:

1. In the discursive understanding of the moral object of
their acts, children are clearly limited by their psychological

development. All children up to a certain age (usually between seven and thirteen) find that a great deal of what they are asked to do by adults eludes their understanding. The moral object of their act then becomes formally avoiding discomfort from punishment or loss from getting the poorer end of a bargain (Kohlberg's preconventional level).

Moral theology knows that there are other dimensions of conscience than this one dimension of discursive rationality. But where theology discerns this discursive rationality at work, it ought now to respect the findings of psychology about the gradualism of understanding and the tentativeness of commitment in childhood and youth (as well as in underdeveloped adults).[32]

2. The reports of developmentalists on the growth patterns in children give us new meaning to and new respect for the frontier zone of "dawning awareness." Kohlberg teaches that persons move gradually from one stage to another, motivated by cognitive dissonance (as explained above). In Piaget's studies, children almost imperceptibly move into firmer, better established capacities for higher operations. Piaget speaks of horizontal decalage, by which he means the development represented by the ability to make broader and broader applications across a wide field of objects of a newly acquired insight gained in a much narrower application.[33] There is such a thing as "both knowing and not knowing" at the same time—and it is a state characterized by enormous potentiality rather than by ignorance, malice, or uncooperativeness.

Confronted by this frontier zone of cognition, educators have in the past quite often overlooked the potential of this very special human quality, or even misinterpreted it as ignorance or stupidity. It is very important that we should recognize this frontier of "dawning awareness" for what it is. Particularly in moral matters, we need to avoid laying blame or shame on the person in the transition of growth to a new stage. For the lower level of thinking or behavior that a learning situation discloses as inadequate, nonetheless remains a substantial resource for this person to draw upon. Developmental psychology is, in my estimation, correct in recommending that such moments are met most responsibly by a combination of an accepting trust of the person and a challenging invitation to a higher but accessible level of activity.

I would apply this principle to the area of adolescent sexuality (particularly in males) by referring to adolescent masturbation as a posture that our tradition considers seriously inadequate as a terminal moral stance. Nonetheless, the movement from latency into puberty is a movement which, given our culture, is predictably going to entail some (perhaps even lengthy) periods of masturbation, both as sexual exploration and as relief from sexual tension.[34] Not only is it more productive morally and psychically to encourage the adolescent male to accept his sexuality and his tension and own it as his *de facto* state, than it is to reject him as willfully malicious. It is also more likely that the ideal of a mature chastity (which no-one acquires in any other manner except gradually) will be communicated more nobly when it can find its place realistically within the world of real tensions and limited resources that the adolescent knows undeniably to be his own.

As an application of the theme of "dawning awareness," this problem of adolescent sexuality demonstrates that a good deal of what is on the agenda of moral development for an adolescent falls through the sieve of stages of moral reasoning. Much of life is initiation into a world that feels right on the basis of experience. As such, only patience and the commendation of not-yet-adequate but nonetheless true developments of moral capacity will be the responsible way to treat many moments of childhood and adolescent growth.

3. The developmentalist position is based fundamentally

upon a pervasive trust in the orientation of the human organism toward what is for its good or integrity. As I have commented elsewhere,[35] this attitude is reminiscent of the natural-law tradition of high scholasticism, where natural law means reason's participation in the eternal law (and where *reason* means not some reified entity in an invisible ivory tower but the effective unification of the organism in a dynamic movement toward something true and something good).

This actualizing tendency, however, is endangered or obliterated by powerful social forces that distort the understanding of freedom and corrupt much of our natural orientation to wholeness. Critics from a number of fields point out many of these distortions, which include debilitating competitiveness, empty exaltation of materialism, false seeking of power for its own sake, and a multiplication of experts through specialization that leads to social fragmentation. In the face of these determinisms, developmental psychology holds out to us some hope of resolving them in some other fashion than that worst of options, a fascist or totalitarian control. The demonstration of the power and acuity of the actualizing powers of the human personality represents what may be the best hope for the coming generation, charged with the synthesis of this half century of discoveries.

The developmentalists' confidence in the orientation toward wholeness leads me to reflect that, in the face of the real determinisms that destroy our freedom, we need to see our ethical position as one of doing the best we can within an arena of tensions which are not going to disappear. No one is going to make the world unified, moral, and sinless with the wave of a wand or the proclamation of a new set of decrees. We will go on existing within tensions of various kinds:

(a) in tension between a *freedom* that is autonomous independence, allowing us the concrete experience of our own original selves—and *freedom* that is the integration of our already achieved gifts with the interior life of grace in the Holy Spirit;

(b) in tension between *communion* as the ideal of a community based on love and the kingdom of God ... and *communion* that too easily degenerates into an impoverished faddism (aesthetically) or into conformity (morally);

(c) in tension between *justice,* the rule of law as a socially enforced insistence on the common good, equity in a society of partners ... and *love* as the interior rule of spontaneous recognition and willing of the good which each person participates in from the eternal source of goodness;

(d) the tension between *institutions* and their need for consistency and predictability in human affairs ... and the *freshness of human originality,* which continues to yearn for structures of meaning and realizations of ideal that exceed our historic achievements.

To affirm these tensions is to refuse to collapse moral and political life one-sidedly into either authoritarianism, on the one hand, or superficial romanticism, on the other. Proposition 13 and Lasch's *Culture of Narcissism*[36] are vivid examples of tendencies that clearly opt for one of these extremes. While living in tension may often be less than satisfying, for a developmentalist this tension is a sign that a meaningful autonomy has entered into the realm of one's moral consciousness and provoked a level of responsibility that could be truly characterized as adult.

What Other Tasks of Conscience Formation Remain?

To conclude this necessarily complex reflection on moral development education and moral theology, I will simply list some dimensions of conscience formation that remain to be attended to outside but parallel to the developmental framework.

First, I would say that the contribution that developmental theory does make is to provide a remedy for *legalism*. By legalism I mean a moral posture where one sees only a single value as relevant to the direction of moral experience, viz., the precept of law or commandment or rule, or the advice of an authority. Such a position is morally unsatisfactory, since it lacks one of the major dimensions of a moral act—its capacity to witness to the openness of personal experience to the movement of the transcendent divine Spirit of God. Let me be clear in insisting that I am not proposing *anarchy* as an alternative to legalism: From what we have said about the meaning of autonomy in psychology, I am merely pointing out that an adult moral attitude that is socially constructive and truly loving must be sure of itself, not always looking over its shoulder for reassurance. And some familiarity with the stages of Piaget and Kohlberg is the best cure for this kind of legalism that I can imagine.

Second, beyond the realm of reasoning out difficult decisions in disputed matters, a large part of ethics deals with what I have repeatedly called one's *moral landscape*. By this imaginative phrase I mean to indicate that difficult-to-describe focus that constitutes a person's fundamental attitudes to the world and to relations. A truly Christian ethics *is* Christian precisely because a person's moral landscape contains a lot of symbols that speak of the transcendent within the visible structure of the created world. This is why the liturgy, art, music, and media of a community are central to the formation of conscience. Perfectly correct linguistic formulas about the nature of the Church and its values will communicate little or nothing to someone for whom the gestures, symbols, and ideas spoken of are merely words. Living symbols are both visible and invisible, both here and hereafter, both articulate and mute. And as we are learning from the experience of fifteen years of liturgical renewal, a symbol is not communicated by explaining it to death in words. Symbols live because of the honesty of their form and the respect that a community brings to them as a shared celebration of life.

Third, I believe there are bodily training components to conscience formation which moral development theory and its rationalism fail to appreciate. A curious example, perhaps, but a relevant one is peer interaction in the form of organized play. I believe children and teenagers are learning something about virtue in a gym class when they learn physical games. Curiously, a large part of what they learn is not only that they can control their physical bodies and musculature (which is important), but also that they can reinvent the game within the mutual understanding of peer cooperation. (Little League ironically both fulfills and defeats this purpose by correctly encouraging the peer interaction, but incorrectly failing to leave the adolescent participants on their own to discover their capacity to appropriate the rules as their own.) In training, it is not the mere repetition of external acts that forms the habit underlying virtue; it is external acts that have a true inner motivation (what St. Thomas called *interior acts* in the Prima Secundae of his *Summa*). The student who unwillingly attends the stations of the cross on a Lenten Friday learns as little as the Little Leaguer who sits, hangdog, in the dugout waiting for the ordeal of this insane game to be over so that he can satisfy his parents. In either case, working to elicit inner cooperation is as important as the physical training of the exterior act.

Fourth, conscience formation includes what we have always meant by "an informed conscience," i.e., a vital awareness of how this religious society conceives its responsibilites according to its historic tradition. But an informed conscience is not just knowing answers in verbal formulas. Rather it must mean cognitive autonomy in accepting the Church's answers on the basis of owning their meaning. Again the point is that we must work as hard for that interior understanding as for the retention of the formulas.

Fifth, conscience formation must provide a generous support for prayer and spiritual dialogue. We are great for telling people how important personal prayer is; but only a very small minority of our Christian people actually build one another up in sharing their own spontaneous prayer. Prayer can be learned in the liturgical community. But, of course, for that to happen the participation must be theologically intelligent and generously shared. I suspect at this moment, this is the dimension which we have most neglected—at least for children and adolescents. Where children are logically heteronomous (not yet autonomous), they are often very active symbolically. An entire realm of research (not touched on in the body of this paper) has established the importance of symbolic richness in the child of four to twelve years old.[37] One very important way in which we touch this symbolism is in the spontaneous piety of prayer and religious images in the home. And again, we have far to go to assure that these popular images are both theologically correct and aesthetically challenging so as to develop a fuller openness to the transcendent through symbolism and not a retardation of the imagination through sentimental literalism.

As a final word, I will simply say that I hope that my opening comment about moral theologians is clearer now than it was an hour ago. The goal of our human growth as well as the goal of our growth in the Spirit of God is that we become witnesses to the life that is in us in its fullness. No one can prescribe for me how to become Paul. My moral theologian friends—in loving communion with the people of God served by the Church's magisterium—do, however, describe to me the challenge of becoming fully and authentically the original word that God speaks in the creative dialogue that is the Christian moral life.

Notes

1. A balanced statement of the view that the responsible person generates values with a "freedom that creates culture" is found in J. H. Walgrave, *Person and Society: A Christian View* (Pittsburgh: Duquesne University Press, 1965). See esp. chs. 1 and 5. See also the interesting study of Alfons Decken, *Process and Permanence in Ethics: Max Scheler's Moral Philosophy* (New York: Paulist Press, 1974).

2. See, e.g., the *Nicomachean Ethics,* bk. 1, ch. 3 (1095 a1-12) in *The Basic Works of Aristotle,* R. McKeon, ed. (New York: Random House, 1941), pp. 936-37.

3. Kierkegaard spoke of the aesthetic, moral, and religious dimensions of human existence. Many introductions to his works explain these categories. See the interesting parallel made by L. Monden, *Sin, Liberty and Law* (New York: Sheed and Ward, 1965) with his categories of the instinctive, the moral, and the Christian-religious (ch. 1).

4. See L. Kohlberg, "Moral Stages and Moralization" in T. Lickona, ed., *Moral Development and Behavior* (New York: Holt, Rinehart and Winston, 1976), p. 31-53. Lickona's pages of references (pp. 364-402) contain most of Kohlberg's bibliography plus much other relevant material.

5. See Jack R. Fraenkel, "The Kohlberg Bandwagon: Some Reservations," in P. Scharf, ed., *Readings in Moral Education* (Minneapolis: Winston Press, 1978), p. 250 f.

6. See C. E. Curran, *Catholic Moral Theology in Dialogue* (Notre Dame, Ind.: Fides, 1972), ch. 3, esp. pp. 71-78. Also R. A. McCormick, "Abortion: Rules for Debate," *America* (July 15, 1978), pp. 26-30.

7. Curran, p. 78.

8. T. Luckmann, *The Invisible Religion* (New York: Macmillan, 1967). Cf. G. Baum, *Religion and Alienation* (New York: Paulist Press, 1975), pp. 238-63.

9. P. L. Berger, *Pyramids of Sacrifice* (Garden City: Anchor Books,

1976). Chapter 2 describes "the capitalist ideology of development" in terms that support my description of rationalistic reductionism. See pp. 41-2 especially.

10. J. Walgrave, "The Essence of Modern Fundamental Theology," in *Concilium,* vol. 46, (New York: Paulist Press, 1969), p. 81-91, speaks of the movement from apologetic fundamental theology, characteristic of the manualist tradition, to one that roots its claims in an appeal to religious experience(s).

11. This phrase, found at the beginning and the end of the Epistle to the Romans, has become a category of contemporary religious reflection of some importance. Cf. *Dei Verbum,* "Dogmatic Constitution on Divine Revelation," *Vatican* II *The Conciliar and Post-Conciliar Documents,* A. Flannery, ed., (Collegeville, Minn.: Liturgical Press, 1975), para. 5, p. 752.

12. The real issue here, it seems to me, is in what sense a refined theological awareness of true moral responsibility is prerequisite to sinning and to the confession and forgiveness of sins. We need to avoid making childhood confession part of a cultural package which environmentally reinforces an instinctive, unconscious, and taboo morality-of-fear. See, e.g., L. Monden, *Sin, Liberty and Law.* On the other hand, the forgiving-loving aspects of the sacrament of reconciliation are clearly dimensions into which children can be meaningfully and positively initiated just as we initiate them into other dimensions of the Christian community's life. Re: recent legislation on this topic, see T. F. Sullivan, "The First Confession: Law and Catechesis," *America* (September 10, 1977), pp. 128-131. The example I give in my text is prompted by comments of E. Schillebeeckx, "Theological Reflections on Religio-Sociological Interpretations of Modern 'Irreligion'," *Social Compass* 10, no. 3 (1963): 258.

13. See L. Kohlberg, "Education, Moral Development, and Faith," *Journal of Moral Education* 4, no. 1 (1974): 14-15.

14. L. Kohlberg, "Stages of Moral Development as a Basis for Moral Education," in *Moral Education: Interdisciplinary Approaches,* C. M. Beck, ed. (New York: Newman, 1971), p. 62 f. Also L. Kohlberg, "From Is to Ought," in *Cognitive Development and Epistemology,* T. Mischel, ed. (New York: Academic Press, 1971), pp. 214-15.

15. S. Hauerwas et al., *Truthfulness and Tragedy* (Notre Dame, Ind.: University of Notre Dame Press, 1977), p. 23.

16. I develop this argument in my article "Conscience: Developmental Perspectives from Rogers and Kohlberg," *Horizons* 6, no. 1 (1979): 1-25.

17. Among authors concerned with the question of developmental structures of self-appreciation and self-awareness, see articles by M. L. Hoffman, J. Gilligan, and E. L. Simpson in *Moral Development and Behavior,* (n. 4 above).

18. P. J. Philibert, "Moral Development Research: Its Achievements and Its Limitations," *Catholic Library World* (December, 1979), forthcoming.

19. A number of these criticisms are summarized in H. Muson, "Moral Thinking: Can It Be Taught?" *Psychology Today* (February 1979).

20. See J. Aronfreed, "Moral Development from the Standpoint of a General Psychological Theory," in *Moral Development and Behavior,* p. 56.

21. See S. Hauerwas, (n. 15 above), p. 23: ". . . the standard account places us in the odd position of excluding pleasure as an integral aspect of doing the good"; p. 24: ". . . genuine disinterest reflects a non-interest in the self occasioned by the lure of a greater good or a more beautiful object than we can create or will into existence. In this sense we are not able to choose to conform to the moral point of view, for it is a gift." Cf. C. R. Rogers and B. Stevens, *Person to Person* (New York: Pocket Books, 1971), pp. 4–21, where Carl Rogers's theory of an *organismic valuing process* complements a "natural" theory of appetite as an *indicator* of *the good.*

22. See H. Furth, *The World of Grownups* (New York: Elsevier, 1979); J. Youniss, "Dialectical Theory and Piaget on Social Knowledge," *Human Development* 21, no. 4 (1978): 234–47; J. Youniss, *Friends and Parents in Social Development* (Chicago: University of Chicago Press, 1980) (in press); J. Loevinger, *Ego Development* (San Francisco: Jossey-Bass, 1976).

23. For a broad treatment of transactional analysis, see M. James and D. Jongeward, *Born to Win* (Reading, Mass.: Addison-Wesley Publishing Co., 1971).

24. J. Piaget, *The Moral Judgment of the Child* (New York: Free Press, 1965). (First published in English, London: Kegan Paul, 1932).

25. Cf. the further elucidation of this point in P. J. Philibert, "Leadership for Responsibility," *Liturgy* 24, no. 3 (May-June 1979): 12–17.

26. A presentation of this strategy-theory is summarized in Kohlberg's "Foreword" to *Readings in Moral Education* (n. 5 above).

27. See, e.g., Aronfreed (n. 20) and Fraenkel (n. 5).

28. See P. J. Philibert, "Conscience: Developmental Perspectives," (n. 16 above).

29. This is Kohlberg's phrase. For a Piagetian account of this phenomenon, see T. Mischel, "Piaget: Cognitive Conflict and the Motivation of Thought," in *Cognitive Development and Epistemology*, (n. 14 above), p. 311 f., esp. p. 323–33.

30. B. Häring, *Free and Faithful in Christ*, vol. I: *General Moral Theology* (New York: Seabury Press, 1978), p. 244. Häring puts Kohlberg's contribution into a broad Christian theological context in pp. 243–59.

31. The new *National Catechetical Directory* makes a place for memorization as a method in childhood catechesis, with the understanding, of course, that the repetition that undergirds memorization take place in a context of growing "cognitive autonomy" (as I use this phrase here).

32. See my "Conscience: Developmental Perspective," p. 20: "The child begins by needing initiation and reassurance in the activities of life. The child's locus of authority (in important matters at least) is outside himself. Only gradually does the self substantially process practical understandings and shape decisions. In this dimension of conscience which is *autonomy*, we witness what is without doubt a developmental reality."

33. "*Horizontal decalage* refers to a repetition which takes place within a single period in development": J. H. Flavell, *The Developmental Psychology of Jean Piaget* (Princeton, N.J.: Van Nostrand, 1963), p. 22.

34. See the assessment in *Sexuality and Man*, compiled and edited by the Sex Information Education Council of the United States (New York: Scribner's, 1970), p. 61 f.

35. P. J. Philibert, "L. Kohlberg's Use of Virtue in His Theory of Moral Development," *International Philosophical Quarterly* 15,4 (1975), p. 455 f.

36. C. Lasch, *The Culture of Narcissism* (New York: W. W Norton, 1979). Lasch argues that contemporary Americans have become obsessed with themselves; they hunger not for personal salvation, but psychic security. Cf. the still prophetic comments about the dangers of our moral climate in Y. Congar, *Laity, Church and World* (Baltimore: Helicon, 1960), pp. 3–4.

37. A magisterial statement of this theme can be found in Erik H. Erikson, *Toys and Reasons* (New York: W. W. Norton, 1977); see also Erikson's *Childhood and Society* (New York: W. W. Norton, 1963). Likewise, Bruno Bettelheim, *The Uses of Enchantment: The Meaning and Importance of Fairy Tales* (New York, Alfred A. Knopf, 1976).

Part Six
Christian Perfection: The Goal of Moral Living

The Call to Perfection: God's Grace, Charity, and the Christian Life

Jordan Aumann O.P.
The Angelicum University
Rome

The Second Vatican Council has been characterized as a pastoral council rather than a doctrinal one. Although the two aspects are not and should not be considered as mutually exclusive, since doctrine and life should form a synthesis, the pastoral emphasis has great significance for the theology of Christian perfection. The fathers of the Council made a serious effort to understand the needs and problems of the contemporary world; they then formulated guidelines for applying the gospel teaching to those needs and problems.

Like Christian anthropology in the best sense of the word, the documents of Vatican II constantly refer to the Church as the people of God; the sacraments and the liturgy are always discussed in terms of the faithful, for whom they were instituted; the ministry of priests and bishops is defined in terms of service to the people. Whereas in the past it may have been necessary to defend the doctrines of the Church and to define the Church itself as a visible, hierarchical society, the emphasis since Vatican II has been on the persons who constitute the Church as the Mystical Body of Christ. This is as it should be, for according to St. Augustine, the faithful are the Church, and the Church is Christ.

In the context of the spiritual life, Vatican II promulgated two statements that are fundamental in any discussion of the Christian life. The first, appearing in *Lumen Gentium,* reaffirms the traditional doctrine on the vocation of all Christians to holiness:

> Therefore all in the Church, whether they belong to the hierarchy or are cared for by it, are called to holiness, according to the Apostle's saying: "For this is the will of God, your sanctification" (I Thess. 4:3; cf. Eph. 1:4).
>
> The Lord Jesus, divine teacher and model of all perfection, preached holiness of life (of which he is the author and maker) to each and every one of his disciples without distinction: "You, therefore, must be perfect, as your heavenly Father is perfect" (Matt. 5:48).
>
> It is therefore quite clear that all Christians in any state or walk of life are called to the fullness of the Christian life and to the perfection of love, and by this holiness a more human manner of life is fostered also in earthly society (*Lumen Gentium,* 39-40).[1]

The foregoing statement should serve not only to correct any misapprehension on the part of Christians—especially diocesan priests and the laity—concerning the obligation to strive for personal holiness; but it is also a reminder to bishops, priests, and deacons that they can no longer restrict their preaching to "salvation" sermons. The entire ministry of preaching, and of catechetics as well, must be oriented to the formation of holy Christians. The people of God is a *plebs sancta Dei.*

The second statement that pertains directly to the spiritual life is really the summation of the theme that runs through most of the documents of Vatican II: Jesus Christ, mediator and head of the Mystical Body, is the source of all grace and holiness, and as model and exemplar, he is the only authentic pattern of Christian holiness. For the sake of brevity we cite only one passage, again from *Lumen Gentium:*

> By communicating his Spirit, Christ mystically constitutes as his body those brothers and sisters of his who are called together from every nation.
>
> In that body the life of Christ is communicated to those who believe and who, through the sacraments, are united in a hidden and real way to Christ....
>
> All the members must be formed in his likeness, until Christ be formed in them (cf. Gal. 4:19). For this reason we, who have been made like to him,... are taken up into the mysteries of his life, until we reign together with him (cf. Phil. 3:21; II Tim. 2:11; Eph. 2:6; Col. 2:12) (*Lumen Gentium,* 7).

Christian spirtuality may therefore be described as participation in the mystery of Jesus Christ through grace, faith, and charity, and imaging that same Christ, as an adult person and according to one's state in life and particular graces and charisms. St. Thomas Aquinas stated the same truth more succinctly when he said: "Grace was conferred on Christ as the universal principle of all those who have grace."[2]

The Life of Grace

Jesus Christ came that we might have life, and the life that he gives us is sanctifying grace. St. Peter did not hesitate to describe it as a sharing in the divine nature of God himself (2 Pt. 1:4) and for that reason the Fathers of the Church called it "divinization." These concepts imply—and rightly so—that sanctifying grace derives its meaning ultimately from uncreated grace, which is God, just as, according to St. John, the love that is charity is first of all God's love for us (cf. 1 Jn. 4:7-10). And precisely because sanctifying grace is a sharing in uncreated grace, it raises us to a supernatural level; it makes us children of God and brothers and sisters of Christ, and it changes us into living temples of the Trinity.

It is axiomatic in theology that grace does not destroy nature but perfects it.[3] Indeed, it so permeates the nature of the person who receives it that it becomes the mode of living and acting that is proper to the individual.[4] Thus grace becomes, as it were "connatural," and by an intrinsic necessity the infused supernatural virtues and the gifts of the Holy Spirit flow from sanctifying grace.[5] It is commonly held by theologians today that the infused supernatural virtues are substantially supernatural, but they operate in a human mode, while the gifts of the Holy Spirit are supernatural both in their substance and in their mode of operation. Thus the supernatural organism of the spiritual life is comprised of sanctifying grace, the infused supernatural virtues, and the gifts of the Holy Spirit, and all these elements are given with the very first infusion of grace at baptism.

Because the perfection of the human person is God-centered and is, indeed, a sharing in the very nature and life of God, we must conclude with Cardinal Wojtyla:

> Moral perfection is the principal and central act of human nature; all other perfections of the person, in one way or another, are reduced to this, and only through this can they become human perfections in the true sense of the word.[6]

Unfortunately, those who deny the supernatural order brand this as a "dehumanizing of the human person" and an "alienation from humanity." Yet these same critics would likely admit that a person should, when possible, choose the higher and better good, which means that the individual must necessarily reject the goods or values that are opposed to it or incompatible with it.

Those who deny the orientation of the human person to the supernatural, to the life of grace, have offered a variety of systems that claim to reveal the true identity of the human person and promise personal fulfillment and perfection. First of all, there is the system of *Marxist humanism,* with its roots in Hegel and cultivated by Engels, Marx, and Bloch; it is nothing more than economic materialism. Cardinal Wojtyla saw very clearly that one of the central points of Marxist anthropology—that of alienation—was used as a battle cry to promote the struggle against everything that, in the words of the Marxists, "dehumanized" the human person. As they saw it, the alienation was caused not only by the socioeconomic structure with private ownership of the means of production, and not only by the State that protected this structure, but also by every form of religion. For that reason the Cardinal warned that Catholics should be aware of these facts when they assert that the gospel serves as a basis in the struggle for liberation.[7]

The second system, which gained numerous followers even among theologians, is the *dialectic humanism* of Feuerbach, Scheler, Buber, Marcel, and Nédoncelle. The proponents of this anthropology would restrict the development of the individual to personal encounter and the formation of community. Of all the systems promulgated, perhaps this is the one that has attracted the most followers from persons of every walk of life and religious affiliation.

The *psychoanalytic humanism* of Freud is the third system to capture the attention of modern Christians. His excessively simplistic explanation of the human person and of conscious and subconscious actions in terms of the libido was soon contested even by some of his disciples, but the Freudian influence is still perceptible in the theories of some contemporary theologians.

The fourth and last system offered to modern man is the *naturalistic humanism* of Hobbes, Rousseau, and Russell, who overestimated the natural goodness of the human person, at least implicitly denied the dogma of original sin, and accepted as permissible any type of behavior that the individual feels will contribute to personal fulfillment. If followed to its logical conclusion, this system would likewise have to deny personal sin and guilt.

If taken in their entirety, none of the foregoing systems suffices to "liberate" the human person or to lead one to fulfillment and perfection. As early as 1932 Jacques Maritain sounded a warning:

> In the present day, naturalism has so ruined and subverted nature that there is no possible healing for nature itself, no possible return to the stable order of reason, save by a full and complete recognition of the rights of the supernatural, the absolute, the demands of the Gospel and of living faith.[8]

The ultimate meaning and purpose of human nature cannot be understood by metaphysics or ethics alone. Therefore, no system of philosophical anthropology can reveal to human beings their true destiny or project with clarity the image of their ultimate perfection and fulfillment. It is only in the revealed word of God, accepted in faith, that one finds a definitive answer. We should not reject or prescind from the valid findings of the various philosophical anthropologies, but as Christians we must heed the words of the fathers of Vatican II:

> It is only in the mystery of the Word made flesh that the mystery of man truly becomes clear.... Christ the Lord, Christ the new Adam ... fully reveals man to himself and brings to light his most high calling.... He who is the "image of the invisible God" (Col. 1:15) is himself the perfect man who has restored in the children of Adam that likeness to God which had been disfigured ever since the first

sin. Human nature, by the very fact that it was assumed, not absorbed, in him, has been raised in us
also to a dignity beyond compare. For, by his incarnation, he, the Son of God, has in a certain way
united himself with each man (*Gaudium et Spes* 22).

The foregoing statement brings us back to our earlier statement concerning the spiritual life as a sharing in the mystery
of Jesus Christ. We can be holy and perfect only in the measure
that we imitate and are conformed to Christ. For if it is the will
of God that we be holy, it is likewise his will that "we become
one in faith and in the knowledge of God's Son, and form that
perfect man who is Christ come to full stature," and that we
"profess the truth in love and grow to the full maturity of
Christ the head" (Eph. 4:13, 15).

The Love That Is Charity

Having seen that our perfection consists in configuration to
Jesus Christ through sanctifying grace and a faith that works
through love, we are in a position to ask what is the love that is
charity. It is a question that must be asked, if only because love
has many faces.

We should note in passing that it is common doctrine that
charity is the primary element in the perfection of the Christian life. Sanctifying grace bestows what we call a "substantial
perfection" or a perfection in our very being, since it is a participation in the nature and life of God. But the dynamic element must be sought in the infused supernatural virtues, since
they are the spiritual faculties of operation in the Christian
life. Normally we describe the role of charity as follows: Christian perfection consists primarily in the elicited act of charity
or in the act of charity imperating the other virtues. Hence the
saying: It is not what you do that makes you holy, but the love
with which you do it. This means that the acts of all the other

infused virtues derive their value and merit from their being motivated by charity. It also signifies that Christian perfection is the perfection of charity.

Charity is love, but there are several kinds of love, and not all of them comply with the requisites of charity. The classical division of love among the theologians is that of concupiscible love (love of a thing) and benevolent love (love of a person). When two persons love each other with benevolent love, that constitutes friendship.[9]

In modern times, however, there has been a tendency to use different and more relevant terms for the various types of love. Thus, "need" love refers to the love of some good for oneself, and this love is usually characteristic of infants and children (as a love of sensate objects) and of adolescents (emotional love). "Gift" love, on the other hand, is the love that marks maturity. It is a love that gives, without asking a return.[10] Gift love between two persons constitutes friendship.

The question now is: Which of the various kinds of love is charity? St. Thomas Aquinas stated succinctly that charity is friendship.[11] In other words, charity is benevolent love, gift love, and friendship love. But this does not mean that there is no allowance made for love of self. The truth is that we are bound by the love of charity to love God and self and neighbor. We are also impelled by our very nature and by the virtue of hope to desire our ultimate end, which is God. Throughout the course of history there have been those who insisted that love of God alone is charity, and that all love of self is excluded, but this doctrine has consistently been condemned by the Church and by orthodox theology. There is, however, a priority or order of charity. We are commanded to love God above all else, secondly to love ourselves in view of our ultimate end in glory, and lastly to love our neighbor.

The perfection of charity, like the perfection of any virtue, is attained by degrees. Moreover, there is no definite terminus or limit to our growth in charity, since it is a supernatural virtue flowing from the supernatural principle of sanctifying grace. The only limit to our possible growth in charity is death, beyond which there is no more merit or growth in grace. During this life, however, an individual can and should grow in love.

Various spiritual writers and theologians have attempted to designate the various stages or degrees of growth in perfection and charity. They are all helpful as general guidelines, whether one uses the classical division of the purgative, illuminative, and unitive stages, or the division into incipient, advanced, and perfect charity. In the course of his preaching ministry, Christ himself indicated that there are degrees of perfection and stages of growth in charity.

Thus, when the Pharisees asked him which is the greatest commandment of the Law, he replied: "You shall love the Lord your God with your whole heart, with your whole soul, and with all your mind. And the second is like it: You shall love your neighbor as yourself" (Mt. 22:37-38). The first part of this statement is found in Deuteronomy 6:5; the second part in the Golden Rule of the pagan philosophers; therefore it is not a specifically Christian precept. It serves, however, as a starting point in the gradual perfection of love of God and of neighbor.

The second degree of charity taught by Christ is recorded in Matthew 25:40, where Christ described the Last Judgement: "I assure you solemnly, as often as you did it for one of my least brothers, you did it for me." Jesus is not only telling his disciples to see him in their neighbor, but he is asking them to perform all their service to their neighbor for and because of Christ. In the first statement, Jesus asked that they love their neighbor as they love themselves; now he is telling them to love their neighbor as they love Christ.

This is not yet the summit of perfection in love, however. At the Last Supper, in his farewell sermon to his chosen ones, Jesus said: "This is my commandment: love one another as I have loved you" (Jn. 15:12). Now the measure of love is to love without measure, for the command is to love as Jesus loved us. The saints and mystics who have reached this intensity of charity have considered themselves channels of divine love, and they no longer experience the love that is charity as their own love, but as God's love working through them. They have reached the mystical experience wherein charity is perfected by the gift of wisdom, and it is the Holy Spirit who now works in and through them.

Christian Perfection

We have mentioned mystical experience, and that serves as a point of transition to a consideration of the relation between Christian perfection and mystical activity. There is a consensus among modern theologians that Christian perfection consists primarily and essentially in the perfection of charity, that is, in the elicited act of charity and in charity as imperating the other virtues. It is likewise commonly admitted that the fullness of Christian perfection in this life requires the operation of the gifts of the Holy Spirit, and that the operation of the gifts is the constitutive principle of the mystical experience. We would stress the phrase *constitutive principle* in order to prescind from all concomitant and extraordinary phenomena that may accompany the mystical experience. And since the gifts of the Holy Spirit operate in a divine mode, with the Spirit himself as principal agent, the soul is in a passive or receptive condition as regards the activity. The mystical experience itself may be a positive awareness of the divine presence and action (as in infused contemplation or the mystical touches), or it may be a negative awareness (as in the passive purgations). The latter is, nevertheless, a true mystical activity because the soul is, as we say, *patiens divina* under the motion of the Holy Spirit through his gifts.

The mystical activity and experience, however, are not restricted to the mystical state any more than ascetical activity is confined to the ascetical phase of the spiritual life. Fr. John Arintero, an author with great authority in spiritual theology, repeatedly insisted on this particular point:

> What truly constitutes the mystical state is the predominance of the gifts of the Holy Spirit... over simple, ordinary, vivified faith, with its corresponding works of hope and charity. The predominance of the latter over the former characterizes the ascetical state.
>
> But sometimes the good ascetic, moved by the Holy Spirit, can proceed mystically, although he may not advert to it; and so also, on the other hand, the mystics, however elevated they may be, when the Holy Spirit withdraws from them for some time, ... must proceed and do proceed after the manner of ascetics.[12]

We turn now to the question concerning the relation between Christian perfection and the mystical state. For those few theologians who hold for an "ascetical perfection" as distinct from a "mystical perfection," the mystical state is either the goal of a few select souls or else it is completely extraordinary, a *gratia gratis data*. On the other hand, those who maintain that there is but one and the same perfection for all, with the ascetical and mystical phases as two stages on the same path to perfection, conclude that all who reach the perfection of Christian life are in the mystical state.

We have already seen that charity is the primary element of Christian perfection, and that it is perfected by the actuation of the gifts of the Holy Spirit. But the actuation of the gifts is the constitutive element of mystical activity. Therefore, if a soul attains to the perfection of charity, it is in the mystical state. But we hasten to state again that this does not mean that mystical activity is continuous in the mystical state; it means

simply that in the mystical state the soul is habitually receptive to the movement of the Holy Spirit through his gifts.

The spiritual life is essentially an interior life, a life of the
spirit. Even charity, the primary element in Christian holiness, consists basically in an interior dynamism and only sec-
ondarily in the acts that flow from charity. Now closely related
to the interior life is the practice of prayer, for prayer as a
spiritual exercise is the language of love. The question has
been posed and argued as to whether or not there is a distinction between infused contemplative prayer and mystical activity and experience; further, whether all who attain Christian
perfection will necessarily receive infused contemplative
prayer. To discuss the first question, we shall have to say something about the grades of prayer.

Two things should be noted at the outset. First, although we
divide prayer into ascetical prayer and mystical prayer, it is
possible, as we have already admitted, that a soul in the ascetical phase may receive the gift of infused contemplation. This is
the explicit teaching of St. Teresa of Ávila, the Church's
greatest authority on the theology of prayer. She says: "I must
tell you that, while repeating the Paternoster or some other
vocal prayer, it is quite possible for the Lord to grant you perfect contemplation."[13] The reason is that a person in the ascetical phase may at a given time have such an intense affective
love of God that it is properly disposed for the action of the Holy
Spirit upon its prayer life. This constitutes what we have described as a mystical act, and is not restricted to the mystical
state.

Second, there is no definitive classification of the grades or
types of prayer because the differentiation in mental prayer is
based more on the intensity of charity than on self-contained
categories or types of prayer. Nevertheless, it is necessary to
formulate some kind of division, however general.

For our purposes it suffices to list the grades of ascetical mental prayer as discursive meditation, affective prayer, and the prayer of simplicity (also called acquired contemplation and the prayer of loving gaze). All of these types of ascetical prayer are within the power of the individual soul, and therefore the prayer of simplicity can be attained by all who faithfully practice prayer with the help of ordinary grace. It should be noted in passing that neither St. Teresa nor St. John of the Cross speak exactly this way about the grades of ascetical prayer. Affective prayer is described in detail by St. Francis de Sales, and the *prayer of simplicity* is a term popularized by the French school in the seventeenth century.

Mystical prayer also admits of a variety of types, and some authors place them all under the generic title *infused contemplation*. The most compact division is that of infused contemplation, prayer of quiet, and prayer of union, although the prayer of union also admits of degrees or grades: simple union, ecstatic union, conforming union, and transforming union. Infused contemplation is an absorption of the intellect in the divine object; the prayer of quiet is a captivation of the will; the prayer of union is a gradual and ever more intense union of all the faculties in God.

It is readily admitted by all theologians that infused contemplation is a mystical activity, being the result of the actuation of the gifts of the Holy Spirit. It is not evident, however, that each and every mystical act or experience involves infused contemplation. The gifts of the Holy Spirit perfect and complete the infused virtues by giving them the divine mode of operation they lack as virtues. But the virtues perfect the human being's activities in both the active and the contemplative pursuits that characterize human existence. Consequently, there are gifts that pertain to the active or apostolic life, and there are gifts that pertain to the contemplative life. We are indebted to Jacques Maritain for insisting on this distinction in the operation of the gifts, and also for defending the

opinion that mystical activity as such does not necessarily include infused contemplation.

We likewise have a statement from John Arintero that
seems to be in accord with the conclusion stated above:

> But those who, because of their state of life, are con-
> tinually occupied with works for God and, over-
> whelmed with occupations, scarcely find the time to
> be recollected, can truly advance in Christian per-
> fection and arrive at a certain conforming union by
> the practice of good works, the exercise of the virtues
> that their profession requires, the ever indispens-
> able prayer—even though it is vocal—and the prac-
> tice of the presence of God.[14]

It is quite another matter, however, when we come to the
second question proposed above, namely, whether all who attain Christian perfection and the mystical state will experience infused contemplative prayer. Not all the saints were con-
templatives; indeed some of them were eminently apostolic.
Moreover, if there are gifts of the Holy Spirit that perfect the
virtues of the active or apostolic life, it would seem that a
person totally dedicated to the active life would be able to enter
the mystical state without experiencing infused contemplative
prayer. It may seem so, but it isn't so.

Following in the tradition of Pseudo-Dionysius, St. John of
the Cross speaks of a "dark and obscure contemplation" that is
experienced by the soul in the periods of passive purgation.
This may seem to some theologians to be an unwarranted extension of the term *infused contemplation,* but the Mystical
Doctor frequently correlates infused contemplation with mystical experience, even when it is the negative experience of the
dark nights. The divine object is in itself clear and distinct, but
the soul has contact with the divine through faith and for that
reason the contemplation is night to the soul.[15] As the soul

approaches the transforming union, the contemplative experience becomes more clear, but for St. John of the Cross the essential note in contemplative activity is not that something is seen but that the soul is united with God through faith vivified by charity.

The theological reasons for asserting that all who attain Christian perfection and the mystical state will experience infused contemplation can be found in the doctrine we have already expounded. The state of Christian perfection is a mystical state, signifying the habitual disposition to be moved by the operation of the gifts. The primary and essential element in Christian perfection is charity, which is perfected by the gift of wisdom. But the gift of wisdom bestows on the soul a savory knowledge of God, and this is a contemplative act. Therefore, infused contemplation is a concomitant phenomenon of the mystical state and Christian perfection.

This doctrine has been clearly stated and summarized by John Arintero, and the following quotation serves as an appropriate conclusion for this article:

> Charity, indeed, to be stirred to life and to grow, needs to be revived with the fire of holy meditation (Ps. 38:4). It never reaches the perfection required until it is established in the mystical "cellar" of contemplation through the sublime gift of wisdom, which makes us enjoy and appreciate divine things, know them from experience, and judge with certitude and according to God, of human affairs.
>
> Hence the essential perfection and true efficacy of the works of zeal of the active life come from the latter's being more or less informed and stimulated by the contemplative life.... And if the external work of the active life is already a proof of love and merits love's reward, this in itself is accidental; the true, essential reward depends chiefly on the degree

of charity that is fostered. But it is manifested much better in the interior work of contemplation than in the external works of action. For this reason the contemplative life is in itself more excellent than the active life. . . . Consequently, the perfect and fruitful active life presupposes contemplation as its support and counterpoise and as the source of all its true efficacy.[16]

Notes

1. Quotations from the English translation of the documents of Vatican Council II were edited by Austin Flannery O.P. and published by Dominican Publications, Dublin, Ireland.
2. *Summa Theologiae* III, q. 7, a. 8.
3. *Summa Theologiae* I, q. 1, a. 8, ad 2; q. 2, a. 2, ad 1.
4. Cf. Karol Wojtyla, *Educazione all'Amore* (Milano: Ed. Logos, 1978), p. 51.
5. Cf. *Summa Theologiae* I-II, q. 110, a. 2.
6. Wojtyla, p. 51.
7. Karol Wojtyla, *L'Evangelizzazione e l'uomo interiore* (Roma: CRIS, 1974), p. 30.
8. Jacques Maritain, Introduction to *St. John of the Cross,* English trans. (London: Sheed and Ward, 1932).
9. Cf. *Summa Theologiae* II-II, q. 23, a. 1.
10. C. S. Lewis, *The Four Loves* (New York: Harcourt, Brace and World, 1960), pp. 12-13.
11. *Summa Theologiae* II-II, q. 23, a. 1.
12. John G. Arintero, *Cuestiones misticas* (Salamanca: Fides, 1920), p. 663.
13. St. Teresa of Avila, *The Way of Perfection,* chap. 25.
14. John G. Arintero, *The Mystical Evolution,* Jordan Aumann, trans. (St. Louis: B. Herder, 1948). vol. 2, p. 391.
15. St. John of the Cross, *The Ascent,* bk. 2 chaps. 2 and 32; *The Dark Night,* bk. 2, chaps. 2 and 5.
16. John G. Arintero, *Grados de Oracion* (Salamanca: Fides, 1920), p. 665.

Authors' Biographies

WILLIAM CARDINAL BAUM is the former Archbishop of Washington, D.C. He grew up in Missouri and attended Kenrich Seminary in St. Louis, and later received advanced theological studies in Rome. He has long been active in ecumenical affairs and currently serves as the chairman of the Bishops' Committee on Doctrine. He also served on the Bishops' Committee in charge of drafting the 1976 pastoral letter, *To Live in Christ Jesus,* a pastoral on the moral life. He was chosen in 1980 to head the Vatican's education congregation.

RICHARD ROACH, S.J., teaches moral theology at Marquette University. He holds a doctorate from Yale University and is also a graduate of the Jesuit Theologate in Toronto, Canada, where he studies under Bernard Lonergan. He has written for such journals a *Heythrop Journal, The Way,* and *Communio.* He has been particularly interested in the work of C. S. Lewis, Elizabeth Anscombe, and Peter Geach.

DONALD MC CARTHY is a priest of the Archdiocese of Cincinnati, where he teaches moral theology at Mt. St. Mary's of the West Seminary. He has been very active in the field of bioethics and serves as a board member of the John XXIII Center. He had edited several works in medical ethics, among them *The Ethics of Fetal Research,* and he has authored a work on the care of the dying for the United States Catholic Conference. He is active in the natural family planning movement and lectures frequently on this topic throughout the country.

He holds a doctorate in philosophy from the University of Dallas. Recently, he joined the staff of the Pope John XXIII Medical-Moral Center in St. Louis.

REV. LOUIS BOUYER is a member of the Congregation of the Oratory. An internationally famous theologian, he is the author of numerous important studies, including *An Introduction to the Spiritual Life, A History of Christian Spirituality,* and *A Dictionary of Theology.* His most recent work in French is an outstanding work in Christology which will soon be published in English.

PROFESSOR JOHN M. FINNIS is Professor of Law at University College, Oxford University. A native of Australia, he holds a doctorate in philosophy from the University of Adelaide and a doctorate in law from Oxford. He has written frequently on the subject of the natural law and is the author of a new study of this important subject, *Natural Law and Natural Rights* (Oxford University Press, 1980). He was one of the principal contributors to *The Teachings of Christ.*

WILLIAM E. MAY is associate professor of moral theology at The Catholic University of America. He is the author of several books and booklets, among them *Human Existence, Medicine and Ethics,* and *The Nature and Meaning of Chastity,* and writes frequently for professional journals. He recently finished a book on marriage and sexual morality, *Sex, Marriage, and Chastity.*

RONALD LAWLER, O.F.M., CAP. is Director of the Center for Thomistic Studies, University of St. Thomas, Dallas, Texas. He is the editor of *The Teachings of Christ* and the author of several important essays and books among them *Philosophy and Ethical Analysis.* He was the first president of the Fellowship of Catholic Scholars.

JOHN R. CONNERY, S.J. is a noted Jesuit moral theologian. He wrote "Notes of Moral Theology" for Theological Studies for several years while he taught at the Chicago Jesuit Theologate. He served as provincial of the Chicago province of the Jesuits and is the author of a scholarly study of *Abortion in the Catholic Tradition*.

JOSEPH M. BOYLE, JR., is associate professor of philosophy at St. Thomas College, St. Paul. A graduate of Georgetown, he has written many articles in philosophical and theological journals and is the co-author of *Freedom of Choice: A Self Referential Argument* and of *Life and Death with Liberty and Justice*. The latter is a massive and important study of euthanasia.

FREDERICK S. CARNEY is professor of Christian Ethics at the Perkins School of Theology, Southern Methodist University. He is one of this nation's leading Protestant moral theologians and has written important articles for *Journal of Religious Ethics, Hastings Center Report* and other journals.

GERMAIN G. GRISEZ is the newly appointed Harry Flynn Professor of Christian Ethics at Mt. St. Mary's Seminary, Emmitsburg, Md. Professor Grisez formerly taught at Georgetown University and at Camion College, the University of Regina. He is the author of several important books, among them Abortion: *The Myths and Realities and the Arguments* and, with Joseph Boyle, of *Freedom of Choice and Life and Death with Liberty and Justice*.

REV. WILLIAM SMITH is a priest of the archdiocese of New York, where he teaches moral theology at St. Joseph's Seminary, Dunwoodie. He holds an S.T.D. from the Catholic University of America and is the author of a number of important articles and likewise contributes a column on moral issues to National Catholic Register.

PAUL PHILIBERT, O.P. teaches at the Catholic University of America, where he holds a joint appointment to the Dept. of Religion and Religious Education and to the Boystown Center. He specializes in the area of moral development and is an authority on the work of developmental psychologists such as Lawrence Kohlberg and Jean Piaget. He seeks to understand and criticize their work in the light of principles grounded in the thought of St. Thomas.

JORDAN AUMANN, O.P., is professor of spiritual theology at the Angelicum University in Rome. He is the author of several studies in spiritual theology and has published widely in theological and popular journals.

MANUEL MIGUENS, O.F.M. is a Doctor of Sacred Scripture and an internationally noted biblical scholar. He is the author of important studies on the virgin birth and on other new Testament questions.

Index